In this volume, prominent American and European scholars explore the historical shaping of psychological discourse. Speaking from several disciplinary standpoints, they direct attention to the ideological, intellectual, political, economic, and literary forces that enter into the cultural construction of mental life. In its explorations, the volume not only challenges the reality of the taken-for-granted world of everyday life, but raises fundamental questions concerning the potential of psychological science to establish historically independent knowledge of mental process.

Contributions to the volume treat a variety of subjects, including the emotions, cognition, the concept of child development, psychotherapy, gender differences, and knowledge. Additional chapters represent firsthand accounts of historical change in psychological movements.

**Historical dimensions
of psychological discourse**

Historical dimensions
of psychological discourse

Edited by

CARL F. GRAUMANN

University of Heidelberg

KENNETH J. GERGEN

Swarthmore College

CAMBRIDGE
UNIVERSITY PRESS

Published by the Press Syndicate of the University of Cambridge
The Pitt Building, Trumpington Street, Cambridge CB2 1RP
40 West 20th Street, New York, NY 10011-4211, USA
10 Stamford Road, Oakleigh, Melbourne 3166, Australia

First published 1996

Printed in the United States of America

Library of Congress Cataloging-in-Publication Data

Historical dimensions of psychological discourse : edited by Carl F.
Graumann, Kenneth J. Gergen.
p. cm.
ISBN 0-521-48021-3
1. Psychology – History. I. Graumann, Carl F. (Carl Friedrich),
1923– . II. Gergen, Kenneth J.
BF81.H55 1996
150'.9 – dc20   95-30666

A catalog record for this book is available from the British Library.

ISBN 0-521-48021-3 Hardback

Contents

Contributors

Kurt Danziger
Department of Psychology
York University
Downsview, Ontario M3JIP3
Canada

Lorraine Daston
% Prof. Gerd Gigerenzer

Kenneth J. Gergen
Department of Psychology
Swarthmore College
Swarthmore, PA 19081

Gerd Gigerenzer
Max-Planck-Institut für Psychologische
Forschung
Leopoldstr. 24
80802 Munich
Germany

Carl F. Graumann
Psychologisches Institut
Universität Heidelberg
Hauptstrasse 47-51
69117 Heidelberg
Germany

William Kessen
Department of Psychology
Box 11A Yale Station
New Haven, CT 06520

Suzanne Kirschner
12 Fainwood Circle
Cambridge, MA 02139

Catherine Lutz
Department of Anthropology
University of North Carolina
Chapel Hill, NC 27599

Jill Morawski
Department of Psychology
Wesleyan University
Middletown, CT 06457

Brigitte Niestroj-Kutzner
Psychologisches Institut der FU Berlin
Habelschwerdter Allee 45
D-14195 Berlin
Germany

Harry Peeters
Department of Psychology
Tilburg University
5000 LE Tilburg
Netherlands

Nikolas Rose
Department of Sociology
Goldsmith's College
University of London, New Cross
London SE14 6NW
England

Irmingard Staeuble
Psychologisches Institut der FU Berlin
Habelschwerdter Allee 45
D-14195 Berlin
Germany

vii

1   Psychological discourse in historical context: An introduction

Kenneth J. Gergen and Carl F. Graumann

As a child of modernist culture, psychological science has treated historical inquiry with little more than tolerant civility. Psychology has been an enterprise struggling to develop a compelling rationale, seeking to establish productive paradigms, and desirous of the respect of more established sciences. From its vantage point, the discipline had no history worthy of extensive attention. Further, because of its newly fashioned commitment to empiricism, preceding scholarship of the mind was necessarily impaired. In an important sense the past was a shroud to be cast away. Psychologists might scan the preceding centuries in search of interesting hypotheses, but the results would most likely confirm the widely shared suspicion that contemporary research was far superior in its conclusions. To be sure, there were reasons for sustaining a small cadre of historians, but their task was ancillary to the scientific project itself. Theirs was primarily to chronicle the progress of the science, along with the deeds that would secure for posterity the contributions of the visionaries and achievers.

Although psychology as a discipline has remained robustly committed to 1930s conceptions of its nature as science, historically oriented psychologists have ceased to be content with their role as company scribes. Rather, as the conceptions of science and of history have evolved more generally in academic culture, historical psychologists – joined by psychologically oriented historians – have vitally transformed the view of their mission. And this newly emerging view of historical analysis has dramatic implications for the conception of psychological science and its future. At their extreme, contemporary arguments reverse the positions of master and servant. Rather than scientific research serving as the originating master of knowledge, to which history must necessarily be the servant, we find that historical analysis furnishes the necessary prerequisite for any form of sophisticated psychological inquiry. On these grounds, scientific theory cannot extricate itself from history; rather, psychological understanding is itself a servant to historical and cultural processes. Without a reflexive understanding of historical context, the field moves aimlessly into the future.

To appreciate the force and implications of such views, it is useful to

1

consider three important lines of contributing inquiry: the erosion of empiricist foundationalism, the social construction of knowledge, and ideological critique.

The demise of empiricist foundations

In large measure psychology's marginalization of history can be attributed to its commitment to a foundationalist – and, more specifically, empiricist – account of its activities. From the late 1900s through the flowering of logical empiricism in the present century, it was widely believed that the success of the sciences was not aleatory but systematic. The productive/predictive achievements of the sciences must be evidence of an underlying logic – a rational foundation on which all future investigation could rest. The 1930s movement toward a unified science perhaps best epitomizes this optimistic stance. In any case, with such views undergirding the endeavors of psychological scientists, there was good reason for rigging full sail for the horizons of prediction and control. Of what but passing interest was the historical wake?

Yet, if we now scan the philosophical shores, we find virtually none of the optimism that dominated the early decades. The search for philosophical foundations of knowledge is moribund; the ancillary investment in analytic philosophy is rapidly eroding; indeed, it is now unclear to many philosophers whether the very problem of epistemology is more than a cultural/ linguistic artifact. From midcentury on, the philosophy of science became increasingly dominated by an articulate and incisive range of critiques. Effective arguments were first formulated against pivotal beliefs in the inductive basis of theoretical propositions (Hanson, 1958; Popper, 1959), the separation of analytic from synthetic propositions (Quine, 1953), word–object correspondence (Quine, 1960), the logic of falsification (Quine, 1953), the interdependence of theory and prediction (Toulmin, 1961), and the applicability of the covering law model to human action (White, 1978). As the storm gathered, the critique grew bolder. Kuhn (1962) persuasively argued against the empirical incommensurability of competing theories; Feyerabend (1976) demonstrated the independence of scientific progress from rationally grounded method; Habermas (1971) challenged the nonpartisan character of scientific theory. As most philosophers now conclude, whatever is left of the philosophy of science, it is decidedly *postempiricist*.

Nor have the implications of this erosion of philosophical foundations been entirely neglected by psychologists and related scholars in the philosophy of social science. Koch (1963) was one of the first to explore the problematics of logical empiricism when applied to psychological science. Winch (1946) and Taylor (1964) convincingly demonstrated the impossibility of strictly behavioral description, and argued for the restoration of human agency. In a related vein, phenomenological psychologists have emphasized the meaning-dependent intentionality of human activity, bringing into focus both the historicity and sociality of psychological process (Graumann, 1988; Kockelmans, 1987). Extending the emphasis on agency, Harré and Secord (1972) have opted for an ethogenic orientation to psychology, one that views individual behavior not as a function of universal laws of behavior but as rule-governed. With a similar emphasis on the historical and cultural contingency of human action, Gergen (1982) has argued that the psychological sciences are temporally embedded and launched inquiry into a historically sensitive psychology (Gergen and Gergen, 1984).

As a result of this erosion in foundations, the argument for science over (or without) history begins to lose force. It does so both generally and specifically. More generally, without rational grounds, the scientific orientation to understanding loses its claim to superiority over other voices. The presumptions of mechanical causality, the experimental evaluation of theory, and cumulative knowledge are all placed in question. Competing accounts of human action, including a historical orientation to explanation, not only gain in credibility but open the field to a rich array of alternatives. Further, by resorting to a historical understanding of its own activities – their benefits and liabilities for society – the field is provided with a means of reflecting on its boundaries and potentials. No longer can the productivity of the science be properly assessed on empiricist grounds – with its narrow and misleadingly neutral focus on the winnowing of truth claims – but professional endeavors are opened to discussion in terms of their political, economic, ethical, and aesthetic impact on the evolving culture.

Yet, there is a very specific way in which these corrosive attacks on empiricist foundationalism pave the way for a renaissance of historical analysis. Popper's (1959) celebrated *The Logic of Scientific Discovery,* confronted the sciences with a profound enigma: How are we to account for the origin of theoretical conceptualizations? It was abundantly clear that an inductive orientation to theory construction was impossible. There was no means by which one could derive abstract propositions from untutored observation. Popper's answer to this question was to distinguish between a "context of discovery," and a "context of justification." Whereas matters of justification were the just provenance of foundationalist philosophy, the process of discovery was left unarticulated. The question was frontally addressed, however, in Norbert Hanson's *Patterns of Discovery* (1958), and the answer was of resounding consequence. As Hanson proposed, theories were not derived from facts, but rather the reverse. The scientist approaches the world with a theoretical lens already in place, and it is by peering at the world through this lens that various contours come into view. Much the same line of reasoning was also featured in Kuhn's (1962) work on the structure of scientific revolutions, a topic to which we shall return shortly.

The importance thus assigned to the theoretical forestructure fully reverses the priorities traditionally assigned to science versus history. Rather than serving as a record of science past, historical analysis acquires the role of arbitrating the future. The selection of theory – the privileging of one form of intelligibility over others – can no longer be justified on the basis of existing facts. What we take to be the facts are already saturated with theoretical perspectives. Rather, the selection of theory is optimally considered in terms of historical lodgment. What are the consequences, both scientifically and culturally, of previous theoretical commitments? What were the conditions under which these outcomes were achieved? How do existing circumstances differ from those of the past? What are the likely repercussions, both scientifically and culturally, of now embracing one form of theory as opposed to another? Failing to address such issues is to fall prey to culturally sedimented assumptions, to reify existing paradigms, and to foreclose on alternative futures.

The social construction of science

With the erosion of logical foundations of science, a space was created for an alternative conception of scientific activity. This space was a rapidly filled by historians of science and sociologists of knowledge. Heralded by Ludwik Fleck's *Genesis and Development of a Scientific Fact* (1935/1979), and Polanyi's (1962) exploration of science as a societal subculture, the landmark volume is Kuhn's *The Structure of Scientific Revolutions* – a work that effectively replaced philosophy of science with social analysis. Kuhn's work not only challenged the traditional view of science as a rationally grounded enterprise in which the accumulation of objective knowledge was secure. The strong emphasis placed on scientific subcultures and their commitment to incommensurable paradigms invited a uniquely social explanation of what we take to be scientific progress. Feyerabend's volume, *Against Method* (1976), added force to the Kuhnian exposition. Traditional standards of rationality were shown to be irrelevant (if not obfuscating) to scientific advances.

Intertextual to this adventure were arguments being advanced in the sociology of knowledge. Peter Winch's *The Idea of a Social Science* (1946) demonstrated the ways in which theoretical intelligibilities are not so much descriptive as they are constitutive of social life. Berger and Luckmann's *The Social Construction of Reality* (1966) effectively replaced scientific objectivity with a conception of socially informed subjectivity. It was thus that by the mid-1970s sociologists Barnes (1974) and Bloor (1976) could outline the possibilities for a "strong programme" in the sociology of knowledge, whereby virtually all scientific accounts could be traced to social process. While the strong program may overstate the case, there have been enormous efforts since this period to explore the microsocial processes from which scientific knowledge is generated, and the sociocultural setting as it impregnates scientific knowledge (Mendelsohn & Elkana, 1981). Attention has variously been directed, for example, to the discursive practices of scientific communities (Mulkay & Gilbert, 1982), scientific knowledge claims as forms of symbolic capital (Bourdieu, 1977), the social practices accounting for inductive inference (Collins, 1985), group influences on the way data are construed (Collins & Pinch, 1982; Graumann, 1994), and the locally situated and contingent character of description (Knorr-Cetina, 1981).

To the extent that scientific intelligibility is derived from social processes, historical reflexivity becomes an essential component of the scientific process. If psychologists' accounts of their activities are cast solely in terms of the logic of science, the result is an impoverished form of self-evaluation and a myopic conception of the craft. One is rendered insensitive to the social history – both external to and within the discipline – that shapes the existing practices. To believe, for example, that the shift from behaviorist to cognitive forms of explanation in psychology was demanded by the evidence is to narrow radically the range of what is desirable research. By contrast, to understand this shift in terms of parallel transformations in the intellectual and cultural context, and as it reflects the political dynamics of the discipline, is to loosen the grasp of cognitive explanation. Such explanation may now be seen as optional, as "one form of among many," and consideration may be extended to alternative candidates.

Knowledge as ideology

Further impetus to the erosion of empiricist foundations, and the emergence of a social view of science, is supplied by a third important movement. The 1950s writings of the Frankfurt School scholars – including Horkheimer, Adorno, and Marcuse – placed logical empiricist science under attack for its failure to sustain means for self-evaluation, and particularly its possible failings with respect to cultural conditions. Extending earlier Marxist critiques, linkages were seen between positivist science, capitalism, and bourgeois liberalism. At issue, then, were the oppressive forms of life that the scientific world view seemed to generate. Such concerns were vastly expanded during the 1960s and 1970s, when the sciences were held partisan to the subjugating efforts of the U.S. military in Southeast Asia. The claims to value-free knowledge were no longer viable. The floodgates to ideological criticism were thus opened, and an enormous body of writing has since flourished throughout the sciences. To the class biases detailed by Marxist writings, critics have come to see the logic and practices of science as saturated with racist, sexist, individualist, and Western prejudices. Noteworthy explorations of such biases in psychology include the writings of

Szasz (1963), Sampson (1978), Billig (1982), Hare-Mustin and Marecek (1988), and Wexler (1983).

It is scarcely surprising that scholars engaged in the three movements outlined here – opposing foundations of science, building toward a social view of science, and generating an ideological critique – should ally themselves with each other. Feminist critics, for example, have made ample use of social and rhetorical analyses in their exploration of androcentric biases, and social analysts often employ ideology as a useful explanatory device in their accounts of scientific movements. However, it is important to underscore the pivotal place of Foucault's writings (especially 1978, 1979), first in linking the concerns of the three movements and, second, in demonstrating the value of a historical perspective in giving them a consequential edge. Foucault's analyses of historically contingent structures of understanding (l'episteme); his depictions of the hegemonic tendencies of various "discursive regimes" such as religion, science, and the law; and his concern with the close relationship between knowledge – as a body of discourse – and the distribution of power in society unite the interests of scholars across these movements. As Foucault's writings make clear, any separation between the philosophy of science, social theory, and ideological critique is artificial and ultimately obfuscating. Further, by elaborating on the hegemonic tendencies of discursive regimes – along with the institutions they sustain – Foucault elucidates the importance of historical study. As his own work demonstrates, such scholarship need not be subservient to existing regimes of power, but is an important means of challenging the otherwise unlimited expansion and solidification of existing beliefs and institutions.

As we find, then, sensitivity to the ideological consequences of scientific commitments, combined with the steadily expanding chorus of critique within the culture, underscores the importance of the kinds of historical analyses outlined here. When the science is evaluated in terms of its own discourse – regarding its capabilities to enhance truth claims, improve mensurational technologies, generate effective interventions, and the like – then issues of political, ideological, and cultural consequence vanish from the table. The exploration of these issues requires a specifically historical consciousness, a deep sense of the culture's traditions, sensitivity to the evolutions of its institutions, and a grasp of what might be changed in the quest for enhancement of the human condition.

The challenge of postempiricist history of psychology

As the major intellectual movements of recent decades converge, their mutually supporting affinities essentially reconstitute the character and potentials of historical inquiry. In the context of psychological science, this reformulation is of major consequence. The vast body of psychological research has attempted to transcend both history and culture, to discover regularities, and to formulate laws and principles that stand outside the contingencies of time and local meaning. However, in order to achieve this goal, it has been necessary to arrogate the local and the particular to the status of the universal – to treat the momentary actions of persons in particular cultural and historical circumstance as manifestations of the transcendent. The emerging critiques reframe this quest for the eternal in historical perspective and, in doing so, demonstrate its limitations and dangers. Most important, the new sensitivity promises to restore the historical grounds on which the scientific process is carried out, and thus supply an enriched dialogue for charting the future.

Distilling further from the preceding, we may recognize three prominent and distinctive features of this emergent brand of what may be called "postempiricist history." First is the attempt to substantially broaden the criteria for evaluating the discipline's commitments and potentials. If the range of empiricist yardsticks (e.g., prediction, measurement, statistical reliability) is dangerously narrow, an attempt must be made to place the discipline's efforts in their larger historical and cultural context, opening them, for example, to considerations of ideological investments, distributions of power and privilege, and contribution to cultural meaning systems. Second, such work attempts to use historical analysis to free the discipline from the constraints of what is taken for granted – from the grasp of everyday scientific or cultural objectivity. This aim is related to a third, that of opening the discipline to the consideration of alternatives. Given the problems and prospects of the existing investments, what might be gained through alternative theories, practices, and forms of research or writing? In these ways historical analysis ceases to be merely a repository of moribund artifacts but, rather, serves as the major context for reflexivity and emancipation.

In significant degree these various lines of critique have already begun to reshape the character of historical writing in psychology. Historical analysts increasingly abjure the task of scientific record keeping and seek forms of scholarship that reflect the challenges wrought by a failed foundationalism and new sensitivities to the role of history in creating the future. Perhaps the initial inspiration for much of this work was Koch's (1963) treatment of the failures of logical empiricism when applied to psychological understanding. The work of Samelson (1979), Lewin (1983), Sarason (1981), Graumann and Sommer (1984), and Graumann and Moscovici's interdisciplinary study group on "historical change in social psychology," (Graumann & Moscovici, 1986a, 1986b, 1987) have vitally extended this genre of critical history. More recent entries into the dialogue include Ash and Woodworth's edited volume (1987) on the social basis of psychology's development, Leary's (1990) collection of papers on metaphor in the history of psychology

Morawski's (1988) edited work on the development of the concept of experimentation, and Danziger's (1990) exegesis of the concept of the subject in psychological research. In important respects, these all represent contributions to an emerging corpus of postempiricist history of psychology.

Psychological discourse in historical perspective

The present volume represents a further extension of work within the postempiricist genre of historical scholarship in psychology. It shares much with the preceding forms of analysis. In particular, the chapters join in the existing skepticism of the grand narratives of foundational science, and in the attempt to comprehend developments in psychology in terms of the broader intellectual and social context. Further, they also attempt to use historical inquiry to restore choice to professional investments, and to open new vistas of psychological inquiry. At the same time, the present essays differ from much preceding work in two important respects. The first is in their primary focus on psychology's conceptions of the person. Rather than treating as their subject matter the professional trajectory of single individuals, the rise and fall of various schools of thought, the developments of various methods and their assumptions, or the cultural ideologies embedded in psychological research and practice – all targeted by many of the preceding analyses – the present essays are largely concerned with conceptions of individual psychological functioning. What are the root assumptions regarding mental life, the forestructure of beliefs that guide research, that privilege certain methods over others, and that favor existing forms of professional and social practice? How are we to understand why psychologists embrace certain conceptions of the mind as opposed to others? In particular, what are the sociopolitical processes at work within the profession, and within broader cultural history, that bring certain conceptions into focus while suppressing the alternatives? And, what are the ramifications – both for the discipline and the culture alike – of commitments to various conceptions of the mental? Such issues are central to the essays composing the volume.

This focus on conceptions of the mind also broadens the range of literature relevant to the historical analysis of psychology. Existing scholarship makes ample use of research in neighboring histories of political, cultural, and intellectual processes. However, the present focus on conceptions of psychological being welcomes into the disciplinary dialogue new registers of inquiry. Particularly relevant are historians' explorations of earlier conceptions of mental functioning and their relationship to a broader sociocultural process. The work of Aries (1962) on changing conceptions of the child, Badinter (1980) on the history of maternal love, Corbin (1986) on the sense of smell, Delumeau (1990) on the sense of guilt, the work of the Stearns on anger (Stearns & Stearns, 1986) and jealousy (Stearns, 1989), along with edited volumes by Lynch (1990) and Stearns and Stearns (1986), are particularly noteworthy. Similar in their liberating implications are anthropological writings treating variations in conceptions of the person. Psychologists' consideration of their disciplinary commitments stand to benefit greatly from the insights of Geertz (1973) and Shweder (1991) on cultural variations in the concept of the self, Rosaldo (1980) and Lutz (1988) on differences in the conception of emotion, and others concerned with elucidating features of indigenous psychologies (see, e.g., Heelas & Lock, 1981; Kondo, 1990).

A second emphasis of the present volume significantly distinguishes it from many of its postempiricist predecessors. The focus on conceptions of mind in psychology might traditionally be placed under the rubric of intellectual history. Such conceptions are obviously manifest in theoretical formulations, and such formulations serve as the intellectual content of psychology. However, much of the present work is distinct in displacing such terms as "theory," "concepts," and "intellectual content" in favor of a language of "discourse." The primary reason for doing so is that it allows historical analysis to draw from a far broader range of conceptual resources. The emphasis on discourse shifts the focus away from particular individuals and institutions, and foregrounds the function of language within communities of interlocutors. The overarching concern, then, is with the language of the mind and the ways in which it functions both within the discipline and society – along with the relations between them. In this way, the psychological historian adds substantially to the existing repository of analytic resources. Specifically, the analyst can conveniently draw from the domains of *semiotics,* with its emphasis on systems of circulating and interrelated signs (Bakhtin, 1981; Rimmon-Kenan, 1983); *poststructural literary theory,* and its concerns with the creation of meaning within communities (Fish, 1980) and textual histories (Derrida, 1976); *ordinary language philosophy,* with its focus on the communal rule systems from which psychological terms acquire their meaning (see especially Wittgenstein, 1980); *pragmatic study of language,* with its emphasis on the social uses of language (see especially Coulter, 1979, 1989); and the *rhetoric of inquiry,* with its treatments of metaphor, narrative, and other tropes in the formation of effective writing (Kearns, 1987; McClosky, 1985; Simons, 1990). In effect, by placing the primary emphasis on discourse, the conceptual resources available for historical analysis are enormously enriched.

Organization of the volume

The chapters are organized into four sections. In the initial section the chapters are primarily concerned with the development of psychology in the twentieth century, with an emphasis on the social dynamics of psychological discourse. Kurt Danziger, whose landmark volume, *Constructing the Subject* (1990), served as an important precursor to the present volume, opens with a consideration of the ways in which psychological discourse is embedded within – and often determined by – disciplinary research practices. These practices, in turn, are related to the ideological ambience and cultural context. In the following chapter Gerd Gigerenzer illustrates these themes. He proposes that the major metaphors of contemporary cognitive psychology are borrowed from misleading logics of earlier statistical discourse. In effect, the research tools became objectified within theories about mental functioning.

Kenneth Gergen's chapter shifts the emphasis from research procedures to the politics and poetics of theoretical commitment. He finds the history of emotions research to be a battle among competing metaphors, with high stakes deriving from the acceptability of this discourse within both the academy and the culture. The concern with the relationship between the discourse of the discipline and its cultural surrounds is again amplified in Carl Graumann's chapter (chapter 5). As Graumann proposes, the language of the psyche is undergoing continuous elaboration and transformation both within the discipline and within the culture more generally. There is substantial transfer of concepts across the boundary of culture and discipline, but the uses and transformations in these domains are disparate and harbor differing moral implications.

In Part II the emphasis shifts from discourse dynamics to the use of historical analysis in generating critical sensitivity. Nikolas Rose's chapter sets the stage with a broad discussion of the potentials inherent in a critical history of psychology. His principal concern is with the use of history in altering the distribution of power. However, Rose also sees critical history as a means of altering epistemic assumptions and disciplinary practices. The concern with power is amplified by Catherine's Lutz's discussion in chapter 7. Lutz has done extensive work on the cultural construction of emotion (see especially her volume *Unnatural Emotions* [1988]). Her concern in this chapter is with the gendered character of emotions discourse and the ways in which such discourse sustains an androcentric distribution of power. Jill Morawski, another prominent figure in the development of a postempiricist history of psychology (see especially her edited volume, *The Rise of Experimentation in American Psychology* [1988]), completes this section with an analysis of the ways in which psychological discourse is shaped by cultural values, and in turn, the way it reinforces and sustains these values through its texts. In an analysis of early textbooks in psychology, Morawski demonstrates the rhetorical techniques used to create the reality of psychological discourse.

The essays composing Part III of the volume are all concerned with early antecedents of contemporary assumptions. In chapter 9, Lorraine Daston, a historian of science, documents the way in which the concept of intelligence has been gendered, even since the seventeenth century. As she proposes, assumptions of female intelligence derive in large measure from conceptions of nature in general, and the female body in particular. Suzanne Kirschner's contribution (chapter 10) further explicates the connection between early history and contemporary assumptions. She demonstrates that the Judeo-Christian tradition furnishes a significant forestructure from which grounding suppositions of human development in general, and psychoanalytic theory in particular, are derived. Harry Peeters, a major contributor to European historical psychology (see, e.g., Peeters, 1994), then traces the concept of mental illness over several centuries, attending particularly to the social, practical, and intellectual conditions that have shaped conceptions and treatment of nonnormative action. To close this section, Brigitte Niestroj considers how the concept of the woman as mother has changed across European history, and particularly how these changes are related to alterations in the concept of human reason and the significance of child development.

The final section of the volume serves as an experiment in historical inscription. The vast bulk of historical writing is conducted in the third-person voice. The historian is situated as an observer of those who produce history. Here, however, we include two contributions by historically oriented psychologists who have actively participated in significant historical movements. In chapter 13, Irmingard Staeuble reflects in the first person on the dramatic rise and decline of critical psychology, a movement that once promised to reshape radically the character of European psychology. The final chapter is offered by William Kessen, whose writings have been of pivotal importance in sensitizing psychology to the historical contingency of its subject matter. Here Kessen reflects on the cultural history that paved the way for the universalist aspirations of twentieth-century psychology, and he considers the future of psychology as its long-standing romance with historical transcendence is terminating.

References

Aries, P. (1962) *Centuries of childhood: A social history of family life*. Trans. R. Baldick. New York: Vintage.

Ash, M. A., & Woodward, W. R. (Eds.) (1987) *Psychology in the twentieth-century, thought and society*. Cambridge: Cambridge University Press.

Badinter, E. (1980) *Mother love, myth and reality*. New York: Macmillan.

Bakhtin, M. (1981) *The dialogic imagination*. Austin: University of Texas Press.

Barnes, B. (1974) *Scientific knowledge and sociological theory*. London: Routledge & Kegan Paul.

Berger, P., & Luckmann, T. (1966) *The social construction of reality*. New York: Doubleday/ Anchor.

Billig, M. (1982) *Ideology and social psychology*. Oxford: Blackwell.

Bloor, D. (1976) *Knowledge and social imagery*. London: Routledge & Kegan Paul.

Bourdieu, P. (1977) *Outline of a theory of practice*. Cambridge: Cambridge University Press.

Collins, H. M. (1985) *Changing order*. London: Sage.

Collins, H. M., & Pinch, T. J. (1982) *The social construction of extraordinary science*. London: Routledge & Kegan Paul.

Corbin, A. (1986) *The foul and the fragrant: Odor and the French social imagination*. Cambridge, MA: Harvard University Press.

Coulter, J. (1979) *The social construction of the mind*. New York: Macmillan.

Coulter, J. (1989) *Mind in action*. Oxford: Blackwell.

Danziger, K. (1990) *Constructing the subject, historical origins of psychological research*. Cambridge: Cambridge University Press.

Delumeau, J. (1990) *Sin and fear: The emergence of a western guilt culture, thirteenth–eighteenth centuries*. Trans. E. Nicholson. New York: St. Martin's Press.

Derrida, J. (1976) *Of grammatology*. Baltimore: Johns Hopkins University Press.

Feyerabend, P. K. (1976) *Against method*. New York: Humanities Press.

Fish, S. (1980) *Is there a text in this class? The authority of interpretive communities*. Cambridge, MA: Harvard University Press.

Fleck, L. (1935/1979) *Genesis and development of a scientific fact*. Chicago: University of Chicago Press.

Foucault, M. (1978) *The history of sexuality* (Vol. 1). New York: Pantheon.

Foucault, M. (1979) *Discipline and punish: The birth of the prison*. New York: Random House.

Geertz, C. (1973) *The interpretation of cultures*. New York: Basic Books.

Gergen, K. J. (1982) *Toward transformation in social knowledge*. New York: Springer-Verlag.

Gergen, K. J., & Gergen, M. M. (Eds.) (1984) *Historical social psychology*. Hillsdale, NJ: Lawrence Erlbaum.

Graumann, C. F. (1988) Der Kognitivismus in der Sozialpsychologie – Die Kehrseite der Wende. *Psychologische Rundschau, 39*, 83–90.

Graumann, C. F. (1994) Die Forschergruppe. Zum Verhältnis von Sozialpsychologie und Wissenschaftsforschung. In W. Sprondel (Ed.), *Die Objektivität der Ordnungen und ihre kommunikative Konstruktion*. Frankfurt: Suhrkamp (pp. 67–92).

Graumann, C. F., & Moscovici, S. (Eds.) (1986a) *Changing conceptions of crowd mind and behaviour*. New York: Springer-Verlag.

Graumann, C. F., & Moscovici, S. (Eds.) (1986b) *Changing conceptions of leadership*. New York: Springer-Verlag.

Graumann, C. F., & Moscovici, S. (Eds.) (1987) *Changing conceptions of conspiracy*. New York: Springer-Verlag.

Graumann, C. F., & Sommer, M. (1984) Schema and inference: Models in cognitive social psychology. In J. R. Royce & L. P. Mos (Eds.), *Annals of theoretical psychology, 1*. New York: Plenum Press (pp. 31–76).

Habermas, J. (1971) *Knowledge and human interest*. Boston: Beacon Press.

Hanson, N. R. (1958) *Patterns of discovery*. Cambridge: Cambridge University Press.

Hare-Mustin, R., & Marecek, J. (1988) The meaning of difference, gender theory, postmodernism, and psychology. *American Psychologist, 43*, 455–464.

Harré, R., & Secord, P. (1972) *The explanation of social behaviour*. Oxford: Blackwell.

Heelas, P., & Lock, A. (Eds.) (1981) *Indigenous psychologies*. London: Academic Press.

Kearns, M. S. (1987) *Metaphors of mind in fiction and psychology*. Lexington: University Press of Kentucky.

Kessen, W. (1979) The American child and other cultural inventions. *American Psychologist, 34*, 815–820.

Knorr-Cetina, K. D. (1981) *The manufacture of knowledge*. Oxford: Pergamon.

Koch, S. (1963) Epilogue. In S. Koch (Ed.), *Psychology: A study of a science. Vol. III*. New York: McGraw-Hill (pp. 729–783).

Kockelmans, J. J. (Ed.) (1987) *Phenomenological psychology: The Dutch School*. Dordrecht: Nijhoff.

Kondo, D. K. (1990) *Crafting selves, power, gender, and discourses of identity in a Japanese workplace.* Chicago: University of Chicago Press.

Kuhn, T. S. (1962) *The structure of scientific revolutions.* Chicago: University of Chicago Press.

Leary, D. (Ed.) (1990) *Metaphors in the history of psychology.* Cambridge: Cambridge University Press.

Lewin, M. (Ed.) (1983) *In the shadow of the past: Psychology portrays the sexes.* New York: Columbia University Press.

Lutz, C. (1988) *Unnatural emotions.* Chicago: University of Chicago Press.

Lynch, O. (Ed.) (1990) *Divine passions: The social construction of emotion in India.* Berkeley: University of California Press.

McClosky, D. N. (1985) *The rhetoric of economics.* Madison: University of Wisconsin Press.

Mendelsohn, E., & Elkana, Y. (Eds.) (1981) *Sciences and cultures.* Dordrecht: Reidel.

Morawski, J. G. (Ed.) (1988) *The rise of experimentation in American psychology.* New Haven: Yale University Press.

Mulkay, M., & Gilbert, G. N. (1982) What is the ultimate question? Some remarks in defense of the analysis of scientific discourse. *Social Studies of Science, 12,* 309–319.

Peeters, H. F. M. (1994) *Hoe veranderlijk is de mens? een inleiding in de historische psychologie.* Nijmegen: SUN.

Polanyi, M. (1962) *Personal knowledge.* London: Routledge & Kegan Paul.

Popper, K. R. (1959) *The logic of scientific discovery.* London: Hutchinson.

Popper, K. R. (1963) *Conjectures and refutations.* New York: Harper.

Quine, W. V. O. (1953) *From a logical point of view.* Cambridge, MA: Harvard University Press.

Quine, W. V. O. (1960) *Word and object.* Cambridge, MA: MIT Press.

Rimmon-Kenan, S. (1983) *Narrative fiction.* London: Methuen.

Rosaldo, M. (1980) *Knowledge and passion: Illongot notions of self and social life.* Cambridge: Cambridge University Press.

Rose, N. (1988) *The psychological complex.* London: Routledge & Kegan Paul.

Rose, N. (1992) *Governing the soul.* London: Routledge.

Samelson, F. (1979) Putting psychology on the map: Ideology and intelligence testing. In A. R. Buss (Ed.), *Psychology in social context.* New York: Irvington (pp. 78–93).

Sampson, E. E. (1978) Psychology and the American ideal. *Journal of Personality and Social Psychology, 35,* 767–782.

Sarason, S. (1981) *Psychology misdirected.* New York: Free Press.

Shweder, R. (1991) *Thinking through cultures.* Cambridge, MA: Harvard University Press.

Simons, H. W. (Ed.) (1990) *Case studies in the rhetoric of the human sciences.* Chicago: University of Chicago Press.

Stearns, C. Z., & Stearns, P. N. (1986) *Anger: The struggle for emotional control in America's history.* Chicago: University of Chicago Press.

Stearns, C. Z., & Stearns, P. N. (Eds.) (1988) *Emotion and social change: Toward a new psychohistory.* New York: Holmes and Meier.

Stearns, P. N. (1989) *Jealousy: The evolution of an emotion in American history.* New York: New York University Press.

Szasz, T. S. (1963) *Law, liberty and psychiatry: An inquiry into the social uses of mental health practices.* New York: Macmillan.

Taylor, C. (1964) *The explanation of behavior.* London: Routledge & Kegan Paul.

Toulmin, S. (1961) *Foresight and understanding.* New York: Harper and Row.

Wexler, P. (1983) *Critical social psychology.* Boston: Routledge & Kegan Paul.

White, H. (1978) *Tropics of discourse.* Baltimore: Johns Hopkins University Press.

Winch, P. (1946) *The idea of a social science.* London: Routledge & Kegan Paul.

Wittgenstein, L. (1980) *Remarks on the philosophy of psychology* (Vols. 1–2). Ed. G. E. M. Anscombe & G. H. von Wright. Oxford: Blackwell.

Part I

Disciplining psychological discourse

2 The practice of psychological discourse

Kurt Danziger

For some time I have been trying to make sense of the history of psychological discourse. When I first began to occupy myself seriously with this task, I assumed, along with just about everyone else, that a historical account of psychological discourse would have to focus primarily on the concepts and theories that seemed to form the essential content of this discourse. Of course, I knew that, at least since the last quarter of the nineteenth century, psychologists had been quite busy doing other things than contributing to theoretical discourse. They had fervently embraced laboratory activity and become increasingly involved in an array of technologies for the production of psychological knowledge. But as experimental and other techniques supposedly related to theory as means to ends, they presumably played only a subsidiary role in the history of psychological discourse. Certainly, the traditional histories of the discipline, as much as they addressed themselves to theoretical problems, tended to treat the realm of methodology as relatively unproblematic, as being governed by self-evident principles of instrumental rationality and linear technical progress.

It soon became clear to me, however, that it was only possible to cling to this received view if one steadfastly closed one's eyes to a barrage of historical evidence. For example, the way in which the topics of psychological discourse were consistently redefined so as to fit the Procrustean bed of a very limited range of allowable procedures suggested that it was often the procedures that dictated theoretical formulations rather than the other way around. If one looked at those texts that actually formed the lifeblood of intradisciplinary discourse, namely, the empirical research reports published in the journal literature, it seemed that the rules about what could be done in the actual practice of psychological investigation often decided what could and what could not be discussed, what had to be regarded as problematic and what could be taken for granted, and so on. The link between these rules of practice and psychological theory was neither simple nor obvious.

At the very least, there seemed to be an underdetermination of methodological rules by theory that was analogous to the better-known underdetermination of theory by data. The general features of a theoretical problem or position did not necessarily prescribe a particular style of investigative practice. For example, there is no necessary connection between a behavioristic theoretical framework and a research practice based on constructing measures of interindividual variance, although historically the two arose at approximately the same time. Neither J. B. Watson nor B. J. Skinner employed this form of practice, though many who regarded themselves as behaviorists did. Commitment to a behaviorist position is quite compatible with a considerable range of investigative practice. Similarly, being committed to mentalistic theories does not automatically direct one to the use of a particular variant of introspection, or any use of introspection at all. Modern mentalists usually reject introspective practices altogether, and the way in which Wundt understood this practice was quite different from its use in the practice of "systematic experimental introspection" which appeared at the beginning of the twentieth century (Danziger, 1980).

It seems then that the realm of practice enters psychological discourse in a relatively autonomous manner and not simply as a derivative of theory. If this is true in the case of the theoretically oriented discourse of psychological research, it holds even more strongly in the case of so-called applied psychology where the theoretical element has often been quite weak and sometimes nonexistent. Here the core of the psychological contribution is often clearly constituted by a set of socially significant practices, like mental testing, which may or may not be surrounded by a penumbra of theoretical discourse.

These and other considerations soon convinced me that the theme of practice would have to occupy a place in the history of psychological discourse that was not subordinate to theory. If the historical role of practice cannot be reduced to an instrumental function, questions about its true historical role must be placed on the agenda. Such a project seems to be strongly encouraged by some recent developments in the history and philosophy of science that point in the same direction. Ian Hacking (1983), for example, has argued that in the natural sciences experiment has a life of its own and is not necessarily driven by theory. There are several kinds of experimentation, and the relationship between theory and practice is complex and variable. Often, practice plays a constitutive role in theory development. More recently, Timothy Lenoir (1988) has reviewed a body of literature that contributes to an understanding of these issues. In this work scientific practice is analyzed on its own terms and not simply as a logical extension of scientific theory. That appears to be a necessary preliminary to understanding scientific discourse, not as a logical monologue, but as a socially embedded dialogue between theory and practice.

In what follows I intend to examine three aspects of the discourse–practice relationship in psychology. First, some comment is necessary on the way in which large parts of psychological discourse have become a discourse *of* psychological practice, presenting features of that practice as though they were real features of the object investigated. Second, the disciplinary discourse *about* practice needs to be examined in order to reveal its ideological features. Third, the possibilities of an alternative discourse about psychological practice will be explored.

Disciplinary discourse as a discourse of practice

Compared with most other sciences, mainstream psychology has long been characterized by a somewhat peculiar relationship between theory and practice. An important clue to the peculiarity of that relationship is provided by the principle of "operationism." There is no other discipline in which this principle ever assumed anything remotely like the prominence it assumed in psychology. Even today it remains an unquestioned methodological rule for scientific work throughout most of the discipline, published criticisms (Leahy, 1980, 1983) notwithstanding. "Operationism," as it is understood in psychology, has long been unique to that discipline and to certain trends in the other social sciences for which psychology has functioned as a model.

The version of operationism that is in vogue in psychology defines the relationship of theory and practice by reducing the former to the latter. Intelligence *is* what intelligence tests test. The practice defines the concept. When engaged in psychological research, investigators are supposed to define each of their theoretical concepts in terms of the practical procedures required to make them sensuously manifest.

Even though this rule cannot be strictly followed, the attempt to follow it suffices to impose a certain cast on a great deal of theoretical discourse in psychology. What this discourse is often limited to are interrelationships among operationally defined theoretical entities. In many areas of psychology, notably in social psychology, personality, and the psychology of individual differences, one will find little of the elaborate modeling of unobservable but real processes that is so characteristic of the natural sciences. Instead, one finds sets of relationships among entities that are entirely defined by the interventions of the psychologist. These interventions may take the form of the administration of personality scales or other kinds of mental tests, or of instructions and manipulations in a social psychological laboratory. But in each case these interventions define the reality that "operationalized" theoretical discourse is about.

How did psychologists end up with this decidedly peculiar form of scientific practice? Is it because they drank too deeply at the well of logical positivism, taking too seriously and too literally the canons of a dubious philosophy of science? The historical record suggests a rather different interpretation. Operationism as a doctrine appeared in the mainstream psychological literature in 1935 (Stevens, 1935). It was immediately taken up by several of the leading lights of American psychology, men like Boring, Hull, Spence, and Tolman. But was this a sudden and widespread conversion? Did it make a profound difference to the kinds of psychological theory that these men and their associates propounded and to the type of research that they advocated? Far from it. The fundamental approach of what has come to be known as neobehaviorism had been essentially worked out by 1935 (Hull, 1935; Tolman, 1932). The subsequent appearance of the term "operational" in the discourse of neobehaviorism represented little more than a rhetorical device. Reference to the doctrine of operationism provided a welcome rationalization of what American psychologists were doing in any case (Rogers, 1989, 1990). Their discovery of operationism was rather like the experience of Molière's character who discovered that he had been speaking prose all his life. The extremely rapid elevation of operationism into the canon of psychological research practice and its subsequent imperviousness to criticism suggest that what it rationalizes constitutes a very fundamental aspect of that practice.

If we are to gain some historical insight into the origins of this fundamental aspect, we will have to extend our inquiry backward to the period before 1935, when the practice subsequently rationalized as "operational" actually came into being. We will then find that a truly decisive transformation of both the discourse and the practice of American psychology occurred during the second and third decades of the twentieth century (Danziger, 1990). At that time there took place an astounding metamorphosis of psychology from a rather esoteric academic hobby into a scientific discipline that was seriously expected to play a major role in improving social life.

The language of psychology now began to show clear signs of change. Behaviorism was certainly part of this change, but it would be a mistake to equate the change itself with the rise of a particular school. Watsonian behaviorism managed to express some of the changes that were affecting the disciplinary discourse of psychology, but it also expressed a concern with issues that were not necessarily important to most American psychologists. Although many members of the profession were not unsympathetic to Watson's agenda, they were not exactly card-carrying behaviorists either. Far more representative of mainstream attitudes than Watson was the immensely influential Columbia psychologist R. S. Woodworth, who, when he asked himself whether he was a behaviorist, essentially decided that he didn't know and didn't much care (Woodworth, 1939).

In 1921 Woodworth authored what was to become by far the most successful undergraduate text of the time (Winston, 1988), followed by the authoritative graduate text, *Experimental Psychology,* of 1938. He called his approach "stimulus–response psychology," and this, rather than Watsonian behaviorism, defined the key features of disciplinary discourse for several decades.

The earlier text established a fundamental axiom of psychological discourse and practice, namely, that all individual action, whether overt or covert, was to be conceptually represented and studied in terms of the stimulus–response schema. This formula was based on a particular definition of the object of psychological investigation, a specific prescription for the way in which such investigation was to be conducted, and a limitation on the language of psychological discourse. First of all, it was taken as axiomatic that all behavior was produced by stimuli, and that the task of the psychologist was essentially the production of an inventory of stimulus–response links. This involved a dissection of both the internal and the external world of the organism into discrete functional units, called stimuli, and the dissection of all individual action into discrete units, called responses.

What needs emphasizing here is the fundamental role played by the psychologist's practice in constituting both stimuli and responses. These units were decidedly not natural kinds but were the product of the psychologist's investigative intervention. Neither the perceptual world nor the stream of behavior naturally presented itself as divided up into distinct units, let alone units that spontaneously arranged themselves into measurable scales. Producing these latter kinds of units required a great deal of ingenuity on the part of the psychologist. Yet – and this is the key point – stimuli and responses were always discussed as though they were features of the objective world and not artifacts of psychological procedure.

Not that there was anything particularly strange about this aspect of psychologists' discursive practice. Overlooking the contribution of scientists' intervention to the constitution of objectivity had been a common feature of late nineteenth-century science. What did set stimulus–response psychology apart from general practice in the natural sciences, however, was its insistence that the kinds of units produced by the psychologist's own activity were the ultimate building blocks of that aspect of reality which the science of psychology took as its object. Stimuli and responses were all there was! In physics or genetics constructed measures would be regarded as indicators of objective features, but they would never be *identified* with the underlying processes and entities whose nature science was intended to elucidate. The real objects of scientific investigation were conceptualized as protons and electrons, gemmules or genes, and these were not identical with the measures that scientists constructed in order to study them.

Not so in stimulus–response psychology. Here the structural features of psychologists' research activity were explicitly held to define the structure of everything that they investigated. In general, psychological investigation conformed to the stimulus–response format. The subject in such investigations would be presented with some specially constructed situation and then certain aspects of his or her reaction to that situation would be measured. Stimulus–response psychology insisted that the structure of the reality that the discipline took as its object could not differ from the structure of its investigative situations. The establishment of relationships among measures constructed in the course of psychological investigation was held to exhaust the task of psychological science and to define the limits of disciplinary discourse. That discourse would henceforth have to restrict itself to categories exhaustively defined by the practice of psychological investigators. This was operationism without the label.

Modern psychology had begun life with an object of investigation, the individual consciousness, that it had inherited from a certain cultural and philosophical tradition. It contrived to apply certain procedures of experimentation and quantification to the study of the preexisting object. But once the disciplinary apparatus of investigation had been institutionalized, the possibility emerged of allowing this apparatus, rather than tradition, to define the objects of psychological science. The realization of this possibility was inseparably bound up with an increase in the social influence of the practitioners of psychological science. It was *their* practice that was to play the constituting role in defining the structure of psychological reality. In this sense the discourse of psychology became a discourse of practice, the practice of the experts.

But that development would not have been as successful as it was if the new language of psychology had not had a certain appeal to social interests outside the discipline. By limiting itself to a language that directly reflected the practical manipulations of experts, the new psychology pandered to dreams of "social control" within which most social problems were transformed into individuals' problems that could be solved by applying the appropriate technological fix. For the new psychological discourse that spread so rapidly in North America during the years following World War I, psychological reality was defined as the sum of the possibilities of expert psychological manipulation.

In the 1930s the new psychological discourse was transformed into what can only be described as the "official" language of American psychology. An important part of this process was the neutralization of the earlier stimulus–response language because it had simplistic and mechanistic connotations that were not universally acceptable. In any case, the retention of two distinct terms, stimulus and response, had become redundant, because it was generally recognized that these terms referred to functional properties, so that one and the same event – for example, an organism's movement – could be simultaneously a response to a stimulus and a stimulus to another response.

The new terminology substituted the language of "variables" for that of stimulus and response. What had previously been somewhat audaciously referred to as a stimulus was now more cautiously categorized as an "independent variable." Similarly, responses became "dependent variables." This switch had several advantages. First of all, the historical link with an out-of-date quasi-reflexological schema was finally broken. This gave the language of dependent and independent variables a greater apparent degree of theoretical neutrality than the language of stimuli and responses. It was therefore better suited to become the common language of disciplinary consensus. Different interpretations of what variables represented were permissible, as long as all psychologists agreed that the units of their investigative practice were "variables." Second, the language of variables could accommodate the practice of psychologists who were engaged in establishing correlations among measures – for example, personality traits – that had not been experimentally manipulated and hence were not expressible in the language of stimulus and response. The new language was thus broader in scope and more flexible.

In spite of this flexibility, the principle that the object of psychological investigation had to be constituted by the constructive activity of the psychologist was enforced more tightly by the new language than it had been by the old. In stimulus–response psychology, what went on between observable stimuli and responses was designated as pertaining to the "organism." This was expressed in the well known S-O-R schema. Although Woodworth had made it clear that intraorganismic events, including thoughts, must be conceptualized as internal stimuli and responses, this extension of the stimulus–response structure to unobservable events was left to discursive elaboration and was not expressed in the terminology of the S-O-R schema itself. That was rectified in the language of variables, where the place of intraorganismic events was taken by "intervening variables." These were thought of as forming the links between independent and dependent variables, much as the O terms had linked stimulus and response in the older scheme. The difference was that whereas "organism" carried no necessary structural implications, the term "intervening variables" made it clear that whatever was postulated as going on within the individual had to conform to the structural limitations of a "variable." Not only was the practice of psychological investigation to be limited to the exploration of relationships among "variables," but psychological theory was now unable to speak of postulated processes except insofar as their structure conformed to the schema implicit in the language of variables.

The adoption of the language of variables within American psychology was part of a historical process for which no specific individual bears a unique responsibility. However, just as Woodworth's role is worthy of special note in connection with the stimulus–response psychology of the

1920s, so one must recognize the contribution of certain key figures to the discourse of the 1930s that led to the general adoption of the language of variables. Hull and his followers were important, but they did not start the fashion. That distinction must go to another leading neobehaviorist, E. C. Tolman, who, in his pathbreaking *Purposive Behavior in Animals and Men* (1932), provided a convincing example of how the language of variables could be used as a disciplinary metalanguage that permitted a systematic comparison of the claims of different psychological systems. He not only gave an account of his own system in terms of independent, dependent, and intervening variables, but attempted to fit Titchenerian structuralism, gestalt psychology, and Spearman's individual psychology into the same bed of Procrustes. Other prominent neobehaviorists soon joined this discourse. It provided a convenient medium for pursuing their internal disagreements, and a far-from-level playing field for settling accounts with positions that did not conform to the neobehaviorist ethos. In the area of psychological theory this kind of framework reached its baroque culmination in Sigmund Koch's multivolume *Psychology: A Study of a Science* (1959).

By 1936 Tolman had made the connection between the language of variables and operationism. In a paper presented that year he elaborated his scheme in the form of a set of linear relationships linking "intervening variables" to observed variables and pointed out that "this schema is . . . a pretty fair summary of what psychology today is actually, operationally, doing" (Tolman, 1951, p. 119). He called his approach "an operational behaviorism," a term that is surely descriptive of a great deal of psychology, even after behaviorism as such had ceased to be fashionable. The point was that the practical construction of "variables" by the psychologist was to be accepted as the ultimate meaning conferring activity for all permissible psychological concepts. The other major principle of operational behaviorism, according to Tolman, was the assertion "that the ultimate interest of psychology is solely the prediction and control of behavior" (1951, p. 129), a principle that was of course enshrined in the schema of independent and dependent variables. That schema was to fix the fundamental parameters of "scientific" psychological discourse for a long time to come. It was a discourse that took its terms from the investigative practice of the psychologist and used them to impose a very particular structure on any aspect of psychological reality that could be talked about. Because psychological practice was solely dedicated to the task of predicting and controlling behavior, the hypothetical constructs of this type of psychology never advanced beyond expressions for possibilities of behavioral manipulation.

The result was an extraordinary impoverishment of psychological language. During the centuries preceding the rise of contemporary psychology, the natural languages used by the practitioners of this science had developed rich semantic resources for dealing with the subtleties of human conduct and experience. Practicing psychology, however, meant superimposing on this language a new technical language within which only a vastly reduced range of circumstances pertaining to human subjectivity could be expressed. Thus, a world of collectively experienced meanings would be reduced to the category of social attitudes, the complexities of individual development would become confined within the paradigm of social learning, and any kind of directedness in human conduct would be handled in terms of simple reifications like drive or motivation.

Psychology became divided up into such domains as "social attitudes," "social learning," "motivation," and others of the same type. These domains were constituted entirely by the investigative practices of psychologists. What marked off the objects investigated within one domain from those of another domain were the procedures used to construct each category of object. But insofar as they were experimental, these procedures were all designed to optimize the demonstration of the general effectiveness of various kinds of manipulation. By making their theoretical discourse a reflection of their procedures, psychologists produced a language whose terms gave expression to little else but various possibilities of manipulation. Thus, terms like "social attitudes" and "social stimuli" simply were abstracted from a universe of human relatedness and meaningful experience to represent certain possibilities of manipulative influence inherent in some human situations.

But even under the specially prepared conditions of psychological experimentation, the effects of influence could only be displayed against an unavoidable background of information that potentially cast doubt on the ubiquity of the influence model. The psychologists' procedures rendered such information harmless by translating it into statistical error supposedly due to the operation of "individual differences." Other investigations could then focus on these individual differences, conceived as sources of resistance to limitless and arbitrary experimental manipulation.

Almost from its beginnings, modern psychological practice embarked on its characteristic bifurcation into experimentation, which sought to maximize the demonstration of manipulative effects, and mental testing, which sought to minimize such effects. All that this meant was that the manipulation involved in the construction and standardization of tests and testlike instruments remained relatively hidden. The categories of this branch of psychology, including such well-known examples as "intelligence," "test anxiety," and personality "traits," were, if anything, even more closely tied to specific psychological practices than the categories of the experimentalist. But whereas the latter expressed possibilities of short-term unidirectional influence, the categories of "individual differences" expressed possibilities of social selection based on notions of long-term resistance to change. The criteria employed in the construction, standardization, and administration of tests aimed to produce instruments that would maximize the demonstration of such intraindividual limits to change. These limits were not however conceptualized in terms of individual situations but in terms of a grading of the output of many individuals on a unitary scale that was equally valid for them all. By defining its categories solely in terms of these practices, the discourse of "individual differences" replaced a vast linguistic domain potentially relevant to human individuality with the rather limited language of grading and selection.

It should be noted, however, that the emaciated technical language of the discipline retained a highly equivocal relationship to lay discourse. Had they been absolutely loyal to the prescriptions that governed their use of psychological terms, practitioners of the discipline should have avoided the use of inherently fuzzy lay terms and restricted themselves to the use of rigorously defined technical neologisms. However, in general, they did not do this but continued to use terms like "intelligence," "emotionality," "habit," and "memory," even though their disciplinary ideology actually precluded the use of such terms in any everyday sense. Moreover, they freely promoted the translation of technical terms like "reinforcement," "stimulus," and "information" into everyday equivalents. Had they acted otherwise, their work would have lost most of its popular appeal and apparent relevance to human affairs. So a curious ambiguity came to characterize the discourse of the discipline. As the occasion demanded, key terms would be used either in a restricted technical or some lay sense, and frequently the same text might move from the one to the other without fanfare. One important result of this was the insertion into some areas of lay discourse of usages that had had a technical origin. In this way disciplinary practices could acquire a cultural significance that went far beyond a merely instrumental use of specific psychological techniques.

Discourse about practice

The next question to ask is how psychologists' discourse about their practice has reflected their actual practice. If one does not limit oneself to the contemporary scene but applies this question to the century spanned by the history of the discipline, one cannot avoid being struck by some strange lacunae in psychologists' discourse about their own practice. A major blind spot emerges in connection with the social aspects of psychological practice. Although psychologists did occasionally reflect on the macrosocial context in which they operated, the discipline's first century was nearly over before it began to dawn on its practitioners that they operated in a microsocial context that might well have a crucial influence on the results of their investigations. I am referring to the fact that psychological investigations involving human subjects are conducted in situations that are intrinsically social in nature. Not only do human individuals participate in these situations as social beings, but the situations themselves are highly structured in terms of written and unwritten rules and regulations. Psychological investigation is therefore a social practice, not only in the same sense that all science is a social practice, involving a scientific community interacting with its society and culture, but also in the sense that access to its primary object of investigation usually requires some social interaction with that object.

The discourse of psychology has never been characterized by a readiness to accommodate this topic. For most of its history, the topic was simply ignored. In 1933 the *Psychological Review* did actually publish a very insightful article on the issue (Rosenzweig, 1933), but the silence that followed it was deafening. Nothing more was said about the matter for at least three decades. Then a flood of literature on the social psychology of the psychological experiment began to appear (Suls and Rosnow, 1988). This obviously represented some kind of belated reception of the topic into the corpus of psychological discourse, although it is noteworthy that the issue was assimilable only as a *psychological* issue to be further investigated by psychological (i.e., experimental) methods. The question of the social nature of psychology's investigative practice is not, however, a psychological question that requires a psychological answer in terms of the psychology of experimental subjects or experimenter expectancy effects. It is a question of the nature and historically situated character of the institutionalized arrangements that constitute the investigative situations within which psychological knowledge is generated.

Of course, the literature of the discipline has always had room for texts about investigative practice. Beginning with the second volume of Wundt's *Logik* (1883) and continuing all the way to contemporary treatises on experimental design, there is an intradisciplinary discourse on the practice of investigation that is as remarkable for what it leaves out as for what it focuses on. What is typically left out, of course is any reflection on psychological practice as a historically situated, institutionalized activity. Instead, one finds a technical discourse of methodology that abstracts from the social nature of the process of investigation and presents the situation of the investigator in purely rational terms. This discourse is constructed around logical relationships among items of evidence and between evidence and hypothesis. In other words, psychological investigation appears in this discourse not as a species of social practice but as a manipulation of symbols governed by purely rational considerations. There is little doubt that this literature hides the socially constructive nature of psychological investigation from the practitioners, a function that is further reinforced by the way in which methodological prescriptions are presented as impersonal laws that have no human authors (Gigerenzer and Murray, 1987).

What I would like to put on the agenda is the development of an alternative discourse of psychological research practice, one that is adequate to those crucial aspects that conventional methodological discourse leaves out. Such an alternative discourse would have to provide an account of the social structure of investigative situations in terms of the interaction among the participants in those situations. There is, for example, the question of power relationships in these situations. Conventionally, the power of the investigator is, of course, assumed. Without this power to dispose, the advice purveyed by methodological texts would be so much hot air. But typically the power of the investigator goes unexamined. What are the reasons for it? Is it inherent in the very nature of psychological investigation, as contemporary texts imply? Apparently not, for in the early years of what was undoubtedly psychological investigation, the experimenter was little more than a technical assistant to the subject, who was the source of the data yielded by the experiment (Danziger, 1985). Is the power of the experimenter based on a necessary gap between his knowledge of what is going on and that of the subject? Perhaps, but this gap was not a feature of most psychological experimentation until after World War I. It has to be built into the investigative situation; it is not one of its necessary features. If that is so, one must ask, why build it in? And having built it in, what are its consequences for the process of knowledge generation?

The reasons for the experimenter's power may not coincide with its social source. That may have little to do with the microsociology of the experiment and everything to do with the investigator's status in a broader social framework. The power differential in the investigative situation may simply reflect the power differential between experts and lay persons, between adults and children, between clinicians and patients. If that is the case, to what extent does the structure of research situations resemble the structure of other investigative situations, clinical examinations or school examinations, for example? What consequences do the structural features of the investigative situation have for the nature and applicability of the knowledge products yielded by these situations? Such questions arise within a discourse about psychological practice that is rather different from the intradisciplinary discourse of technique. It is different because it targets disciplinary practice as a form of social practice and therefore raises the question of its relationship to other forms of social practice.

This does not mean that questions of technique are not to be addressed. The distinguishing feature of technical discourse is not that it concerns itself with questions of technique, but that it concerns itself with such questions within a purely instrumentalist framework. Techniques of investigation are employed in the service of certain knowledge goals; but in technical discourse these goals have to be taken for granted. Not all human knowledge is of the same type, and the kind of knowledge aimed for determines the range of potentially suitable techniques. The kinds of psychological knowledge that are employed in everyday life or in a counseling context are fundamentally different from the kind of knowledge aimed for in experimental personality research, for example. Much of the first two kinds of knowledge is of an implicit kind, depending on practical reason, or "knowing of the third kind" (Shotter, 1990), and is inseparable from the person who possesses it. By contrast, scientific knowledge is necessarily formulated in public symbols and is completely separate from its originator.

Another relevant distinction is that between the source of knowledge and the utilization of knowledge. This is particularly important in the case of psychology. In the natural sciences there is always a disjunction between a nonhuman source of knowledge and a human agency that utilizes this knowledge. But for psychological knowledge there are a number of possibilities. Source and utilization may be the same, as in self-knowledge. However, in most psychological research the people who are the sources of knowledge are not the ones who utilize it. Knowledge is produced by the investigators for their own purposes. Subjects are not usually in a position to utilize such knowledge. But it is also possible to set up investigative situations designed to yield knowledge that will be directly utilized by the subjects of the investigation, insight therapy being a case in point.

Going beyond technical discourse

The appropriate means or methods of knowledge acquisition will depend on knowledge goals and on their effect on the structure of the knowledge-generating situation. There is, for example a "technique" of psychoanalysis just as there is a "technique" of experimental personality research, although there is no overlap between the two. But in the respective technical literatures a particular knowledge goal is taken for granted so that specific methods need be considered only in their instrumental aspects. Taking one's knowledge goal for granted, however, means operating with an unproblematic concept of knowledge that abstracts from the social embeddedness of human knowledge. There is no such thing as knowledge in general, only different forms of knowledge that are pursued and utilized for specific purposes by particular groups of people. Against this kind of background a rather different discourse of practice emerges than the one we are accustomed to in our disciplinary "how to" literature. It is a fundamental characteristic of the latter that it reifies the knowledge goals of the investigator in the form of natural properties of the object of investigation. Then the practices of investigation appear to be merely instrumental accommodations to fixed features of an independent object. The way in which the practice of investigation constructs the kind of object it needs to work with is thereby removed from view.

For example, discussions of different techniques of "psychological (or psychophysical) measurement" tend to imply that there are objective features out there that naturally exist in some amount, and the investigator merely has to find the best way to capture this fact. But this sort of account assigns altogether too passive a role to the investigator. It treats the "raw data" produced in the experimental situation as being in some sense isomorphic with something that exists independently of that situation. But these "raw data" are far from raw! They are the product of a most elaborate artifice that includes a set of highly structured instruments, extremely specific instructions to the subject, and a complex social situation in which the subject has accepted playing by certain rules. That the raw data are in a form that lends itself to certain operations of measurement is the direct result of the prior mobilization of an extended social apparatus. Before one can measure, one must be able to count. But in order to count, there must be something to count, there must be information in a form that lends itself to counting. The practices by which such a form is imposed may be called "arithmetization." They can be used without directly affecting the behavior of any human individual, as in the content analysis of texts, but much more frequently in psychology their application involves a profound influence on the behavior of experimental subjects. They agree to limit themselves to responses of "equal" or "unequal," "greater" or "smaller," for example.

My purpose in emphasizing this well-known state of affairs is not to argue against the use of quantitative data in psychology. I am, however, concerned about the widespread tendency to use such data blindly and unreflectively, and to use them as a basis for various absurd knowledge claims. The discipline seems condemned to such blindness as long as its only recognized form of discourse about practice remains the discourse of technique.

Fortunately, a more reflective kind of discourse about psychological practice is emerging that works with categories of practice that capture the ways in which the practitioners impose a distinctive form on their knowledge products. "Arithmetization" is only one of these categories. I will mention a few others briefly by way of illustration.

There is, for example, the practice of "serialization" by which a serial form is imposed on the behavior of laboratory subjects. By this I mean a form in which behavior appears as a linear sequence of discrete acts, each unit in the sequence being formally equivalent to every other unit. Early examples of this are to be found in the Ebbinghaus method of studying memory by means of responses to items in a list, the responses being themselves structured as a temporal sequence of separate occasions, called "trials" (Danziger, 1990). Going through old research reports one can trace the emergence of the concept of a "trial" as the practice of serialization takes hold, and as a consequence of this a clear distinction between a "trial" and an "experiment," the latter referring to a set of trials linked in a sequence. Insofar as studies of serial learning achieved paradigmatic status within the discipline, all behavior came to be conceptualized as having a serialized form. The employment of attitude and other scales ensured the production of serialized analogues of human behavior that fit the basic model. Serialization is, of course, related to arithmetization, but it is not identical with it. Both are categories of a shaping process that molds human behavior while attempting to study it.

The molding may be quite direct, as in the examples I have mentioned, or it may be indirect. This is what often happens in the practice of "normalization" (Rose, 1990), where elements of behavior are detached from the life of a particular individual and subjected to a statistical order produced by the aggregation of analogous elements contributed by different individuals. Examples are provided by intelligence and personality testing as well as by the constitution of developmental norms and by attitude measurement. One of the features that these practices have in common is the setting up of normative statistical distributions within which each individually contributed element has its precise place (Hacking, 1990). Historically, this involved a profound change of perspective on individual behavior, for the significance of any element of behavior now derived from its place in such normative distributions rather than from its place in the life story of an individual (Danziger, 1990).

As an investigative practice, normalization involves the use of standardized response categories to which individuals must adapt themselves. A certain molding of individual behavior is therefore part of this practice, though it should be noted that a large part of the molding takes place after the subjects of the investigation have left the scene. This stage of investigative practice, known as data processing, reminds us that the ultimate target of experimental intervention consists of the record left behind by the experimental subject, not the subject's behavior as such. The latter is molded in a certain way in order to produce a particular type of record. Such a record then provides opportunities for further constructive practices.

But investigative practice does not end there. The reconstructed record of the investigation and its results must be translated into the form of a research article publishable through very specific channels. At this stage a new set of practices is brought to bear, which are literary and rhetorical. In large part these practices have been codified in disciplinary prescriptions that are as explicit and precise as the prescriptions of texts on research methodology. The *Publication Manual of the American Psychological Association* is a prize example of a literary form that has been brilliantly analyzed by Charles Bazerman (1988). One of the major effects of the literary devices applied at this stage of investigative practice is to hide the constructive nature of research activity from view and to simulate a descriptive account of natural events. Another important function of such texts is that of "universalization," the conveying of the impression that what is being described is not merely of local but of universal significance (Hornstein and Leigh Star, 1990). All psychological investigations are historically unique events involving a specific set of individuals at a particular time and place. Yet, in the great majority of cases, the reports of these investigations seek to establish a universal rather than a local significance. This involves a set of reporting practices that decontextualize both the procedures used and the persons who were subjected to these procedures (Danziger, 1988).

Conclusion: The contextualization of psychological practices

These highly condensed illustrations must suffice to convey something of the flavor of an emerging discourse that takes the investigative practices of psychology as its object. In conclusion I would like to raise a set of broader issues that this discourse seems to have placed on the agenda. These issues concern the social and historical contextualization of psychological practices. It is obvious that the practices we are talking about do not function in a social vacuum. On the one hand they are the practices of groups with a specific social identity, but on the other hand they are closely related to a broad spectrum of social practices whose significance extends far beyond the limited area of psychological investigation.

It is fairly clear, for example, that mental testing has some features that are similar to those found more generally in the social practice of examination, both medical and academic. The kinds of categories I have been discussing, such as arithmetization and normalization, permit a relatively fine-grained analysis of the similarities, and also the differences, between mental testing and more traditional examination practices. It then becomes possible to treat the history of psychological testing as part of a broader history of examination practices and to raise questions about the social changes of which changes in examination practices are a part. It may well be the case that its practices integrate the discipline even more firmly into the broader culture than its theoretical concepts.

But the links between psychological tests and other forms of examination are only one example of similar links that are likely to exist between various psychological practices and practices associated with other segments of social life. Quite generally, we need to inquire into possible homologies between procedures characteristic of various forms of psychological investigation and procedures typically associated with various bureaucratic, administrative, and industrial institutions. The forms imposed on human behavior in such institutions may have a great deal in common with the constraints that typically operate in psychological investigation.

Ultimately, this kind of analysis becomes relevant to concerns about the scope of psychological knowledge. Our discipline has had to labor under the burden of a false ideal of universal knowledge or, more precisely, under the burden of a false dichotomy between general laws of human nature and the unique individual case. This dichotomy used to be popularized in terms of the distinction between the nomothetic and the idiographic approach (Allport, 1937). Although these terms are no longer in general use, the distinction to which they refer is still widely credited. Discussions about the scope of psychological knowledge still seem to proceed on the assumption that the only alternative to universal generalizations is to be found in descriptions of unique individuals. Most investigators equate their scientific mission with a preference for the universal over the unique.

In terms of the discourse of practice, however, this is a false dichotomy. If we strip away the rhetorical devices by means of which investigators commonly establish universalistic claims for their findings, we are left with bits of local knowledge. There is a sense in which a psychological investigation is indeed a historically unique event like any other life event. Nevertheless, it may be legitimate to generalize from such events. The question is, what warrants such generalizations? Traditionally, psychologists have grounded their generalizations on their faith in a constant human nature that operates according to the same principles from one situation to another. That faith provides a basis for universalistic generalizations only if we make the additional, usually implicit, assumption that the system we are describing is essentially a closed system that operates in the same way irrespective of larger systems of which it may be a part.

In contrast to this traditional view, I want to suggest that the practices of investigation serve to embed individuals in a supraindividual system of rules and constraints that provide a *necessary* framework for their conduct. I emphasize "necessary," because the individual never functions outside some such framework. If that is so, then the search for laws of human nature *in vacuo* is futile, and the only kinds of generalizations we can aspire to are those that describe human functioning within particular sets of rules and constraints. The scope of such generalizations will extend only as far as the scope of the practices that establish a particular system of constraints. If homologies exist between certain investigative practices and more widely encountered institutional practices – as I have suggested here – then generalization from experimental to real-life situations may indeed be legitimate in certain cases and may even turn out to have some empirical validity. But these would not be universalistic generalizations. Their scope would be limited by the scope of the practices that define the framework within which they hold. An adequate understanding of practices of investigation, therefore, seems to provide the foundation for a more realistic alternative to the traditional ideal of universalistic psychological knowledge.

References

Allport, G. W. (1937). *Personality: A Psychological Interpretation*. New York: Holt.
Bazerman, C. (1988). Codifying the social scientific style: The APA Publication Manual as a behaviorist rhetoric. In C. Bazerman, *Shaping Written Knowledge: The Genre and Activity of the Experimental Article in Science*. Madison: University of Wisconsin Press (pp. 257–277).
Danziger, K. (1980). The history of introspection reconsidered. *Journal of the History of the Behavioral Sciences, 16,* 241–262.
Danziger, K. (1985). The origins of the psychological experiment as a social institution. *American Psychologist, 40,* 133–140.
Danziger, K. (1988). A question of identity: Who participated in psychological research. In J. G. Morawski (Ed.), *The Rise of Experimentation in American Psychology*. New Haven: Yale University Press (pp. 35–52).
Danziger, K. (1990). *Constructing the Subject: Historical Origins of Psychological Research*. Cambridge: Cambridge University Press.
Gigerenzer, G., and Murray, D. J. (1987). *Cognition As Intuitive Statistics*. Hillsdale, N.J.: Lawrence Erlbaum.
Hacking, I. (1983). *Representing and Intervening*. Cambridge: Cambridge University Press.
Hacking, I. (1990). *The Taming of Chance*. Cambridge: Cambridge University Press.
Hornstein, G. A., and Leigh Star, S. (1990). Universality biases: How theories about human nature succeed. *Philosophy of the Social Sciences, 20,* 421–436.
Hull, C. L. (1935). The conflicting psychologies of learning – a way out. *Psychological Review, 42,* 491–516.
Koch, S. (1959). *Psychology: A Study of a Science*, Vols. 1–6. New York: McGraw-Hill.
Leahy, T. H. (1980). The myth of operationism. *Journal of Mind and Behavior, 1,* 127–143.
Leahy, T. H. (1983). Operationism and ideology: Reply to Kendler. *Journal of Mind and Behavior, 4,* 81–89.
Lenoir, T. (1988). Practice, reason, context: The dialogue between theory and experiment. *Science in Context, 2,* 3–22.
Rogers, T. B. (1989). Operationism in psychology: A discussion of contextual antecedents and an historical interpretation of its longevity. *Journal of the History of the Behavioral Sciences, 25,* 139–153.
Rogers, T. B. (1990). Antecedents of operationism: A case history in radical positivism. Paper presented at the Canadian Psychological Association meeting, Ottawa.
Rose, N. (1990). *Governing the Soul: The Shaping of the Private Self*. London: Routledge.
Rosenzweig, S. (1933). The experimental situation as a psychological problem. *Psychological Review, 40,* 337–354.
Shotter, J. (1990). *Knowing of the Third Kind*. Utrecht: ISOR, University of Utrecht.
Stevens, S. S. (1935). The operational definition of psychological concepts. *Psychological Review, 42,* 517–527.
Suls, J. M., and Rosnow, R. L. (1988). Concerns about artifacts in psychological experiments. In J. G. Morawski (Ed.), *The Rise of Experimentation in American Psychology*. New Haven: Yale University Press (pp. 163–187).
Tolman, E. C. (1932). *Purposive Behavior in Animals and Men*. New York: Century.
Tolman, E. C. (1951). Operational behaviorism and current trends in psychology. Proceedings of the Twenty-fifth anniversary celebration of the inauguration of graduate studies at the University of Southern California, 1936. Reprinted in E. C. Tolman, *Collected Papers in Psychology*. Berkeley: University of California Press (pp. 115–129).

Winston, A. S. (1988). *Cause* and *experiment* in introductory psychology: An analysis of R. S. Woodworth's textbooks. *Teaching of Psychology, 15,* 79–83.

Woodworth, R. S. (1921). *Psychology.* New York: Holt.

Woodworth, R. S. (1938). *Experimental Psychology.* New York: Holt.

Woodworth, R. S. (1939). Four varieties of behaviorism. In *Psychological Issues: Selected Papers of Robert S. Woodworth.* New York: Columbia University Press (pp. 128–135).

Wundt, W. (1883). *Logik,* vol. 2: *Methodenlehre.* Stuttgart: Enke.

3   From tools to theories:
Discovery in cognitive psychology

Gerd Gigerenzer

Let us look at scientific inquiry as "an ocean, continuous everywhere and without a break or division," in Leibniz's words (1690/1951, p. 73). Hans Reichenbach nonetheless divided this ocean into two great seas, the context of discovery and the context of justification. Philosophers, logicians, and mathematicians claimed justification as a part of their territory and dismissed the context of discovery as none of their business, or even as "irrelevant to the logical analysis of scientific knowledge" (Popper, 1959, p. 31). Their sun shines over one part of the ocean and has enlightened us about matters of justification, but the other part of the ocean still remains in a mystical darkness where imagination and intuition reign, or so it is claimed. Popper, Braithwaite, and others ceded the dark part of the ocean to psychology and, perhaps, sociology; but few psychologists have fished in these waters. Most did not dare or care.

In this chapter, I will argue that discovery can be understood by heuristics (not a logic) of discovery. I will propose a heuristic of discovery that makes use of methods of justification, thereby attempting to bridge the artificial distinction between the two. Furthermore, I will attempt to demonstrate that this discovery heuristic may not only be of interest for an a posteriori understanding of theory development, but also may be useful for understanding limitations of present-day theories and research programs and for the further development of alternatives and new possibilities. The discovery heuristic that I call the "tools-to-theories heuristic" (see Gigerenzer & Murray, 1987) postulates a close connection between the shining and the dark part of Leibniz's ocean: Scientists' tools for justification provide the metaphors and concepts for their theories.

The power of tools to shape, or even to become, theoretical concepts is an issue largely ignored in both the history and philosophy of science. Inductivist accounts of discovery, from Bacon to Reichenbach and the Vienna School, focus on the role of data, but do not consider how the

This article is a shortened and slightly revised version of my article "From Tools to Theories: A Heuristic of Discovery in Cognitive Psychology," *Psychological Review*, 1991, *98*, 254–267. Reprinted with the permission of the American Psychological Association.

data are generated or processed. Nor do the numerous anecdotes about discoveries, such as Newton watching an apple fall in his mother's orchard while pondering the mystery of gravitation, Galton taking shelter from a rainstorm during a country outing when discovering correlation and regression toward mediocrity, and the stories about Fechner, Kekulé, Poincaré, and others that link discovery to beds, bicycles, and bathrooms. What unites these anecdotes is the focus on the vivid but prosaic circumstances; they report the setting in which a discovery occurs, rather than analyzing the process of discovery.

The question, Is there a logic of discovery? and Popper's (1959) conjecture that there is none have misled many into assuming that the issue is whether there exists a logic of discovery or only idiosyncratic personal and accidental reasons that explain the "flash of insight" of a particular scientist (Nickles, 1980). I do not think that formal logic and individual personality are the only alternatives, nor do I believe that either of these is a central issue for understanding discovery.

The process of discovery can be shown, according to my argument, to possess more structure than thunderbolt guesses but less definite structure than a monolithic logic of discovery, of the sort Hanson (1958) searched for, or a general inductive hypothesis-generation logic (e.g., Reichenbach, 1938). The present approach lies between these two extremes; it looks for structure beyond the insight of a genius, but does not claim that the tools-to-theories heuristic is (or should be) the only account of scientific discovery. The tools-to-theories heuristic applies neither to all theories in science nor to all cognitive theories; it applies to a specific group of cognitive theories developed after the so-called cognitive revolution, in the past three decades.

Nevertheless, similar heuristics have promoted discovery in physics, physiology, and other areas. For instance, it has been argued that once the mechanical clock became the indispensable tool for astronomical research, the universe itself became understood as a kind of mechanical clock, and God as a divine watchmaker. Lenoir (1986) shows how Faraday's instruments for recording electric currents shaped the understanding of electrophysiological processes by promoting concepts such as "muscle current" and "nerve current."

Thus this discovery heuristic boasts some generality both within cognitive psychology and within science, but this generality is not unrestricted. Since there has been little research in how tools of justification influence theory development, the tools-to-theories heuristic may be more broadly applicable than I am able to show in this chapter. If my view of heuristics of discovery as a heterogeneous bundle of search strategies is correct, however, this implies that generalizability is in principle bounded.

What follows has been inspired by Herbert Simon's notion of heuristics

of discovery, but goes beyond his attempt to model discovery with programs such as BACON that attempt to induce scientific laws from data
(e.g., Langley et al., 1987). My focus is on the role of the tools that process
and produce data, not the data themselves, in the discovery and acceptance
of theories.

How methods of justification shape theoretical concepts

My general thesis is twofold. (1) Scientific tools (both methods and instruments) suggest new theoretical metaphors and theoretical concepts, once
they are entrenched in scientific practice. (2) Familiarity with the tools
within a scientific community also paves the way for the general acceptance
of the theoretical concepts and metaphors inspired by the tools.

By "tools" I refer to both analytical and physical methods that are used
to evaluate given theories. Analytical tools can be either empirical or nonempirical. Examples of analytical methods of the empirical kind are tools
for data processing such as statistics; examples of the nonempirical kind
are normative criteria for the evaluation of hypotheses such as logical
consistency. Examples of physical tools of justification are measurement
instruments such as clocks. In this chapter, I focus on analytical rather than
physical tools of justification and, among these, on techniques of statistical
inference and hypothesis testing. My topic here will be theories of mind,
and how social scientists discovered them after the emergence of new tools
for data analysis, rather than of new data.

In this context, the tools-to-theories heuristic consists in the discovery of
new theories by changing the conception of the mind through the analogy of
the statistical tool. The result can vary in depth from opening new general
perspectives, albeit mainly metaphorical, to sharp discontinuity in specific
cognitive theories caused by the direct transfer of scientists' tools into
theories of mind.

A brief history follows. In American psychology, the study of cognitive
processes was suppressed in the early twentieth century by the allied forces
of operationalism and behaviorism. The operationalism and the inductivism
of the Vienna School, inter alia, paved the way for the institutionalization
of inferential statistics in American experimental psychology between 1940
and 1955 (Gigerenzer, 1987a; Toulmin & Leary, 1985). In experimental
psychology, inferential statistics became almost synonymous with scientific
method. Inferential statistics, in turn, provided a large part of the new
concepts for mental processes that have fueled the so-called cognitive revolution since the 1960s. Theories of cognition were cleansed of terms such as
restructuring and insight, and the new mind has come to be portrayed
as drawing random samples from nervous fibers, computing probabilities,

calculating analyses of variance, setting decision criteria, and performing utility analyses.

After the institutionalization of inferential statistics, a broad range of cognitive processes, conscious and unconscious, elementary and complex, was reinterpreted as involving "intuitive statistics." For instance, W. P. Tanner and his co-workers assumed in their theory of signal detectability that the mind "decides" whether there is a stimulus or only noise, just as a statistician of the Neyman-Pearson school decides between two hypotheses (Tanner & Swets, 1954). In his causal attribution theory, Harold H. Kelley (1967) postulated that the mind attributes a cause to an effect in the same way as behavioral scientists have come to do, namely, by performing an analysis of variance and testing null hypotheses. These two influential theories show the breadth of the new conception of the "mind as an intuitive statistician" (Gigerenzer, 1994; Gigerenzer & Murray, 1987). They also exemplify cognitive theories that were suggested not by new data but by new tools of data analysis.

In what follows, I shall give evidence for three points. First, the discovery of theories based on the conception of the mind as an intuitive statistician caused discontinuity in theory rather than being merely a new, fashionable language: It radically changed the kind of phenomena reported, the kind of explanations looked for, and even the kind of data that were generated. This first point illustrates the profound power of the tools-to-theories heuristic to generate quite innovative theories. Second, I will provide evidence for the "blindness" or inability of researchers to discover and accept the conception of the mind as an intuitive statistician before they became familiar with inferential statistics as part of their daily routine. The discontinuity in cognitive theory is closely linked to the preceding discontinuity in method, that is, to the institutionalization of inferential statistics in psychology. Third, I will show how the tools-to-theories heuristic can help us to see the limits and possibilities of current cognitive theories that investigate the mind as an "intuitive statistician."

Discontinuity in cognitive theory development

What has been called the "cognitive revolution" (Gardner, 1985) is more than the overthrow of behaviorism by mentalist concepts. The latter have been continuously part of scientific psychology since its emergence in the late nineteenth century, even coexisting with American behaviorism during its heyday (Lovie, 1983). The cognitive revolution did more than revive the mental; it has changed our concepts of what the mental means, often dramatically. One source of this change is the tools-to-theories heuristic, with its new analogy of the mind as an intuitive statistician. To show the discontinuity within cognitive theories, I will briefly discuss two areas in which an entire statistical technique, not only a few statistical concepts, became a model of mental processes: stimulus detection and discrimination, and causal attribution.

What intensity must a 440-Hz tone have to be perceived? How much heavier than a standard stimulus of 100 gms must a comparison stimulus be, in order for a perceiver to notice a difference? How to understand the elementary cognitive processes involved in those tasks, known today as "stimulus detection" and "stimulus discrimination"? Since Herbart (1816), such processes have been explained by using a threshold metaphor: Detection occurs only if the effect an object has on our nervous system exceeds an absolute threshold, and discrimination between two objects occurs if the excitation from one exceeds that from another by an amount greater than a differential threshold. E. H. Weber and G. T. Fechner's laws refer to the concept of fixed thresholds; Titchener (1896) saw in differential thresholds the long-sought-after elements of mind (he counted ca. 44,000); and classic textbooks such as Brown and Thomson's (1921) and Guilford's (1954) document methods and research.

Around 1955, the psychophysics of absolute and differential thresholds was revolutionized by the new analogy between the mind and the statistician. W. P. Tanner and others proposed a "theory of signal detectability" (TSD), which assumes that the Neyman-Pearson technique of hypothesis testing describes the processes involved in detection and discrimination. Recall that in Neyman-Pearson statistics, two sampling distributions (hypotheses H_0 and H_1) and a decision criterion (which is a likelihood ratio) are defined, and then the data observed are transformed into a likelihood ratio and compared with the decision criterion. Depending on which side of the criterion the data fall, the decision "reject H_0 and accept H_1" or "accept H_0 and reject H_1" is made. In straight analogy, TSD assumes that the mind calculates two sampling distributions for "noise" and "signal plus noise" (in the detection situation) and sets a decision criterion after weighing the cost of the two possible decision errors (Type I and Type II errors in Neyman-Pearson theory, now called "false alarms" and "misses"). The sensory input is transduced into a form that allows the brain to calculate its likelihood ratio, and depending on whether this ratio is smaller or larger than the criterion, the subject says "no, there is no signal" or "yes, there is a signal." Tanner (1965) explicitly referred to his new model of the mind as a "Neyman-Pearson" detector, and, in unpublished work, his flow charts included a drawing of a homunculus statistician performing the unconscious statistics in the brain (Gigerenzer & Murray, 1987, pp. 43–53).

The new analogy between mind and statistician replaced the century-old concept of a fixed threshold by the twin notions of observer's attitudes and observer's sensitivity. Just as Neyman-Pearson technique distinguishes between a subjective part (e.g., selection of a criterion dependent on cost–benefit considerations) and a mathematical part, detection and discrimination became understood as involving both subjective processes, such as attitudes and cost-benefit considerations, and sensory processes. Swets, Tanner, and Birdsall (1964, p. 52) considered this link between attitudes and sensory processes to be the "main thrust" of their theory. The analogy between technique and mind made new research questions thinkable, such as, How can the mind's decision criterion be manipulated? A new kind of data even emerged: Two types of errors were generated in the experiments, false alarms and misses, just as the statistical theory distinguishes two types of error.

As far as I can tell, the idea of generating these two kinds of data (errors) was not common before. The discovery of TSD was not motivated by new data; rather, the new theory motivated a new kind of data. In fact, in their seminal paper, Tanner and Swets (1954, p. 401) explicitly admit that their theory "appears to be inconsistent with the large quantity of existing data on this subject," and proceed to criticize the "form of these data."

The Neyman-Pearsonian technique of hypothesis testing was subsequently transformed into a theory of a broad range of cognitive processes, ranging from recognition in memory (e.g., Murdock, 1982; Wickelgreen & Norman, 1966) to eyewitness testimony (e.g., Birnbaum, 1983) to discrimination between random and nonrandom patterns (e.g., Lopes, 1982).

My second example concerns theories of causal reasoning. In Europe, Albert Michotte (1946/1963), Jean Piaget (1930), the gestalt psychologists, and others had investigated how certain temporal–spatial relationships between two or more visual objects, such as moving dots, produced phenomenal causality. For instance, the subjects were made to "perceive" that one dot launches, pushes, or chases another. After the institutionalization of inferential statistics, Harold H. Kelley (1967) proposed in his "attribution theory" that the long-sought laws of causal reasoning are in fact the tools of the behavioral scientist: R. A. Fisher's analysis of variance (ANOVA). Just as the experimenter has come to infer a causal relationship between two variables from calculating an analysis of variance and performing an F-test, the man in the street infers the cause of an effect by unconsciously doing the same calculations. By the time Kelley discovered the new metaphor for causal inference, about 70% of all experimental articles already used ANOVA (Edgington, 1974).

The theory was quickly accepted in social psychology; Kelley and Michaela (1980) report more than 900 references in one decade. The vision of the Fisherian mind radically changed the understanding of causal reasoning, the problems posed to the subjects, and the explanations looked for. I list a few discontinuities that reveal the fingerprints of the tool. (1) ANOVA needs repetitions or numbers as data in order to estimate variances and covariances. Consequently, the information presented to the subjects in studies of causal attribution consists of information about the frequency of events (e.g., McArthur, 1972), which played no role in either Michotte's or Piaget's work. (2) Whereas Michotte's work still reflects the broad Aristotelian conception of four causes (see Gavin, 1972), and Piaget (1930) distinguished 17 kinds of causality in children's minds, the Fisherian mind concentrates on the one kind of causes for which ANOVA is used as a tool (similar to Aristotle's "material cause"). (3) In Michotte's view, causal perception is direct and spontaneous and needs no inference, as a consequence of largely innate laws that determine the organization of the perceptual field. ANOVA, in contrast, is used in psychology as a technique for inductive inferences from data to hypotheses, and the focus in Kelley's attribution theory is consequently on the data-driven, inductive side of causal perception.

The latter point illustrates that the specific use of a tool, that is, its practical context rather than its mathematical structure, can also shape theoretical conceptions of mind. To elaborate on this point, let us assume that Harold Kelley had lived one and a half centuries earlier than he did. In the early nineteenth century, significance tests (similar to those in ANOVA) were already being used by astronomers (Swijtink, 1987). But they used their tests to reject data, so-called outliers, and not to reject hypotheses. At least provisionally, the astronomers assumed that the theory was correct and mistrusted the data, whereas the ANOVA mind, following the current statistical textbooks, assumes the data to be correct and mistrusts the theories. So, to our nineteenth-century Kelley, the mind's causal attribution would have seemed expectation-driven rather than data-driven: The statistician homunculus in the mind would have tested the data and not the hypothesis.

These two areas – detection and discrimination, and causal reasoning – may be sufficient to illustrate some of the fundamental innovations in the explanatory framework, in the research questions posed, and in the kind of data generated. The spectrum of theories that model cognition after statistical inference ranges from auditory and visual perception to recognition in memory, and from speech perception to thinking and reasoning (see Gigerenzer & Murray, 1987).

To summarize: The tools-to-theories heuristic can account for the discovery and acceptance of a group of cognitive theories in apparently unrelated subfields of psychology, all of them sharing the view that cognitive processes can be modeled by statistical hypothesis testing. Among these are several highly innovative and influential theories that have radically changed our understanding of what "cognitive" means.

Before the institutionalization of inferential statistics

There is an important test case for the present hypotheses (1) that familiarity with the statistical tool is crucial to the discovery of corresponding theories of mind and (2) that the institutionalization of the tool within a scientific community is crucial for the broad acceptance of those theories. That test case is the era before the institutionalization of inferential statistics. Theories that conceive of the mind as an intuitive statistician should have a very small likelihood of being discovered, and even less likelihood of being accepted. The two strongest tests are cases where (1) someone proposed a similar conceptual analogy and (2) someone proposed a similar probabilistic (formal) model. The chances of theories of the first kind being accepted should be small, and the chances of a probabilistic model being interpreted as "intuitive statistics" should be similarly small. I know of only one case each, which I will analyze after defining first what I mean by the term "institutionalization of inferential statistics."

Statistical inference has been known for a long time, but not used in theories of mind. In 1710, John Arbuthnot proved the existence of God using a kind of significance test; as mentioned earlier, astronomers used significance tests in the nineteenth century; G. T. Fechner's statistical text *Kollektivmasslehre* (1897) included tests of hypotheses; W. S. Gosset (using the pseudonym "Student") published the t-test in 1908; and Fisher's significance testing techniques, such as ANOVA, as well as Neyman-Pearsonian hypothesis testing methods have been available since the 1920s (see Gigerenzer et al., 1989). Bayes' theorem was known since 1763. Nonetheless, there was little interest in these techniques in experimental psychology before 1940 (Rucci & Tweney, 1980).

The statisticians' conquest of new territory in psychology started in the 1940s. By 1942, Maurice Kendall could comment on the statisticians' expansion: "They have already overrun every branch of science with a rapidity of conquest rivalled only by Attila, Mohammed, and the Colorado beetle" (p. 69). By the early 1950s, half of the psychology departments in leading American universities offered courses on Fisherian methods and had made inferential statistics a graduate program requirement. By 1955, more than 80% of the experimental articles in leading journals used inferential statistics to justify conclusions from the data (Sterling, 1959), and editors of major journals made significance testing a requirement for the acceptance of articles submitted (e.g., Melton, 1962).

I shall therefore use 1955 as a rough date for the institutionalization of the tool in curricula, textbooks, and editorials. What became institutionalized as the logic of statistical inference was a mixture of ideas from two opposing camps, those of R. A. Fisher, on the one hand, and Jerzy Neyman and Egon S. Pearson (the son of Karl Pearson) on the other.

Discovery and rejection of the analogy

The analogy between the mind and the statistician was first proposed before the institutionalization of inferential statistics, in the early 1940s, by Egon Brunswik at Berkeley (e.g., Brunswik, 1943). As Leary (1987) has shown, Brunswik's probabilistic functionalism was based on a very unusual blending of scientific traditions, including the probabilistic world view of Hans Reichenbach and members of the Vienna School, and Karl Pearson's correlational statistics.

The important point here is that in the late 1930s Brunswik changed his techniques for measuring perceptual constancies, from calculating (nonstatistical) "Brunswik ratios" to calculating Pearson correlations, such as "functional" and "ecological validities." In the 1940s, he also began to think of the organism as "an intuitive statistician," but it took him several years to spell out the analogy in a clear and consistent way (Gigerenzer, 1987b).

The analogy is this: The perceptual system infers its environment from uncertain cues by (unconsciously) calculating correlation and regression statistics, just as the Brunswikian researcher does when (consciously) calculating the degree of adaptation of a perceptual system to a given environment. Brunswik's "intuitive statistician" was a statistician of the Karl Pearson school, like the Brunswikian researcher. Brunswik's "intuitive statistician" was not well adapted to the psychological science of the time, however, and the analogy was poorly understood and generally rejected (Leary, 1987).

Brunswik's analogy came too early to be understood and accepted by his colleagues of the experimental discipline; it came before the institutionalization of statistics as the indispensable method of scientific inference, and it came with the "wrong" statistical model, correlational statistics. Correlation was an indispensable method not in experimental psychology, but rather in its rival discipline, known as the Galton-Pearson program, or, as Lee Cronbach (1957) put it, the "Holy Roman Empire" of "correlational psychology."

The schism between the two disciplines had been repeatedly taken up in presidential addresses before the APA (Dashiell, 1939; Cronbach, 1957) and had deeply affected the values and the mutual esteem of psychologists (Thorndike, 1954). Brunswik could not succeed in persuading his colleagues from the experimental discipline to consider the statistical tool of the competing discipline as a model of how the mind works. Ernest Hilgard (1955), in his rejection of Brunswik's perspective, did not mince words: "Correlation is an instrument of the devil" (p. 228).

Brunswik, who coined the metaphor of "man as intuitive statistician," did not survive to see the success of his analogy. It was accepted only after statistical inference became institutionalized in experimental psychology, and with the new institutionalized tools rather than (Karl) Pearsonian statistics serving as models of mind. Only in the mid-1960s, however, did interest in Brunswikian models of mind emerge (e.g., Brehmer & Joyce, 1988; Hammond et al., 1975).

Probabilistic models without the "intuitive statistician"

My preceding point was that the statistical tool was accepted as a plausible analogy of cognitive processes only after its institutionalization in experimental psychology. My second point is that although some probabilistic models of cognitive processes were advanced before the institutionalization of inferential statistics, they were not interpreted using the metaphor of the "mind as intuitive statistician." The distinction I draw here is between probabilistic models that use the metaphor and ones that do not. The latter kind is illustrated by models that use probability distributions for perceptual judgment, assuming that variability is caused by lack of experimental control, measurement error, or other factors that can be summarized as experimenter's ignorance. Ideally, if the experimenter had complete control and knowledge (such as Laplace's demon), all probabilistic terms could be eliminated from the theory. This does not hold for a probabilistic model that is based on the metaphor. Here, the probabilistic terms model the ignorance of the mind rather than that of the experimenter. That is, they model how the "homunculus statistician" in the brain comes to terms with a fundamentally uncertain world. Even if the experimenter had complete knowledge, the theories would remain probabilistic, since it is the mind that is ignorant and needs statistics.

The key example is L. L. Thurstone, who in 1927 formulated a model for perceptual judgment that was formally equivalent to the present-day theory of signal detectability (TSD). But neither Thurstone nor his followers recognized the possibility of interpreting the formal structure of their model in terms of the "intuitive statistician." Like TSD, Thurstone's model had two overlapping normal distributions, which represented the internal values of two stimuli and which specified the corresponding likelihood ratios, but it never occurred to Thurstone to include the conscious activities of a statistician, such as the weighing of the costs of the two errors and the setting of a decision criterion, in his model. Thus neither Thurstone nor his followers took the – with hindsight – small step to develop the "law of comparative judgment" into TSD. When Duncan Luce (1977) reviewed Thurstone's model 50 years later, he found it hard to believe that nothing in Thurstone's writings showed the least awareness of this small but crucial step. Thurstone's perceptual model remained a mechanical, albeit probabilistic, stimulus-response theory without a homunculus statistician in the brain. The small conceptual step was never taken, and TSD entered psychology by an independent route.

To summarize: There are several kinds of evidence for a close link between the institutionalization of inferential statistics in the 1950s and the subsequent broad acceptance of the metaphor of the mind as an intuitive statistician: (1) the general failure to accept, and even to understand, Brunswik's "intuitive statistician" before the institutionalization of the tool, and (2) the case of Thurstone, who proposed a probabilistic model that was formally equivalent to one important present-day theory of "intuitive statistics," but was never interpreted in this way; the analogy was not yet seen. Brunswik's case illustrates that tools may act at two levels: First, new tools may suggest new cognitive theories to a scientist; and, second, the degree to which these tools are institutionalized within the scientific community to which the scientist belongs can prepare (or hinder) the acceptance of the new theory. This close link between tools for justification on the one hand and discovery and acceptance on the other reveals the artificiality of the discovery–justification distinction. Discovery does not come first, and justification afterward. Discovery is inspired by justification.

How heuristics of discovery may help in understanding limitations and possibilities of current research programs

In this section I will argue that the preceding analysis of discovery is of interest not only for a psychology of scientific discovery and creativity (e.g., Gardner, 1988; Gruber, 1981; Tweney, Dotherty, & Mynatt, 1981), but also for the evaluation and further development of current cognitive theories. The general point is that institutionalized tools like statistics are not theoretically inert. Rather they come with a set of assumptions and interpretations that may be smuggled in Trojan horse fashion into the new cognitive theories and research programs. One example was mentioned: The formal tools of significance testing are interpreted in psychology as tools for rejecting *hypotheses,* assuming that the data are correct, whereas in other fields and at other times the same tools were interpreted as tools for rejecting *data* (outliers), assuming that the hypotheses were correct. The latter use of statistics is practically extinct in experimental psychology (although the problem of outliers routinely emerges) and, therefore, also absent in theories that liken cognitive processes to significance testing. In cases like these, analysis of discovery may help to reveal "blind spots" associated with the tool and, as a consequence, new possibilities for cognitive theorizing.

I will illustrate this potential in more detail using examples from the "judgment under uncertainty" program of Daniel Kahneman, Amos Tversky, and others (see Kahneman, Slovic, & Tversky, 1982). This stimulating research program emerged from the earlier research on human information processing by Ward Edwards and his co-workers. In Edwards's work, the dual role of statistics as a tool and a model of mind is again evident: Edwards, Lindman, and Savage (1963) proposed Bayesian statistics for scientific hypothesis evaluation and considered the mind as a reasonably good, albeit conservative, Bayesian statistician (e.g., Edwards, 1966). The judgment-under-uncertainty program also investigates reasoning as "intuitive statistics," but focuses on so-called errors in probabilistic reasoning. In most of the theories based on the metaphor of the "intuitive statistician," statistics or probability theory is used both as normative and as descriptive of a cognitive process (e.g., both as the optimal and the actual mechanism for speech perception and human memory; see Massaro, 1987, and Anderson & Milson, 1989, respectively). This is not the case in the judgment-under-uncertainty program; here, statistics and probability theory are used only in the normative function, whereas actual human reasoning has been described as "biased," "fallacious," or "indefensible" (on the rhetoric, see Lopes, 1991).

In the following, I will first point out two assumptions that became associated with the statistical tool in the course of its institutionalization in psychology, neither of them being part of the mathematics or statistical theory proper. Then I will show that these assumptions reemerge in the judgment-under-uncertainty program, resulting in severe limitations on that program. Finally, I will suggest how this hidden legacy of the tool could be eliminated to provide new impulses and possibilities for the research program.

The first assumption can be called "There is only one statistics." Textbooks on statistics for psychologists (usually written by nonmathematicians) generally teach statistical inference as if there existed only one logic of inference. Since the 1950s and 1960s, almost all texts teach a mishmash of R. A. Fisher's ideas tangled with those of Jerzy Neyman and Egon S. Pearson, but without acknowledgment. The fact that Fisherians and Neyman-Pearsonians could never agree on a logic of statistical inference is not mentioned in the textbooks, nor are the controversial issues that divide them. Even alternative statistical logics for scientific inference are rarely discussed (Gigerenzer, 1987a). For instance, Fisher (1955) argued that concepts like Type II error, power, the setting of a level of significance before the experiment, and its interpretation as a long-run frequency of errors in repeated experiments are concepts inappropriate for scientific inference – at best they could be applied to technology (his pejorative example was Stalin's). Neyman, for his part, declared that some of Fisher's significance tests are "worse than useless" (since their power is less than their size; see Hacking, 1965, p. 99). I know of no textbook written by psychologists for psychologists that mentions and explains this and other controversies about the logic of inference. Instead, readers are presented with an intellectually incoherent mix of Fisherian and Neyman-Pearsonian ideas, but a mix presented as a seamless, uncontroversial whole: *the* logic of scientific inference (for more details see Gigerenzer, 1993; Gigerenzer et al., 1989, chap. 3 and 6; Gigerenzer & Murray, 1987, chap. 1).

The second assumption that became associated with the tool during its institutionalization is "There is only one meaning of probability." For instance, Fisher and Neyman-Pearson had different interpretations of what a level of significance means. Fisher's was an epistemic interpretation, that is, that the level of significance tells us about the confidence we can have in the particular hypothesis under test, whereas Neyman's was a strictly frequentist and behavioristic interpretation, which claimed that a level of significance tells us nothing about a particular hypothesis, but about the relative frequency of wrongly rejecting the null hypothesis if it is true in the long run. Although the textbooks teach both Fisherian and Neyman-Pearsonian ideas, these alternative views of what a probability (such as level of significance) could mean are generally neglected – not to speak of the many other meanings that have been proposed for the formal concept of probability (Hacking, 1965).

These assumptions, characteristic of the practical context in which the statistical tool has been used, reemerge at the theoretical level in current cognitive psychology, just as the tools-to-theories heuristic would lead us to expect.

Assumption 1: There is only one statistics, which is normative

Tversky and Kahneman (1974) described their judgment-under-uncertainty program as a two-step procedure. First, subjects are confronted with a reasoning problem, and their answer is compared with the "normative" or "correct" answer, supplied by statistics and probability theory. Second, the *deviation* between the subject's answer and the "normative" answer, also called a "bias of reasoning," is explained by some "heuristic" of reasoning.

One implicit assumption at the heart of this research program says that statistical theory provides exactly one answer to the "real world" problems presented to the subjects. If this were not true, the deviation between subjects' judgment and the "normative" answer would be an inappropriate explanandum, because there are as many different deviations as there are statistical answers. Consider the following problem:

A cab was involved in a hit-and-run accident at night. Two companies, the Green and the Blue, operate in the city. You are given the following data:

(i) 85% of the cabs in the city are Green and 15% are Blue. (ii) A witness identified the cab as a Blue cab. The court tested his ability to identify cabs under the appropriate visibility conditions. When presented with a sample of cabs (half of which were Blue and half of which were Green), the witness made correct identifications in 80% of the cases and erred in 20% of the cases.

Question: What is the probability that the cab involved in the accident was Blue rather than Green? (Tversky & Kahneman, 1980, p. 62)

The authors inserted the values specified in this problem into Bayes' formula and calculated a probability of .41 as the "correct" answer; and, despite criticism, they have never retreated from that claim. They saw in the difference between this value and the subjects' median answer of .80 an instance of a reasoning error, known as *neglect of base rates*. But alternative statistical solutions to the problem exist.

Tversky and Kahneman's reasoning is based on one among many possible Bayesian views – which the statistician I. J. Good (1971), not all too seriously, once counted up to 46,656 in number. For instance, using the classical principle of indifference to determine the Bayesian prior probabilities can be as defensible as Tversky and Kahneman's use of base rates of "cabs in the city" for the relevant priors, but leads to a probability of .80 instead of .41 (Levi, 1983). Or if we apply Neyman-Pearson theory to the cab problem, we get solutions between .28 and .82, depending on the psychological theory about the witness's criterion shift – the shift from witness testimony at the time of the accident to witness testimony at the time of the court's test (Birnbaum, 1983; Gigerenzer & Murray, 1987, pp. 167–174).

There may be more arguable answers to the cab problem, depending on what statistical or philosophical theory of inference one uses. Indeed, the range of possible statistical solutions is about the range of subjects' actual answers. The point is that none of these statistical solutions is the only correct one to the preceding problem, and therefore it makes little sense to use the deviation between a subject's judgment and one of these statistical answers as the psychological explanandum.

Statistics is an indispensable tool for scientific inference, but, as Neyman and Pearson (1928, p. 176) pointed out, in "many cases there is probably no single best method of solution." Rather, several such theories are legitimate, just as "Euclidean and non-Euclidean geometrics are equally legitimate" (Neyman, 1937, p. 336). My point is: The *idée fixe* that statistics speaks with one voice has reappeared in research on intuitive statistics. The highly interesting judgment-under-uncertainty program could progress beyond the present point, if (1) subjects' judgments rather than deviations between judgments and a so-called normative solution are considered as the data to be explained, and if (2) various statistical models are proposed as competing hypotheses of problem-solving strategies rather than one model as *the* general norm for rational reasoning. The willingness of many researchers to accept the claim that statistics speaks with one voice is the legacy of the institutionalized tool, not of statistics per se.

Note the resulting double standard: Many researchers on "intuitive statistics" argue that their subjects should draw inferences from data to hypotheses by using Bayes' formula, although they themselves do not. Rather, the researchers use the institutionalized mixture of Fisherian and Neyman-Pearsonian statistics to draw their inferences from data to hypothesis.

Assumption 2: There is only one interpretation of probability

Just as there are alternative logics of inference, there are alternative interpretations of probability that have been part of the mathematical theory since its inception in the mid-seventeenth century (Daston, 1988; Hacking, 1975). Again, both the institutionalized tool and the recent cognitive research on probabilistic reasoning exhibit the same blind spot concerning the existence of alternative interpretations of probability. For instance, Lichtenstein, Fischoff, and Phillips (1982) have reported and summarized research on a phenomenon called "overconfidence." Briefly, subjects were given questions such as "Absinthe is (a) a precious stone, (b) a liqueur"; they chose what they believed was the correct answer and then were asked for a confidence rating in their answer, for example, 90% certain. When people said they were 100% certain about individual answers, they had in the long run only about 80% correct answers; when they were 90% certain, they had in the long run only 75% correct answers, and so on. This discrepancy was called "overconfidence" and was explained by general heuristics in memory search, such as "confirmation biases," or general motivational tendencies such as an "illusion of validity."

My point is that two different interpretations of probability are compared: degrees of belief in single events (i.e., that *this answer* is correct) and relative frequencies of correct answers in the long run. Although eighteenth-century mathematicians, like many of today's cognitive psychologists, would have had no problem in equating the two, most mathematicians and philosophers since then have. For instance, according to the frequentist point of view, the term "probability," when it refers to a single event, "has no meaning at all for us" (Mises, 1957, p. 11) because probability theory is about relative frequencies in the long run. Thus, for a frequentist, probability theory does not apply to single-event confidences, and therefore no confidence judgment can violate probability theory. To call a discrepancy between confidence and relative frequency a *bias* in probabilistic reasoning would mean comparing apples and oranges. Moreover, even subjectivists would not generally think of a discrepancy between confidence and relative frequency as a bias (see Kadane & Lichtenstein, 1982, for a discussion of conditions). For a subjectivist such as Bruno de Finetti, probability *is* about single events, but rationality is identified with the internal consistency of probability judgments. As de Finetti (1931/1989, p. 174) emphasizes: "However an individual evaluates the probability of a particular event, no experience can prove him right, or wrong; nor in general, could any conceivable criterion give any objective sense to the distinction one would like to draw, here, between right and wrong."

Nonetheless, the literature on "overconfidence" is largely silent on even the possibility of this conceptual problem (but see Keren, 1987). The question about research strategy is whether to use the deviation between degrees of belief and relative frequencies (again considered as a "bias") as the explanandum, or to accept the existence of several meanings of "probability" and to investigate the kind of conceptual distinctions that untutored subjects make. Almost all research has been done within the former research strategy. And, indeed, if the issue were a general tendency to overestimate one's knowledge, as the term "overconfidence" suggests – for instance, as a result of general strategies of memory search or motivational tendencies – then asking the subject for degrees of belief or for frequencies should not matter.

But it does. In a series of experiments (Gigerenzer, Hoffrage, & Kleinbölting, 1991; see also May, 1987) we gave subjects several hundred questions of the absinthe type and asked them for confidence judgments after every question was answered (as usual). In addition, after each 50 (or 10, 5, and 2) questions we asked the subjects how many of those questions they believed they had answered correctly – that is, we requested frequency judgments. This design allowed comparison both between their confidence in their individual answers and true relative frequencies of correct answers, and between judgments of relative frequencies and true relative frequencies. Comparing frequency judgments with the true frequency of correct answers showed that overestimation or "overconfidence" disappeared in 80% to 90% of the subjects, depending on experimental conditions. Frequency judgments were precise or even showed underestimation. Ironically, after each frequency judgment, subjects went on to give confidence judgments (degrees of belief) that exhibit what has been called "overconfidence."

As in the preceding example, a so-called bias of reasoning disappears if a controversial norm is dropped and replaced by several descriptive alternatives, statistical models, and meanings of probability, respectively. Thus probabilities for single events and relative frequencies seem to refer to different meanings of confidence in the minds of our subjects. This result is inconsistent with previous explanations of the alleged bias by general heuristics or a generally mistaken self-evaluation, and has led to the theory of probabilistic mental models (Gigerenzer et al., 1991). Untutored intuition seems to be capable of making conceptual distinctions of the sort statisticians and philosophers make (e.g., Cohen, 1986; Lopes, 1981; Teigen, 1983). And it suggests that the important research questions to be investigated are, How are different meanings of "probability" cued in everyday language? and How does this affect judgment? rather than, How can we explain the alleged bias of "overconfidence" by some general deficits in memory, cognition, or personality?

The same conceptual distinction can help us to understand other kinds of judgments under uncertainty. For instance, Tversky and Kahneman (1982, 1983) used a personality sketch of "Linda" that suggested she was a feminist. Subjects were asked which is more probable, (1) that Linda is a bank teller, or (2) that Linda is a bank teller and active in the feminist movement. Most subjects chose (2), which Tversky and Kahneman (1982) called a "fallacious" belief, to be explained by their hypothesis that people use a limited number of heuristics – in the present case, representativeness (the similarity between the description of Linda and the alternatives (1) and (2), respectively). Subjects' judgments were called a "conjunction fallacy," since the probability of a conjunction of events (bank teller and active in the feminist movement) cannot be greater than the probability of one of its components.

As in the preceding example, this normative interpretation neglects two facts. First, in everyday language, words like "probable" legitimately have several meanings, just as terms like "if . . . then" and "or" do. The particular meaning seems to be automatically cued by content and context. Second, statisticians similarly have alternative views of what probability is about. In the context of some subjectivist theories, choosing (2) truly violates the rules of probability; but for a frequentist, judgments of singular events such as in the Linda problem have nothing to do with probability theory: As the statistician G. A. Barnard (1979) objected, they should be treated in the context of psychoanalysis, not probability (p. 171).

Again, the normative view explicit in the term "conjunction fallacy" is far from being uncontroversial, and progress in understanding reasoning may be expected by focusing on subjects' judgments as explanandum rather than on their deviations from a so-called norm. As in the previous example, if problems of the Linda type are rephrased as involving *frequency* judgments (e.g., How many out of 100 cases that fit the description of Linda are (1) bank tellers, and (2) bank tellers and active in the feminist movement?), then the so-called conjunction fallacy decreases from 77% to 27%, as Fiedler (1988) has shown. "Which alternative is more probable?" is not the same as "Which alternative is more frequent?" in the Linda context. Tversky and Kahneman (1983) themselves found a similar result, but they maintained their normative claims and treated the disappearance of the phenomenon merely as "attempts to combat" the fallacy, as an exception to the rule (p. 293).

Discussion

New technologies have been a steady source of metaphors of mind: "In my childhood we were always assured that the brain was a telephone switchboard. ('What else could it be?')," recalls John Searle (1984, p. 44). The tools-to-theories heuristic is more specific than general technology meta-phors. Scientists' tools, not just any tools, are used to understand the mind. Holograms are not social scientists' tools, but computers are, and part of their differential acceptance as metaphors of mind by the psychological community may be a result of psychologists' differential familiarity with these devices in research practice.

The computer, serial and parallel, is another case study for the tools-to-theories heuristic – a case study that is in some aspects different (Giger-enzer & Goldstein, 1996). For instance, John von Neumann (1958) and others explicitly suggested the analogy between the serial computer and the brain. But the main use of computers in psychological science was first in the context of justification: for processing data, making statistical calcula-tions, and as an ideal, endlessly patient experimental subject. Recently, the computer metaphor and the statistics metaphors of mind have converged, both in artificial intelligence and in the shift toward massively parallel computers simulating the interaction between neurons.

The examples of discovery I gave in this chapter are modest instances compared with the classical literature in the history of science treating the contribution of a Copernicus or a Darwin. But in the narrower context of recent cognitive psychology, the theories discussed here count as among the most influential. In this more prosaic context of discovery, the tools-to-theories heuristic can account for a group of significant theoretical innova-tions. And, as I have argued, this discovery heuristic can both open and foreclose new avenues of research, depending on the interpretations attached to the statistical tool. My focus was on analytical tools of justifica-tion, and I have not dealt with physical tools of experimentation and data processing. Physical tools, once familiar and considered indispensable, also may become the stuff of theories. This holds not only for the hardware (like the software) of the computer, but also for theory innovation beyond recent cognitive psychology. Smith (1986) argued that Edward C. Tolman's use of the maze as an experimental apparatus transformed Tolman's conception of purpose and cognition into spatial characteristics, such as cognitive maps. Similarly, he argued that Clark L. Hull's fascination with conditioning machines has shaped Hull's thinking of behavior as if it were machine design. With the exception of Danziger's (1985, 1987, 1990) work on chang-ing methodological practices in psychology and their impact on the kind of knowledge produced, however, there seems to exist no systematic research program on the power of familiar tools to shape new theories in psychology.

Discovery reconsidered

Let me conclude with some reflections on how the present view stands in relation to major themes in scientific discovery.

Data-to-theories reconsidered. Should we go on telling our students that new theories originate from new data? If only because "little is known about how theories come to be created," as J. R. Anderson introduces the reader to his *Cognitive Psychology* (1980, p. 17)? Holton (1988) noted the tendency among physicists to reconstruct discovery with hindsight as originating from new data, even if this is not the case. His most prominent example is Einstein's special theory of relativity, which was and still is celebrated as an empirical generalization from Michelson's experimental data – by such eminent figures as R. A. Millikan and H. Reichenbach, as well as by the textbook writers. As Holton demonstrated with firsthand documents, the role of Michelson's data in the discovery of Einstein's theory was slight, a conclusion shared by Einstein himself.

The strongest claim for an inductive view of discovery came from the Vienna Circle's emphasis on sensory data (reduced to the concept of "pointer readings"). Carnap (1928/1969), Reichenbach (1938), and others focused on what they called the "rational reconstruction" of actual discovery rather than on actual discovery itself, in order to screen out the "merely" irrational and psychological. For instance, Reichenbach reconstructed Einstein's special theory of relativity as being "suggested by closest adherence to experimental facts," a claim that Einstein rejected, as mentioned above (see Holton, 1988, p. 296). It seems fair to say that all attempts logically to reconstruct discovery in science have failed in practice (Blackwell, 1983, p. 111). The strongest theoretical disclaimer concerning the possibility of a logic of discovery came from Popper, Hempel, and other proponents of the hypothetico-deductive account, resulting in the judgment that discovery, not being logical, occurs irrationally. Theories are simply "guesses guided by the unscientific" (Popper, 1959, p. 278). But rational induction and irrational guesses are not exhaustive of scientific discovery, and the tools-to-theories heuristic explores the field beyond.

Scientists' practice reconsidered. The tools-to-theories heuristic is about scientists' practice, that is, the analytical and physical tools used in the conduct of experiments. This practice has a long tradition of neglect. The very philosophers who called themselves logical empiricists had, ironically, no interest in the empirical practice of scientists. Against their reduction of observation to pointer reading, Kuhn (1970) has emphasized the theory-ladenness of observation. Referring to perceptual experiments and gestalt switches, he says, "scientists see new and different things when looking with familiar instruments in places they have looked before" (p. 111). Both the logical empiricists and Kuhn were highly influential on psychology (see Toulmin & Leary, 1985), but neither view has emphasized the role of tools and experimental conduct. Their role in the development of science has been grossly underestimated until recently (Danziger, 1985; Lenoir, 1988).

Through the lens of theory, we are told, we can understand the growth of knowledge. But there is a recent move away from a theory-dominated account of science that pays attention to what really happens in the laboratories. Hacking (1983) argued that experimentation has a life of its own, and that not all observation is theory-laden. Galison (1987) analyzed modern experimental practice, such as in high-energy physics, focusing on the role of the fine-grained web of instruments, beliefs, and practice that determine when a "fact" is considered to be established and when experiments end. Both Hacking and Galison emphasize the role of the familiarity experimenters have with their tools, and the importance and relative autonomy of experimental practice in the quest for knowledge. This is the broader context in which the present tools-to-theories heuristic stands: the conjecture that theory is inseparable from instrumental practices.

In conclusion, my argument is that discovery in recent cognitive psychology can be understood beyond mere inductive generalizations or lucky guesses. More than that, I argue that for a considerable group of cognitive theories, neither induction from data nor lucky guesses played an important role. Rather, these innovations in theory can be accounted for by the tools-to-theories heuristic. So can conceptual problems and possibilities in current theories. Scientists' tools are not neutral. In the present case, the mind has been recreated in their image.

References

Anderson, J. R. (1980). *Cognitive psychology and its implications*. San Francisco: Freeman.

Anderson, J. R., & Milson, R. (1989). Human memory: An adaptive perspective. *Psychological Review, 96,* 703–719.

Barnard, G. A. (1979). Discussion of the paper by Professors Lindley and Tversky and Dr. Brown. *Journal of the Royal Statistical Society (A), 142,* 171–172.

Birnbaum, M. H. (1983). Base rates in Bayesian inference: Signal detection analysis of the cab problem. *American Journal of Psychology, 96,* 85–94.

Blackwell, R. J. (1983). Scientific discovery: The search for new categories. *New Ideas in Psychology, 1,* 111–115.

Brehmer, B., & Joyce, C. R. B. (Eds.) (1988). *Human judgment: The SJT view*. Amsterdam: North-Holland.

Brown, W., & Thomson, G. H. (1921). *The essentials of mental measurement*. Cambridge: Cambridge University Press.

Brunswik, E. (1943). Organismic achievement and environmental probability. *Psychological Review, 50,* 255–272.

Carnap, R. (1969). *The logical structure of the world,* trans. by R. A. George. Berkeley: University of California Press. (Originally published 1928.)

Cohen, L. J. (1986). *The dialogue of reason*. Oxford: Clarendon Press.

Cronbach, L. J. (1957). The two disciplines of scientific psychology. *American Psychologist, 12,* 671–684.

Danziger, K. (1985). The methodological imperative in psychology. *Philosophy of the Social Sciences, 16,* 1–13.

Danziger, K. (1987). Statistical method and the historical development of research practice in American psychology. In L. Krüger, G. Gigerenzer, & M. S. Morgan (Eds.), *The probabilistic revolution,* vol. 2: *Ideas in the sciences*. Cambridge, MA: MIT Press, 35–47.

Danziger, K. (1990). *Constructing the subject: Historical origins of psychological research.* Cambridge: Cambridge University Press.

Dashiell, J. F. (1939). Some rapprochements in contemporary psychology. *Psychological Bulletin, 36,* 1–24.

Daston, L. J. (1988). *Classical probability in the enlightenment.* Princeton, NJ: Princeton University Press.

de Finetti, B. (1989). Probabilism. *Erkenntnis, 31,* 169–223. (Originally published 1931.)

Edgington, E. E. (1974). A new tabulation of statistical procedures used in APA journals. *American Psychologist, 29,* 25–26.

Edwards, W. (1966). *Nonconservative information processing systems.* University of Michigan, Institute of Science and Technology. Report 5893-22-F.

Edwards, W., Lindman, H., & Savage, L. J. (1963). Bayesian statistical inference for psychological research. *Psychological Review, 70,* 193–242.

Fechner, G. T. (1897). *Kollektivmasslehre* [The measurement of collectivities]. Leipzig: W. Engelmann.

Fiedler, K. (1988). The dependence of the conjunction fallacy on subtle linguistic factors. *Psychological Research, 50,* 123–129.

Fisher, R. A. (1955). Statistical methods and scientific induction. *Journal of the Royal Statistical Society (B), 17,* 69–78.

Galison, P. (1987). *How experiments end.* Chicago: University of Chicago Press.

Gardner, H. (1985). *The mind's new science.* New York: Basic Books.

Gardner, H. (1988). Creative lives and creative works: A synthetic scientific approach. In R. J. Sternberg (Ed.), *The nature of creativity.* Cambridge: Cambridge University Press, 298–321.

Gavin, E. A. (1972). The causal issue in empirical psychology from Hume to the present with emphasis upon the work of Michotte. *Journal of the History of the Behavioral Sciences, 8,* 302–320.

Gigerenzer, G. (1987a). Probabilistic thinking and the fight against subjectivity. In L. Krüger, G. Gigerenzer, & M. S. Morgan (Eds.), *The probabilistic revolution,* vol. 2: *Ideas in the sciences.* Cambridge, MA: MIT Press, 11–33.

Gigerenzer, G. (1987b). Survival of the fittest probabilist: Brunswik, Thurstone, and the two disciplines of psychology. In L. Krüger, G. Gigerenzer, & M. S. Morgan (Eds.), *The probabilistic revolution,* vol. 2: *Ideas in the sciences.* Cambridge, MA: MIT Press, 49–72.

Gigerenzer, G. (1993). The Superego, the Ego, and the Id in statistical reasoning. In G. Keren & C. Lewis (Eds.), *A handbook for data analysis in the behavioral sciences: Methodological issues* (pp. 311–339). Hillsdale, NJ: Erlbaum.

Gigerenzer, G. (1994). Where do new ideas come from? In M. A. Boden (Ed.), *Dimensions of creativity* (pp. 55–74). Cambridge, MA: MIT Press.

Gigerenzer, G., & Goldstein, D. G. (1996). Mind as computer: The birth of a metaphor. *Creativity Research Journal,* in press.

Gigerenzer G., Hoffrage, U., & Kleinbölting, H. (1991). Probabilistic mental models: A Brunswikian theory of confidence. *Psychological Review, 98,* 506–528.

Gigerenzer, G., & Murray, D. J. (1987). *Cognition as intuitive statistics.* Hillsdale, NJ: Lawrence Erlbaum.

Gigerenzer, G., Swijtink, Z., Porter, T., Daston, L., Beatty, J., & Krüger, L. (1989). *The empire of chance: How probability changed science and everyday life.* Cambridge: Cambridge University Press.

Good, I. J. (1971). 46,656 varieties of Bayesians. *American Statistician, 25,* 62–63.

Gruber, H. (1981). *Darwin on man: A psychological study of scientific creativity.* 2nd ed. Chicago: University of Chicago Press.

Guilford, J. P. (1954). *Psychometric methods.* 2nd ed. New York: McGraw-Hill.

Hacking, I. (1965). *Logic of statistical inference.* Cambridge: Cambridge University Press.

Hacking, I. (1975). *The emergence of probability.* Cambridge: Cambridge University Press.

Hacking, I. (1983). *Representing and intervening*. Cambridge: Cambridge University Press.

Hammond, K. R., Stewart, T. R., Brehmer, B., & Steinmann, D. O. (1975). Social judgment theory. In M. F. Kaplan & S. Schwartz (Eds.), *Human judgment and decision processes*. New York: Academic Press, 271–312.

Hanson, N. R. (1958). *Patterns of discovery*. Cambridge: Cambridge University Press.

Herbart, J. F. (1816). *Lehrbuch zur Psychologie*. Hamburg and Leipzig: G. Hartenstein. 2nd ed., 1834, translated by M. K. Smith, as J. F. Herbart, *A textbook in psychology*. New York: Appleton.

Hilgard, E. R. (1955). Discussion of probabilistic functionalism. *Psychological Review, 62,* 226–228.

Holton, G. (1988). *Thematic origins of scientific thought*. 2nd ed. Cambridge, MA: Harvard University Press.

Kadane, J. B., & Lichtenstein, S. (1982). *A subjectivist view of calibration*. Decision Research Report No. 82–6. Eugene, OR: Decision Research, A Branch of Perceptronics.

Kahneman, D., Slovic, P., & Tversky, A. (Eds.) (1982). *Judgment under uncertainty: Heuristics and biases*. Cambridge: Cambridge University Press.

Kelley, H. H. (1967). Attribution theory in social psychology. In D. Levine (Ed.), *Nebraska symposium on motivation. Vol. 15*. Lincoln: University of Nebraska Press.

Kelley, H. H., & Michaela, I. L. (1980). Attribution theory and research. *Annual Review of Psychology, 31,* 457–501.

Kendall, M. G. (1942). On the future of statistics. *Journal of the Royal Statistical Society, 105,* 69–80.

Keren, G. (1987). Facing uncertainty in the game of Bridge: A calibration study. *Organizational Behavior and Human Decision Processes, 39,* 98–114.

Kuhn, T. (1970). *The structure of scientific revolutions*. 2nd ed. Chicago: University of Chicago Press.

Langley, P., Simon, H. A., Bradshaw, G. L., & Zytkow, J. M. (1987). *Scientific discovery*. Cambridge, MA: MIT Press.

Leary, D. E. (1987). From act psychology to probabilistic functionalism: The place of Egon Brunswik in the history of psychology. In M. S. Ash & W. R. Woodward (Eds.), *Psychology in twentieth-century thought and society*. Cambridge: Cambridge University Press, 115–142.

Leibniz, G. W. von (1951). The horizon of human doctrine. In P. P. Wiener (Ed.), *Selections*. New York: Scribner, 73–77. (Originally published after 1690.)

Lenoir, T. (1986). Models and instruments in the development of electrophysiology, 1845–1912. *Historical Studies in the Physical Sciences, 17,* 1–54.

Lenoir, T. (1988). Practice, reason, context: The dialogue between theory and experiment. *Science in Context, 2,* 3–22.

Levi, I. (1983). Who commits the base rate fallacy? *Behavioral and Brain Sciences, 6,* 502–506.

Lichtenstein, S., Fischoff, B., & Phillips, L. D. (1982). Calibration of probabilities: The state of the art to 1980. In D. Kahneman, P. Slovic, & A. Tversky (Eds.), *Judgment under uncertainty: Heuristics and biases*. Cambridge: Cambridge University Press, 306–334.

Lopes, L. L. (1981). Decision making in the short run. *Journal of Experimental Psychology: Human Learning and Memory, 7,* 377–385.

Lopes, L. L. (1982). Doing the impossible: A note on induction and the experience of randomness. *Journal of Experimental Psychology: Learning, Memory, and Cognition, 8,* 626–636.

Lopes, L. L. (1991). The rhetoric of irrationality. *Theory and Psychology, 1,* 65–82.

Lovie, A. D. (1983). Attention and behaviorism – fact and fiction. *British Journal of Psychology, 74,* 301–310.

Luce, R. D. (1977). Thurstone's discriminal processes fifty years later. *Psychometrika, 42,* 461–489.

Massaro, D. W. (1987). *Speech perception by ear and eye*. Hillsdale, NJ: Lawrence Erlbaum.

May, R. S. (1987). *Realismus von subjektiven Wahrscheinlichkeiten*. Frankfurt am Main: Lang.

McArthur, L. A. (1972). The how and what of why: Some determinants and consequents of causal attribution. *Journal of Personality and Social Psychology, 22*, 171–193.

Melton, A. W. (1962). Editorial. *Journal of Experimental Psychology, 64*, 553–557.

Michotte, A. (1963). *The perception of causality*. London: Methuen. (Originally published 1946.)

Mises, R. von. (1957). *Probability, statistics, and truth*. London: Allen and Unwin.

Murdock, B. B., Jr. (1982). A theory for the storage and retrieval of item and associative information. *Psychological Review, 89*, 609–626.

Neumann, J. von (1958). *The computer and the brain*. New Haven: Yale University Press.

Neyman, J. (1937). Outline of a theory of statistical estimation based on the classical theory of probability. *Philosophical Transactions of the Royal Society (A), 236*, 333–380.

Neyman, J., & Pearson, E. S. (1928). On the use and interpretation of certain test criteria for purposes of statistical inference. Part I. *Biometrika, 20A*, 175–240.

Nickles, T. (1980). Introductory essay: Scientific discovery and the future of philosophy of science. In T. Nickles (Ed.), *Scientific discovery, logic, and rationality*. Dordrecht: Reidel, 1–59.

Piaget, J. (1930). *The child's conception of causality*. London: Kegan Paul.

Popper, K. (1959). *The logic of scientific discovery*. New York: Basic Books.

Reichenbach, H. (1938). *Experience and prediction*. Chicago: University of Chicago Press.

Rucci, A. J., & Tweney, R. D. (1980). Analysis of variance and the "second discipline" of scientific psychology: A historical account. *Psychological Bulletin, 87*, 166–184.

Searle, J. (1984). *Minds, brains and science*. Cambridge, MA: Harvard University Press.

Smith, L. D. (1986). *Behaviorism and logical positivism*. Stanford, CA: Stanford University Press.

Sterling, T. D. (1959). Publication decisions and their possible effects on inferences drawn from tests of significance or vice versa. *Journal of the American Statistical Association, 54*, 30–34.

Swets, J. A., Tanner, W. D., & Birdsall, T. G. (1964). Decision processes in perception. In J. A. Swets (Ed.), *Signal detection and recognition in human observers*. New York: Wiley, 3–57.

Swijtink, Z. G. (1987). The objectification of observation: Measurement and statistical methods in the nineteenth century. In L. Krüger, L. J. Daston, & M. Heidelberger (Eds.), *The probabilistic revolution*, vol. 1: *Ideas in history*. Cambridge, MA: MIT Press, 261–285.

Tanner, W. P., Jr. (1965). *Statistical decision processes in detection and recognition*. Technical Report, Sensory Intelligence Laboratory, Department of Psychology, University of Michigan.

Tanner, W. P., Jr., & Swets, J. A. (1954). A decision-making theory of visual detection. *Psychological Review, 61*, 401–409.

Teigen, K. H. (1983). Studies in subjective probability IV: Probabilities, confidence, and luck. *Scandinavian Journal of Psychology, 24*, 175–191.

Thorndike, R. L. (1954). The psychological value systems of psychologists. *American Psychologist, 9*, 787–789.

Thurstone, L. L. (1927). A law of comparative judgement. *Psychological Review, 34*, 273–286.

Titchener, E. B. (1896). *An outline of psychology*. New York: Macmillan.

Toulmin, S., & Leary, D. E. (1985). The cult of empiricism in psychology, and beyond. In S. Koch (Ed.), *A century of psychology as science*. New York: McGraw-Hill, 594–617.

Tversky, A., & Kahneman, D. (1974). Judgment under uncertainty: Heuristics and biases. *Science, 185*, 1124–1131.

Tversky, A., & Kahneman, D. (1980). Causal schemata in judgments under uncertainty. In M. Fishbein (Ed.), *Progress in social psychology. Vol. 1*. Hillsdale, NJ: Lawrence Erlbaum, 49–72.

Tversky, A., & Kahneman, D. (1982). Judgments of and by representativeness. In D. Kahneman, P. Slovic, & A. Tversky (Eds.), *Judgment under uncertainty: Heuristics and biases.* Cambridge: Cambridge University Press, 84–98.

Tversky, A. & Kahneman, D. (1983). Extensional versus intuitive reasoning: The conjunction fallacy in probability judgment. *Psychological Review, 90*, 293–315.

Tweney, R. D., Dotherty, M. E., & Mynatt, C. R. (Eds.) (1981). *On scientific thinking.* New York: Columbia University Press.

Wickelgreen, W. A., & Norman, D. A. (1966). Strength models and serial position in short-term recognition memory. *Journal of Mathematical Psychology, 3*, 316–347.

4 Metaphor and monophony in the twentieth-century psychology of emotions

Kenneth J. Gergen

Attempts to define the emotions and elucidate their character have ornamented the intellectual landscape for over two thousand years. Two characteristics of this continuing colloquy are particularly noteworthy: first, the presumption of palpability and, second, the interminability of debate. In the former case, until the present century there has been little doubting the obdurate existence of the emotions. In the second book of the *Rhetoric,* Aristotle distinguished among 15 emotional states; Aquinas's *Summa Theologiae* enumerated 6 "affective" and 5 "spirited" emotions; Descartes distinguished among 6 primary passions of the soul; the eighteenth-century moralist, David Hartley, located 10 "general passions of human nature"; and the major contributions by recent theorists, Tomkins (1962) and Izard (1977), describe some 10 distinctive emotional states. In effect, the cultural history is one in which there is unflinching agreement regarding the palpable presence of emotional states within persons.

At the same time, these deep ontological commitments are also matched by a virtual cacophony of competing views on the character of the emotions – their distinguishing characteristics, origins, manifestations, and significance in human affairs. For Aristotle the emotions constituted "motions of the soul"; for Aquinas the emotions were experienced by the soul, but were the products of sensory appetites; Descartes isolated specific "passions of the soul," these owing to movements of the "animal spirits" agitating the brain. For Thomas Hobbes (1651), the passions were constitutive of human nature itself, and furnished the activating "spirit" for the intellect, the will, and moral character. In his *Treatise on Human Nature* (1739), David Hume divided the passions into those directly derived from human instinct (e.g., the desire to punish our enemies) and those which derive from a "double relation" of sensory impressions and ideas. A century later, both Spencer's *Principles of Psychology* and Darwin's *The Expression of the*

I wish to thank David Schaub and Rebeckah Flowers for their valuable assistance in this research, and the William Fulbright Foundation, Washington, DC, and Fundacion Interfas, Buenos Aires, for making the funds and facilities available for its completion. An earlier draft of the present paper appears in *History of the Human Sciences,* 1995, *8,* 1–23.

Emotions in Man and Animals attempted to place the emotions on more seemingly certain biological grounds.

This interminability of debate is most effectively illustrated by considering the "objects of study" themselves, that which is identified as an emotion. For example, Aristotle identified *placability, confidence, benevolence, churlishness, resentment, emulation, longing,* and *enthusiasm* as emotional states no less transparent than *anger* or *joy*. Yet, in their twentieth-century exegeses, neither Tomkins (1962) nor Izard (1977) recognizes these states as constituents of the emotional domain. Aquinas believed *love, desire, hope,* and *courage* were all central emotions, and, while Aristotle agreed in the case of *love,* all such states go virtually unrecognized in the recent theories of Tomkins and Izard. Hobbes identified *covetousness, luxury, curiosity, ambition, good naturedness, superstition,* and *will* as emotional states, none of which qualify as such in contemporary psychology. Tomkins and Izard agree that *surprise* is an emotion, a belief that would indeed puzzle most of their predecessors. However, where Izard believes *sadness* and *guilt* are major emotions, they fail to qualify in Tomkins analysis; simultaneously, Tomkins sees *distress* as a central emotion, where Izard does not.

There is a certain irony inhering in these two features of emotional debate – palpability and interminability. If the emotions are simply there as transparent features of human existence, why should univocality be so difficult to achieve? Broad agreement exists within scientific communities concerning, for example, chemical tables, genetic constitution, and the movements of the planets; and where disagreements have developed, procedures have also been located for pressing the nomenclature toward greater uniformity. Why, then, is scientific convergence so elusive in the case of emotions? At least one significant reason for the continuous contention derives from a presumptive fallacy, namely Whitehead's fallacy of misplaced concreteness. One suspects that we labor in a tradition in which we mistakenly treat the putative objects of our mental vocabulary as palpable, where it is the names themselves that possess more indubitable properties. Because there are words such as love, anger, and guilt, we presume that there must be specific states to which they refer. And if there are not, we presume that continued study of the matter will set the matter straight. Two thousand years have been insufficient to achieve this end, and one is ineluctably led to suppose that there are no such isolable conditions inside individuals to which such terms refer (or at a minimum, the terms are not determinant markers of such states).

This latter possibility has become far more reasonable within recent years, and particularly with the development of ordinary language philosophy. Wittgenstein's *Philosophical Investigations* was the major stimulus in this case, both questioning the referential base for mental predicates and offering an alternative way of accounting for such discourse. As Wittgenstein (1980) asks, "I give notice that I am afraid. – Do I recall my thoughts of the past half hour in order to do that, or do I let a thought of the dentist quickly cross my mind in order to see how it affects me; or can I be uncertain of whether it is really fear of the dentists, and not some other physical feeling of discomfort?" (p. 32e). The impossibility of answering such a question in terms of mental referents for emotion terms demands an alternative means of understanding mental terms. This understanding is largely to be found in Wittgenstein's arguments for use-derived meaning. On this view, mental predicates acquire their meaning through various language games embedded within cultural forms of life. Mental language is rendered significant not by virtue of its capacity to reveal, mark, or describe mental states, but from its function in social interchange. The challenge posed by these ideas to traditional dualistic theories of knowledge was effectively extended in the works of Ryle (1949) and Austin (1962). Other scholars, such as Kenny (1963) and Anscombe (1976), went on to explore the various functions, problems, and philosophical challenges of mental state terms in their everyday usage.

As the Wittgensteinian view is extended, the possibility of falsifying scientific propositions about emotional states becomes increasingly problematic (see Gergen, 1994). This problematization is fortified by a substantial body of writing in both the history of science and the sociology of knowledge, demonstrating the sociocultural processes at work in rendering various scientific claims intelligible and acceptable. The important point for the present offering is that together these various arguments invite consideration of the reality posits of scientific psychology, independent of the methods and findings typically employed as justificatory bases within the field. It is within this context that I wish, then, to sketch with broad strokes the vicissitudes of emotional discourse in scientific psychology of the present century. As I shall propose, emotion terms have largely served political purposes within professional psychology, strategically situating the discipline (or its various subcultures) in relationship to the academy, to the general public, and to its own membership. What psychology has had to say about the emotions, or in many instances failed to say, is not – and in principle cannot be – the result of careful and controlled observation. Rather its varying scientific postures can be traced, in large measure, to the intellectual and cultural circumstances in which professional life is played out.

Caveats are required: I am not proposing that the present account is conclusive. This is but a preliminary sketch, and there are many other influences to which inquiry should also be directed. Nor am I proposing that all inquiry into the emotions is the result of consciously considered strategies. Rather, I am generating a lens through which coherent sense may be derived from an otherwise chaotic morass of particulars. Finally, the present analysis is largely confined to developments in mainstream psychology in the United States. There are other stories to be told about the development of psychology in the context of an embattled Europe, and as well in the many tributaries of American psychology.

Prolegomenon on power/knowledge

Foucault's (1978, 1979) writings on knowledge and power are an effective entry to the present analysis. Language, for Foucault, serves as a major medium for carrying out relations. Because language constitutes what we take to be the world, and rationalizes the form of reality thus created, it also serves as a socially binding force. By acting within language, relations of power and privilege are sustained. And, by engaging in the further circulation of a form of language, the array of power relations is further extended. Thus, as disciplines such as psychology, psychiatry, and sociology are developed, so do they operate as discursive regimes. They specify a world and a normative domain of relevant action. As these languages are further elaborated and disseminated, so then is the configuration of power extended. In this sense, power relations possess a productive capacity. The relevance of this perspective for psychology has been effectively demonstrated in Rose's (1985, 1990) analyses of psychological theory and measurement as forms of cultural control.

Yet, there is a strong tendency in Foucault's work to treat discursive regimes as unitary forms. That is, regimes tend to be treated as internally coherent and hegemonically accelerated. As Foucault (1979) proposes, beginning in the eighteenth century and extending into the present,

the formation of knowledge and the increase of power regularly reinforce(d) one another in a circular process. . . . First the hospital, then the school, then, later the workshop were not simply "reordered" by the disciplines: they became, thanks to them, apparatuses such that any mechanism of objectification could be used in them as an instrument of subjection, and any growth of power could give rise in them to possible branches of knowledge; it was this link, proper to the technological system that made possible within the disciplinary element the formation of clinical medicine, psychiatry, child psychology, educational psychology, and the rationalization of labor. It is . . . a multiplication of the effects of power through the formation and accumulation of new forms of knowledge. (p. 224)

This line of argument has also been fortified by much Marxist theory, particularly as inspired by Althusser, of a unified, hegemonic order.

The view I wish to propose, and indeed which might be supported with alternative quotes from Foucault's capillary view of power, is that life within what we take to be the existing regimes is seldom unitary. Rather, regimes themselves are composed of variegated discursive practices, drawn from sundry contexts, ripped from previous ecologies of usage and stitched awkwardly together to form what – with continued usage and considerable suppression – is seen as a *coherent* view ("a discipline"). Ontologies and rationalities are thus only apparently and momentarily univocal; they harbor multiple tensions and contradictions even for those who dwell within. In a sense, I wish to augment (or shift the emphasis of) a Foucauldian perspective with important theses from Bakhtin (1981) and Derrida (1976). While Bakhtin points to the hybrid or *heteroglossial* character of any given domain of language, Derrida's writings emphasize the failure of any language to carry autonomous meanings – to stand independent of its multiple signifying traces. The present analysis agrees, then, with Raymond Williams's (1980) view that "Hegemony is not singular. Its own internal structures are highly complex, and have continually to be renewed, recreated and defended; and by the same token . . . they can be continually challenged and in certain respects modified" (p. 38). The present concern is the history of these internal movements in psychological science – their challenges, conflicts and evolutions – from the prebehaviorist period through contemporary constructionism.

Metaphor and the politics of emotion

The status of psychological study at the turn of the century was a tenuous one. Scholars both in Europe and the United States were struggling to achieve recognition for a uniquely psychological science, independent of its philosophic forbears, and independent of adjoining and already established sciences (particularly medicine and biology). At the same time, if such a discipline were to achieve sanction within the academy, its rationale would have to achieve intelligibility in these very disciplines, as in others. Moreover, such a discipline should ideally enjoy the affirmation of a broader, educated public. This was particularly so in the United States, with its strong emphasis on the pragmatic outcomes of scholarly work (Manicas, 1987). In terms of the present analysis, the central challenge for psychology, then, was to generate forms of self-representation that could simultaneously appeal to audiences both within the academy and the educated public – in addition to its own membership.

It is within this context that we may consider the status of emotions discourse. At the outset, such discourse serves as symbolic capital of high order. Given the long history of scholarship on the emotions, particularly within philosophy and later in medicine and biology, there was little doubting the existence of emotions in human makeup. And, for the fledgling discipline to claim independent, but allied, investigation into the emotions would be a potentially powerful self-justificatory device. Similarly, because of long-standing beliefs in the emotions more generally within the culture, a discipline that could finally illuminate their character and function would purchase promise in providing useful information and services to the society.

At the same time, to annex the discourse of emotions was not without its dangers. Strong claims to probity on matters of the emotion could threaten the investments of the more established disciplines, thus fostering political enmity. Further, for psychology to employ the established forms of description and explanation could simultaneously threaten its claims to being a separate or independent discipline. In addition to these problems, emotions discourse also served as the mainstay for cultural romanticism. The romanticist rhetoric was becoming increasingly suspect – not only in certain sectors of philosophy, but within the sciences more generally. For a discipline aspiring to scientific status to grant the emotions a central place in its vocabulary of explanation could be hazardous. In effect, there were treasures to be gained in appropriating the discourse of the emotions, but the course could be perilous.

There was extant a rich and compelling vocabulary on which psychological investigation could proceed. Of particular importance, Averill (1990) distinguishes among five major metaphors available to psychological science from preceding centuries of dialogue: emotions as (1) *inner feelings* (experiences), (2) *physiological responses,* (3) *animal impulses* in human nature, (4) *diseases of the mind,* and (5) *driving forces* (vital energy). The metaphors were also wedded to estimable traditions. First, the nineteenth-century writings of Bain, Darwin, and Spencer, among others, defined the emotions as biological processes (drawing from the related metaphors of emotions as physiological responses, and as animal impulses in human nature). The biological view was advantageous for a fledgling discipline, inasmuch as it would ally psychological study with the *Naturwissenschaften* as opposed to the new and more tentative breed of the *Geisteswissenschaften.* In contrast, there was also a long heritage – drawing from the works of Descartes, Hartley, and Cabanis – that defined the emotions largely in terms of internal sensations (the metaphor of inner feelings). It is this tradition that lent strong support to the efforts of nineteenth-century German psychologists to establish psychology as a science sui generis. For figures such as Fechner, Lehmann, Wundt, and Hamilton, the primary emphasis was thus placed on the emotions as elements of conscious experience.

Finally, a third tradition – more allied to the artistic community than to the biological and philosophical – granted the emotions a preeminent position in human makeup. This, the romanticist tradition, treated the emotions as the fundamental wellsprings for human action. For them these sources of energy were beyond the penetration by (mere) conscious sensation or reasoning. This was essentially the tradition of Goethe, Herder, and Nietzsche, and of Shelley, Keats, and Byron. It was also a tradition of special promise to practitioners of psychology, to those who functioned not in the impersonal conditions of the laboratory, but in the hospital or consultation room. For this was preeminently a tradition broadly shared within the culture. To speak this language would be most effective in the public sphere.

Faced with these options, how should the discipline proceed? In a broad sense, the choice was between a monophonic and a polyphonic intelligibility. In the former instance, one could select a single metaphor from the available array and, within the theoretical and research contexts, extend its intelligibility to full fruition. There were both advantages and liabilities in doing so. Each of the existing metaphors offered a major means of rendering an emotional world intelligible, and the full expansion of its linguistic implicature offered the possibility of a complete, coherent, and rhetorically powerful theory. Further, an effective monophonic account would either denigrate the significance of the alternatives, appropriate them, or fully erase their ontologies. For example, a theory that claims the emotions fundamentally to be *inner feelings,* can place physiology in a secondary position (as mere accompaniment or a reductionist parallel), and can function unproblematically without reference to impulses, diseases, or driving forces. Similarly, with the full expansion of the *physiological* metaphor, "feelings" become either a secondary manifestation or fully suspect; animal impulses can be appropriated as physiology at an imprecise level of description, and the metaphor of driving force becomes so much poetry. The *driving-force* theorist can reduce feelings and physiology to the status of manifestations of the driving force, can claim such discourses to be reductionistic (and largely irrelevant) descriptions, and can claim fully explanatory potential without reference to animal impulses.

Yet, the monophonic account is also purchased at a price. For psychology to lay claim to either the physiological or biological metaphors would encroach on neighboring disciplines and disclaim rights to independent status. The disease metaphor is highly circumscribed, and the driving force metaphor would ally the field too closely with romanticism. The metaphor of inner feelings had been particularly appealing in establishing psychology as an independent discipline in the German context. However, such a metaphor reduces psychology to the study of conscious states, and thus in the American context failed to meet the standards of pragmatic utility. If the field is to appeal to other disciplines without encroaching on their self-definitions, and if it is to acquire credibility both within and outside the academy, the more favorable choice would seem to be polyphony. That is, the most rhetorically powerful discourse should be one that harbors multiple metaphors. Whether this is indeed a winning option is revealed in the following.

The early impulse toward polyphony

At the turn of the century, psychology as an academic discipline in the United States was struggling toward recognition. The American Psychological Association was organized in 1892 with 31 members, only a minority of whom identified themselves professionally as psychologists. If such a field was to justify itself through its accounts of mental life, how was it to proceed? From the preceding, there is much to be gained by appropriating the discourse of emotion; and there is more to be gained in this early stage by amalgamating metaphors than in monophony. Polyphonic models were also available for the undertaking. Within the immediately preceding decades, Lotze and Fechner in Germany and Lange in Denmark had attempted to integrate mind and body into a single theory of emotion. For each, there was an interactive relationship between the mind as sensorium and determinantly linked physiological processes; for each, psychological and biological inquiry were interdependent. For American psychology, William James's work was thus of pivotal significance. Not only did his 1890 treatise, *The Principles of Psychology,* suggest the contours of a unified discipline – a mutually fortifying synthesis – but his theory of emotion demonstrated the possibility by integrating two of the root metaphors into a single formulation. Consider the famous passage:

Bodily changes follow directly the perception of the exciting fact and . . . our feeling of the same changes as they occur *is* the emotion. Common sense says we lose our fortune, are sorry and weep; we meet a bear, are frightened and run. . . . The hypothesis here to be defended says that this order of sequence is incorrect. . . . (Rather) we feel sorry because we cry, afraid because we tremble. (pp. 449–450)

As is clear, the emotions are the by-product of two interacting conditions, a biological event on the one side, and a pattern of sensations on the other. In effect, James linked the discourses of physical and sensory reality in such a way that emotional life could not be understood by a more reductionistic discipline. Both were required. One could surmise, then, the possibility of a unified psychology, a discipline requiring its own identity outside biology, but safely allied with this more established tradition.

But would it be possible to forge a second alliance, this time with the more pragmatically promising enterprise of clinical treatment? There were hopes extant even in 1896, with the development of the first psychological clinic at the University of Pennsylvania, that clinical practitioners could be integrated into a unified psychology. However, there were at least two major hurdles to be traversed. First, strongly committed to psychoanalytic theory, psychiatric practitioners were struggling to gain their own identity and public sanction. The practitioners in this case were also medical doctors as opposed to laboratory researchers. In effect, psychologists confronted an alterior subculture with its own centripetal force. Both related to and rationalizing these sociopolitical barriers, were discursive differences – primary among them the root metaphors for describing the emotions. The psychiatric view of emotions as life forces and the practices associated with this metaphor were not easily integrated into the biosensory formulations of the experimentalist. However, with some hope of integration, Sigmund Freud was invited in 1908 to speak to an estimable group of American psychologists. And in 1918 Robert Woodworth's *Dynamic Psychology* was published, a volume that attempted to integrate the psychodynamic views into the experimental account.

Yet, these were indeed uneasy alliances, for each attempt to integrate, collate, or combine necessarily left significant traces of the root metaphors. The extended discourse surrounding, substantiating, and constituting the metaphoric center remained undigested. The result was a continuous tension: By reverting to monophony, any subculture could brandish Occam's razor and claim a pure and powerful access to the emotions. Such was the case as the experimental work of Sherrington (1906) and Cannon (1914) were used to discredit James and replace his theory with single foundation in neurophysiology. The senses were, then, epiphenomenal – simply biological processes at a gross level of description. Further, the clinically oriented psychologists found that too much was sacrificed in *Dynamic Psychology*'s translation of life urges into experimental abstractions. Thus, the journal *Psychological Clinic* contemptuously dismissed the volume as "brass instrument psychology," with the instruments "cunningly concealed" from the public. Finally, the Jamesian emphasis on sensations was difficult to cash out in terms of broader pragmatic demands. The invitation to polyphony was insufficient, then, to impede the rapacious discourse of behaviorism.

Behaviorism and the sacrifice of emotion

As broadly recognized, there was a close association between the ascendance of behaviorist psychology in the 1930s and the bold moves of philosophers of science toward foundations for a unified science (Koch, 1963). For academic psychologists in particular, the availability of principles of scientific rationality were particularly consequential. Still struggling for recognition and reputation, and unable to forge viable linkages among biological, human experimental, and practitioner enclaves, the possibility of modeling itself on a philosophically grounded model of science was an attractive one. Such a move would allow psychological inquiry to lay claim to independent scientific status. Because the conception of a unified science would ensure its connection to the natural sciences, no specific alliance with biology was essential. And because empiricist foundationalism gave hope that fundamental principles of human activity could be discovered, then any responsible clinical practice would necessarily be derived from the more basic science. In effect, there was a strong rationale for establishing psychology as an independent and basic science, from which could be developed a profusion of practical applications – in the clinic, schools, industry, the military, and so on. In retrospect, one must suppose that this family of arguments was a powerful one: Between 1930 and 1960 the ranks of the American Psychological Association expanded some twentyfold.

Yet, how were the emotions to be regarded by this foundational form of psychological science? To appreciate the fate of the emotions in this era, we must further consider the scientific model that psychologists appropriated from the philosophy of science. Central components of this received view were particular conceptions of observation, causality, and methodology. That which most clearly aligned the new psychology with the natural sciences was to be its emphasis on observables. Each of its theoretical conceptions, insofar as possible, was to be linked through a series of "operational definitions" to observable behaviors of the organism. In this way the discipline could replace the interminable and embarrassing imbroglios over the nature of the "inner world," with facts open to public observation and reliable replication. And, because overt behavior was clearly material, where "mindstuff" was dubitable at best, the discipline could claim ultimate unity with the natural sciences.

The centrality of observation was closely linked to a mechanical view of causality (Hollis, 1977). If the goal of the science is to predict the behavior of organisms, and the commitment to observation is preeminent, then the favored explanatory model is that of Humean causality: behavior as a consequence of observable antecedents. Teleology and intentionality, as alternative explanatory forms, are rendered suspect because of their necessary reference to inner (nonobservable) impulses. And, with mechanical causality as the strong preference for the new science, the optimal research method is experimentation. It is only in the context of the laboratory experiment, in particular, that the scientist can systematically control the antecedent conditions ("independent variables"), and trace their "causal effects," on behavioral outcomes ("dependent variables").

With these commitments in place, the fate of the emotions is virtually sealed. First, if the chief focus of the science is publicly observable behavior, then mental states and conditions are shunted to the margins of the discipline, at best "hypothetical," and at worst obfuscating folklore. Because the emotions are commonly viewed as constituents of the subjective world (the metaphor of inner sense), their status as "objects of study" is threatened. And, if they are primarily biological processes, as many argued, their status in psychological science is equally problematic. The prescribed forms of study in this case are primarily neurological and biochemical. Nor were the emotions easily absorbed into a science committed to a conception of mechanical causation. Theorists did argue that emotions are "triggered" by environmental stimuli, but on most traditional accounts the emotions themselves are inherent or instinctual. For example, if emotions are vital life forces with the capacity to drive or motivate thought and action, they function as unmoved movers. They are outside the system of antecedent–consequent contingency. One might observe their effects in natural settings, or compare the emotional tendencies of various species, but these are scarcely inviting topics for laboratory experimentation. In effect, with the assent of behaviorism the emotions largely vanished from the agenda of scientific psychology.

For radical behaviorists such as B. F. Skinner (1938), all mental state terms could properly be eradicated from the discipline. For more liberal behaviorists, the emotions made but fleeting entry into professional consciousness. For example, in F. H. Allport's volume, *Social Psychology* (1924), considered by many to have shaped the next 30 years of social psychological research, only 15 of the 453 pages are devoted to "feelings and emotion." Further, the treatment is primarily couched in terms of the biological metaphor. As to the origin of "feelings," Allport proposes, "The cranio-sacral division of the autonomic nervous system, supplemented under certain conditions by the cerebro-spinal system, innervates those responses whose return afferent impulses are associated with the conscious quality of pleasantness. The sympathetic division produces visceral responses which are represented in the consciousness as unpleasantness" (p. 90). Much the same view is taken in Myerson's volume, *Social Psychology,* published ten years later. No chapter is given over to the emotions in social life, and the few relevant pages of the volume are built around the view that "the expression of emotion in the sense of the enormous changes which take place and become visible as rage, fear, etc. and which come to consciousness as the *affect,* arise largely through the hypothalamus" (p. 158). In the highly popular and more cognitively oriented text of the 1950s, Krech and Crutchfield's *Theory and Problems of Social Psychology,* there is no organized treatment of emotion; it is simply a term associated in unsystematic fashion to the concept of motivation.

Neobehaviorism and the return of the interior

The reasons for the softening grasp of radical behaviorism on psychological science are many and complex. However, as Koch (1963) outlines the case, psychologists themselves found the demands of a rigorous positivism too restrictive. Broad debate over the problems inherent in a strict operationalism, for example, led to a liberalization of views. Strong cases were made in favor of a family of "hypothetical constructs," terms that stood in for possible psychological processes but were not to be confused with the processes themselves. The chief function of such terms was to link independent and dependent variables in a systematic way. This liberalization of behaviorism – or the emergence of *neobehaviorism* – opened a respectable way for psychology to readmit the psychological interior to the science.

Perhaps the pivotal work for mainstream psychology was that of Clark Hull and his colleagues at Yale's Institute for Human Relations. Hull's careful and intellectually commanding work served as a model for *psychology as science*. His quasi-mathematical formulations for a theory of learning incorporated an increasing number of formal terms for a hypothetical interior. And, while there was no scientific purpose served by freighting such terms with cultural content, the possibility of a distinctly psychological treatment of the emotions was slowly reawakened when Hull articulated a concept of *primary drive* in his widely heralded, *Principles of Behavior*. Although primarily interested in the organism's acquisition of behavior patterns, Hull required an explanation for the organism's state of basic activation. This was accomplished first by borrowing from the biological metaphor the concept of tissue needs necessary for survival. The choice of a *needs* discourse was particularly auspicious, in this case, because needs, as opposed, for example, to *instincts,* can be related to environmental conditions ("hunger needs can be sated"), and the model thus retained an allegiance to the mechanistic metatheory. At the same time, however, Hull set out to establish a fully psychological theory. Thus, needs at the biological level were reinscribed as drives at the psychological level. Primary drives were thus based on a few simple organismic needs (hunger, thirst, pain avoidance, etc.), but, once placed into theoretical orbit, operated with explanatory efficacy without further reference to biological conditions.

While drawing sustenance from the biological metaphor, the conception of primary drive also carries strong traces of the romanticist metaphor of vital energy. By successfully exploiting this tradition, psychoanalysts had successfully ensconced themselves within the medical profession. However, with the concept of drive now granted scientific respectability, the door was open not only for scientific psychology to reclaim the discourse of emotion, but for appropriating psychoanalytic formulations – of demonstrating that the basic tenets of psychoanalytic theory were consistent with the more scientifically well grounded theories of neobehaviorism. The most significant attempt of this kind was Dollard and Miller's 1950 volume, *Personality and Psychotherapy*. As these authors proposed, by drawing on the energic wellsprings of the primary drives, new dispositions (secondary drives) could – under a particular combination of antecedent conditions – be established. Thus, for example, fear is "an innate response to a (pain) stimulus" (p. 69). However, if the painful stimulus is associated with a previously neutral cue, the neutral cue will come to produce fear (now a secondary drive). By extending assumptions such as these, psychotherapy can be properly envisioned as a form of learning laboratory.

With this opening for the development of emotionlike constructs in scientific psychology, the metaphor of emotion as driving force was reinscribed in dozens of volumes, including Young's *Motivation and Emotion,* Symonds's *Dynamic Psychology,* Leeper and Madison's *Understanding Personality,* and Cofer's *Motivation and Emotion.* Such volumes succeeded in tracing the major Freudian concepts – along with a broad array of common emotion terms (including love) – to a drive formulation. Yet, the monophonic claim to superiority also stood as a challenge to those invested in alternative discourses. If the emotions were now legitimate objects of study, there were other long-standing metaphors to which allegiance could be claimed. The old battle lines were soon reactivated. In 1964, D. E. Berlyne was given the opportunity to inscribe the first chapter on emotions ever to appear in the prestigious *Annual Review of Psychology.* The title of this entry into the 15th volume of the series, "Emotional Aspects of Learning," seems to leave the behaviorist imprimatur unquestioned. As Berlyne begins, "Psychologists are, on the whole, following a suggestion reiterated since 1934 by Duffy. She contended that terms like 'emotion' have outlived their usefulness. We should, she feels, give them up and recognize that all behavior, including 'emotional' behavior, has both a 'directive' aspect and an 'energy-mobilization' (or to use newer terms, 'activation' or 'arousal') aspect, with distinguishable determinants" (p. 115). Berlyne concurs with this view, but through a series of subtle interpolations, points the way to replacing the metaphor of driving force with a physiological discourse.

As Berlyne reasons, if emotions are essentially internal drives, and drives are fundamentally biological, then neurological investigation of brain stimulation constitutes a contribution to our understanding of emotion. By then reviewing research on the reticular formation, the limbic system, and the lateral hypothalamus as they "arouse" the organism, the way was again opened to replace "drive" with physiology. And when physiology becomes the basis of learning, then psychological theorizing about learning becomes superfluous. Behaviorist theory is placed in jeopardy; the physiological metaphor is resuscitated. Further conflict, however, would be postponed until the cognitive movement reached maturity.

The cognitive revolution: Suppression and suspiration

With interior process once again reinstated, the neobehaviorist program was slowly eclipsed by a broad and enthusiastic resuscitation of mental discourse – particularly the discourse of reason. Although there are many reasons for what became known as the "cognitive revolution" in psychology, just as in the case of behaviorism, this investment can be traced in part to psychology's dependency on a philosophy of science with its major roots in the Enlightenment. The twin philosophical movements on which Enlightenment epistemology largely rests are the empiricist and rationalist. Empiricist philosophy of science (drawing from Locke, Hume, and the Mills) gives primary voice to the former (e.g., the preeminent role of observation), whereas the rationalist tradition (drawing from Descartes, Leibniz, and Kant) is placed in a secondary but nevertheless essential position (e.g., the role of induction and deduction). In many respects, the behaviorist and neobehaviorist movements in psychology recapitulate at the theoretical level the empiricist emphasis in the philosophy of science. That is, the theories of human psychology represent reformulations of the empiricist metatheory that informs the behaviorist and neobehaviorist projects of science (Gergen, 1994). However, these movements simultaneously left unexplored the rationalist contribution to the reigning metatheory. Unexplored was the implicit implicature, in which rational processes could be credited with a contribution to human action – not simply pawns to antecedent conditions, but possessing intrinsic properties with their own demands on action. Thus, the drama of Piaget's (1952) genetic epistemology, Chomsky's (1958) critique of the Skinnerian theory of language, and his subsequent advocacy of inherent syntactical knowledge (Chomsky, 1968) was a significant demotion in the causal powers attributed to "the stimulus world." These theories granted active mental operations the central role in directing human action. The floodgates were now open, and the literature soon abounded in research and theory on intrinsic cognitive process.

In terms of inquiry into the emotions, however, the initial effect of the cognitive movement was full-scale suppression. To render the ontology of "cognition" both intelligible and compelling favored a family of metaphors that either obscured or failed to recognize a domain of emotions. Although centrally concerned with the problem of "mental representation," the traditional epistemological metaphor of "mind as mirror" (Rorty, 1979) was unserviceable. The metaphor again granted too much credit to the demands of the stimulus world. Rather, cognitive theorists required fresh metaphors – and particularly those which could grasp the imagination of the *scientific* community. It is thus that much cognitive theory incorporated, for example, the metaphor of rationality as statistical process; when operating optimally, rational thought approximated the principles of statistical analysis (see Gigerenzer and Murray, 1987). Also compelling was a family of metaphors drawn from engineering (servomechanisms, feedback loops, networks) and physics (the hologram). However, perhaps the dominant metaphor for the cognitive theorist, and one that adds the strength of allegiance to the field of artificial intelligence, is the computer (see Hoffman, Cochran, and Nead's 1990 review). When the internal world is constituted by computational devices, addresses, locations, data structures, formats, and other forms of information processing, the emotions are erased from the ontology of the interior. Thus, between Berlyn's 1964 entry and 1986, not a single chapter on the emotions appeared in the *Annual Review of Psychology*.

Yet, a psychology without emotion would not only fail to draw public advantage from this symbolic capital but, more locally, would reduce the dependency of clinical practitioners on "mainstream" science. The major challenge, then, was to develop a theory that would allow the emotions to be appropriated by cognitive theory. This was furnished by Stanley Schachter's (Schachter, 1964; Schachter and Singer, 1962) *two-factor theory* of emotion. Schachter's formulation carried the traces of both the James and Hull formulations. Like James, he cleanly separated biology from psychology. At the same time he was able successfully to reframe the sensory metaphor. Rather than viewing conscious experience as a passive recording (in this case of the biological interior), the psyche was granted status as an active interpreter of the world and self. Cognitive process did not so much reflect as determine the nature of emotional experience. Similar to Hull, Schachter resorted to an amorphous concept of *undifferentiated arousal*. In effect, the biological system furnished energy in the form of generalized activation, and the cognitive system (rather than sensing messages from biology as in the case of James) operated in a "top down" manner to define its character. For Schachter (1964), cognition "exerts a steering function. . . . It is the cognition which determines whether the state of physiological arousal will be labeled 'anger,' 'joy,' or whatever" (p. 51).

Not only did Schachter's polyphonic account open up a means for cognitive theorists to annex an important discourse – without threatening the preferred explanatory fulcrum – but it also promised riches in practical/ therapeutic application. Of particular importance was the conception of cognitive attribution. Thus, rather than treating actual states of emotion, motivation, pain, and the like, these states were deontologized, and the practitioner was invited to focus on attributional tendencies or styles. Under what conditions did the individual attribute pain, anger, romantic love, and so on to the self, and how could therapists help the client to reconceptualize these conditions in more promising ways. (See, e.g., Harvey and Ickes, 1976; Harvey and Weary, 1985.) Perhaps the most articulate application of the cognitive perspective to psychotherapy is contained in Aaron Beck's (1976) *Cognitive Therapy and the Emotional Disorders*. Published almost 15 years after the initial appearance of Schachter's work, Beck's study alters the explanatory structure, so that the individual does not cognize undifferentiated arousal (a view that had come under considerable attack) but cognizes the situation. It is this cognition that has an automatic eliciting effect on the emotional response. "The thesis that the special meaning of an event determines the emotional response forms the core of the cognitive model of emotions and emotional disorder. The meaning is encased in cognition" (p. 52). In effect, while a biological propensity is recognized, cognitive process remains regnant.

In many respects, Schachter's theory did much the same as William James's at the turn of the century to generate a vision of unification among psychologists, biologists, and the mental health practitioners – yet, with psychology firmly at the helm. Also similar to James, this vision was not to be realized. Schachter's polyphonic account not only brought emotions into the analytic eye once again but also the residual traces of competing metaphors. The turn-of-the-century metaphors had scarcely been lost; they were not only present in the common vernacular, but various professional enclaves (e.g., comparative psychologists, psychobiologists, ethological psychologists) had continued to elaborate their potentials outside the mainstream. These enclaves, were also energized by the cognitivists' penchant for removing the emotions from the ledger. It was with a sense of righteous indignation – and possibly an eye toward establishing a unique professional profile – that the earlier metaphors were once again resuscitated. Leventhal and Tomarken's (1986) chapter in the *Annual Review of Psychology,* "Emotion: Today's Problems," is illustrative:

Much of the conflict and confusion in this area stems from an unwillingness to grant independent conceptual status to emotion. This "begrudging" attitude has three components: (a) the behavioristic legacy and its suspicion of subjective concepts; (b) the traditional cognitive hold on our thinking in which emotion is a combination of arousal and cognition . . . ; and (c) the reluctance of cognitively oriented scientists to view an emotion as anything more complex than a "stop" or interrupt rule in the simulation of mental operations. . . . Admitting a richer concept of emotion to the lexicon could generate major upheavals in cognitive theory as emotions theory addresses the growing theoretical and empirical knowledge in neuroscience and molecular biology. (p. 566)

With this concluding sentence, the biological metaphor again springs to life. Support is garnered in this case from a variety of studies in brain lateralization. Research is used to argue that the right cortical hemisphere plays a major role in the control and expression of moods, and the recognition of emotion in others. The left hemisphere is said to be "nonemotional" (Tucker, 1981). It was noted earlier that the biological metaphor could be segmented, the one viewing emotions as physiological events and the other as animal behavior. Armed with the second metaphor, another phalanx of investigators attempted to identify emotions as intrinsic patterns of organismic expression. Perhaps the most widely heralded of these endeavors are those of Paul Ekman and his colleagues, who – following in Darwin's footsteps – amassed data to prove that the expression of "the basic" emotions in human beings is universal (Ekman, 1982). These efforts were also supported by animal behavior specialists who argued for the evolutionary benefits derived from various emotional expressions (cf. Eibel-Eibelsfeldt, 1979; Plutchick, 1980). The two biological metaphors are finally collapsed –

or at least, a harmony is sought – in the Blanchard and Blanchard's contribution to the 1988 volume of the *Annual Review of Psychology*.

The drive energy metaphor has also reappeared in full regalia. This is unabashedly so in the therapeutic community, where popular-selling volumes on the primal scream, cocounseling, and 12-step programs celebrate the elemental force of the emotions. More subtly, the metaphor has resurfaced in a number of scholarly treatises attempting not so much to replace the cognitive and the biological views, as to perform interpolations in which motivational forces are given a primary role. For example, in the broad overview of Frijda (1986), the emotions are treated as forms of action potential (with traces of unleashed drives). "The emotions," he writes, "can be defined as modes of relational action readiness, either in the form of tendencies to establish, maintain, or disrupt a relationship with the environment or in the form of modes of relational readiness as such" (p. 71). Similarly, in his elaborate integration of the literature, Lazarus (1991) not only stresses the concept of emotion as motivation (drawing from the seventeenth-century concept of the passions), but posits a vast array of innate "action tendencies" that determine the course of anger, envy, love, sadness and so on.

Thus, in spite of the generalized hegemony of the cognitive movement, we find that as emotion has returned full force as a discursive object, the profession is once again fragmented. The fault lines are precisely those of the century's beginning. Differing camps construct research programs, generate literatures, hold conferences, and generally organize themselves around contrasting tropes. Illustrative of this climate of contestation is George Mandler's (1984) troubled query,

Is there a cohesive psychology of emotion? . . . It may be symptomatic that the best summary was provided by Madison Bentley. He knew in 1928 what too many psychologists still fail to accept today, that there is no commonly, even superficially, acceptable definition of what a psychology of emotion is about. . . . Bentley concludes: "Whether the term (emotion) stands for a psychological entity upon which we are all researching I do not know. Whether it is the common subject of our varied investigations I am not sure enough to be dogmatic." (p. 16)

Social constructionism and the metaphoric inflection

Thus far we find that as various movements in psychology have gained ascendance – within the discipline, within the academy more generally, or within the broader cultural and economic context of mental health practice – emotional discourse has been shaped or suppressed accordingly. The different metaphors of the emotions have variously served to justify, credit, excoriate, build allegiances, sustain effective relations, and secure employment for a broad array of disciplinary subcultures. Abundant traces of earlier contests remain, as discursive regimes wax and wane in strength.

However, the story does not thereby terminate. There is yet a final chapter to be added, one that dramatically alters the rhetorical landscape. We confront now the possible emergence of a new form of monophony.

For early behaviorists, the absence of research on emotions seemed largely derived from a commitment to a logical empiricist metatheory. However, since the 1950s logical empiricist philosophy has become subject to increasing criticism, and since the 1960s there has been a general erosion of interest in projects designed to establish rational foundations of scientific method. Moving from the more conservative critiques, for example, of Popper and Quine, to the more radical incursions of theorists such as Kuhn and Feyerabend, philosophy has entered what most consider a "postempiricist" phase. This erosion of confidence in the philosophical justification for scientific psychology has also invited a broad-scale critique of the science and fostered lively discussion of a "new psychology."[1]

As many now recognize, perhaps the chief contender for a successor project to logical empiricism is some form of social constructionism. Drawing importantly from emerging developments most prominently in the history of science, the sociology of knowledge, ethnomethodology, rhetorical studies of science, symbolic anthropology, feminist theory, and poststructuralist literary theory, social constructionism is not so much a foundational theory of knowledge as an antifoundational dialogue. Primary emphases of this dialogue are placed on the social-discursive matrix from which knowledge claims emerge and from which their justification is derived; the values/ideology implicit within knowledge posits; the modes of informal and institutional life sustained and replenished by ontological and epistemological commitments; and the distribution of power and privilege favored by disciplinary beliefs. Much attention is also given to the creation and transformation of cultural constructions; the adjudication of competing belief/value systems; and the generation of new modes of pedagogy, scholarly expression, and disciplinary relations.

Given these investments – in loosening the grip of the empiricist world view, and building toward a positive alternative – what posture can constructionist psychologists take toward the emotions? In this instance none of the central metaphors of the preceding century are felicitous. The biological, the sensory (and its cognitive derivative), and the energic metaphors each conflict with the assumptions of constructionist metatheory. The earlier metaphors, instantiated at the theoretical level, blunt the impetus toward change at the level of metatheory. To enumerate the most prominent failings: (1) Each of the traditional metaphors essentializes the emotions – treating them as biological, sensory-cognitive, or energic givens – there in nature, to be interrogated by science. In effect, the metaphors portend the existence of an obdurate domain outside the realm of social construction. (2) Each metaphor derives from and rationalizes a dualistic conception of human functioning. Not only is dualism a primary constituent of the empiricist view of knowledge (with the mental representations of individuals serving as the locus of knowledge), but favors psychological explanations of human action as opposed to the microsocial explanations central to constructionism. (3) In their focus on individual process, each of the metaphors favors an ideology of the self-contained individual, a commitment that most constructionists see as inimical to cultural well-being. Feminist critics have been particularly vocal in their critiques of the biological metaphor, and its contribution to the cluster of androcentric binaries that valorize reason, culture, and masculinity, at the expense of emotion, nature, and femininity.

Confronted with the unattractive options offered by the tradition, and desirous of appropriating this significant discursive realm, it has been necessary for constructionists to draw from alternative repositories of cultural intelligibility. The result is a resuscitation of a family of interrelated but (until now) more marginal metaphors within the culture. Primary among these are life as theater (*the dramaturgic*), as game (*the ludic*), as literature (*the narrative*), and as cultural ritual (*the tribal*). These metaphors not only furnish the constructionist with a novel and intelligible set of alternatives to the discourses favored by empiricist psychology, but simultaneously function to reinforce the social constructionist alternative to empiricist metatheory. The metaphors thus carry a dual function, serving as explanatory vehicles in scholarly research on the emotions, and as rhetorical supports for the overarching attempts at metatheoretical ascendance.

To elaborate, each of the new metaphors first draws attention away from individual, psychological process, and gives primacy to the social sphere: to the play (see, e.g., Sarbin, 1986; Averill, 1982), the game (Bailey, 1983), the text (Gergen and Gergen, 1988), or the tribal ritual (Rosaldo, 1980; White and Kirkpatrick, 1985). In effect, psychological explanations are replaced by processes of cultural meaning-making. Second, the kind of essentialism posited by the empiricists is placed in critical relief, as each of the metaphors views the emotions as socially constituted – with emotional action paralleling, for example, the performance of Hamlet (the dramaturgic), or hitting a "home run" in baseball (the ludic); to achieve an emotion is thus similar to writing a climax to a short story (the narrative), or participating in a *rite de passage* (the tribal). There simply is no reality of emotion independent of the community of interlocutors.

Further, each of these metaphors operates against the empiricist claims of universality – casting aspersions on formulations of human functioning that discount history and culture. Rather, each invites sensitivity to the sociocultural circumstances giving rise to various forms of emotional performance. Constructionist scholarship thus lays special emphasis on the specific cultural functions played by various emotional expressions (see, e.g., Lutz, 1988), and the historical conditions giving rise to various forms of emotion (Badinter, 1980; Stearns, 1989). Finally, each of these metaphors opens the way to social critique. The empiricist family of metaphors was all consistent with a world of Humean causality; individual behavior is simply a causal byproduct of antecedent conditions (physiology, stimuli, human constitution). Persons themselves have no responsibility for their actions. For constructionists, such a view of human action not only favors the status quo ("people simply do what they must do"), but leads to myopic claims of ethical neutrality. Yet, the alternative metaphors of the stage, the game, the text, and the tribe all emphasize the optional nature of the actions in question. Contemporary patterns of action are scarcely required, and they could be otherwise (see, e.g., Lutz and Abu-Lughod, 1990). Further, it is one of the responsibilities of the scholar to challenge problematic patterns of action, to engage in forms of social critique.

Conclusion

The view of a unitary hegemonic discourse, subtly expanding and subverting alternative intelligibilities, scarcely fits the history of American psychology. Rather, we find a discipline that is at once attempting to legitimate itself with respect to differing audiences (the academic and the general populace in particular), and fraught with internecine warfare concerning the image of science. Further, these investments are significantly manifest in the theoretical content of the field. As emphasized here, the view taken of "the emotions" is scarcely neutral – derived from a preexistent observation base – but plays an important role in the varying attempts at professional ascendance. The metaphoric construction of the emotions thus serves to buttress or reinforce claims to legitimacy. In certain cases, claims to superior position have lent themselves to theories that exclude or marginalize emotions discourse. However, because "the emotions" are integral to the culturally sedimented belief systems, exclusionary projects are limited in life-span. They are vulnerable to competing movements that, by reinstating the emotions, gain important cultural advantage. There is, then, substantial institutional power derived from compelling metaphors of the emotions. While various movements in psychology have attempted to eradicate the emotions, the resilience and resurgence of the discourse reveals the overarching significance of the broader context of meaning.

Further, when emotions discourse has played a central role in justifying the scientific project, it has confronted an obfuscating polyphony. A variety of compelling metaphors has been available for elaboration. However, attempts at a polyphonic blending have not sutured the conflicting figurations. And, with variegated metaphors still creditable, the temptation toward monophonic reductionism remains ever salient. The move toward a social constructionist science significantly alters the political complex. Constructionists abandon each of the traditional metaphors – and thus both the long-standing tendencies toward polyphony and monophony. Rather, the constructionist relies on a family of textually related metaphors that blur the distinction between polyphony and monophony. And, while these metaphors are not likely to carry rhetorical weight within the natural science domain, they are highly congenial with the shift toward a *human* (as opposed to a *behavioral*) science more generally within the academy. We thus confront a new array of tensions, the results of which are certain to ramify throughout forthcoming disquisitions on emotion.

Note

1 See, for example, Armistead (1974), Harre and Secord (1972), and Gergen (1994a).

References

Allport, F. H. (1924) *Social psychology*. New York: Houghton Mifflin.
Anscombe, G. E. M. (1976) *Intention*. Oxford: Blackwell.
Armistead, N. (Ed.) (1974) *Reconstructing social psychology*. Baltimore: Penguin.
Austin, J. L. (1962) *Sense and sensibilia*. London: Oxford University Press.
Averill, J. R. (1982) *Anger and aggression: An essay on emotion*. New York: Springer-Verlag.
Averill, J. R. (1990) Inner feelings, works of the flesh, the beast within, diseases of the mind, driving force, and putting on a show: Six metaphors of emotion and their theoretical extensions. In D. E. Leary (Ed.), *Metaphors in the history of psychology*. Cambridge: Cambridge University Press, pp. 104–132.
Badinter, E. (1980) *Mother love, myth and reality*. New York: Macmillan.
Bailey, F. G. (1983) *The tactical uses of passion*. Ithaca, NY: Cornell University Press.
Bakhtin, M. (1981) *The dialogic imagination*. Austin: University of Texas Press.
Beck, A. T. (1976) *Cognitive therapy and the emotional disorders*. New York: Meridian.
Berlyne, D. E. (1964) Emotional aspects of learning. In *Annual Review of Psychology*. Palo Alto: Annual Reviews.
Blanchard, C. C., and Blanchard, R. J. (1988) Ethoexperimental approaches to the biology of emotion. In *Annual Review of Psychology*. Palo Alto: Annual Reviews.
Cannon, W. B. (1914) The interrelations of emotions as suggested by recent psychological researches. *American Journal of Psychology, 25,* 256–282.
Chomsky, N. (1959) A review of B. F. Skinner's *Verbal behavior. Language, 35,* 26–58.
Chomsky, N. (1968) *Language and mind*. New York: Harcourt, Brace and World.
Cofer, C. (1972) *Motivation and emotion*. Glencoe, IL: Scott Foresman.
Derrida, J. (1976) *Of grammatology*. Baltimore: Johns Hopkins University Press.
Dollard, J., and Miller, N. (1950) *Personality and psychotherapy*. New York: McGraw-Hill.
Eibel-Eibelsfeldt, I. (1979) *Love and hate*. New York: Holt, Rinehart and Winston.
Ekman, P. (Ed.) (1982) *Emotion in the human face*. Cambridge: Cambridge University Press.
Foucault, M. (1978) *The history of sexuality*, Vol. 1. New York: Pantheon.
Foucault, M. (1979) *Discipline and punish: The birth of the prison*. Trans. A. Sheridan. New York: Vintage.
Frijda, N. H. (1986) *The emotions*. Cambridge: Cambridge University Press.
Gergen, K. J. (1993) Textual considerations in the scientific construction of human character. In J. V. Knapp (Ed.), *Literary character*. Lanham, MD.: University Press of America, pp. 365–379.
Gergen, K. J. (1994) *Toward transformation in social knowledge,* 2nd ed. London: Sage.

Gergen, K. J. (1994a) *Realities and relationships: Soundings in social construction.* Cambridge, MA: Harvard University Press.

Gergen, K. J., and Gergen, M. M. (1988) Narratives and the self as relationship. In L. Berkowitz (Ed.), *Advances in experimental social psychology,* Vol. 21. New York: Academic Press, pp. 17–66.

Gigerenzer, G., and Murray, D. J. (1987) *Cognition as intuitive statistics.* Hillsdale, NJ: Erlbaum.

Harre, R., and Secord, P. F. (1972) *The explanation of social behaviour.* Oxford: Blackwell.

Harvey, J. H., and Ickes, W. J. (Eds.) (1976) *New directions in attribution research.* New York: Halstead.

Harvey, J. H., and Weary, G. (Eds.) (1985) *Attribution: Basic issues and applications.* Orlando, FL: Academic Press.

Hoffman, R. R., Cochran, E. L., and Nead, J. M. (1990) Cognitive metaphors in experimental psychology. In D. E. Leary (Ed.), *Metaphors in the history of psychology.* Cambridge: Cambridge University Press.

Hollis, M. (1977) *Models of man.* Cambridge: Cambridge University Press.

Izard, C. E. (1977) *Human emotions.* New York: Plenum.

James, W. (1890) *Principles of psychology,* Vol. 1. New York: Henry Holt.

Kenny, A. (1963) *Action, emotion and will.* London: Routledge and Kegan Paul.

Koch, S. (1963) Epilogue. In S. Koch (Ed.), *Psychology: A study of a science,* Vol. 3. New York: McGraw-Hill, pp. 411–491.

Krech, D., and Crutchfield, R. S. (1948) *Theory and problems of social psychology.* New York: McGraw-Hill.

Lazarus, R. S. (1991) *Emotion and adaptation.* New York: Oxford University Press.

Leeper, R. N., and Madison, P. (1959) *Toward understanding personality.* New York: Appleton-Century-Crofts.

Leventhal, H., and Tomarken, A. J. (1986) Emotion: Today's problems. In *Annual review of psychology.* Palo Alto: Annual Reviews.

Lutz, C. (1988) *Unnatural emotions.* Chicago: University of Chicago Press.

Lutz, C., and Abu-Lughod, L. (1990) *Language and the politics of emotion.* Cambridge: Cambridge University Press.

Mandler, G. (1984) *Mind and body: Psychology of emotion and stress.* New York: Norton.

Manicas, P. T. (1987) *A history and philosophy of the social sciences.* Oxford: Blackwell.

Myerson, A. (1934) *Social psychology.* New York: Prentice-Hall.

Oatley, K., and Jenkins, J. M. (1992) Human emotions: Function and dysfunction. In *Annual review of psychology.* Palo Alto: Annual Reviews.

Piaget, J. (1952) *The origins of intelligence in children.* New York: Norton.

Plutchik, R. (1980) A general psychoevolutionary theory of emotion. In R. Plutchik and H. Kellerman (Eds.), *Emotion, theory research and experience.* New York: Academic Press.

Rorty, R. (1979) *Philosophy and the mirror of nature.* Princeton: Princeton University Press.

Rosaldo, M. (1980) *Knowledge and passion.* Cambridge: Cambridge University Press.

Rose, N. (1985) *The psychological complex.* London: Routledge and Kegan Paul.

Rose, N. (1990) *Governing the soul.* London: Routledge.

Ryle, G. (1949) *The concept of mind.* London: Hutchinson.

Sarbin, T. R. (1986) Emotion and act: Roles and rhetoric. In R. Harre (Ed.), *The social construction of emotions.* Oxford: Blackwell, pp. 211–239.

Schachter, S. (1964) The interaction of cognitive and physiological determinants of emotional state. In L. Berkowitz (Ed.), *Advances in experimental social psychology,* Vol. 1. New York: Academic Press, pp. 379–399.

Schachter, S., and Singer, J. (1962) Cognitive, social and physiological determinants of emotional state. *Psychological Review, 69,* 379–399.

Sherrington, C. S. (1906) *The integrative action of the nervous system.* New Haven: Yale University Press.

Skinner, B. B. (1938) *The behavior of organisms: An experimental analysis.* New York: Appleton-Century-Crofts.

Stearns, P. N. (1989) *Jealousy: The evolution of an emotion in American history.* New York: New York University Press.

Symonds, P. M. (1949) *Dynamic psychology.* New York: Appleton-Century-Crofts.

Tomkins, S. (1962) *Affect, imagery, and consciousness,* Vol. 1. New York: Springer.

Tucker, D. M. (1981) Lateral brain function, emotion, and conceptualization. *Psychological Bulletin, 89,* 19–46.

White, G., and Kirkpatrick, J. (Eds.) (1985) *Person, self and experience: Exploring Pacific ethnopsychologies.* Berkeley: University of California Press.

Williams, R. (1980) *Problems in materialism and culture.* London: Verso.

Wittgenstein, L. (1978) *Philosophical investigations.* Oxford: Blackwell.

Wittgenstein, L. (1980) *Remarks on the philosophy of psychology.* Ed. G. H. von Wright and H. Nyman. Oxford: Blackwell.

Woodworth, R. S. (1918) *Dynamic psychology.* New York: Columbia University Press.

Young, P. T. (1961) *Motivation and emotion: A survey of the determinants of human and animal activity.* New York: Wiley.

5 Psyche and her descendants

Carl F. Graumann

A century of psychology

Every now and then the closing century has been named the century of psychology. Whether this label is justified is still too early to say. But among the many names this century was given at its beginning, some had at least a psychological flavor or were meant to relate to psychology. When LeBon spoke of the era of the masses, William Stern of the century of individuality, Ellen Key of the century of the child, they named and fixed topics of public concern that, although not exclusively psychological, contributed to the growth of interest in the new science of psychology. Psychology, from its infancy in the late nineteenth century, had made children and development, character and personality, and the mind and behavior of crowds key topics of concern. Crowd psychology and psychoanalysis, and also the more academically respectable child and personality psychologies, very soon after the turn of the century contributed to at least the educated public discourse. The influx of psychological words and phrases has had its ups and downs, but today, at the end of the century, we may state that it is still going on, so that at least psychological discourse has become a characteristic feature of the twentieth century.

Whenever we join a social gathering, open a paper of the rainbow press or an illustrated magazine, listen to so-called educational broadcasts or watch television talk shows, we can rely on being confronted with a jargon or lingo that looks or sounds "psychological," although in many cases this "psychotalk" only bears a slight resemblance to the professional language of psychology lectures and textbooks. While the latter in its hermetic technicality may remain incomprehensible "psychologese" to the so-called layperson, the former is quite common and even familiar to the larger part of the nonprofessional public. Both types of language we must consider to be variants of psychological discourse. Instead of drawing sharp dividing lines,

Parts of this chapter are based on papers presented at the International Science Forum of Heidelberg University in January and at the Bellagio Study and Conference Center in August 1991. For critical comments I am grateful to both audiences and, above all, to Ken Gergen.

we should consider that there is a considerable two-way traffic between these two subsets or manifestations of psychological discourse, but either one will hardly be mistaken for the other. The layperson will not be able to follow the professionals' discourse, and scientists will abhor and reject what they regard as vulgarizations of scientific terms and ideas. But if both registers are rightly named "psychological," the double question is of what they have in common and in which respects they differ.

Realizing that both the language of psychological science and that of psychologizing in everyday life are broad topics, I can deal with the problem of the two-faced psychological discourse only very selectively. Because I consider the academic as well as the everyday variant of psychological discourse as descending from a common ground or source, I shall approach the topic in three perspectives.

First, I shall very briefly refer to the origin of psychological discourse in the literal sense of "psychology" – that is, the *logos* of the *psyche* (soul, mind) as these Greek terms were used in contexts of a prescientific, mainly philosophical, psychology. Second, I will, again briefly, draw the reader's attention to what became of the *psyche* (soul, mind) when psychology in the modern sense became established as an individual science (*Einzel-wissenschaft*), when, as the serious joke aptly states, psychology first lost its "soul" and then went out of its "mind." In a third step I will then discuss psychological discourse in everyday life, as it is used mainly for evaluative and ultimately moral purposes. For this is the overall thesis of this chapter: Originally, psychological discourse was inseparable from *moral discourse;* it certainly was value-committed. The separation began when psychology was transformed into a science. Briefly stated, the "scientification" of psychology implied an effort at demoralizing moral issues. But while it may be true that, at least in its ideal scientific form, psychological discourse attempts to be "moral- and value-free," the use of psychological terms in everyday life and, mainly, the strategy that will be described as "psychologizing" continue to be a special kind of moralizing. But, if it is permissible to consider both registers of psychological discourse as descendants of an originally unitary one, we must, at least functionally, distinguish between these two modern offsprings.

The *logos* of the *psyche*

Psyche has become such a rare word in our modern language that one is almost inevitably referred to its classical antique usages if one encounters it or is daring enough to use it occasionally. Before it came to be a key term in what I would prefer to call a philosophical anthropology, *psyche* had both a biological and a mythological meaning. The latter has remained so dominant that in some encyclopedias of the nineteenth century it is still the only usage listed; thus, in a German *Handwörterbuch der philosophischen Wissenschaften* (Krug, 1832) the entry *"Psyche"* merely refers the reader to *"Amor."* The basic biological usage of *psyche* as breath (equivalent to *pneuma*) is very close to the philosophical Aristotelian meaning of *psyche* as the life-giving, life-sustaining, or animating principle or agent. I shall disregard here what has later on been interpreted as Aristotle's "psychology" (mainly taken from his *Politics,* the two major *Ethics,* and his *Rhetoric*) and focus instead on *De Anima,* from which little book we may consider a few conceptions (or rather interpretations) that, for a long time, influenced psychological discourse.

For Aristotle, *psyche,* as a vital force, is inseparable from the living body (in its nutritive, perceptive, and locomotor functions). A psychology, based on *De Anima,* is part of the natural sciences, here the life sciences (cf. Robinson, 1976). *Psyche* and mind (*nous*) are not identical. Although the latter resides in the former, they are different in kind: Whereas the soul perishes with the body, mind survives (which attribute was later on ascribed to the soul). Without discussing details of the *psyche,* of its sensory, motor, and rational faculties, it is for the modern reader interesting to see that, for Aristotle, *psyche* is treated as something that can be analyzed in and by itself without embedding it in the person's conduct and relatedness to his or her social context. It is man's inner nature as such that is made the topic of this early psychology, and it is to this interiority that our attention is directed, leaving everything outside that is exterior to the soul. One could not say that Aristotle's *psyche* is worldless, nutritive, and perceptive as it is functionally, but the scope of investigation is entirely inside the soul or the mind, respectively. I do not maintain that Aristotle was the first thinker to conceive of human nature in terms of a fundamental inside–outside *polarity,* which has always been the most powerful metaphor of psychological discourse (and as far as I know this is cross-culturally so); but *De Anima* has subsequently become a model of what I would call an immanentist psychology preoccupied with what is inside the (animal or human) body without itself having physical or material reality.

Although this is already a post-Aristotelian interpretation of the soul, the immaterial, the fleeting, the evanescent, the invisible have become permanent characteristics of the soul up to the present day. To this mixture of the mythological, the biological, and the metaphysical conceptions of *psyche,* we must add the consequences of its Christianization: The vital principle was transformed into the "soul" as the immortal spiritual and substantial part of the person. It is mainly because discourse on the soul had for centuries been a predominantly theological, at least religious, affair that the soul (*die Seele, l'âme*) and, with it, its Greek equivalent, *psyche,* were not admitted to the new scientific universe of discourse when psychology endeavored to become a modern science.[1]

Psyche's metamorphoses in psychological science

Consciousness

Instead of *psyche* and *Seele,* which were kept out of scientific bounds, two very close relatives were admitted to the realm of the rapidly developing psychological discourse, namely either their substantivated adjectives, *das Psychische* and *das Seelische,* or the compound *das Seelenleben.* The latter's English equivalent is "mental life," a more acceptable expression than "mind," which, in turn, was much more admissible than "soul," to which William James (1890/1950, 181) ironically referred as "this much-despised word." But right from the beginning of the "New Psychology," *das Seelische* (or mental life) was equated with consciousness (*Bewußtsein*) and psychology very soon was defined as the science of consciousness. Since the history of the concepts of consciousness and *Bewußtsein* have been presented several times (cf. Diemer, 1971; Graumann, 1966, 1984; Pongratz, 1967), only a few features of the first modern successor to *psyche* need to be indicated.

The first feature, the most relevant for the guiding thesis of this chapter, is to be seen in the fact that both the English and the German word go back to Latin *conscientia,* which term originally did not yet distinguish between knowing oneself (*sibi conscius esse*) and *conscience* (moral consciousness). Even today the French have just one word (*conscience*) for both *conscience psychologique* and *conscience morale* (Robert, 1976). *Bewußtsein,* the German equivalent of Latin *conscientia,* coined by Christian Wolff in his 1719 metaphysics, was meant to emphasize knowledge, the noetic functions of the mind at the expense of the moral ones. For Wolff, a rationalist philosopher in the tradition of Descartes and Leibniz, reason, the power of the *cogito,* constituted knowledge. When consciousness was, later on, made the subject matter of the new psychology and was said to coincide with the mental, it still carried with it the rational flavor of the dominating *cogito.* This rationality was even strengthened by the ideas of nineteenth-century voluntarism; it was volition that Wilhelm Wundt considered to be the prototype of consciousness. Furthermore, all the "facts of consciousness," the mental states and processes, were treated as strictly inner affairs, accessible only to the various methods of introspection. We know from the history of modern psychology that the emphasis on interiority led to a kind of encapsulation which made data from introspection, if they carried any reference, unacceptable.[2] Hence, scientific psychology endorsed what its metaphysical predecessor had launched: the idea that discourse on the *psyche,* even in its secularized gestalt, refers to strictly interior, self-contained states and processes of individuals.[3] To the extent that such conscious states and processes can only be identified and described by individuals, psychology as *Bewuβtseinswissenschaft* (science of consciousness) was, almost by definition, a strictly *individualist* branch of knowledge.

Immediate experience (Erleben)

Already in the early years of modern psychology, even within the oeuvre of Wilhelm Wundt, psychological discourse gradually changed from *Bewuβtsein,* first to *Bewuβtseinserlebnisse,* then to *Erlebnisse* and *Erleben.* While it is impossible to render *Erleben* fully into English, "immediate experience" being the closest approximation, it is nevertheless important to remember that German-language psychology, for at least half a century, was the *Wissenschaft vom Erleben und Verhalten,* that is, the science of (immediate) experience and behavior. I am sure that the untranslatability of *Erleben* has to do with a special German cultural tradition containing elements of romanticism, vitalism, and historicism (cf. Gadamer, 1975; Graumann, 1984). The verb *erleben* itself, about as old as psychology, is a resultative form of *leben* (live) and also connotes the immediacy of what we experience ourselves.[4] In a semantic differential analysis (Graumann, 1965), *Erleben* proves more emotional, deep, individual, intimate, full, strong, and diffuse than "consciousness," which is experienced as more constant, rational, serious, and sober. Belonging to the semantic field of life and living, *Erleben* is certainly the richer and more comprehensive manifestation of human existence than consciousness. Correspondingly, the period of German psychology as *Erlebniswissenschaft* (in the first half of the century) showed more concern for emotionality than earlier and later periods. The favorite method of study was, significantly enough, that of *Erlebnisdeskription,* that is, experiential or phenomenological description.

Perhaps the most significant change that was brought about by understanding the psychical as immediate experience was opening consciousness to the world, diverting the psychologist's interest from a person's mental interior to the world-as-it-is-experienced, the phenomenal world, as paradigmatically studied by the early gestalt psychologists. Since then (some) psychologists have felt free to do professionally what everybody had always done in everyday discourse, namely to talk of the world "outside" in perceptual, emotional, motivational, or actional terms: to speak of the "charm" of a face, the "grace" of a gesture, the "perils" of a narrow mountain road, of the "challenge" of a peak. Not only beauty is acknowledged to be in the eyes of the beholder; experiential qualities in general are understood as correlates of mental states (as, e.g., Lewin's "valences" [Lewin, 1935]) or of specific behavior patterns (as, e.g., Tolman's discriminanda, manipulanda, and utilitanda [Tolman & Brunswik, 1935]). Since descriptions of the psychological qualities of the world had been integrated into the professional's discourse, psychological description was no longer confined to "inner man."

Behavior

After the beginning of the century, interest in animal and human behavior was added to that of consciousness and experience and, at least in some countries and for several decades, became not only the predominant but the exclusive field of psychological research. In its strong resentment against "mentalistic" conceptions of psychology and in its popular appeal, at least for the American public, behavioral conceptions had a strong impact on psychological discourse in general. The ease with which the superfluous word "behavior" could, and still can, be added to any other word designating animal or human activities (from crowding to milling, from dating to mating, from littering to energy-saving behavior) is at least indicative of the belief in the ubiquitous potency of psychology alias behavioral science.

What "behavior," so far the most distant descendant of *psyche,* still has to do with its repressed or even denigrated ancestor, and why representatives of a "behavioral science" have tolerated being called "psychologists" are interesting stories in themselves. Behavior, the key term of this branch of psychology, originally was, and in the educational field still is, a moral concept. In its originally reflexive form it meant to conduct oneself in a proper manner, that is, according to moral standards. Only by virtue of this meaning does the imperative "Behave!" make any sense. Again, when "behavior" was introduced into biology and psychology as a general term for an organism's responses to stimulation, the result was to "demoralize" it, which, linguistically as well as psychologically, meant the loss of reflexivity. This, however, was in anticipation of a more radical loss, namely of consciousness or of mind, at least as a subject matter of psychology, which discipline then concentrated on "outer man" and on what could be observed, measured, and inferred from outside, without giving up the self-contained individualism of the much-criticized psychology of consciousness.

Cognition

In the meantime, we have had another "turn," another "revolution," and behavior is no longer successor to *psyche*'s throne. The new pretender, for some already the new sovereign, is cognition or even information processing. Despite some borrowings from mentalist discourse, the most recent psychology is not a return to a psychology of consciousness, say, on a higher level. The new spirit and the language are largely taken from the computer technology of information processing. The guiding metaphor has rightly been named the computational metaphor; its "elective affinities" are the new cognitive sciences. Maybe it is too early to assess the degree of relationship with psychological predecessors. But at present this lineage rather derives from *nous,* from the rational faculties and from an individualist conception of the mind-soul, again with a resulting suppression of the emotional, motivational, unconscious, and *Erlebnis* aspects of psyche.

To summarize: Since the beginning of modern psychology, we have had a rather rapid succession of eponyms, following the soul or *psyche*. Considering the *substantial* oscillation between such different *logoi* of *psyche,* such different types of psychological discourse, it is difficult to predict the next shift and the time of its emergence. In order to do that we need to know more about the social and intellectual conditions of such changes. This analysis has hardly begun and, at the present time, is still descriptive rather than explanatory. We observe that an emphasis on the rational and conscious aspects of the *psyche* (as in early "mentalism") was followed by an emphasis on the irrational and unconscious (as in the emotionalism of *Erlebniswissenschaft* and in psychoanalysis). We observe that an exclusive concern for inner events, accessible only to one's own introspection (as in the structuralist version of "mentalist" psychology), is abruptly followed by an equally exclusive consideration of outer behavior, accessible to third persons' observations (as in the various forms of "behaviorism"), which, in turn, has meanwhile been replaced by the "cognitivist" effort to reenact conceptions of mental processes by means of computer programs. The principle of such shifts and turns seems to be that what is a meaningful aspect of the *psyche* is converted into an absolute. Once absolutized, it evokes its opposite which, in turn, tends to become sovereign. The result is a series of "isms" (Graumann, 1988, 1991). Why this is so, and why in psychology much more so than in other social sciences, is still an open question. In any case, the fashionlike variation in psychological key terms is a problem that calls for the concentrated effort of the historiography, semantics, and sociology of psychology.

Psychology in everyday discourse

Psychological key terms

We must now turn our attention to lay-psychological discourse, to psychotalk and psychologizing in everyday life. I shall, for the present purpose, largely ignore that mentioning "psychology" and matters "psychological" sometimes refers people to what professional psychologists do or what is going on in a science named psychology. Everybody knows that some such science exists and may have heard or read that professionals trained in this field work in clinics, schools, and industry and are offering their services to authorities, agencies, corporations, and individuals. However, what these professionals actually do often remains opaque or vague. It may have to do with tests or with lying on a couch, with marketing or with rationalization. There is no clear-cut professional image as for a dentist, a surgeon, or even a priest, although the media provide the public with regular doses of professional psychology. Willy-nilly we receive a kind of minimum daily requirement of psychology for our educational, marital, extramarital, and other interpersonal or personal problems, receiving advice perhaps on how to reduce weight, stop smoking, enjoy aging, and prepare for dying. While some of these psychological messages sound strange, even outlandish, and are therefore resented and rejected, many sound familiar since they coincide with the lore and wisdom handed down from generation to generation for use in situations like pregnancy, birth, disease, death, or other critical life events.

Here it is hardly possible to distinguish between lore and science, between what we have always "known" and what may properly be called psychological technology. As a result it is difficult to distinguish between folk and professional psychology. The distinction is difficult or impossible mainly for three reasons: the vocabulary used in folk as well as professional psychology is often identical; a good portion of the social lore has, critically checked, indeed entered psychological technology; and, inversely, through the mechanisms of vulgarization scientific knowledge has diffused into the common "stock of knowledge" (Schütz, 1953) and is contained in many "social representations" (Moscovici, 1961).

Although an investigation of the interaction between scientific and folk psychology for obvious reasons is difficult to undertake, it is feasible in areas where a period can be fixed in which new terms were coined (e.g., frustration, repression, conditioned reflex, or achievement motivation) and were subsequently diffused and scattered in the vernacular till they attained the status of everyday words. Without being able to clarify the genealogy and etymology of psychological terms in the vernacular, we can still try to answer some questions regarding the usage of such terms and the functions of everyday psychological discourse. One way to approach the topic is to identify the situations or contexts in which the psychological vocabulary is used. Before we try to do this we should take a brief look at the key terms of what once used to be the study of mind.

The word *psyche* is still occasionally used when we refer to the nonphysical aspects of the human being. But when we say "It is his or her *psyche*" or "it is psychical" (at least in German this is intellectual talk), we refer to something sensitive, delicate, vulnerable, residing invisibly in a body, "deep down inside." And if, in colloquial German, we refer to a person as a *Psychi,* we discriminate him or her as a "freak." In English, the psychical, lying outside the sphere of the physical and of physical science, has even adopted a spiritualist meaning but may still be an object of so-called "psychical research."

More common, however, is "mental" discourse. Besides the common usage as the adjective relating to mind, to state "it's mental" or even to speak of a "mental case," clearly refers to a deficiency or disorder in the psychiatric sense. A "mental patient," however, is not necessarily a person "sick" in mind *(geisteskrank)* as the term "mental disease" suggests. His or her behavior may merely impress others as odd, fantastic, unusual, or "deviant." More often than not it seems to be difficult to decide whether the disorder we meet with is "mental" or "social." At least in some societies persons who are socially or politically "deviant" run the risk of ending up as "mental patients." In many cases we say "mental" only to indicate that there are no physical or visible signs. That applies to making "mental notes" as well as to committing "mental cruelty."

Although many usages of "mind" are indispensable in everyday language, if we want to refer to the mental capacities or functions of perceiving, intending, deciding, or remembering, the English counterpart of the mind, the "soul," is a much more delicate and less frequent word, and so is German *Seele* and French *l'âme*. While it has been banned from psychological science, it has been retained in religious, poetic, and erotic discourse; but it seems generally to be on the retreat in everyday talk. Still, it sometimes means something like the guiding principle and the center or the "heart" of things. Free speech, for example, can be the "soul of democracy"; a person may be "the soul of the department." If we compare the usage of "mind" with "soul" in ordinary language, "mind" seems to contrast with (heart and) "soul," "mind" being more rational and cognitive, whereas "soul" suggests intimacy, emotionality, and expressiveness. If we call a person a dear or poor soul, we mean *Gemüt,* the qualities that express and arouse sentiment rather than intellect. The oldest meaning of soul as a spiritual principle may be obsolescent in ordinary language, but the recent Afro-American Soul (with the capital S) is the most distinctive indication that the soul still is a spiritual, moral, and expressive force. And only recently students in Germany convened a humanistic conference under the slogan "Against a soulless psychology!"

There seems to be a central tendency in the ordinary usage of psychological key terms: Denoting something as "mental" in English (*psychisch* in German) frequently means something tender, frail, deficient, or even sick. The state of mind of a healthy, attentive, and contented person would not be characterized as "mental." But if a person looks glum, strained, and irritated, the cause might be "mental." We may even say that, in ordinary language, the "psychological" in general is frequently associated with the weak, soft, delicate, or vulnerable. If we conclude that, for instance, an executive's assistant is a "good psychologist," we usually mean to say that he or she knows the "weak sides," the foibles, and, above all, the vanities of his or her employer and knows how to use his or her knowledge. Being a "good psychologist" in nonprofessional discourse implies the knowledge and the skill of how to influence or even to manipulate others. In this context it is interesting to know that the ability to look through a person's "facade" or "mask" is part of the social representation of a good psychologist to such a degree that people still believe that psychology students are trained in these skills at the university. Although academic psychology has long given up the claim to be the art of unmasking, of revealing the "true" character of a person, this is still a popular notion, going back to conceptions of psychology as once held by Friedrich Nietzsche and Sigmund Freud. Here we have one of the crucial points where, expressed by the same word "psychologist," the modern scientific and the popular notions diverge.

There is one other difference between the scientific and the everyday usage of psychological terms. We know that *psyche,* "soul," even "mind" are not technical terms nor hypothetical constructs of modern psychological science. When the layperson uses these words, we can often recognize from the contexts and purposes of such practice that these words are still used in some of their original philosophical meanings, however simplified and distorted their popularizations may appear. Reference to the soul (mind or *psyche*) as an inner principle or, at least, an invisible inner state, as contrasted with the visibly, tangibly behaving and directly manipulable outer physical body, still implies a dimension of innerness that permits not only of talking meaningfully about "inner man" but even of the latter's "innermost," which sometimes becomes audible as one's "inner voice," where consciousness still coincides with conscience. In contrast, a cognition, if defined at all, is a theoretical construct rather than an element of our inner mental life.[5]

While the everyday uses and meanings of psychological key words are rather far away from the universe of academic psychological discourse and reasoning, there is, however, one overlapping area. Our innermost, where we are "our very selves," we also conceive of as a sphere not to be invaded, a sphere whose privacy is recognized by others, whose protection against "transgressors" or "trespassers" is consensually considered to be legitimate, in some countries even guaranteed by constitution or by law. This inner sphere of privacy has also been recognized and made a topic of research in personality and social psychology. It figures as the central (or core) part of certain personality models to be distinguished from more peripheral parts (cf. Lewin, 1935). It is at least presupposed in the study of self-disclosure (Jourard, 1971) and has been central to the sociopsychological research on privacy (Kruse, 1980). Considering that conceptions of an inner structure or organization of personality date back to antiquity, it is difficult to decide whether ancient lay notions of human interiority have infiltrated academic discourse or the latter has diffused into the layperson's language.

The psychological vocabulary and its usage

So far we have dealt only with the fate of the headwords or key terms of psychology. But our everyday discourse is interspersed, sometimes saturated, with a huge variety of mental terms. They are not, as in science, constitutive of, but certainly essential for, the everyday universe of discourse. It would be difficult to find a representative language sample of interpersonal communication without a substantial part of mental terms.

The mere fact that our language is so rich in mental words and phrases may be taken as the cultural acknowledgment of the conscious character of human subjectivity. Having commerce with others and oneself is having commerce with conscious beings. Without going into the philosophical controversy about the *reality* of mental states, it is, for the present purpose, sufficient to state that, because people communicate effectively by using mental terms, they mutually refer to something that they posit to be real. However, when we make use of mental terms, do we always address our own or other people's intentions, feelings, memories, beliefs, or attitudes? Let us consider a few examples. I announce a future action by the expression of an "intention." You confirm an agreement by uttering your "willingness" or "resolution." She assures him of their close mutual relationship by offering words of "love" and "longing." Equally, I like to hear about your "intentions," "willingness," and "love," if I want to know what to expect from you.

What is the function of these words? For which purpose do we use them at all? There is no simple answer. In many cases we indeed mean to refer our interlocutor to a mental state if we have the impression that it is relevant for the other one to know. The phrase "I love you" may (but must not) be meant as the expression of an inner state, of a feeling I wish to communicate and, possibly, share. Also, "you are jealous" may be a contention about a partner's state of mind and a challenge to react accordingly. That, however, is not always the case. "I want to know what to expect" contains three mental terms; at least, "want," "know," and "expect" are also terms for mental processes. But this sentence does not necessarily refer the hearer to three different mental states of the speaker, who merely presses for a decision. If, according to speech-act theory (Searle, 1969), referring someone to something presupposes the existence and the identifiability of the referent, many mental expressions will not be referential, unless we would assume a one-to-one correspondence between mental terms and mental states – an utterly improbable relationship. The rule seems to be that one and the same mental term or phrase may serve referential as well as other communicative purposes, depending on (linguistic) *context* and (social) *situation*. The utterance, for instance, "I am afraid," if spoken by a child asked to go into a dark basement room, may refer the parent to the child's state of apprehension or fear. At the same time, the sentence conveys the answer "No!" The utterance, however, "I am afraid not," if given as an answer to the question "Can you loan me a hundred dollars?" is a more or less polite "No" or "Sorry," although occasionally it may also betray a person's fear of separating from his or her money.

If the assumption is valid that we have to rely on the context and the situation to be sure that mental terms and phrases also carry mental reference, it is also safe to assume that the more personal a situation is the higher the probability that interlocutors mean to refer to their partner's, their own, or third persons' mental states because in such situations thoughts, feelings, preferences, aversions, memories, and dreams do become interesting. The prototype of a highly, or even exclusively, personal situation may be the case of two lovers mutually exploring one another's mind or soul – a way of becoming familiar and intimate with one another. There are, however, other situations in which this highly personal discourse is neither expected nor considered to be in good taste. Nevertheless, we occasionally meet persons who, by means of a very personal language, try to inquire into another person's moods, feelings, sentiments, and motives when these are not volunteered. It may be that some individuals are flattered if others seem to be interested in their mental life. But it will equally happen that such enticements into "self-disclosure" are resented as an indecent "invasion of privacy." Whichever obtains, those who like to intrude verbally into other persons' "inner spheres" as well as those who are embarrassed by such psychological curiosity, confirm the social reality of both the inside–outside metaphor of mind and a boundary between these two psychological "regions." As we know from research on privacy and on self-disclosure, communication across this boundary is socially regulated and so is interpersonal discourse. We should not hesitate to recognize such rules of discourse as basically moral rules.

The socially ambiguous tendency to gain "insight" into the inner life of another person who is not an intimate, is certainly a case for a differential psychology. But the recent spread of "psychotalk" in everyday social life will probably have to be explained by two related public trends: the spread of clinical "psychologese" (correlated with the apparently incessant growth of psychotherapies) and the popularity of television talk shows, for which personal or even intimate questions and "outings" have become significant features.

We have now come close to what I shall call psychologizing in the narrow sense of the word.

Psychologizing in everyday discourse

Psychologizing in interpersonal relations

In order to understand psychologizing, it may be helpful to start with a basic definition and an exemplification. The generally accepted meaning of psychologizing is the explanation or interpretation in psychological, especially psychodynamic, terms of matters that in themselves are not, or not exclusively, of a psychological nature. Similar to "psychologism" (the much criticized usage of psychological concepts in professional fields outside psychology),[6] the point in psychologizing is its usage in contexts and situations where reference to a speaker's or writer's mental states is unwarranted or, at least, surprising. If, for example, in a matter-of-fact discussion one of the participants, instead of responding to an opponent's statement, reacts to his mental makeup by referring to the presumably affective or motivational state "behind" his adversary's argument, we speak of psychologizing. In general, psychologizing is the rhetorical device of not reacting directly to an act or to the proposition of a speech act (Searle, 1969) but referring to the alleged psychological "background" of this act, that is, to the actor's conscious or unconscious mental states.

Psychologizing ad hominem may serve different purposes. It may be the overwhelming interest in a person's mental life rather than his or her achievements. Psychologizing may be a technique of avoiding a critical issue. It may also be a case of verbal aggression if the motives or intentions hinted at are morally questionable or socially undesirable. Inversely, it may be used in defense if we refer to our own (or our friends') basically positive mental dispositions in accounting for criticized behavior.

Since in interpersonal as well as in public situations the evaluative accounting for others' and one's own behavior seems to be one of the major functions of psychologizing, it is important to see how such accounting is achieved. Whenever we refer to a person's mental dispositions or traits, we not only address features that we consider to be general and permanent. We also conceive of traits as essential features of a person that tell us who the person "really" is. Stealing something easily makes a person a "thief." Once labeled a "thief," he will remain a "thief" even if he stops stealing. If an observed act would contradict the attributed trait, we may argue "the exception proves the rule." The disposition, although invisible, tends to become the more powerful psychological reality than a person's merely contingent behavior, which, furthermore, can be dissimulated.

The social power of psychologizing originates in this *indeterminacy* of the relation between mental dispositions and actual behavior, which is wide open for interpretation. Alleging, alluding, insinuating, deriding, and suspecting are social and rhetorical techniques of interpersonal aggression aiming at questionable motives or traits. Inversely, we may appeal to "positive" dispositions if we try to defend a controversial conduct. I may have done something stupid or inappropriate, but I must not take full responsibility since I can account for it by referring to pertinent mental states or traits. I may either excuse my misbehavior by apologetic reference to a temporary state of mind, such as inattention, preoccupation with a problem, grief, or stress. Or I try to justify what I did by relating my behavior to underlying positive personality dispositions such as open-mindedness, good faith, and kindheartedness, which sometimes "make me do" inconsiderate things. Here, appealing to mental traits is like pleading for mitigating circumstances, as if one's character was a fixed given entity that others as well as I myself have to take into account. The self-assertive proposition, "It's the way I am," which we occasionally present half apologetically, half defiantly, refers our interlocutor to such a last instance or *ultima ratio*.[7]

In all these cases, the function of mental references is the diversionary maneuver of directing an interlocutor's attention from the actual matter at stake to an allegedly relevant mental state or trait. The presupposition is that referring to mental dispositions is referring to the "true" character of a person.

Psychologizing in public discourse

From the fact that psychologizing presupposes the existence of an individual (other or self) to whose mental states we refer, it does not follow that psychologizing is restricted to interpersonal communication. It is equally practiced with respect to social groups and categories, which, in conclusion, I will demonstrate with examples from public discourse. If we are critical of a social movement or a political party, we may, in direct intentionality, argue against the program of the party or movement. We may, however – and this is frequently done in political debates – use the linguistic strategy of psychologizing. Yet, if we are up against a party, the government, or the Socialists, Jews, or feminists, we can only psychologize if we, first of all, personify and personalize.

We single out an individual who for us personifies, that is, represents the whole category or even embodies the spirit of a movement, and it is toward him or her that we can assume a given attitude, be it of admiration, of critique, or of contempt. Just as historically individuals like Robespierre became the personification of Jacobinism or, generalized, of revolutionary terror, or Eichmann became the personification of a racist ideology ending up in genocide, we may, if we are confronted with a social issue or movement, concentrate our attitude toward that movement and its ideology on a person whom *pars pro toto* we consider to embody its significant features.

Sometimes this figure is a socially accepted representative of the group, sometimes he or she is a personification ad hoc, for a given purpose: the urgently needed addressee of a critique or the target of a political or police measure, as when someone is alleged to be the leader of, or the moving force behind, a collective movement. Mainly in so-called conspiracies it is essential to identify someone to be held responsible for a development considered harmful for the established order (Graumann & Moscovici, 1987).

This tendency toward personification does not only serve the need of having someone or some group to blame. It is also endorsed and augmented by the modern media, mainly by television. The necessity to visualize political, economic, and other social trends and events in a concrete audio-visual manner inevitably leads to the presentation of persons who are either introduced as agents, victims, or eye witnesses or belong to the mixed category of experts. What they say and how they say it is often the only palpable concretization of an otherwise invisible occurrence. Once a person has been made a salient representative of a social category or current, one requirement of psychologization is met: We have to do with an individual. Only now we can personalize, that is, endow our personification of a cause or trend with personal, or psychological, qualities. The figure that stands for a supraindividual – for example, social state of affairs – is furnished with traits, habits, attitudes, and motives, and may thus become the target of psychologizing in political discourse. Personalization is not necessarily individualization. Mainly in the public discourse it very often is typification.

Although many of the terms that are exchanged in political and other controversies are psychological because we may characterize persons with them, they are also elements of social stereotypes. To refer to somebody as a socialist, a capitalist, a macho, or a feminist implies the attribution of a set of typical traits that need not be explicitly mentioned. The attributes at least of popular types are "well known," irrespective of their validity. Referring to persons as mere instances of a (stereo)type or social category results in deindividuation and discrimination (Graumann, 1995). We no longer mean a person's individual makeup but what he or she has in common with all other "instances." The rhetorical and literary technique of typing or typifying persons, which dates from antiquity, refers to mentality rather than individuality, if by mentality we understand a general mental set or disposition that is presumed to be characteristic of a whole social category.[8]

Psychological discourse: A tentative conclusion

Discourse referring to social stereotypes and to mentalities of groups and classes seems to be a very distant relative of the original discourse about the human *psyche*. But it is "psychological" in the original sense that, now as before, we tend to refer to a vital force, inseparable from and activating the living body, acting from the inside on the outside world. We still refer to something which, although invisible, tender, and vulnerable, due to its dispositional potency is ascribed a reality that for many is more trustworthy than manifest behavior. This, of course, is the esteem in which the mental is held in everyday discourse, not in scientific psychology.

What I tried to show is that in philosophy and, above all, in scientific psychology *psyche* has had many and various descendants, but that in its descent to the lowlands of everyday discourse it has preserved more of its origin than through the metamorphoses *psyche* underwent and is still undergoing in the science named psychology. I have argued that a distinctive feature is the basically evaluative and, in the special case of psychologizing, moralizing usage of mental terms.

Looking back, however sketchily, into the development of psychological discourse and pointing to some of the major functions of everyday mental language raise many questions that we have hardly begun to answer. It may be doubtful whether the ending century may legitimately be called the psychological one. Too many other events and problems of human concern may have been and still are more essential for our period. But we certainly had not only a rapid growth of the field and the importance of psychology. At the same time, we witnessed and participated in an impressive diffusion and circulation of psychological terms and phrases in everyday language. From these two secular effects at least two major fields of interdisciplinary research have opened: the study of the internal and external conditions of the rapid succession of psychology's key terms as well as the investigation of the various interactions and interferences between professional and everyday psychological discourse.

Notes

1 With respect to the non-German reader I may disregard the German peculiarity of eighteenth-century *Erfahrungsseelenkunde* or even experimental *Seelenlehre*, where *Seelenkunde* is the Germanization of "psychology" (unsuccessfully reanimated in Felix Krueger's [1933] *Seelenwissenschaft*). A comprehensive discussion of the original psychological discourse will have to include the usages of "mind" as a quasi-equivalent of German *Seele,* not however of English soul. What in German philosophy is the *Leib–Seele* problem is, in corresponding English texts, the mind–body problem. But to enter into this comparative philological analysis requires an expertise beyond this author's capacity.

2 In its purest form immanentist psychology was represented by Titchener (1929/1972), for whom referring to something extramental in an introspective report was committing the "stimulus-error."

3 The quasi-autonomous interiority of consciousness did not remain a theoretical construction of scientific psychology. When William James's (1890/1950) conception of the "stream of consciousness" became a narrative technique of modern fiction (as in Schnitzler's *Leutnant Gustl* [1901] or in Joyce's *Ulysses* [1922]) he literary access to the freely flowing and floating ideas, images, and words had to be the in :rior monologue.

4 "Resultative" is a linguistic term denoting verbs that are expressive of result. About *Erleben* as the result of *Leben,* cf. Gadamer, 1975; Graumann, 1965, 1984.

5 If I may once more include German usage, we have there the practically untranslatable conception of *Innerlichkeit* (literally "innerliness"), which is more of a culture than a state of mind, an amalgam from experiences of medieval mysticism, eighteenth-century romanticism, nineteenth-century sentimentalism, and modern forms of emotionalism. Its psychological basis, however, is the "soul," unadulterated by intellectual or external intrusion, the warmth and piousness of "inner man," as expressed in devotion and intimacy.

6 While psychologism in logic was finally overcome by Husserl (1900–1901), we still find it occasionally in epistemology (Piaget, 1950) and sociology (Homans, 1974). Also the psychoanalytic infiltration of many fields in the humanities must be regarded as a special variety of psychologism.

7 For the accountability of conduct in general, cf. Semin & Manstead, 1983.

8 This generalization or transfer of the psychological-mental to social groups and categories is not restricted to folk psychology. Although psychology has traditionally been defined as the scientific study of individual (experience and) behavior, we have had psychological descriptions and explanations of sociocultural systems and types in *Völkerpsychologie,* typologies, studies of "basic personality," of national character, and – outside psychology – mentality research.

References

Aristotle (1961) *On the Soul.* Oxford: Clarendon.

Diemer, A. (1971) Bewußtsein. In J. Ritter (ed.), *Historisches Wörterbuch der Philosophie* (Vol. 1, pp. 888–896). Basel: Schwabe.

Gadamer, H. G. (1975) *Wahrheit und Methode* (4th ed.). Tübingen: Mohr.

Graumann, C. F. (1965) Bewußtsein – Erleben – Verhalten. *Ruperto Carola, 37,* 90–95.

Graumann, C. F. (1966) Bewußtsein und Bewußtheit. In W. Metzger (ed.), *Handbuch der Psychologie* (Vol. I, ,1, pp. 79–127). Göttingen: Hogrefe.

Graumann, C. F. (1984) Bewußtsein und Verhalten. Gedanken zu Sprachspielen der Psychologie. In H. Lenk (ed.), *Handlungstheorien interdisziplinär III,* 2nd Halbband (pp. 547–573). Munich: Fink.

Graumann, C. F. (1988) Der Kognitivismus in der Sozialpsychologie – Die Kehrseite der "Wende." *Psychologische Rundschau, 39,* 83–90.

Graumann, C. F. (1991) Wiederannäherung an Psychologie. In K. Grawe, R. Hänni, N. Semmer, & F. Tschan (eds.), *Über die richtige Art, Psychologie zu betreiben (pp. 3–12).* Göttingen: Hogrefe.

Graumann, C. F. (1995) Discriminatory discourse. *Patterns of Prejudice, 29,* 69–83.

Graumann, C. F., & Moscovici, S. (eds.) (1987) *Changing Conceptions of Conspiracy.* New York: Springer-Verlag.

Homans, G. C. (1974) *Social Behavior: Its Elementary Forms* (rev. ed.). New York: Harcourt Brace Jovanovich.

Husserl, E. (1900–1901). *Logische Untersuchungen.* Halle: Niemeyer.

James, W. (1890/1950). *The Principles of Psychology.* 2 Vols. New York: Dover

Jourard, S. M. (1971) *Self-Disclosure: An Experimental Analysis of the Transparent Self.* New York: Wiley.

Krueger, F. (1933) Die Lage der Seelenwissenschaft in der deutschen Gegenwart. *Bericht über den 13. Kongreß der Deutschen Gesellschaft für Psychologie 1933* (pp. 9–38). Jena: Fischer.

Krug, W. T.. (1832) *Allgemeines Handwörterbuch der philosophischen Wissenschaften* (Vol. 3). Leipzig: Brockhaus.

Kruse, L. (1980) *Privatheit als Problem und Gegenstand der Psychologie.* Bern: Huber.

Lewin, K. (1935) *A Dynamic Theory of Personality*. New York: McGraw-Hill.

Moscovici, S. (1961) *La psychanalyse. Son image et son public*. Paris: Presses Universitaires de France.

Piaget, J. (1950) *L'épistémologie génétique*. Paris: Presses Universitaires de France.

Pongratz, L. J. (1967) *Problemgeschichte der Psychologie*. Bern: Francke.

Robert, P. (1976) *Dictionnaire alphabétique & analogique de la langue française*. Paris: S.N.L.

Robinson, D. N. (1976) *An Intellectual History of Psychology*. New York: Macmillan.

Schütz, A. (1953) Common-sense and scientific interpretation of human action. *Philosophy and Phenomenological Research, 14*, 1–37.

Searle, J. (1969) *Speech acts*. Cambridge: Cambridge University Press.

Semin, G. R., & Manstead, A. S. R. (1983) *The Accountability of Conduct*. London: Academic Press.

Titchener, E. B. (1929/1972) *Systematic Psychology: Prolegomena*. Ithaca, NY: Cornell University Press.

Tolman, E. C., & Brunswik, E. (1935) The Organism and the Causal Texture of the Environment. *Psychological Review, 42*, 43–77.

Wolff, Chr. (1719) *Vernünftige Gedanken von Gott, der Welt und der Seele des Menschen, auch aller Dinge überhaupt*. Halle: Rengerische Buchhandlung. Reprint of the 1751 edition: Hildesheim: Olms, 1983.

Part II

History as culture critique

6   Power and subjectivity: Critical history and psychology

Nikolas Rose

Psychology, history, subjectivity

The human being is not the eternal basis of human history and human culture but a historical and cultural artifact. This is the message of studies from a variety of disciplines, which have pointed in different ways to the historical and cultural specificity of our modern Western conception of the person. In such societies, the self is construed as a naturally unique and discrete entity, the boundaries of the body enclosing, as if by definition, an inner life of the psyche, in which are inscribed the experiences of an individual biography. But modern Western societies are unusual in construing the self as such a natural locus of beliefs and desires, with inherent capacities, as the self-evident origin of actions and decisions, as a stable phenomenon exhibiting consistency across different contexts and times.[1] They are also unusual in grounding and justifying their apparatuses for the regulation of conduct upon such a conception of the self: law, with its notions of responsibility and intent; morality, with its valorization of authenticity and its emotivism; politics, with its emphasis on individual rights, individual choices, and individual freedoms.[2] It is in these societies that psychology has been born as a scientific discipline, as a positive knowledge of the self, and a particular way of speaking the truth about selves and acting upon them.[3]

How should one construe the relation between "the history of the self" and the history of psychology. It is tempting to place the history of the self and the history of psychology within a common history of *mentalities*. Both would thus be seen as elements in a new way of thinking about persons, emerging, perhaps, out of a centuries-long process of the intensification of intimacy and the constitution of domains of privacy. Recent studies of the history of private life have certainly helped us understand the ways in which a variety of domains of privacy were gradually distinguished from a public sphere, yet at the same time were regulated by public codes and represented publicly according to precisely specified conventions.[4] But we cannot recapture a history of subjectivity from these historical traces. To purport to

103

read *through* these documents and images to discover the real inner life of the persons who composed them, or the persons who figure in them, would be to fall victim to a hermeneutic illusion: We would merely infuse those long dead others with our own preconceptions under the guise of "interpretation." The same applies to the texts that compose the archive of psychology, past and present: We can never retrace the path from these words on paper, disciplined and regulated by codes of knowledge, explanatory assumptions, and ethical values, to some "real" state of the human soul prior to its capture by thought.

I would like to suggest a different approach to the relations between the historicity of the self and the history of psychology. This would not embrace this relation within a global process of the transformation of culture or mentality. Nor would it aspire to the recapture of the lost referent. For the traces, texts, procedures, and practices that have surrounded, explained, and addressed the human person are more than merely *representations,* whether this be of subjective reality or of cultural beliefs. They are more positive and productive than this. They give form to a whole variety of beliefs, aspirations, dreams, hopes, and fears. They have been enmeshed within the diverse norms that have been elaborated by moralists and pedagogues for the evaluation of the capacities and conduct of the self. They have been bound up with the programs, projects, and techniques through which authorities have sought to shape and reform selves. They underpin the regimes of judgment and calculation through which persons understand and act upon themselves and their lives. And they have helped compose a body of critical reflections on the problems of governing persons that would simultaneously satisfy the demands of social order, harmony, tranquillity and well-being and accord with their true nature as human beings.

From this perspective, psychology cannot be understood as merely a theoretical discipline. Rather, the term should be seen as indexing an assortment of ways of thinking and acting, practices, techniques, forms of calculation, routines and procedures, and skilled personnel. Further, an analysis of psychology cannot begin by accepting the limits of a discipline as defining, as of right, a coherent and bounded domain. The discipline of psychology is certainly not unified at the level of its object, its concept, its theoretical harmony, its "paradigm"; the unity it has acquired since the end of the nineteenth century is pedagogic and institutional. More significantly, there are strategic relations and thematic links between psychological modes of thinking about and acting upon persons and those in other discourses – criminology, political philosophy, statistics, medicine, and psychiatry. In these complex relations, psychology has been a participant and beneficiary of new kinds of reflection upon the world and the persons that inhabit it. Psychology, that is to say, has been bound up with the production of new domains of objectivity. It has made certain old things thinkable in new ways, and made certain new things thinkable and practicable.

How should we do the history of psychology

How might one do a history of such a complex of thought and action?[5] I would like to propose some criteria for a "critical" history of psychology. Such a critical history of psychology can, crudely, be distinguished from two other kinds of history of psychology: "recurrent" histories and "critiques." The term recurrent history comes from Georges Canguilhem.[6] He uses it to describe – not necessarily pejoratively – the ways in which scientific disciplines tend to identify themselves partly through a certain conception of their past. This kind of history – which is familiar from textbooks and authoritative tomes usually called something like "The History of Psychology" and beginning with the Greeks – operates by distinguishing the "sanctioned" from the "lapsed." The sanctioned past is arranged in a more or less continual sequence, as that which led to the present and anticipated it, that virtuous tradition of which the present is the inheritor. It is a past of genius, precursors, influences, obstacles overcome, crucial experiments, discoveries, and the like. Opposed to this sanctioned history is a lapsed history. This is a history of false paths, errors and illusions, prejudice and mystification. Consigned to this history of error are all those books, theories, arguments, and explanations associated with the past of a system of thought but incongruous with its present. Recurrent histories take the present as both the culmination of the past and the standpoint from which its historicity can be displayed. Recurrent histories are more than "ideology"; they have a constitutive role to play in most scientific discourses. For they use the past to help demarcate that regime of truth that is contemporary for a discipline – and in doing so, they not only use history to police the present, but also to shape the future.[7]

Alternatively, history can be written as critique. The different versions of critique share a common ambition: to delegitimate the present of the discipline by exposing its past, and hence to write a different future. Historical critiques of psychology written from *within* the discipline have traced a history in which progress toward a conceptually or morally virtuous psychology has been blocked or distorted, by the incursion of obstacles – political, ideological, moral, methodological. These have prevented psychology from becoming what it should be. History here is used to resurrect a lost potential, to reactivate a forgotten destiny, to inscribe the possibility of an alternative future into the present by means of the past.[8] Historical critiques written from *outside* psychology have tended to reduce the scientificity of the discipline to a kind of shadow play, in which the vicissitudes of knowledge claims are merely the ghostly projection of outside forces. Some have seen psychology, like other scientific disciplines, as a space in which the social, professional, and cognitive interests of scientists are played out; psychology and psychologists merely exemplify the fact that all knowledge is constituted by human interests.[9] In a stronger version, a history is traced in which the development and destiny of science in capitalist societies is bound up with a range of attempts to conquer nature in order to control it. Psychology here is seen as embodying a series of attempts to master persons in order better to manipulate them. Psychological knowledge is a servant of power, and history unmasks this servitude disguised as objectivity, this manipulative ambition disguised as rationality. Psychology here is seen as an example of, and an instrument of, a general process of domination at the service of powerful economic interests.[10] Critique is also the mode in which cultural historians have tended to approach psychology, treating it as an index of more general social malaise: narcissism, the tyranny of intimacy, the "me" generation, the decline of spiritual and communal values, the search for certainty in an epoch when god is dead, the mark of a doomed quest for authenticity. Psychology here is merely a symptom of the mentality of an age that has seen the birth of the inward-looking, isolated, self-sufficient individual, for whom truth is neither collective nor sacred but personal.[11]

Critique poses significant questions concerning the relations between knowledge and society, between truth and power, between psychology and subjectivity. However, it does so in a rather reductive manner. Psychology, for critique, is socially significant merely in that it serves functions, manipulates persons, enforces adaptation, legitimates status, disguises lack, provides false comforts, and the like. Against the idea of critique, I would like to pose the notion of a *critical* history. Such an endeavor would be critical not in the sense of pronouncing guilty verdicts, but in the sense of opening a space for careful analytical judgment.[12] A critical history, that is to say, is a way of utilizing investigations of the past to enable one to think differently about the present, to interrogate that in our contemporary experience which we take for granted, through an examination of the conditions under which our current forms of truth have been made possible.

Such a critical history of the constitutive relations between the psychological, the social, and the subjective would certainly concern itself with power. But it would view psychology as more than a sign, symptom, exemplar, or effect of power relations. Power in the case of psychology would not be thought of in negative or instrumental terms, as that which manipulates, denies, serves other purposes. Rather, psychology would be viewed from the perspective of the "power effects" that it has made possible. For psychology, like the other "human" sciences, has played a fundamental role in the creation of the kind of present in which we in "the West" have come to live. To address the relations between subjectivity, psychology, and society from this perspective is to examine those fields in which the conduct of the self and its powers have been linked to ethics and morality, to politics and administration, and to truth and knowledge. For such societies have been constituted, in part, through an array of plans and procedures for the shaping, regulation, and administration of the self, that, over the last two centuries, has been inescapably bound to knowledges of the self. And psychology – indeed, all the "psy-" knowledges – have played a very significant role in the reorganization and expansion of these practices and techniques, which have linked authority to subjectivity over the past century, especially in the liberal democratic polities of Europe, the United States, and Australia.

The construction of the psychological

Up until quite recently, historical studies of psychology tended to operate in terms of a distinction between three separate spheres. There was the domain of "reality," which psychology sought to know. This reality was specified in various ways – as the psyche, consciousness, human mental life, behavior, or whatever – but in each case it existed independently from attempts to know it. There was the domain of knowledge, in this case "psychology." Again, what comprised "psychology" varied from account to account, but it generally consisted of psychologists or their precursors, theories, beliefs, books and articles, experiments, and the like. And there was the domain of "society," construed either as "culture" or "world views," or of processes such as "industrialization," which acted as a kind of backdrop to these attempts. Of course, such histories sometimes – though not always – asked questions about the relationships between "psychology" and "society": How had "social" phenomena such as religion, prejudice, or even institutional arrangements such as universities and professions, affected or influenced the development of "psychology"? And they sometimes – though not often – asked how psychological theories and practitioners had affected "society": How and where had they been "applied," to what phenomena, and with what success? But they seldom, if ever, asked questions concerning the relations between the object of psychological knowledge – the mental life of the human individual, subjectivity – and psychological knowledge itself.

Recently writers have successfully challenged this separation of spheres. Psychology, it has been shown, cannot be regarded as a given domain, separate from something called "society" – the processes by which its truths are produced are constitutively "social." And, further, the object of psychology cannot be regarded as something given, independent, that preexists knowledge and which is merely "discovered." Psychology constitutes its object in the process of knowing it. In this sense, as Kurt Danziger has elegantly shown, the "subject" of psychology is "socially constructed" both in the sense of the construction of the discipline and in the sense of the construction of its thought object – the human subject.[13]

Let us agree, then, that the psychological domain is a "constructed" domain. But, in scientific domains less racked by anxieties about their own status and respectability, philosophers and historians of science have long accepted that scientific truth is a matter of construction. What, then, if anything, distinguishes psychology from other fields of scientific knowledge?

Phenomenotechnics

To speak of the "construction" of new realms of scientific objectivity is to recognize that what is entailed is a break *away from the given*. Gaston Bachelard's writings on quantum physics, relativity, and non-Euclidian geometry can help us understand this process. For Bachelard agrees with Nietzsche that "everything crucial comes into being only 'in spite.' . . . Every new truth comes into being in spite of the evidence; every new experience is acquired in spite of immediate experience."

In *The New Scientific Spirit*, Bachelard argues that scientific reason is necessarily a break away from the empirical. Science, he claims, should be understood not as a phenomenology but as "phenomeno-technology": "It takes its instruction from construction." That is to say, science is not a mere reflection on or rationalization of experience. Science, and Bachelard is being both descriptive and normative here, entails the attempt to produce, in reality, that which has already been produced in thought. In scientific thought, "meditation on the object always takes the form of a project. . . . Scientific observation is always polemical; it either confirms or denies a prior thesis, a preexisting model, an observational protocol." And experimentation is essentially a process by which theories are materialized by technical means. For "once the step is taken from observation to experimentation, the polemical character of knowledge stands out even more sharply. Now phenomena must be selected, filtered, purified, shaped by instruments; indeed it may well be the instruments that produce the phenomena in the first place. And the instruments are nothing but theories materialized."[14]

Reality should thus not be understood as some kind of primitive given: "every fruitful scientific revolution has forced a profound revision in the categories of the real."[15] Indeed, Bachelard's notions of epistemological obstacles and of a "psychoanalysis" of scientific reason arise from his injunction that science needs to exercise a constant vigilance against the *seduction of the empirical,* the lure of the given that serves as an impediment to the scientific imagination.

From this perspective, to point to the constructed nature of scientific objectivity is not to embarrass or debunk the project of science, not to "ironize" it, "deconstruct" it, but to define it. Contrary to all forms of empiricism – whether philosophically grounded or based on a valorization of "lay" knowledge and "everyday experience" – for Bachelard scientific reality is *not* in accordance with "everyday thought": Its objectivity is achieved and not merely "experienced." Contemporary scientific reality – and this goes for a science like psychology as much as any other – is the outcome of the categories we use to think it, the techniques and procedures we use to evidence it, the statistical tools and modes of proof we use to justify it. But this does not amount to a delegitimation of its scientific pretensions. It is merely the basis from which we become able to pose questions concerning the means of construction of these new domains of objectivity and their consequences.

Regimes of truth

However, whatever its insights into the technical and material character of the scientific activity, the Bachelardian model is too benign to account for the construction of psychological objectivity. Truth is not only the outcome of construction but of contestation. There are battles over truth, in which evidence, results, arguments, laboratories, status, and much else are deployed as resources in the attempts to win allies and force something into the true.[16] Truth, that is to say, is always enthroned by acts of violence. It entails a social process of exclusion in which arguments, evidence, theories, and beliefs are thrust to the margins, not allowed to enter "the true."

These battles over truth are not abstract, for truth inheres in material forms. To be in the true, facts and arguments must be permitted to enter into complex apparatuses of truth – scholarly journals, conferences, and the like – which impose their own norms and standards on the rhetorics of truths. Truth entails an exercise in alliances and persuasion both within and without the bounds of any disciplinary regime, in which process an audience for truth can be identified and enrolled. And truth entails the existence of a form of life within which such truth might be feasible and operative.[17]

From such a perspective, we can explore the particular conditions under which psychological arguments have been allowed "in the true." The notion of "translation," developed in the work of Bruno Latour and Michel Callon, is helpful in understanding these processes: "By translation we understand all the negotiations, intrigues, calculations, acts of persuasion and violence, thanks to which an actor or force takes, or causes to be conferred on itself, authority to speak or act on behalf of another actor or force; 'Our interests are the same,' 'do what I want,' 'you cannot succeed without me.' "[18] It is through such processes of translation, Latour and Callon suggest, that very diverse entities and agents – laboratory researchers, academics, practitioners, and social authorities – come to be linked together. Actors in locales separated in time and space are enrolled in a network to the extent that they come to understand their situation according to a certain language and logic, to construe their goals and their fate as in some way inextricable.

To understand the "construction of the psychological" does indeed entail an investigation of the ways in which networks that operated under a certain "psychological" regime of truth were formed. One should, however, not overstate the agonistic impetus in such an event: Networks are not established on the basis of a "will to power" on the part of individual or collective actors, nor through a "domination" of networks by particular centers. What is involved, rather, is a process in which certain forms of thinking and acting come to appear to be solutions to the problems and decisions confronting actors in a variety of settings. Nonetheless Callon and Latour are right in rejecting accounts of such processes posed in terms of either the insipid notion of "diffusion of ideas" or the cynical notion of satisfaction of "social interests." Kurt Danziger's meticulous examination of the relation between the deployment of psychology in these practical domains and the psychology of the laboratory has illustrated clearly some of the political and rhetorical processes through which such alliances have been formed, and their consequences for what is to count as valid psychological knowledge. A political and rhetorical labor is involved in constructing a "translatability" between the laboratory, the textbook, the manual, the academic course, the professional association, the courtroom, the factory, the family, the battalion, and so on – the diverse loci for the elaboration, utilization, and justification of psychological statements.

We can distinguish a number of different tactics through which, in the case of psychology, translation has occurred, at one and the same time, simultaneously stabilizing psychological thought and creating a psychological territory. First of all, this has entailed persuasion, negotiation, and bargaining between different social and conceptual authorities, with all the calculations and trade-offs one might expect. Second, it has involved fashioning a mode of perception in which certain events and entities come to be visualized according to particular images or patterns. Third, it has been characterized by the circulation of a language in which concerns come to be articulated in certain terms, solidarities, and dependencies expressed according to certain rhetorics, objectives, and goals identified according to a certain vocabulary and grammar. Fourth, the enrolling of agents into a "psychologized" network entails establishing the linkage between the nature, character, and causes of problems facing various individuals and groups – producers and shopkeepers, doctors and patients – and forming a relation between the problems of one and those of another, such that the two seem intrinsically linked in their basis and their solution.

Mobile and thixotropic associations are thus established between a variety of agents, in which each seeks to enhance its powers by "translating" the resources provided by the association so that it may function to its own advantage.[19] Through adopting shared problem definitions and vocabularies of explanation, loose and flexible linkages can be put in place between those who are separated spatially and temporally, and between events in spheres that remain formally distinct and autonomous. These alliances between the researchers and the practitioners, the producers and the consumers of psychological knowledge, so essential to its construction, impart a particular character to the process of construction of what will count as psychological knowledge.

Disciplinization

The "disciplinization" of psychology from the mid-nineteenth century onward was inextricably linked to the possibility of the building of such alliances. It was through this process that a positive knowledge of "man" became possible; but the conditions of the birth of such a positive knowledge shaped its character in certain very significant respects.

First, perhaps, we can identify the ways in which certain norms and values of a technical nature came to define the topography of psychological truth. Most significant here were *statistics* and *the experiment*. The constitutive role of "tools" and "methods" in the establishment of a psychological regime of truth requires us to redraw Bachelard's diagram of the relation between thought and technique. In the construction of psychological truth, the technical means available for the materialization of theory have played a determining and not a subordinate role. The technical and instrumental forms that psychology has adopted for the demonstration and justification of theoretical propositions have come to delimit and shape the space of psychological thought itself. The disciplinary project of psychology, over the fifty years that followed the establishment of the first psychological laboratories, journals, and societies in the late nineteenth century, was accomplished, to a large extent, in a process that required psychology to jettison its previous modes of justification and adopt "truth techniques" already established in other domains of positive knowledge.

The two truth techniques that were preeminent here were "statistics" and "the experiment."[20] Both exemplify not merely the alliances formed by psychology with other scientific disciplines but also the reciprocal interplay between the theoretical and the technical. Statistics, of course, emerged originally as "science of state," the attempt to gather numerical information

on events and happenings in a realm in order to know and govern them –
the formation of a lasting relation between knowledge and government. Ian
Hacking has argued convincingly that, in the course of the nineteenth
century, the earlier assumption that statistical laws were merely the expression of underlying deterministic events gave way to the view that statistical
laws – the laws of large numbers formulated in the 1830s and 1840s by
Poisson and Quetelet – were laws in their own right that could be extended
to natural phenomena.[21] A conceptual rationale was constructed for the
claim that statistical regularity underlay the apparently disorderly variability
of phenomena.

In the first 30 years or so of psychology's disciplinary project, from the
1870s to the early years of this century, programs for the stabilization of
psychological truths went hand in hand with the construction of the technical devices necessary to demonstrate that truth. In the work of Francis
Galton, Karl Pearson, Charles Spearman, and others, and from the notion
of a "normal distribution" to the devices for calculating correlations, the
relation between the theoretical and the statistical was an internal one.
Statistics were instruments that both materialized the theory and produced
the phenomena that the theory was to explain. Yet within a remarkably
short time, statistical techniques that began as a condensation of the empirical and progressed to being viewed as a materialization of the theoretical
became detached from the specific conceptual rationales that underpinned
them. By the 1920s, statistical laws appeared to have an autonomous existence which was merely accessed by statistical devices. Statistical tests
appeared merely as a neutral means for the demonstration of truth deriving
from a universe of numerical phenomena, which, because untainted by
social and human affairs, can be utilized to adjudicate between different
accounts of such affairs. Not only psychology but also the other "social
sciences" would seek to utilize such devices to establish their truthfulness
and scientificity, to force themselves into the canon of truths, to convince
sometimes skeptical audiences of politicians, practitioners, and academics
of their veridicality, to arm those who professed them with defenses against
criticisms that they were merely dressing up prejudice and speculation in
the clothes of science. From this point forward, the means of justification
come to shape that which can be justified in certain fundamental ways:
Statistical norms and values become incorporated within the very texture of
conceptions of psychological reality.[22]

"The experiment" was also to be embraced by psychology as a means
of "disciplinizing" itself, of lashing together the various constituencies of
practitioners, journal editors, funding bodies, fellow academics, and university administrators into the alliances necessary to force itself into the apparatus of truth. The interminable debate over the relations between the
psychological "sciences" and the "natural sciences" is better understood if

it is removed from the realm of philosophy and relocated in relation to technique.[23] In seeking to establish their credibility with necessary but skeptical allies, British and American psychologists in the early decades of this century were to abandon their attempts to craft an investigative method that answered to a conception of the human subject of investigation as an active participant in the process of generation and validation of psychological facts. The "experimental method" in psychology was not merely sanctified through the attempt to simulate a model for the production and evaluation of evidence derived from (naive) images of laboratories in physics and chemistry. It also arose out of a series of practical measures for the generation and stabilization of data in calculable, repeatable, stable forms: the establishing of psychological laboratories as the ideal site for the production, intensification, and manipulation of psychological phenomena; the separation of the experimenter endowed with technical skills and the subject, whose role was merely to provide a source of data; the attempt to generate evidence in the form of inscriptions amenable to comparison and calculation and the like. As the form of the psychological experiment became institutionalized and policed by the emerging disciplinary apparatus, the social characteristics of the experimental situation were naturalized. The norms of the experimental program had, as it were, merged with the psychological subject itself; in the process the object of psychology was itself disciplined. It became "docile," it internalized the technical means to know it in the very form in which it could be thought.[24] Psychological truths here were no simple materialization of theory; indeed, the reverse is probably closer to the truth. The disciplinization of psychology as a positive science entailed the incorporation of the technical forms of positivity into the object of psychology – the psychological subject – itself.

Psychologization

The "disciplinization" of psychology was intrinsically bound to the "psychologization" of a range of diverse sites and practices, in which psychology comes to infuse and even to dominate other ways forming, organizing, disseminating, and implementing truths about persons. In this process, the regulatory and administrative requirements of an actual or potential constituency of social authorities and practitioners played a key role in establishing the kinds of problems that psychological truths claim to solve and the kinds of possibilities that psychological truths claim to open.

Psychologization does not imply that a single model of the person was imposed or adopted in a totalitarian manner, indeed psychology's celebrated "nonparadigmatic" character ensures a kind of perpetual contestation over the characteristics of personhood. This variability in psychological ways of "making up" persons is a key to the wide-ranging power of psychology, for it enables the discipline to tie together diverse sites, problems, and concerns. The social reality of psychology is not as a kind of disembodied yet coherent "paradigm," but as a complex and heterogeneous network of agents, sites, practices, and techniques for the production, dissemination, legitimation, and utilization of psychological truths.

The production of psychological "truth effects" is thus intrinsically tied to the process through which a range of domains, sites, problems, practices, and activities have "become psychological." They "become psychological" in that they are *problematized* – that is to say, rendered simultaneously troubling and intelligible – in terms that are infused by psychology. To educate a child, to reform a delinquent, to cure a hysteric, to raise a baby, to administer an army, to run a factory – it is not so much that these activities entail the utilization of psychological theories and techniques than that there is a constitutive relation between the character of what will count as an adequate psychological theory or argument, and the processes by which a kind of psychological visibility may be accorded to these domains. The conduct of persons becomes remarkable and intelligible when, as it were, displayed on a psychological screen, reality becomes ordered according to a psychological taxonomy and abilities, personalities, attitudes, and the like become central to the deliberations and calculations of social authorities and psychological theorists alike.

Institutional epistemology

Michel Foucault remarks somewhere that the "psy-" knowledges have a "low epistemological profile." The boundaries between that which "psy" organizes in the form of positive knowledge and a wider universe of images, explanations, meanings, and beliefs about persons are indeed more "perme-able" in the case of "psy" than, say, in the field of atomic physics or molecular biology. But we should not merely pose this question of perme-ability in the form familiar from the history of ideas, in which certain scientific discourses partake of metaphors or key notions that are widely socially distributed. Again, this relation can be posed at a more modest and technical level. In the case of "psy" knowledges, there is an interpenetration of practicability and epistemology. We have already examined some of these relations, but we can investigate the "practical" constitution of psy-chological epistemology in another way. Bachelard argues that scientific thought does not work on the world as it finds it, the production of truth is an active process of intervention into the world. But there is something characteristic about the conditions under which psychological truths have been produced. Psychological epistemology is, in many respects, an *institu-tional epistemology*.[25]

Michel Foucault utilized the notion of *surfaces of emergence* to investigate the apparatuses within which the troubles or problem spaces condensed what were later to be rationalized, codified, and theorized in terms such as disease, alienation, dementia, and neurosis.[26] Such apparatuses – such as the family, the work situation, the religious community – have certain characteristics. They are normative, and hence sensitive to deviation. They provide the focus for the activity of authorities – such as the medical profession – who will scrutinize and adjudicate events within them. And they are the locus for the application of certain grids of specification for dividing, classifying, grouping, and regrouping the phenomena that appear within them.

As far as psychology was concerned, it was within the prison, the courtroom, the factory, the schoolroom, and other similar institutional spaces that the objects were formed that psychology would seek to render intelligible. Psychology disciplinized itself through the codification of the vicissitudes of individual conduct as they have appeared within the apparatuses of regulation, administration, punishment, and cure. Within these apparatuses, psychology would align itself with institutional *systems of visibility*. It was the normativity of the apparatus itself – the norms and standards of the institution, their limits and thresholds of tolerance, their rules and their systems of judgment – that conferred visibility on certain features and illuminated the topography of the domains that psychology would seek to render intelligible. Its conceptions of intelligence, personality, attitudes, and the like would establish themselves as truthful only to the extent that they could be simultaneously practicable, translated back into the disciplinary requirements of the apparatus and its authorities. Hence, to return to Bachelard, the psychologist's meditation on his or her scientific object has not taken the form of a polemical intervention into reality to realize a scientific thesis. Rather, it has been characterized by a range of attempts to rationalize an already existing domain of experience and render it comprehensible and calculable.[27]

However, rendering a preexisting problem space comprehensible and calculable in psychological terms does not leave it in its original state. Psychological ways of seeing, thinking, calculating, and acting have a particular potency because of the *transformations* that they effect on such problem spaces. They confer a certain *simplification* on the range of activities that authorities engage in when they deal with the conduct of conduct. If one considers, say, the transformation of "social work" or the rise of "person-centred" approaches in general medical practice, one can see how psychology, in "rationalizing" the practice, simplifies diverse tasks by rendering them as all concerned with the personhood of the client or patient. Psychology not only offers these authorities a plethora of new devices and techniques – for the allocation of persons to tasks, for the arrangement of the minutiae of the technical aspects of an institution, for architecture, timetables and spatial organization, and for the organization of working groups, leadership, and hierarchy. It also accords these mundane and heterogenous activities a coherence and a rationale, locating them within a single field of explanation and deliberation: They are no longer ad hoc, but purport to be grounded in a positive knowledge of the person. And, in the process, the very notion of authority, and of the power invested in the one who exercises it, is transformed.

The power of psychology thus initially derived from its capacity to organize, simplify, and rationalize domains of human individuality and difference that emerged in the course of institutional projects of cure, reform, punishment, management, pedagogy, and the like. But, in simplifying them, it transforms them in certain fundamental ways. Let me turn to consider some of these transformations.

The *techne* of psychology

Suppose we consider psychology not as merely a body of thought but as a certain form of life, a mode of practicing or acting upon the world. We could then seek to identify what one might term the *techne* of psychology: its distinctive characteristics as skill, art, practice, and set of devices.[28] Here I would like to highlight three aspects of this *techne,* three dimensions of the relations between psychology, power, and subjectivity: first, a transformation in rationales and programs of *government;* second, a transformation in the legitimacy of *authority;* and, third, a transformation in *ethics.*

Government

By government I refer not to a particular set of political institutions, but to a certain mode of thinking about political power and seeking to exercise it: the territory traced out by the multitude of schemes, dreams, calculations, and strategies for "the conduct of conduct" that have proliferated over the past two centuries.[29] Over the course of the twentieth century, psychological norms, values, images, and techniques have increasingly come to shape the ways in which various social authorities think of persons, their vices and virtues, their health and illness, their normalities and pathologies. Objectives construed in psychological terms – normality, adjustment, fulfillment – have been incorporated into programs, dreams, and schemes for the regulation of human conduct. From the "macro" (the apparatuses of welfare, security, and labor regulation) to the "micro" (the individual workplace, family, school, army, courtroom, prison, or hospital), the administration of persons has taken a psychological coloration. Psychology has been embodied in the techniques and devices invented for the government of conduct and deployed not only by psychologists themselves but also by doctors, priests, philanthropists, architects, and teachers. Increasingly, the strategies, programs, techniques, and devices and reflections on the administration of conduct that Michel Foucault terms governmentality or simply government have become "psychologized." The exercise of modern forms of political power has become intrinsically linked to a knowledge of human subjectivity.

Authority

Psychology has been bound up with a transformation in the nature of social authority that is of fundamental importance for the kinds of society we live in "the West." First, of course, psychology has itself produced a range of *new social authorities* whose field of operation is the conduct of conduct, the management of subjectivity. These new authorities, such as clinical, educational, industrial psychologists, psychotherapists, and counselors, claim social powers and status on account of their possession of psychological truths and their mastery of psychological techniques. Second, and perhaps more significant, psychology has been bound up with the constitution of a range of *new objects and problems* over which social authority can legitimately be exercised, and this legitimacy is grounded in beliefs about knowledge, objectivity, and scientificity. Notable here are the emergence of *normality* as itself the product of management under the tutelage of experts and the emergence of *risk* as danger *in potentia* to be diagnosed by experts and managed prophylactically in the name of social security.[30]

Third, the infusion of psychology into already existing systems of authority – that of the commander in the army, the teacher in the school, the manager in the factory, the nurse in the psychiatric hospital, the magistrate in the courtroom, the prison officer in the jail – has transformed them. These forms of authority accumulate a kind of *ethical basis,* through their infusion with the terminology and techniques attributable (in however a dubious and disingenuous manner) to psychology. Authority, that is to say, becomes ethical to the extent that it is exercised in the light of a knowledge of those who are its subjects. And the nature of the exercise of authority is simultaneously transformed. It becomes not so much a matter of ordering, controlling, and commanding obedience and loyalty, but of improving the capacity of individuals to exercise authority over themselves – improving the capacity of schoolchildren, employees, prisoners, or soldiers to understand their own actions and to regulate their own conduct. The exercise of authority, here, becomes a therapeutic matter: The most powerful way of acting upon the actions of others is to change the ways in which they will govern themselves.[31]

Ethics

The history, sociology, and anthropology of subjectivity has been examined in many different ways. Some authors, notably Norbert Elias, have tried to relate changing political and social arrangements, changing codes of personal conduct, and changes in the actual internal psychological organization of subjects.[32] Others have sought to avoid any imputations of internal life to humans, treating linguistic and representational practices as simply repertoires of *accounts* that provide the resources through which subjects make sense, of the actions of themselves and others.[33] I would like to suggest an approach from a rather different perspective. This would examine the changing discourses, techniques, and values that have sought to act upon the minutiae of human conduct, human comportment, and human subjectivity – not just manners but also desires and values – in terms of *ethics*.

An examination of the *techne* of psychology along this ethical dimension would not address itself to "morality" in the Durkheimian sense of a realm of values and its associated mode of producing social integration and solidarity. Rather, it would investigate the ways in which psychology has become bound up with the practices and criteria for "the conduct of conduct."[34] For many centuries manuals concerning manners, books of advice and guidance, and pedagogic and reformatory practices have sought to educate, shape, and channel the emotional and instinctual economy of humans by inculcating a certain ethical awareness into them. But over the past fifty years, the languages, techniques, and personnel of psychology have infused and transformed the ways in which humans have been urged and incited to become ethical beings, beings who define and regulate themselves according to a moral code, establish precepts for conducting and judging their lives, and reject or accept certain moral goals for themselves.

From this perspective, psychology's relation to the self should not be construed in terms of an opposition between etiolated psychological conceptions of the person and real, concrete, creative personhood. This was the theme of so many critiques of the psychology of intelligence, personality, and adaptation in the 1960s and is still a theme in the new "humanist" psychologies. But it is more instructive to examine the ways in which psychology has participated in the construction of diverse repertoires for speaking about, evaluating and acting upon persons, which have their salience in different sites and in relation to different problems, and have a particular relationship to the types of self that are presupposed in contemporary practices for the administration of individuals.[35]

On the one hand, the person has been opened up, in diverse ways, to interventions conducted in the name of subjectivity: the calculable subject, equipped with relatively stable, definable, quantifiable, linear, normally distributed characteristics – the domains of intelligence, personality, aptitude, and the like; the motivated subject, equipped with an internal dynamic orientation to the world, with needs to be shaped and satisfied; the social subject, seeking solidarity, security, and a sense of worth; the cognitive subject in search of meaning, steered through the world by beliefs and attitudes; the psychodynamic subject, driven by unconscious forces and conflicts; and the creative subject, striving for autonomy through fulfillment and choice, according meaning to its existence through the exercise of its freedom. In liberal democratic societies, norms and conception of subjectivity are pluralistic. But the condition of possibility for each version of the contemporary subject is the birth of the person as a psychological self, the opening of a world of objectivity located in an internal "moral" order, between physiology and conduct, an interior space with its own laws and processes that is a possible domain for a positive knowledge and a rational technique.[36]

On the other hand, psychology has been incorporated into the "ethical" repertoire of individuals, into the languages that individuals use to speak of themselves and their own conduct, to judge and evaluate their existence, to give their lives meaning and to act upon themselves. We can analyze these practices of the self along three interrelated axes.[37]

The first axis is that of *moral codes*. Over the past fifty years, and with increasing vociferousness over the past decade, we have witnessed the rise of a language of the self framed in terms of freedom, autonomy, self-fulfillment, and choice. The modern subject is attached to a project of identity and to a secular project of "life-style" in which life and its contingencies become meaningful to the extent that they can be construed as the product of personal choice. It would be foolish to claim that psychology and its experts are the origin of such a moral territory, nor should we see psychological values as mere effects of a more profound cultural transformation. Rather, we need to trace out the ways in which psychological modes of explanation, claims to truth, and systems of authority have participated in the elaboration of moral codes that stress an ideal of responsible autonomy, in shaping these codes in a certain "therapeutic" direction, and in allying them with programs for regulating individuals consonant with the political rationalities of advanced liberal democracies.

This entails an investigation of the languages used in discourses on the conduct of the self, the ethical territory that they map out, the attributes of the person that they identify as of ethical significance, the ways of calibrating and evaluating them they propose, the pitfalls to be avoided and the goals to pursue. We can chart the ways in which psychological norms and values have come to infuse ways of thinking about the conduct of the self in sexual relations and child rearing, in marital relations and family life, in work and in leisure, in the quotidian affairs of house purchase and debt, in dealing with our grief and loss, and in conducting our relations with others.

Within this psychologized version of freedom, persons are enjoined to "work" on themselves – in their relations with their children, their colleagues, their lovers, themselves – in order to "improve their life-style," "maximize their quality of life," release their potential, become free. For the significance of the psychologization of moral codes lies not merely in the images of life they purvey, but also in the links forged between these images and a certain mode of practice on the self, in which psychological constraints on autonomy can be made conscious and amenable to rational transformation, guided by "experts of the soul." The self is not merely an image but a project.

The second axis of investigation concerns *ethical scenarios:* the diverse apparatuses and contexts in which the moral codes are administered and enjoined, and where therapeutic attention can be paid to those who are rendered uneasy by the distance between their experience of their lives and the images of freedom and selfhood to which they aspire. Psychological images and vocabularies have infused all those practices where individual conduct is a matter of concern for others, in the school and the courts, in the visit of the social worker, in the doctor's surgery, in the ward group of the psychiatric hospital, in the interview with the personnel officer. Psychology has also participated in a transformation in the ways in which individuals have come to make their lives meaningful to themselves, to question who they are and who they want to be, to interrogate their relations with others at home, at work, in sport, and in leisure. A range of new contexts has been born in the last four decades of the twentieth century, in which individuals themselves, having however hesitantly come to problematize their lives in psychological terms, seek guidance on their conduct and relations: the analyst's consulting room, the therapeutic group, the counseling session, the marriage guidance encounter, the radio phone-in. A whole variety of new courses and training experiences that seek to instrumentalize a new psychological conception of human relations has been invented. Collectivities from the marital couple to the business meeting have been reconstrued as groups traversed by unconscious forces of projection and identification, allowing not only a new dimension for the explanation of collective troubles but a new range of techniques – from T-groups to group therapy – for managing them therapeutically.[38] A multitude of scenarios has been invented for therapeutic engagement with the human subject, an array of locales for cure, reform, advice, and guidance has been transformed in a psychological direction. And despite the diversity of these scenarios, each nonetheless participates in a single *techne:* A rational technique can now be applied to the way in which each individual conducts his or her own conduct; the management of life has become, potentially, a kind of therapy.

The third aspect of an investigation of the ethical dimension of psychology's *techne* concerns *techniques of the self,* the "models proposed for setting up and developing relationships with the self, for self-reflection, self-knowledge, self-examination, for the deciphering of the self by oneself, for the transformation one seeks to accomplish with oneself as object."[39] Psychology has participated in the invention of a variety of procedures by means of which individuals, using the techniques elaborated by psychological experts, can act upon their bodies, their emotions, their beliefs and their forms of conduct in order to transform themselves, in order to achieve autonomous selfhood. There are techniques for examining and evaluating the self: modes of self-inspection, vocabularies for self-description, ways of rendering the self into thought. These entail *attending to different aspects of the self* – thoughts, feelings, posture, tone of voice – ways of marking differences and making them notable. They entail *ways of disclosing the self* – new ways of speaking not only in the consulting room, but to children, bosses, employees, friends, and lovers. They involve different modes of engaging with the self – an epistemological mode, for example, that searches for past determinants of present states, or an interpretive mode, in which the word or act is understood in terms of its significance in relation to other parties to the interaction. They involve education of the subject in the *languages for evaluating the self,* diagnosing its ills, calibrating its failings and its advances. And they involve *techniques for the curing of the self,* through the purgative effects of catharsis, the liberating effect of understanding, the restructuring effect of interpretation, the retraining of thoughts and emotions. Overarching all these differences, psychological techniques of the self seek to instill in the subject a constant and intense self-scrutiny, an evaluation of our personal experiences, emotions, and feelings in relation to psychological images of fulfillment and autonomy. Within this psychological ethics, the self is obliged to live its life tied to the project of its own identity.

Advanced liberal democracies often measure their civilization in terms of the prominence they give to the values of individuality, freedom, and choice. The norms of autonomy and self-realization that psychology elaborates are integrally bound to this ethicopolitical discourse of individuality, freedom, and choice. Yet what they demonstrate so clearly are the ways in which the elaboration of such norms is intrinsically tied to the inculcation of self-inspection, self-problematization, and self-monitoring. It seems to be the case that one cannot have freedom without experts of subjectivity, we cannot "know ourselves" without some other instance providing the means to that knowledge, we cannot "free ourselves" without the tools provided to us by expertise. Over 50 years ago Robert Musil remarked on a peculiarity of modern times: One can no longer have any experience without so many experts butting in who know so much more about it than oneself.[40]

Today, if the experts do not insist on rights of entry, we offer them invitations, call them on a telephone help-line, or seek them out in their lairs, for we seem to have become unable to understand ourselves without them. And even when they leave our presence, they remain within us and whisper their words of explanation, advice, and warning in our ears. We all incorporate a veritable case conference of experts ready to pronounce on our choices and activities, coaxing us to relate to ourselves as lay psychotherapists, to become amateur administrators of the human soul.

A critical history of psychology

My aim in this chapter has been to suggest, in a necessarily preliminary and abstract way, the way in which one might do a critical history of psychology. Critical history disturbs and fragments, it reveals the fragility of that which seems solid, the contingency of that which seemed necessary, the mundane and quotidian roots of that which claims lofty nobility. It enables us to think *against* the present, in the sense of exploring its horizons and its conditions of possibility. Its aim is not to predetermine judgment, but to make judgment possible.

From this perspective, psychology is significant less for what it is than for what it does. Psychology has altered the way in which it is possible to think about people, the laws and values that govern the actions and conduct of others, and indeed of ourselves. What is more, it has endowed some ways of thinking about people with extra credibility on account of their apparent grounding in positive knowledge. In making the human subject thinkable according to diverse logics and formulas, and in establishing the possibility of evaluating ways of thinking about people by scientific means, psychology also makes human beings amenable to having certain things done to them by others. It also makes it possible for them to do new things to themselves. It opens people up to a range of calculated interventions, whose ends are formulated in terms of the psychological dispositions and qualities of how human individuals conduct themselves, and whose means are inescapably adjusted in the light of psychological knowledge about the nature of humans.

The aim of a critical history of psychology would be to make visible the relations, profoundly ambiguous in their implications, between the ethics of subjectivity, the truths of psychology, and the exercise of power. In the modern period, such a critical history would open a space for thought within which we could examine the constitutive links between psychology – as a form of knowledge, a type of expertise, and a ground of ethics – and the dilemmas in the government of subjectivity that confront liberal democracies.

Notes

1 See, e.g., the discussion in P. Heelas and A. Lock, *Indigenous Psychologies: The Anthropology of the Self,* London, Academic Press, 1981.
2 See, e.g., A. MacIntyre, *After Virtue,* London, Duckworth, 1981.
3 See N. Rose, *The Psychological Complex: Psychology, Politics and Society in England, 1869–1939,* London, Routledge and Kegan Paul, 1985.
4 See, e.g., R. Chartier, ed., *A History of Private Life,* vol. 3: *Passions of the Renaissance,* Cambridge, MA, Harvard/Belknap.
5 I take the formulation in the heading of this section from Ian Hacking's essay, How should we do the history of statistics, *I & C,* 1981, *8,* 15–26.
6 G. Canguilhem, *Etudes d'histoire et de philosophie des sciences,* Paris, Vrin, 1968, and G. Canguilhem, *Ideologie et rationalite,* Paris, Vrin, 1977.
7 The most discussed example is, of course, Edwin Boring, *A History of Experimental Psychology,* London, Century, 1929.
8 For example, the ways in which the work of G. H. Mead has been reexamined by contemporary social psychologists, e.g., R. M. Farr, On the varieties of social psychology: An essay on the relationships between psychology and other social sciences, *Social Science Information,* 1978, *17,* 503–25.
9 As in the writings of the Edinburgh School, e.g., D. MacKenzie, *Statistics in Britain, 1865–1930: The Social Construction of Scientific Knowledge,* Edinburgh, Edinburgh University Press, 1981.
10 As, e.g., in Loren Baritz, *Servants of Power: A History of the Use of Social Science in American Industry,* Middletown, CT, Wesleyan University Press, or Stuart Ewen, *Captains of Consciousness,* New York, Basic Books, 1976.
11 R. Sennett, *The Fall of Public Man,* London, Faber, 1977; P. Rieff, *The Triumph of the Therapeutic,* London, Chatto and Windus, 1966; C. Lasch, *The Culture of Narcissism,* London, Abacus, 1980.
12 There are, of course, many existing contributions to such a project of critical history. Notable is the work of Kurt Danziger, discussed later, and various of the papers collected in A. R. Buss, ed., *Psychology in Social Context,* New York, Irvington, 1979.
13 K. Danziger, *Constructing the Subject,* Cambridge, Cambridge University Press, 1990. See also K. Gergen, The social constructionist movement in modern psychology, *American Psychologist,* 1985, *40,* 266–275.
14 G. Bachelard, *The New Scientific Spirit,* trans. Arthur Goldhammer, Boston, Beacon Press, [1934] 1984. The quotations are from pp. 12–13.
15 Ibid., p. 134.
16 In this paragraph, obviously, I am rather brutally condensing some of the arguments made by Michel Foucault in *The Archaeology of Knowledge,* London, Tavistock, 1972, Orders of Discourse, *Social Science Information,* 1972, *10,* 7–30, and The Politics of Discourse, *Ideology and Consciousness,* 1978, *3,* 7–26. For this first point, Bruno Latour's analyses of battles over scientific truth are instructive; see especially his *Science in Action,* London, Open University Press, 1988.
17 Kurt Danziger's recent studies are exemplary here; see especially *Constructing the Subject.*
18 M. Callon and B. Latour, Unscrewing the Big Leviathan: How actors macrostructure reality and how sociologists help them to do so, in K. Knorr Cetina and A Cicourel, eds., *Advances in Social Theory,* Boston, Routledge and Kegan Paul, 1981, p. 279.
19 "Thixotropic, adj. (of fluids and gels) having a reduced viscosity when stress is applied, as when stirred: thixotropic paints"; *Collins English Dictionary,* London, Collins, 1979.
20 For fuller discussion of these aspects, see, on the role of the "normal distribution," Rose, *The Psychological Complex,* esp. chap. 5; on the "experimental method," Danziger, *Constructing the Subject;* on "statistical tools," G. Gigerenzer, chapter 3, this volume.

21 I. Hacking, *The Taming of Chance*, Cambridge, Cambridge University Press, 1990.

22 Gerd Gigerenzer has traced out a number of these connections. See his contribution to this volume (chapter 3) and G. Gigerenzer, From tools to theories: A heuristic of discovery in cognitive psychology, *Psychological Review*, 1991, *98*, 254–267.

23 My argument concerning the psychological experiment is based upon the work of Danziger, in *Constructing the Subject*.

24 See N. Rose, *Governing the Soul: The Shaping of the Private Self*, London, Routledge, 1990, chap. 12. On "docile objects," see M. Lynch, Discipline and the material form of images: An analysis of scientific visibility, *Social Studies of Science*, 1985, *15*, 37–66.

25 Cf. C. Gordon, The soul of the citizen: Max Weber and Michel Foucault on rationality and government, in S. Whimster and S. Lash, eds., *Max Weber: Rationality and Modernity*, London, Allen and Unwin, pp. 293–316.

26 In *The Archaeology of Knowledge*, p. 41.

27 As I have argued in Calculable minds and manageable individuals, *History of the Human Sciences*, 1988, *1*, 179–200.

28 Engineering the human soul: Analyzing psychological expertise, to *Science in Context*, 1992, *5*, 2, 351–370.

29 M. Foucault, Governmentality, in G. Burchell, C. Gordon, and P. Miller, eds., *The Foucault Effect*, Hemel Hempstead, Harvester, 1991, pp. 87–104.

30 See R. Castel in Burchell et al., *The Foucault Effect*.

31 See my Engineering the human soul.

32 N. Elias, *The Civilizing Process*, Oxford, Blackwell, 1978.

33 R. Harre, *Personal Being*, Oxford, Blackwell, 1983.

34 See M. Foucault, Technologies of the self, in L. Martin et al., eds., *Technologies of the Self*, London, Tavistock, 1988, pp. 16–49.

35 See N. Rose, Governing the enterprising self, in P. Heelas and P. Morris, eds., *The Values of the Enterprise Culture: The Moral Debate*, London, Unwin Hyman, 1991, pp. 141–164.

36 See Rose, *Psychological Complex*.

37 The following remarks are derived from *Governing the Soul*, chap. 18. The schema I use is adapted rather loosely from the later writings of Michel Foucault.

38 See P. Miller and N. Rose, *In Search of Human Relations: A Social and Intellectual History of the Tavistock Clinic and the Tavistock Institute of Human Relations*, London, Routledge, forthcoming.

39 Foucault, Technologies of the self, p. 29.

40 R. Musil, *The Man without Qualities*, Vol. 1, London, Picador, [1930] 1979, pp. 174–175.

7   Cultural politics by other means: Gender and politics in some American psychologies of emotions

Catherine Lutz

The long historical view of psychology as an enterprise with fundamentally sociocultural roots, taken in this book, complements work in anthropology. Early in that discipline's history, the encounter with other peoples' differing assessments of the self and modes of evaluating their compatriots led to the historicizing and relativizing of aspects of Western commonsense psychology. The first wave of such critiques was led by Benedict (1934), whose eloquent work argued for the arbitrariness of contemporary standards of psychological normality. As one of many examples, she described the favorable way Native Americans of the Plains looked upon the widespread institution of the berdache, in which certain men took up women's dress and work at puberty. She goes on to note that societies that condemn such behavior often inaccurately identify the deviant's resulting guilt and stress with personality rather than with social process. And she took the critique still further in concluding *Patterns of Culture* by noting that:

Arrogant and unbridled egoists as family men, as officers of the law and in business, have been again and again portrayed by novelists and dramatists, and they are familiar in every community. . . . their courses of action are often more asocial than those of the inmates of penitentiaries. In terms of the suffering and frustration that they spread about them there is probably no comparison. There is very possibly at least as great a degree of mental warping. Yet they are entrusted with positions of great influence and importance and are as a rule fathers of families. . . . They are not described in our manuals of psychiatry because they are supported by every tenet of our civilization. They are sure of themselves in real life in a way that is possible only to those who are oriented to the points of the compass laid down in their own culture. (1934:277)

Those manuals, she would not be surprised to hear, have been amended in the ensuing half century to exclude homosexuality and to include "premen-

This paper benefited from the comments of Lila Abu-Lughod and Steven Feld. The research on which it is based was conducted with grants from the State University of New York Foundation and the National Institute of Mental Health. Kathryn Beach, Robin Brown, Paula Bienenfeld, and Walter Komorowski assisted in interviewing and transcription, and expert analytic work was provided by Angela Carroll and Marion Pratt.

125

strual dysphoric disorder," "late luteal phase dysphoric disorder," and "self-defeating personality."

Benedict can be seen as having articulated theoretical questions that were reopened on a broad scale only years later, beginning in the mid to late 1970s after Hildred and Clifford Geertz's call for an interpretive approach to the self was first widely made available in anthropology graduate training (H. Geertz 1959; C. Geertz 1973). Their suggestion was that self and emotion are culturally constructed, and that aspects of Western commonsense psychology might blind us to the extent to which people experience themselves and others in distinctive ways.

An academic generation later, a large number of anthropologists began to publish accounts of ethnographic encounters in which these questions were at the forefront (Daniel 1984; Heelas and Lock 1981; Keeler 1987; Myers 1986; Rosaldo 1980, 1984; White and Kirkpatrick 1985; Battaglia 1990; for reviews see Lutz and White 1986; Levy and Wellenkamp 1987; and Besnier 1990). In contrast to one caricature of ethnopsychology as a field concerned simply with disembodied cultural ideas about the self (Shweder 1991:90–91), much of that work has centered instead on observations and accounts of social life rendered in as much of its complexity as possible. It is in the minutiae of social interaction and larger-scale social institutions and movements that most such anthropologists have been interested. Ethnopsychologies are seen as relevant for their role in constituting both. Work in this field has often centered on social conflict – the politics and negotiation of everyday social life – and on the ambiguities and contradictions in concepts of self as deployed in interaction (e.g., Lutz and Abu-Lughod 1990).

Those interested in the cultural framing of self have come to it with a variety of theoretical commitments including psychodynamic approaches (e.g., Levy 1973; Obeyesekere 1985), feminism, and poststructuralism (e.g., Abu-Lughod 1990; Trawick 1990). Some remain convinced of the validity of one of the main, traditional projects of psychological anthropology – the pursuit of a universal science of human nature in cultural context. Many would alternatively agree with Abu-Lughod's caution: "Analyzing emotion discourses as discourses rather than as data for our own 'scientific' discourses on emotion provides us with a technique for avoiding the false attribution of the project of psychologizing to others as it reminds us relentlessly of the social nature of emotion expression" (1990:41).

Ethnographers who have been interested in the diversity of cultural understandings and experiences of subjectivity have often used one or another of two central methods. The first, reflexivity, involves examination of how the ethnographer's own (often "Western") frame for making sense of others' behavior continues to be used in interpreting events in the (often "non-

Western") field setting. All cultural descriptions (and not just those focused on ethnopsychology) are clearly mediated by preexisting notions of the anthropologist, who more often than not has acquired some variants of American ways of viewing such things as emotion or individuality. It is often by accident that these kinds of cultural premises become evident to ethnographers; they blunder their way through social interaction and learn – via their mistakes or the conflicts that ensue – how their neighbors in the field might be otherwise interpreting and valuing events. Description of these often painful moments of learning has been very productive of insight into differing cultural conceptions of self in society (see especially Briggs 1970 and Kondo 1990).

Another central methodological concern has been with language, or rather with speech as the vehicle by which cultural understandings of the self are formulated, negotiated, and have their effects on social life. It is primarily via these speech acts that observers learn about ethnopsychologies. Although anthropological investigations began with a focus on single indigenous terms and their sociocultural ramifications, they quickly moved to include concern with the full range of linguistic operators and speech contexts. This includes such issues as the syntactic coding of ethnopsychological ideas, social or ideological contradictions as played out in ambiguous or veiled speech, and audience reception of emotional messages (Ochs and Schieffelin 1989; Irvine 1990).

This move to examine ethnopsychology has focused on "non-Western" cultures, but other relatively more recent work has looked at some varieties of American psychological notions, lay and scientific. This includes examination of middle-class notions of love and marriage (Quinn 1987), anger (Lakoff and Kovecses 1987), academic and everyday views of emotion more generally (Lutz 1988), and a host of sociocultural practices that inscribe gendered selves (Abu-Lughod 1986; Kondo 1990). My own work has more recently involved looking at the articulation of cultural ideas about the self in racial relations in the United States, particularly via the high-circulation photographs in the *National Geographic* magazine. Experience with the mass media is a central means by which people are enculturated to particular ways of viewing themselves and of distinguishing themselves from others. Psychological discourse is evident both in the magazine's photographs and captions as well as in the transcripts of interviews conducted with a group of Americans who were asked to look at some of the photographs. The cross-ethnic characterizations that go on, particularly in the interviews, are vivid indexes of an American national identity being constructed by contrast to these others. They also show how psychological discourse is used to define the degree of humanness, difference, or deviance of others (Lutz 1995a; see also Lutz 1995b).

One can also look at psychological science as a cultural institution, a task that a number of psychologists and historians have taken up very productively, as this volume attests. To that end, I would like to briefly consider some of the cultural roots of a variety of studies of emotion (from psychology as well as other scientific fields), particularly as they relate to an American system of gender relations. For one of the most important aspects of that category is its association with the female. This means that any discourse on emotion is also, at least implicitly, a discourse on gender.

As both an analytic and an everyday concept in the West, emotion, like the female, has typically been viewed as something natural rather than cultural, irrational rather than rational, chaotic rather than ordered, subjective rather than universal, physical rather than mental or intellectual, unintended and uncontrollable, and hence often dangerous. This network of associations sets emotion in disadvantaged contrast to more valued personal processes, particularly to cognition or rational thought, and the female in deficient relation to her male other. Another and competing theme in Western cultural renditions of emotion, however, contrasts emotion with cold alienation. Emotion, in this view, is life to its absence's death, is interpersonal connection or relationship to an unemotional estrangement, is a glorified and free nature against a shackling civilization. This latter rendition of emotion echoes some of the fundamental ways the female has also been "redeemed," or alternatively and more positively, construed (Lutz 1988).

In this chapter, I explore how emotion has been given a gender in some sectors of American culture and, in the process, make two related arguments. First, I will demonstrate that local or everyday lay discourse on emotion explicitly and implicitly draws links among women, subordination, rebellion, and emotion by examining interview conversations conducted with a small group of American women and men. In particular, I will explore a "rhetoric of control" that frequently accompanies women's (and, to a lesser extent, men's) talk about emotion, and argue that talk about the control or management of emotion is also a narrative about the double-sided nature – both weak and dangerous – of dominated groups. Talk about emotional control in and by women, in other words, is talk about power and its exercise. Second, I will argue that this and further aspects of local discourse are echoed and reproduced in many areas of social and natural scientific discourse that deal with the "emotional female."

Western discourse on emotions constitutes them as paradoxical entities that are both a sign of weakness and a powerful force. On the one hand, emotion weakens the person who experiences it. It does this both by serving as a sign of a sort of character defect (e.g., "She couldn't rise above her emotions") and by being a sign of at least temporary intrapsychic disorganization (e.g., "She was in a fragile state" or "She fell apart"). The person who has "fallen apart," needless to say, is unable to function effectively or forcefully. On the other hand, emotions are literally physical forces that push us into vigorous action. "She was charged up," we say; "Waves of emotion shook his body." Women are constructed in a similar contradictory fashion as both strong and weak (e.g., Jordanova 1980), and I will present evidence from the interviews mentioned earlier that when American women and men talk about emotion, they draw on that similarity to comment on the nature of gender and power. This feature of the emotional and of the female produces frequent discussion in the interviews of the problem of controlling one's feelings. Such discussion is found in both men's and women's discourse, but much more frequently in the latter. I will show that this talk about control of emotions is evidence of a widely shared cultural view of the danger of both women and their emotionality. It is also talk that may mean different things to both the speaker and the audience when it is uttered by women and by men, and this factor will be used to help account for differences in the rate of use of this rhetoric of control. Although both women and men draw on a culturally available model of emotion as something in need of control, they can be seen as often making some different kinds of sense and claims from it.

The material I turn to first was collected in four extended interviews on emotion with fifteen American working- and middle-class women and men. All white, they ranged in age from the early twenties to the mid-seventies and included a bank teller, factory worker, college teacher, retiree, housing code inspector, and stockbroker. Most were parents. The interviews were usually conducted in people's homes, and the interviewers included myself and several graduate students. Each person was interviewed by the same individual for all four sessions, and although a small number of questions organized each session, every attempt was made to have the interviews approximate "natural conversation." Nevertheless, it is clearly important to keep in mind the context of the discourse to be analyzed, as it was produced by a group of people who agreed on letter and phone solicitation "to talk about emotion" for an audience of relative strangers who were also academics and mostly females.[1]

Many people mentioned at one or several points in the interviews that they believe women to be more emotional than men. One example of the variety of ways this was phrased is the account one woman gave to explain her observation that some people seem inherently to be "nervous types." She remembered about her childhood that

the female teachers had a tendency to really holler at the kids a lot, and when I was in class with the male teacher, it seemed like he just let things pass by and it didn't seem to get his goat as fast, and he didn't shout at the same time the female may have in the same instance. . . . I think emotional people get upset faster. I do. And like with men and women, things that are sort of important or bothering me don't bother my husband. . . . I think that's a difference of male and female.

One theme that frequently arises in the interviews is what can be called the "rhetoric of control" (Rosaldo 1977). When people are asked to talk about emotions, one of the most common sets of metaphors used is that in which someone or something controls, handles, copes, deals, disciplines, or manages either or both emotions and the situation seen as creating the emotion. For example:

I believe an individual can exercise a great deal of *control* over their emotions by maintaining a more positive outlook, by not dwelling on the negative, by trying to push aside an unpleasant feeling. I'm getting angry and like I said, he's over being angry, more or less dropped it and he expects me to also. Well we don't have the same temper, I just can't *handle* it that way.

And, in a more poetic turn, one person mused, "sadness . . . dipping, dipping into that . . . just the out-of-*controlness* of things." People typically talk about *controlling* emotions, *handling* emotional situations as well as emotional feelings, and *dealing* with people, situations, and emotions.

The notion of control operates very similarly here to the way it does in Western discourses on sexuality (Foucault 1978). Both emotionality and sexuality are domains whose understanding is dominated by a biomedical model; both are seen as universal, natural impulses; both are talked about as existing in "healthy" and "unhealthy" forms; and both have come under the control of a medical or quasi-medical profession (principally psychiatry and psychology). Foucault has argued that popular views of sexuality – as a drive that was repressed during the Victorian era and gradually liberated during the twentieth century – are misleading because they posit a single essence that is manipulated by social convention. Rather, Foucault postulated, multiple sexualities are constantly produced and changed. A popular discourse on emotional control runs functionally parallel to one on the control of sexuality; a rhetoric of control requires a psychophysical essence that is manipulated or wrestled with and directs attention away from the socially constructed nature of the idea of emotion. In addition, the metaphor of control implies something that would otherwise be out of control, something wild and unruly, a threat to order. To speak about controlling emotions is to replicate the view of emotions as natural, dangerous, irrational, and physical.

What is striking is that women talked about the control of emotion more than twice as often as did men as a proportion of the total speech each produced in the interviews.[2] To help account for this difference, we can ask what the rhetoric of control might accomplish for the speaker and what it might say to several audiences. At least three things can be seen to be done via the rhetoric of emotional control: It reproduces an important part of the cultural view of emotion (and then implicitly of women as the more emotional gender) as irrational, weak, and dangerous; it minimally elevates the social status of the person who claims the need or ability to self-control emotions; and it opposes the view of the feminine self as dangerous when it is reversed, that is, when the speaker denies the need for or possibility of control of emotion. Each of these suggestions can be examined only briefly.

First, this rhetoric can be seen as a reproduction, primarily on the part of women, of the view of themselves as more emotional, of emotion as danger-ous, and hence of themselves as in need of control. It does this first by setting up a boundary – that edge over which emotion that is *un*controlled can spill. A number of people have noted that threats to a dominant social order are sometimes articulated in a concern with diverse kinds of bound-aries (whether physical or social) and their integrity (e.g., Martin 1987; Scheper-Hughes and Lock 1987). One of the most critical boundaries that is constituted in Western psychological discourse is that between the inside and the outside of persons; individualism as ideology is fundamentally based on the magnification of that particular boundary. When emotion is defined as something inside the individual, it provides an important sym-bolic vehicle for voicing the problem of social order. A discourse concerned with the expression, control, or repression of emotions can be seen as a discourse on the crossing back and forth of that boundary between inside and outside, a discourse we can expect to see in more elaborate form in periods and places where social relations appear to be imminently over-turned.

This rhetoric of emotional control goes further than defining and then defending boundaries, however; it also suggests a set of roles – one strong and defensive and the other weak but invasive – that are hierarchized and linked with gender roles. Rosaldo (1984) notes of hierarchical societies that they seem to evince greater concern than do more egalitarian ones with how society controls the inner emotional self and, we can add, with how one part of a bifurcated and hierarchically layered self controls another. The body politic, in other words, is sometimes replicated in the social relations of the various homunculi that populate the human mind, a kind of "mental politic." When cognition outreasons and successfully manages emotion, male–female roles are replicated. When women speak of control, they play the roles of both super- and subordinate, of controller and controllee. They identify their emotions and themselves as undisciplined, and discipline both through a discourse on control of feeling. The construction of a feminine self, this material might suggest, includes a process by which women come to control themselves and so obviate the necessity for more coercive out-side control.

An example is provided by one woman in her late 30s, who talked about the hate she felt for her ex-husband. He began an affair while she was preg-nant and left her with the infant, an older child, and no paid employ-ment:

So I think you try hard not to bring it [the feeling] out 'cause you don't want that type of thing at home with the kids, you know. That's very bad, very unhealthy, that's no way to grow up. So I think now, maybe I've just learned to control it and time has changed the feeling of the hate.

The woman here defines herself as someone with a feeling of hate and portrays it as dangerous, primarily in terms of the threat it poses to her own children, a threat she phrases in biomedical terms (i.e., "unhealthy"). She replicates a view that Shields (1987) found prevalent in a survey of twentieth-century English-language child-rearing manuals; this is the danger that mothers' (and not fathers') emotions are thought to present to children. In addition, this woman's description of her feelings essentializes them as states; as such, they remain passive (see Cancian 1987 on the feminization of love) rather than active motivators, a point to which I will return.

In other cases, people do not talk about themselves, but rather remind others (usually women) of the need to control themselves. These instances also serve to replicate the view of women as dangerously emotional. Another woman spoke about a female friend who still grieved for a son who had died two years previously: "You've got to pick up and go on. You've got to try and get those feelings under control." The "you" in this statement is a complex and multivocal sign (Kirkpatrick 1987), and directs the admonition to control simultaneously to the grieving woman, the female interviewer, the speaker herself, no one in particular, and everyone in a potential audience.

A second pragmatic effect of the rhetoric of emotional control is a claim to have the ability to "rise above" one's emotions or to approve of those who do. Women, more than men, may speak of control because they are concerned about counteracting the cultural denigration of themselves through an association with emotion. "I think it's important to control emotions," they say, and implicitly remind a critical audience that they have the cooler stuff it takes to be considered mature and rational. It is important to note that, as academics, I and the graduate students who conducted the interviews may have been perceived as an audience in special need of such reminders. The speakers would have been doing this, however, by dissociating themselves from emotion rather than by questioning the dominant view both of themselves and of emotion.

Although women may have less access to a view of themselves as masterful individuals, a common aspect of the cultural scheme that is available paints them as masterfully effective with others on joint tasks, particularly interpersonal or emotional tasks (social science versions of this include Chodorow 1978; Parsons and Bales 1955). This subtly alters the meaning of the rhetoric of control; knowledge of what the feelings are that "need" control and of what control should be like is perceived and described as a social rather than an individual process. For example, one woman says: "If you're tied in with a family, . . . you have to use it for guidance how you control your emotions." This is the same woman whose central life problem during the interview period was coping with her husband's ex-wife and family, who lived across the street from her. The regular, friendly contact between husband and ex-wife has left her very unhappy but also unsure about what to do. The ambiguity over who ought to control or regulate what is evident in her description of an argument she had with her husband over the issue.

I was mad. I was mad. And I said, "I don't care whether you think I should [inaudible word] or stay in this at all, it's too, and cause I'm going to say it." And I said, "How dare you tell me how I'm supposed to feel," you know. Bob [her husband] would say, you know, "You got to live with it" or "You got to do this" or "How dare you tell me this, I don't have to put up with anything" or "I don't have to feel this way because you tell me I have to feel this way." You know, it was, in that case Robin is his ex-wife, "and you have to just kind of deal with it," you know, "all the problems that she presents in your own way." And it was almost sort of like saying "You're going to have to like it." Well I don't. I don't, you know. And for a year and a half he kept saying, you know, "You're going to have to like it, this is the way it's going to be, you're going to have to do this, you're going to have to have, be, act, this certain way," you know, act everything hunky-dory, and it wasn't, you know, and I was beginning to resent a whole lot of things. I, I, I resented him for telling me I had to feel that way when I, I wasn't real fond of the situation. I didn't like it. When I would tell him that I didn't like it, it was "It's your problem, you deal with it." I didn't like that, that made me really angry because I was saying. "Help me out here, I don't know how to deal with this."

This woman is frustrated with her husband for failing to join her in a collaborative project of "dealing with" her feelings of resentment. Here control is given away to or shared with others. This strategy of control is more complex and subtle than the simple self-imposition described in other parts of the transcripts so far; it aims to control both the emotions of the self and the attention and assistance of the other. Note also that she speaks of "resenting" or "not liking" (relatively mild terms of displeasure) the overall situation but is most incensed ("mad, mad, mad") about her husband's assumption that she ought not to feel a certain way. She asserts the right to "feel" unhappy about her predicament but is clearly defining that feeling in the standard contemporary sense of a strictly internal and passive event. Nowhere in the interview does she explicitly state or appear to imply that she wants, intends, or ought to act in concert with those feelings. What is being controlled or dealt with, therefore, has already been defined as a relatively innocuous feeling rather than an action tendency.

Finally, the rhetoric of emotional control can also be employed in both idiosyncratic and "reversed" ways that may at least minimally resist the dominant view of emotionality and, thus, of women. A few people, for example, spontaneously spoke about the problem of emotional control, thereby evoking the whole schema we have just been looking at. They went on, however, to define "control" in a way that entailed relatively minimal constraints on emotional communication. One woman, a 28-year-old bank teller, said: "Let me explain control. It's not that you sit there and you take it [some kind of abuse] and, you know, I think controlling them [emotions] is letting them out in the proper time, in the proper place." Perhaps more radically, some women (as well as one of the gay men with whom I spoke) denied having the ability to control some or many of their emotions.[3] One man in his 20s critically described a previous tendency he had to overintellectualize problems and explained that he worked against that tendency because

It wasn't that I wanted to cut off my emotions, I just didn't, they would get out of control, and I found that the more I tried to suppress them, the more powerful they would become. It was like this big dam that didn't let a little out at a time, it would just explode all of a sudden, and I'd be totally out of control.

The question remains, however, of the validity of seeing these latter seemingly resistant uses of the rhetoric of emotional control as "oppositional" forms (Williams 1977). This is certainly a dangerous rhetorical strategy, caught as they (we) are within a hegemonic discourse not of our own making. The opposition to self-control will most likely be absorbed into the existing logic and so come to equal not resistance but simple deficiency or lack (of control). A possibly oppositional intent may have collaborative outcomes to the extent that the denial of self-control is taken by most audiences as a deficit and a confirmation of ideas about women's irrationality.[4]

The culturally constructed emotionality of women is rife with contradiction. The emotional female, like the natural world that is the cultural source of both affect and women, is constructed as both pliant (because weak and a resource for use by civilized man) and ultimately tremendously powerful and uncontrollable (Strathern 1980).[5] Emotionality is the source of women's value, their expertise in lieu of rationality, and yet it is the origin of their unsuitability for broader social tasks and even a potential threat to their children.

There are vivid parallels between this and the cultural meanings surrounding colonialism that Taussig (1984) and Stoler (1985) have described. Looking at early twentieth-century colonists' views of the local Columbian labor force, Taussig describes their alternation between fear and awe of Indians who were perceived as dangerous and powerful figures, on the one hand, and disgust and denigration of their perceived weakness and lack of civilization, on the other. Taussig describes the process as one in which a "colonial mirror" "reflects back onto the colonists the barbarity of their own social relations" (1984:495). In a (certainly less systematic or universally brutal) way, a "patriarchal mirror" can be conceptualized as helping to produce the view of women as emotional – as dangerously "eruptive" and as in the process of weakly "breaking down." A "paradox of will" seems consistently to attend dominating relationships – whether those of gender, race, or class – whereas the subordinate other is ideologically painted as weak (so as to need protection or discipline) and yet periodically as threatening to break the ideological boundary in riot or hysteria. Emotion talk, as evident in these transcripts, shows the same contradictions of control, weakness, and strength. Given its definition as nature, at least in the West, emotion discourses may be one of the most likely and powerful devices for domination.

Demonstrations of the political, moral, and cultural bases of science have been made convincingly in a number of natural and social fields (e.g., Asad 1973; Fausto-Sterling 1985; Haan, Bellah, Rabinow, and Sullivan 1983; Sampson 1981). The sciences of emotion, too, have been a product of their social context, and particularly, a form of political discourse on gender relations. Operating in a field of power struggles for the definition of true womanhood, they constitute a "politics by other means," as Haraway (1986) describes American primatology and most centrally a politics of gender by other means. Much research over the years in biology, psychology, sociology, sociolinguistics, and other fields has been based implicitly on everyday cultural models linking women and emotionality, moving from the assumption of these cultural premises to their "proof." A number naturalize purported gender differences by attributing them to biological or necessary and universal features of the female role in physical and social reproduction. I will briefly examine several areas of research, including the analysis of premenstrual syndrome and mood, sex differences in the recognition of facial expressions of emotion and in aggression, and studies of the affective components and concomitants of motherhood. Feminist critiques of a number of these latter fields have been intensive, and I will draw on them while extending the analysis to the domain of emotion.

Studies of the relationship between mood and hormonal changes have focused on women's (rather than men's) cycles and in the process have discovered the hormonal disease of premenstrual syndrome. This syndrome is characterized by physical pain and mood disturbances and has been attributed by the biomedical research community to hormonal imbalances in the women who suffer from it. The syndrome has been used to explain a host of emotions ranging from irritability and mood swings to depression, anxiety, and panic attacks. A number of feminist critiques (Archer and Lloyd 1985; Fausto-Sterling 1985; Gottlieb 1987; Whatley 1986) have pointed out the weakness of the evidence for this syndrome. Assessment of women's mood is usually based on retrospective self-report via questionnaires (one popular version being titled the "Menstrual Distress Questionnaire"), which allow women to draw on cultural knowledge about the relation between gender, emotion, and hormones. Conversely, studies that disguise the purposes of the questionnaire show no significant premenstrual mood changes. The putative therapeutic effects of hormone injections are taken as primary evidence of the female hormonal basis for mood changes, but these studies have not been "double-blind." As Whatley argues, this biomedical discourse on emotions and gender may "cause us to ignore the fact that our premenstrual mood changes . . . may also correlate more closely to a monthly cycle of low bank balances than of hormonal fluctuations" (1986:183). Moreover, the emotional symptoms of premenstrual syndrome can be seen as a discourse on both the good and the deviant woman, on the necessity of her emotional suffering and the abnormality of, especially, her anger or irritability (Gottlieb 1987), both supposed syndrome symptoms. Normative academic and clinical work on premenstrual syndrome constitutes female emotionality as common and yet as a "symptom" in need of cure. This research draws on the entrenched cultural view of emotions as sited in females, as natural in essence (like but independent of the "naturalness" of females), and as irrational or pathological when they occur.

This line of research follows from and reinvigorates the cultural model in which women are more emotional than men because they are more tied to the biological processes that produce emotion. Wombs, menstruation, and hormones "predict" emotion. A more tacit part of the cultural logic connecting women and emotion may arise from the view of women as biologically inferior both because they menstruate and because they are smaller, weaker, and lack a penis. When viewed as a form of physical chaos or "breakdown," emotion is one other form of biological weakness suffered by women.[6]

A number of people in the interview study just described spontaneously articulated related ideas about the relationship between women, hormones, emotion, and pathology. In several cases, they referred to research as the authoritative source of their assertions, although my argument is that the relationship between everyday and scientific ideas about women and emotion is dialectical rather than an idea system imposed on a previously blank or very different lay model. According to one woman, a 48-year-old telephone operator, "women have been known to have different reactions to the same situation at different times of the month. And that's been a study. I've seen where some women can be downright dangerous, they could be potential killers."

Another field in which some attention has been paid to sex differences is the study of facial expression of emotion. In one sociobiological account, female emotionality is a product of evolution. Babchuk, Hames, and Thompson (1985) interpret studies showing that women are better able than men to read facial expressions of emotions in infants. In their view, this is the result of women's long history of being the primary caretakers of infants and the reproductive value of using these facial cues to detect infant distress. This argument is implausible on many grounds, not the least of which are the redundancy in infants of facial expression and other cues to discomfort, and the theoretically at least equal value of facial expression recognition skills for the prehistoric males, who, in many evolutionary accounts, were engaged primarily in defending the female and infant against threatening and dissembling outsiders. In addition, one of the central studies that demonstrates female superiority in decoding facial expressions of emotion (Hall 1978) has been reanalyzed and shown to account for less than 4% of the variance between individuals in facial expression recognition skills (Deaux 1984, cited in Shields 1987).

Despite its obvious problems, this account of the evolution of facial expression identification is a story with some power, as it draws on entrenched cultural narratives about women, motherhood, children, and love. Here, the first premise is that women are more attuned to emotion in themselves and others. Unlike the premenstrual syndrome studies, however, female emotionality is celebrated here, with emotions taking on their positive sense of the interpersonally engaged, the unalienated. Women's emotionality becomes a skill and an asset. It is significant that the sociobiological account focuses on the use of that asset to detect distress (rather than, for example, threat). Distress, of course, calls for nurturance, whereas other facial expressions (in either infants or adults) might call for flight or defense, but only the former behavior is normative for women and mothers.

Another line of research, on sex differences in aggression, also draws on cultural views of emotion and women. This happens, first, because aggression, at least in the Western cultural view, is seen as retrospectively predictive of anger (Montagu 1978). Anger is the one emotion that is exempted in everyday discourse from the expectation that women feel and express more emotion than men. Every emotion but anger is disapproved in men and, conversely, expected in women (Hochschild 1983). This gender stereotype has been shown to have been thoroughly learned by American children as early as the preschool period (Birnbaum, Nosanchuck, and Croll 1980, cited in Shields 1987). A recent, widely accepted, and often cited set of studies makes the parallel claim to have demonstrated a relationship between levels of the "male" hormone testosterone and aggression. Fausto-Sterling (1985) demonstrates the weakness of the evidence for this claim and questions why it has been taken up so enthusiastically by so many.

The echoes of the lay view in the scientific are followed by the echoes of the scientific view in the lay on this point as well. A professional woman in her 40s in the interview study commented on the association between aggression and gender: "So far the research shows that, yes, little boys are inherently more aggressive than little girls. . . . I think it bothers me that there's a sex link with aggression. There are a couple of sex-linked ones that bother me but . . . but I can't do anything about it."

Some studies that use the cultural logic of engendered emotion focus less on physiological differences to account for emotional ones than on universal functions and roles. In particular, they draw on the notion of women's reproductive role and the nurturing and emotions that supposedly naturally accompany it. From ethological bonding theory (Bowlby 1969) to some schools of feminism (e.g., Ruddick 1980), focus is placed on the natural or inevitable emotional concomitants of motherhood (rather than fatherhood), including particularly the positive emotions of love, caring, and attachment. Bowlby follows the prevailing cultural emphasis on women's emotional qualities when he focuses on the emotions of women and their children. He wants to explain the intensity of the bond between mother and infant, and roots that explanation in an instinctual need for attachment in the infant and fear of separation. Feelings of love for the child on the part of the mother are naturalized (cf. Scheper-Hughes 1985), and disastrous consequences are chronicled should the infant fail to receive sufficient quantities of mother love. These two facets of Bowlby's approach provide the carrot and stick of natural instinct and psychological harm to the child as reasons for continued emphasis on the need for emotionality in women.

Ruddick (1980), on the other hand, identifies "resilient good humor and cheerfulness," "attentive love," and "humility" as among the central features of maternal virtue that follow from (rather than precede) the task of parenting and, by frequent correlation, the task of being female. From these perspectives, women are more deeply embedded in relationships with others (with the mother–infant bond as the primary example and the primary cause). This interpersonal engagement with others is what produces emotion, which is here defined as responses to others with whom one is involved. From the perspective of feminism, male individualism is antithetical to the experience of emotion (see also Chodorow 1978).

The differences between these two perspectives on mothering and emotion are, of course, crucial. Bowlby-style bonding theory naturalizes the connection between women and affect through evolutionary theory and is continuous with earlier theorizing about the elevated moral status of women achieved through their divinely assigned and naturally embedded mothering skills. Feminist theory most often identifies the social division of labor rather than nature as the ultimate source of such emotional differences. Interestingly, however, both kinds of discourse on emotion elevate women (the first to a domestic pedestal, the second to self-esteem and/or the ability to resist patriarchy) by focusing on positive emotions such as love and by using "emotion" in its positive romantic sense of connection and disalienation.

Yet another version of the cultural view of women as emotional is found in the Parsonian normative construction of family roles, in which women are the "expressive expert" and men the "instrumental expert" (Parsons and Bales 1955). These competencies are seen as an outcome of the domestic and market spheres in which the genders differentially participate. Compare this notion, however, with the contradictory view of women's emotional impact on the family noted in the interview example and the child-rearing manual themes described earlier. The point may be that women are expected to be experts in noticing and attending to the emotional needs of others (also per Bowlby), not their own, which are rather objects of control or suppression because they, unlike the emotions of other family members, are defined as dangerous.

Hochschild's (1983) important feminist revision of Parsons and Bales's scheme paints emotion less as a skill than as a form of labor (see also Maher 1984). Women are socially assigned a much heavier burden of emotional labor than are men. Hochschild's ideas contribute to a breaking down of the dichotomy of emotion and thought; they can also extend the notion of women's double day of domestic and wage labor as women are required to contribute both emotional and cognitive labor in both paid and unpaid spheres. In this and other feminist analyses, gender and emotion are related through the relations of production. For Hochschild, emotion is a personal resource that women must self-exploit more than men. It nonetheless remains a psychophysical fact, socially manipulated, rather than a discursive practice that constructs women as more emotional than men.

In sum, social science disciplines women and their psyches. It constructs emotion as an individual and intrapsychic phenomenon and evidences the same concern as lay discourse with the emotionality of women – its frequency, its intensity, its virtues as an emblem of female gender identity, but most of all, its danger and implicitly the need for its control.

In all societies, body disorders – which emotion is considered to be in this society – become crucial indicators of problems with social control and, as such, are more likely to occur or emerge in a discourse concerning social subordinates. Foucault has made the claim that power creates sexuality and its disciplining; similarly, it can be said to create emotionality. The cultural construction of women's emotion can thus be viewed not as the repression or suppression of emotion in men (as many laypeople, therapists, and other commentators argue) but as the creation of emotion in women. Because emotion is constructed as relatively chaotic, irrational, and antisocial, its existence vindicates authority and legitimates the need for control. By association with the female, it vindicates the hierarchical distinction between men and women. And the cultural logic connecting women and emotion corresponds to and shores up the walls between the spheres of private, intimate (and emotional) relations in the (ideologically) female domain of the family and public, formal (and rational) relations in the primarily male domain of the marketplace.

Rubin has remarked of sexuality that "there are historical periods in which [it] is more sharply contested and more overtly politicized" (1984:267). Emotionality has the same historical dynamism, with shifting gender relations often appearing to be at the root of both academic and lay struggles over how emotion is to be defined and evaluated.[7] In other words, the contemporary dominant discourse on emotions – and particularly the view that they are irrational and to be controlled – helps construct but does not wholly determine women's discourse; there is an attempt to recast the association of women with emotion in an alternative feminist voice.

Feminist treatments of the question of emotion (e.g., Hochschild 1983; Jagger 1987; for a review, see Lutz, in press) have tended to portray emotions not as chaos but as a discourse on problems. Some have contested both the irrationality and the passivity of feelings by arguing that emotions may involve the identification of problems in women's lives and are there-fore political. Talk about anger, for example, can be interpreted as an attempt to identify the existence of inappropriate restraint or injustice. Sadness is a discourse on the problem of loss, fear on that of danger. By extension, talk about the control of emotions would be, in this feminist discourse, talk about the suppression of public acknowledgment of prob-lems. The emotional female might then be seen not simply as a mythic construction on the axis of some arbitrary cultural dualism but as an out-come of the fact that women occupy an objectively more problematic posi-tion than does the white, upper-class, northern European, older man who is the cultural exemplar par excellence of cool, emotionless rationality. According to a feminist analysis, whether or not women express their problems (i.e., are emotional) more than men, those women's audiences may hear a message that is an amalgam of the orthodox view and its feminist contestation: "We (those) women are dangerously close to erupting into emotionality/pointing to a problem/moving toward a social critique."

Notes

1 The method used in looking at the transcripts draws on developments in the "cognitive" study of cultural meaning. These focus on the analysis of extended and relatively natural conversations for the cultural knowledge evident in them, if not always explicitly stated (Holland and Quinn 1987). Looking at such things as syntax, metaphor, or the propositional networks underlying the sensibility of sentence order, an analyst can draw inferences about the kinds of models individuals are using or, perhaps more aptly, can draw inferences about the kinds of inferences listeners can make about what the speaker has left unsaid but likely wants understood.

2 There are 180 instances in those parts of the women's transcripts analyzed, and 85 instances in the men's, with each set of transcripts being of approximately equal length.

3 Martin (1990) has examined some American discourses on reproduction and women's bodies and has rigorously uncovered the contradiction between a view of uterine contractions

during childbirth as involuntary and a view of the woman as in fact in control of the labor process. The women she interviewed about their birth experiences spoke very similarly to the women described in this chapter about their sense of control over the physical process and over their cries of pain and pleasure during labor and birth. She notes a class difference, however, with middle-class women speaking with more approval of control than working-class women. We might then expect men also to express more concern with and approval of control of emotion, which is not the case here. This is certainly a problem worthy of more study. Needed is a delineation of what kinds of control of which domains appear to emerge from what kinds of experience within hierarchical systems.

4 Acknowledgment of one's emotionality may mean very different things to female and male audiences. Women may announce to each other shared identity and solidarity, while asserting difference, submission, or defiance when making similar statements to men.

5 Abu-Lughod's (1986) study of the Awlad 'Ali represents the most detailed and eloquent example of how, in another cultural system, the particular *kinds* of emotions allocated to and voiced by women articulate with other aspects of their ideological and social structural positions.

6 This group of studies obviously follows in the tradition of centuries of expert explanations of hysteria. Although there have been many versions of the explanation (such as one nineteenth-century account that diagnosed its origins as an empty womb and a childhood where the restraint of emotion was not taught [Smith-Rosenberg 1972]), they have been organized around the connection between female physiology and mood.

7 The resurgence of interest in emotion from the late 1970s forward, across the social sciences, may in part be the result of the feminist movement's revalorization of all things traditionally associated with women (Margaret Trawick, personal communication). Changing gender relations may also be at the root of the reinvigoration of a long-standing Western discourse on the value of emotional expression; the current debate pits expressionists, for whom healthy emotions are vented ones, against those who would dismiss the latter as "self-indulgent" or "immature." This debate no doubt draws in a complex way, in each concrete context in which it occurs, on the gender ideologies and conflicts of the individual participants.

References

Abu-Lughod, Lila. 1986. *Veiled Sentiments: Honor and Poetry in a Bedouin Society*. Berkeley: University of California Press.

Abu-Lughod, Lila. 1990. Shifting Politics in Bedouin Love Poetry. In Lutz and Abu-Lughod 1990.

Archer, John, and Barbara Lloyd. 1985. *Sex and Gender*. Cambridge: Cambridge University Press.

Asad, Talal, ed. 1973. *Anthropology and the Colonial Encounter*. New York: Humanities Press.

Babchuk, Wayne, Raymond Hames, and Ross Thompson. 1985. Sex Differences in the Recognition of Infant Facial Expressions of Emotion: The Primary Caretaker Hypothesis. *Ethology and Sociobiology* 6:89–101.

Battaglia, Debbora. 1990. *On the Bones of the Serpent: Person, Memory and Mortality in Sabarl Island Society*. Chicago: University of Chicago Press.

Benedict, Ruth. 1934. *Patterns of Culture*. Boston: Houghton Mifflin.

Besnier, Niko. 1990. Language and Affect. *Annual Review of Anthropology* 19:419–451.

Birnbaum, D. A., T. A. Nosanchuck, and W. L. Croll. 1980. Children's Stereotypes about Sex Differences in Emotionality. *Sex Roles* 6:435–443.

Bowlby, John. 1969. *Attachment and Loss*. Vol. 1. London: Hogarth Press.

Briggs, Jean. 1970. *Never in Anger*. Cambridge, MA: Harvard University Press.

Cancian, Francesca. 1987. *Love in America: Gender and Self-Development*. Cambridge: Cambridge University Press.

Chodorow, Nancy. 1978. *The Reproduction of Mothering*. Berkeley: University of California Press.

Daniel, E. Valentine. 1984. *Fluid Signs: Being a Person the Tamil Way*. Berkeley: University of California Press.

Deaux, K. 1984. From Individual Differences to Social Categories: Analysis of a Decade's Research on Gender. *American Psychologist* 39:105–116.

Fausto-Sterling, Anne. 1985. *Myths of Gender: Biological Theories of Women and Men*. New York: Basic Books.

Foucault, Michel. 1978. *The History of Sexuality*. Vol. 1. New York: Pantheon.

Geertz, Clifford. 1973. Person, Time and Conduct in Bali. In *The Interpretation of Cultures*. New York: Basic Books, pp. 360–411.

Geertz, Hildred. 1959. The Vocabulary of Emotion: A Study of Javanese Socialization Processes. *Psychiatry* 22:225–237.

Gottlieb, Alma. 1987. American PMS: A Mute Voice. Paper presented at the annual meetings of the American Anthropological Association, Chicago.

Haan, Norma, Robert Bellah, Paul Rabinow, and William Sullivan. 1983. *Social Science as Moral Inquiry*. New York: Columbia University Press.

Hall, J. 1978. Gender Effects in Decoding Nonverbal Cues. *Psychological Bulletin* 85:845–875.

Haraway, Donna. 1986. Primatology Is Politics by Other Means. In Ruth Bleier, ed., *Feminist Approaches to Science*. New York: Pergamon Press, pp. 77–118.

Heelas, Paul, and Andrew Lock. 1981. *Indigenous Psychologies*. London: Academic Press.

Hochschild, Arlie. 1983. *The Managed Heart: Commercialization of Human Feeling*. Berkeley: University of California Press.

Holland, Dorothy, and Naomi Quinn, eds. 1987. *Cultural Models in Language and Thought*. Cambridge: Cambridge University Press.

Irvine, Judith. 1990. Registering Affect: Heteroglossia in the Linguistic Expression of Affect. In Lutz and Abu-Lughod 1990.

Jagger, Alison. 1987. Love and Knowledge: Emotion as an Epistemic Resource for Feminists. Manuscript in possession of author. Department of Philosophy, University of Cincinnati.

Jordanova, L. J. 1980. Natural Facts: A Historical Perspective on Science and Sexuality. In Carol MacCormack and Marilyn Strathern, eds., *Nature, Culture and Gender*. Cambridge: Cambridge University Press, pp. 42–69.

Keeler, Ward. 1987. *Javanese Shadow Plays, Javanese Selves*. Princeton: Princeton University Press.

Kirkpatrick, John. 1987. Representing the Self as "You" in American Discourse. Paper presented at the annual meetings of the American Anthropological Association, Chicago.

Kondo, Dorinne. 1990. *Crafting Selves*. Chicago: University of Chicago Press.

Lakoff, George, and Zoltan Kovecses. 1987. The Cognitive Model of Anger Inherent in American English. In Dorothy Holland and Naomi Quinn, eds., *Cultural Models in Language and Thought*. Cambridge: Cambridge University Press, pp. 195–221.

Levy, Robert. 1973. *Tahitians: Mind and Experience in the Society Islands*. Chicago: University of Chicago Press.

Levy, Robert, and Jane Wellenkamp. 1987. Methodology in the Anthropological Study of Emotion. In R. Plutchik and H. Kellerman, eds., *The Measurement of Emotions*. New York: Academic Press.

Lutz, Catherine. 1988. *Unnatural Emotions: Everyday Sentiments on a Micronesian Atoll and Their Challenge to Western Theory*. Chicago: University of Chicago Press.

Lutz, Catherine. 1995a. Intentionality, Race and Evolutionism in Photographs of "Non-Westerners." In L. Rosen, ed., *Other Intentions: Cultural Contexts and the Attribution of Inner States*. Santa Fe, NM: School of American Research Press.

Lutz, Catherine. 1995b. Warring Emotions: The Cultural Contradictions of Emotion in Modern Warfare. In C. Ellis and M. Flaherty, eds., *Social Perspectives on Emotion*. Vol. 3. Greenwich, CT: JAI Press, pp. 15–31.

Lutz, Catherine. In press. Feminist Intellectual Labor and Working Definitions of Emotion. In Bradd Shore, ed., *The Emotions: Culture, Psychology, Biology*. Cambridge: Cambridge University Press.

Lutz, Catherine, and Lila Abu-Lughod, eds. 1990. *Language and the Politics of Emotion*. Cambridge: Cambridge University Press.

Lutz, Catherine, and Geoffrey White. 1986. The Anthropology of Emotions. *Annual Review of Anthropology* 15:405–436.

Maher, Vanessa. 1984. Possession and Dispossession: Maternity and Mortality in Morocco. In H. Medick and D. Sabean, eds., *Interest and Emotion*. Cambridge: Cambridge University Press, pp. 103–128.

Martin, Emily. 1990. The Ideology of Reproduction: The Reproduction of Ideology. In F. Ginsburg and A. L. Tsing, eds. *Uncertain Terms: Negotiating Gender in American Culture*. Boston: Beacon Press.

Montagu, Ashley, ed. 1978. *The Learning of Non-Aggression*. Oxford: Oxford University Press.

Myers, Fred. 1986. *Pintupi Country, Pintupi Self*. Washington, DC: Smithsonian Institution Press.

Obeyesekere, Gananath. 1985. Depression, Buddhism and the Work of Culture in Sri Lanka. In A. Kleinman and B. Good, eds., *Culture and Depression*. Berkeley: University of California Press.

Ochs, Elinor, and Bambi Schieffelin. 1989. Language Has a Heart. *Text* 9:7–25.

Parsons, Talcott, and Robert Bales. 1955. *Family, Socialization, and Interaction Process*. Glencoe, IL: Free Press.

Quinn, Naomi. 1987. Convergent Evidence for a Cultural Model of American Marriage. In D. Holland and N. Quinn, eds., *Cultural Models in Language and Thought*. Cambridge: Cambridge University Press, pp. 173–192.

Rosaldo, Michelle. 1980. *Knowledge and Passion*. Cambridge: Cambridge University Press.

Rosaldo, Michelle. 1984. Toward an Anthropology of Self and Feeling. In Richard Shweder and Robert LeVine, eds., *Culture Theory: Essays on Mind, Self and Emotion*. Cambridge: Cambridge University Press, pp. 137–157.

Rosaldo, Renato. 1977. The Rhetoric of Control: Ilongots Viewed as Natural Bandits and Wild Indians. In B. Babcock, ed., *The Reversible World: Symbolic Inversion in Art and Society*, Ithaca, NY: Cornell University Press, pp. 240–257.

Rubin, Gayle. 1984. Thinking Sex: Notes for a Radical Theory of the Politics of Sexuality. In Carol S. Vance, ed., *Pleasure and Danger: Exploring Female Sexuality*. Boston: Routledge & Kegan Paul.

Ruddick, Sara. 1980. Maternal Thinking. *Feminist Studies* 6:70–96.

Sampson, E. E. 1981. Cognitive Psychology as Ideology. *American Psychologist* 36:730–743.

Scheper-Hughes, Nancy. 1985. Culture, Scarcity and Maternal Thinking. *Ethos* 13:291–317.

Scheper-Hughes, Nancy, and Margaret Lock. 1987. The Mindful Body: A Prolegomenon to Future Work in Medical Anthropology. *Medical Anthropology Quarterly* 1:6–41.

Shields, Stephanie A. 1987. Women, Men and the Dilemma of Emotion. In P. Shaver and C. Hendrick, eds., *Sex and Gender*. Newbury Park, CA: Sage, pp. 229–250.

Shweder, Richard A. 1991. *Thinking through Cultures: Expeditions in Cultural Psychology*. Cambridge, MA: Harvard University Press.

Smith-Rosenberg, Carroll. 1972. The Hysterical Woman: Roles and Role Conflict in 19th-Century America. *Social Research* 39:652–678.

Stoler, Anne. 1985. Perceptions of Protest: Defining the Dangerous in Colonial Sumatra. *American Ethnologist* 12:642–658.

Strathern, Marilyn. 1980. No Nature, No Culture: The Hagen Case. In Carol MacCormack and
    Marilyn Strathern, eds., *Nature, Culture, and Gender*. Cambridge: Cambridge University
    Press, pp. 174–222.

Taussig, Michael. 1984. Culture of Terror – Space of Death. Roger Casement's Putumayo
    Report and the Explanation of Torture. *Comparative Studies in Society and History*
    26:467–497.

Trawick, Margaret. 1990. *Notes on Love in a Tamil Family*. Berkeley: University of Califor-
    nia Press.

Whatley, Marianne. 1986. Taking Feminist Science to the Classroom: Where Do We Go from
    Here? In Ruth Bleier, ed., *Feminist Approaches to Science*. New York: Pergamon Press,
    pp. 181–190.

White, Geoffrey, and John Kirkpatrick. 1985. *Person, Self and Experience: Exploring Pacific
    Ethnopsychologies*. Berkeley: University of California Press.

Williams, Raymond. 1977. *Marxism and Literature*. Oxford: Oxford University Press.

8   Principles of selves: The rhetoric of introductory textbooks in American psychology

Jill G. Morawski

All modern sciences employ textbooks as a pedagogical resource; yet despite the ubiquity of this literary genre, science textbooks hold an ambiguous status. While scientists themselves often denigrate textbooks as containing secondhand or false knowledge,[1] these texts nevertheless are taken to represent knowledge that is at once essential to acquire and superior to ordinary accounts of reality. Given scientists' equivocations regarding textbooks, it is not surprising that historians of science have yet to find a place for textbooks in their reconstructions of scientific activities.

This chapter attempts to situate introductory textbooks within the scientific practices of psychology. In particular, the chapter explores some of the ways in which textbooks have played a part in psychology's ongoing mission to propose and defend a particular construction of social reality – a version of social reality that has enabled or maintained certain cultural practices beyond what are taken as the boundaries of scientific psychology. Put another way, this investigation of one scientific entity, textbooks, proceeds from a conception of science as an organized set of technical practices that engage political, economic, and social conditions, and which transform ordinary understandings of those conditions.[2]

Within this conception, textbooks become all the more interesting because they are created as communications between those members who participate in science and those who do not; textbooks, then, become central resources for transforming everyday, nonscientific versions of the world.

Textbooks, along with other psychological writings, are crucial to the disciplinary project of defining and inscribing subjectivity. I will venture to

This research project was initiated while I was a faculty fellow at the Center for Humanities at Wesleyan University, during which time I benefited from conversations with other fellows, especially with Richard Ohmann. I am indebted to Sarah Alvord, Betty Bayer, Ludy Benjamin Jr., and Virginia Johnson, who contributed generously to all facets of the project, and to Robert Steele, who has been ever willing to explore the murkiness of subjectivity with me. Portions of this analysis are reported in, "There Is More to Our History of Giving: The Place of Introductory Textbooks in American Psychology," *American Psychologist,* 1992, *47,* 161–196.

suggest that textbooks' low status has masked their special burdens: Not only have textbooks shrouded inconsistencies and contradictions of this disciplinary project in order to portray psychology as unified and coherent, but they also required a complex dialogue between different subjectivities construed in the texts. In advocating a world that takes subjectivity as an object with characteristics not unlike the "natural" objects of other sciences, and simultaneously claiming superior knowledge of subjectivity, textbook writers had to address and engage the very subjects whose own subjective experiences were to be radically reinterpreted by the science. Textbook authors, then, faced the apparent paradox of denying certain subjectivities while attempting to enlist those very subjectivities in the project of a scientific psychology.

To illustrate these multiple functions of textbooks, I analyze three features of that scientific literary genre. After establishing their growing presence as a cultural commodity in a social world where individuals were turning to a new scientific expertise for guidance and enlightenment, I show how textbooks changed to engage this new audience and their problems of mentation. This analysis makes apparent the emergence of a new discursive format, one that positions readers as ignorant but ultimately capable of a scientific gaze on mental life. Second, I examine how several specific discursive strategies are used to position readers, authors, and others, especially those serving to smooth textual and actual contradictions regarding these subjectivities. I then turn to a selective analysis of illustrations in textbooks of the same period to uncover some of the ways in which subjectivity is constructed as biological, mechanical, and internal. The rhetorical positioning of reader and author subjectivities is necessary but not sufficient for persuading readers that the texts present an authentic *science* of subjective experience. It also is necessary to describe subjectivity as a phenomenon amenable to objective scientific scrutiny, to point to its real existence as something which can be observed, inscribed, measured, and compared.

The "new" psychology textbooks: Embodiment of aspiration

In both a symbolic and a practical sense, disciplinary textbooks represent the state of knowledge at the end of the nineteenth century; they embody industrial innovations (printing and distribution), the democratization of educational institutions, and the segmentation and regularization of formal knowledge. The textbook publishing industry taking form during this period symbolized these cultural changes and aspirations. Thus is Edwin Ginn, the founder of a major textbooks publishing house, described in the company's history: "In his vision he saw millions of children trooping to the elementary schools throughout the land and tens of thousands of earnest students who would be enrolled in the high schools and in the state and private colleges, that, he rightfully believed, would soon be rising in all parts of the Union."[3] Although tinged with the nostalgia of Depression-era America, this description conveys both the visionary and practical aspirations associated with the textbook genre.

If defined as published works that claim to survey the study of psychological phenomena, then introductory psychology textbooks existed even in the early nineteenth century. Appearing at a rate of two or three books per decade, these works were generally used in upper-level college courses in philosophy. Bearing such titles as *The Human Intellect, Mental Philosophy, Rational Psychology,* and sometimes simply *Psychology,* the textbooks were written by academic scholars, usually men trained in theology or philosophy who occupied prestigious positions – such as college presidents – in institutions of higher education.[4] The 1880s marked a noticeable change in publication practices: The number of texts published per decade began to increase dramatically, and their authors now tended to be leading scientists, usually with training in psychology. Few titles retained the words "moral," "understanding," "powers," or "philosophy." In the 1880s there were almost as many textbooks released as had been published in the preceding 30 years: 14 in that decade, 32 in the 1890s, 25 in the first decade of the twentieth century, and 50 in the second.[5]

Using indices of authorship and titling that signaled the beginning of a "new" psychology, the origin of the modern textbook can be dated to or around 1887. Yet these new texts did not differ dramatically in subject headings, nor did the "new" psychology texts contain a vast array of recent experimental findings. Rather, the texts of the 1890s and 1900s retain a similar catalog of subjects: sensation, intellect, perception, judgment, and reasoning. Both pre- and post-1887 texts are concerned with identifying and classifying what counts as psychological reality; they systematically *segment* and *reorder* that reality.

Textbooks of the two areas, however, do differ in substantial ways. These differences result, on the one hand, from the textual and rhetorical features that enable the construal of author, audience, and object of the writing, and on the other hand, from the textual means whereby the intellectual project is tied to visions of cultural well-being and social order. To view textbooks in terms of such practices requires an analysis that goes beyond the conventional ways of reading scientific literature. Guided by techniques of discourse analysis, it is possible to identify patterns of scientific work within the texts. However, discourse analysis typically maintains a problematic distinction between lived experiences and the products of those experiences – commodities. As Michael Apple argues in his study of school textbooks, "This distinction can of course be maintained only on an analytic level, since most of what seem to us to be things – like lightbulbs, cars, records, and . . . books – are really part of a larger social process."[6]

Cultural commodities are social relations between people and, hence, need to be understood in terms of the sociohistorical dynamics of these relations.[7] For the study of books, then, it is necessary not only to examine discursive styles and the economic relations of publishing and educational settings,[8] but also the extended web of social arrangements that mediate the structure and contents of the literary products.[9] Analyses of "written" cultural forms must move between social and economic structures and attend to the social relations constituting those structures and cultural products.

The language and methods of such reading are far from self-evident or agreed upon. Nevertheless, this kind of reading needs to be undertaken with introductory psychology textbooks and, I hope to show, reveals both psychology's enmeshment in a broader cultural project and the importance of textbooks to that project. The social arrangements of readers and authors in these textbooks provide a starting point for tracing the relations between discursive styles and cultural conditions.

Subjects/readers in transition

In 1870, 52,000 students were enrolled in institutions of higher education, and by 1900 enrollment had increased over fourfold to 238,000. (Although most college students were white and male, by 1900 40% of the undergraduate population was female.) There were 563 institutions of higher education in 1870, and 977 in 1900. The faculty increased nearly fourfold during that period, from 5,553 in 1870 to 23,868 in 1900. Prior to 1870 graduate training was virtually nonexistent, and in that year only one doctorate was granted in the nation.[10] By 1904 psychology alone had produced over 100 Ph.D.s and ranked fourth among the sciences in number of degrees conferred.[11] It is more difficult to determine the number of undergraduates who studied psychology. Until the wide-scale adoption of the elective system in the 1890s, students generally were required to take courses in moral philosophy, which usually included a course or coursework in psychology or mental science. By 1904 at least 623 institutions had three or more psychology courses and eight large universities required a psychology course for the B.A.[12] Judging by the increased number of textbooks, professors of psychology, and psychology courses, the number of students who studied psychology during their undergraduate career was substantial.

The student who entered higher education in the last three decades of the nineteenth century lived within a "buzz" of social and economic activity: rapid industrialization, technological innovations (especially in transportation and communication), immigration, urbanization, mass education, and the demise of religious influence. Economic conditions were in an unsteady state, with several depressions and recoveries, while business organizations virtually transformed themselves into hierarchical and inclusive corporate structures. All of these changes implied shifts and proliferation of social relations: between workers and production, between producers and consumers, between ethnic and social classes, between members of families, and between co-workers.[13]

Participants in this culture were situated in a field of tensions and, consequently, the assimilation of culture produced notable anxieties. One set of tensions emerged when the possibilities for vertical mobility, for becoming, in G. Stanley Hall's words, "authorities" (leaders) and not merely "echoes" (workers) coincided with the formation, in all institutions, of corporate hierarchies or broad pyramids where only a few were to reach the peak. Most middle-class individuals would be embodied as what Hall called "corporate members."[14] On another level, the emphasis on ambition, dedication, and self-control – or plain old hard work – existed alongside sanctions for leisure, sport, and permissive consumption of new mass-marketed products. In colleges, study was not supposed to interfere with good times; collective entertainment, whether it be football or fraternities, occupied a significant portion of students' time. Popular literature contributed with accounts of frolic and adventure, and magazines filled the reader with ideas about new products and purchases, not to mention new identities.[15] Finally, the middle-class culture of professionalism privileged firsthand experiences of reality in both work and play. In this spirit, Hall invited readers of *Forum* to partake in the novel experiences of the laboratory, and William James marveled at the "buzz" of experience.[16] However, experience and reality alike were becoming increasingly difficult to locate. The other side of the buzz – and expansion of experiences – was its dynamic complexity, multiplicity, and obscurity. The growing trust in the veracity of scientific knowledge, the faith axiomatic to professionalism, promised ultimate access to reality, yet at the same time the proliferation of new expert knowledges suggested the existence of multiple realities, if not *un*reality. Social science especially challenged the position of reality in its repeated assaults on common sense, proclamations about the subjectivity of ordinary experience, and the insistence on the improbability of autonomous action. As Richard Hofstader reported, 1890s progressives saw reality as hidden and psychic events as "a kind of pale reflex."[17]

Middle-class culture of the late nineteenth century, especially for youth, consisted of anxieties as well as ambition, self-doubt as well as self-control and knowledge, and fragmentation as well as order. If the 1890s are seen only in terms of the professionalization of the sciences, vertical mobility, and progressive attitudes, then we can see how the new psychology served the citizens of this culture by way of offering a utilitarian and reformist as well as scientifically grounded profession. If however, we also acknowledge the ongoing transformations of individual identities and social relations along with the instabilities produced by those transformations, then psychology can be considered as instrumental in the very process of "defining identities appropriate to a changed reality."[18] Psychology was not simply the promise of a science of universal truths (concerning all mankind) or of norms for identifying the abnormal. Psychology did not simply *reflect* social experience by naturalizing and justifying its social codes. Psychology also was in a position to represent *new possibilities,* and to be *constitutive of new identities and social alliances.* The youthful readers of the new psychology textbooks, then, could seek in those volumes not only a potential career path but also a modern guide for experience, one that would locate "real" reality and enhance one's capacity to see and do.

The making of authors and readers

The authors and readers represented in introductory textbooks after 1887 do, indeed, provide a guide for experience and locating reality. They both result from the use of conventional rhetorical strategies, yet the old and new texts differ in their specific discursive aims. The authors of the "old" texts participated in an ageless conversation among men of wisdom. They positioned themselves as caretakers, reformers, and humble transmitters of knowledge which had been fathered through generations, from the Greeks onward. Although the authors of the early texts paid homage to doing "science," improving mental faculties, and aiding education, they gave an egoistic framing to their efforts. They recurrently indicated their personal standpoint and simultaneously supported and illustrated their claims with "experience." "Self" as author and as a set of experiences coalesced in these genealogies of truth. As Hamilton noted in his 1883 textbook, he wrote first for himself and then to furnish "a scientific book such as every American gentleman should have for reading and for reference."[19] The audience imaged in the earlier text likewise was capable of and interested in self-betterment, and although its social and economic status goes unmentioned, its position usually can be inferred: However privileged, these readers are gentle and passively receptive to guidance.[20] Generally, whenever questions are advanced to these gentle readers, the author hastens to provide the answers.

Taking a different purchase, the authors portrayed in the "new" textbooks announce their participation in the escalating action of the new science. In these texts there is a detectable alteration of authorial voice: The self is minimally present either through a strategy of omitting all personal experience and theoretical preferences, or by positioning the self among the many thinkers in psychology. When the self of the author does appear, it is used overtly to establish a "friendly" text, a camaraderie with readers; however, as we shall see later, these occasional self-revelations are important moments in defining subjectivity.

Just as the identity – personal and intellectual – of the author appears to recede in the new textbooks, so the identity and psychology of the reader becomes more precisely marked. Readers are teachers or teachers in training, high school or normal school students, potential lawyers and businessmen, or "ordinary" readers. They are men of action, laboring to examine real life more fully and to master its complexity. To E. A. Kirkpatrick, the reader has no interest in the "thoroughly dried specimens" of the older mental science and its laws, which the student can not observe and verify. "Real knowledge and power" requires that the pupil "observe and analyze the actual processes of his own mind and those of others instead of taking what the author tells him about imaginary mental processes."[21] The reader's ambition, whether to pursue careers in psychology or elsewhere, is aligned with the edict, "a man's reach should exceed his grasp."[22] Even when direct references to readers are absent, these readers are beckoned to acquire the psychologist's standpoint, that is, to acquire the ability to know with certainty the "real" of life experiences. Sometimes this standpoint is offered as an immediate possibility in the form of experiments the reader can perform on his own. More often the standpoint is posed as the motive for reading, and the psychologist's clear vision is only pages away: "with a clean, well-trained eye and the mind's retinal field cleared of all floating specks, the student of Psychology must ever seek the truth, and the truth alone, if he would not be handicapped."[23] From the psychologist's standpoint, "face-to-face experience of actual life is essential." Readers are given the possibility not simply of new psychological experiences but of understanding the "real nature" of those experiences. The trained student shares interests with the trained psychologist who desires to convert consciousness into an object of (indirect but verifiable) knowledge for himself." The author proceeds by assuring readers that "it is not arrogant to claim that the trained psychologist understands not only the child, the idiot, the madman, and the hypnotic subject, but also the artist, the scientist, the statesman, and the thinker, as psychical beings, far better than any of these classes understand each other, or even themselves."[24] Not only are the mental faculties of scientific psychologists presented as the most veridical means of knowing others' realities, but these faculties are attainable by the reader, too, and are taken to be desired by the reader.

Although readers are sometimes invited by textbook authors to become psychologists, more frequently they are identified as members of a special social class of "educated men" who seek knowledge about reality.[25] These men stand apart from the class of "lazy readers."[26] Whether readers are described as potential psychologists or as knowledge holders, their identities have been textually "transplanted" to a desirable location. This move illustrates a long-standing rhetorical device: "If you want an uncultivated man to change his views, transplant him."[27] Not only are the readers' identities elevated; but they are seen as members of an elite audience, another common rhetorical device for persuasion.[28] However, the elite audience portrayed in the new psychology textbook differs from the elite audience in the earlier textbooks: In the "new" books the common man, the motivated man, can by transforming himself thereby include himself within the elite. As one author insisted, even the costly instruments of the new psychology do not prohibit the common person from engaging in this world of knowledge.

Although not always explicit in the texts, readers are assumed to be seeking both self-improvement and mastery over others. They want to become the organizer of experience and the detecting eye, the manager and the surveyor. Self-knowledge was perceived as an obvious ambition: A 1898 textbook posits that "self-control" is "the great end of all education," and a 1911 textbook takes the ability to observe psychological processes to be something "we owe to ourselves as educated members of civilized races."[29] Another text similarly claims that the very function of a textbook is as "guide to the study of his (student's) mind"; however, it also is taken to be instrumental in "dealing with other minds." This other-control is made explicit by claiming that psychology benefits "all individuals interested in studying or controlling human nature."[30]

Beyond this image of reader as ambitious, independent, and aspiring to certain skills, however, are textual messages that insist on passive readers. Questions scattered throughout the text, study problems, and experiments to be performed – all devices that are purportedly innovations befitting the truly enthusiastic reader – actually limit action and preclude the possibility of cognitive independence. The answers to most study questions in the books require no more than rote learning, and the experiments usually have a single correct outcome. Occasionally authors claim to be using simplified language or omitting complex information.[31] Later I will return to this contractory underside of the new reader.

The new authors and readers prepared the way for new understandings – or a new reality – of psychological phenomena. In fact, these new actors at once relied on and fashioned particular rationalities and subjectivities. They enabled certain experiences and social roles; they also determined the containment or denial of other possibilities. Students were invited simultaneously to be consumers of the new psychology and its potential producers; they were offered roles that promised control over other individuals, a special experience of self, and a veridical grasp of reality. What these new roles enabled, in fact, was a different reality, one that specified certain relations between perceiving individuals, between individuals and what comes to be taken as reality, and within individuals. The rhetorical contrivance of readership (and authorship) played upon culturally salient desires and ambitions in order to entice the individual reader. However, the subjectivity made real through these methodological practices differed from the subjectivity of readers described in texts. Psychology's success in undermining commonsense knowledge and in marketing an apparently unsavory model of subjectivity depended on the readers' dissociation from that subjectivity.

Subjectivities: One and the other

Just as the persuasiveness of introductory textbooks depended on particular confections of reader and author, so too it relied upon cultural imagery and beliefs. Authors drew upon a cache of cultural understandings, and in doing so were not just limited to ordinary conceptions of human nature, but also drew on conceptions supplied by other sciences. Their selections from these cultural ideas and ideals, however, were not arbitrary but were determined by the scientific model of subjectivity which they were propounding. Numerous historical studies have documented this subjectivity – a purportedly objective construal of subjective experience – as self-contained or highly individuated, self-monitoring, asocial, mechanistic, trait-bearing (manifesting certain distinct and measurable qualities), and dedicated to rational and logical functions yet ill-equipped for producing them.[32] At first glance this needy if independent subjectivity contrasts with the ambitious, competent, and potentially masterful subjectivity attributed to textbook readers. The contradiction in subjectivities could be explained simply on rhetorical grounds: Some assurance or diversion was needed in order to persuade an audience that the new psychology, which slighted personal experience and offered an apparently inhumane model of humanity, nevertheless offered accurate knowledge. And to some extent this rhetorical strategy is apparent. The reader and author, as members of an elite community, were set apart from "others," especially in those texts where the reader is invited to partake in the psychologist's gaze (to be like, if not to be, an actual psychologist). Those who had not acquired appropriate skills were "poverty stricken," wrote Robert Yerkes in his 1911 textbook, and thus "Millions of human beings – unfortunate but all unconscious of what they are missing – go through life blind to the psychological world."[33] By counterposing the reader and the mass of others (note the economic language of this juxtaposition), intertextual contradictions concerning subjectivity are eased.

The easing of these textual contradictions depended not only on rhetorical contrivances but also on the presence of a master of subjectivity – a socially elevated observer of psychological reality. Perhaps the textual contradictions found between the subjectivity of the reader and "others" actually functioned positively in the larger social landscape, an economic world best served by subjectivities which were at once ambitious and submissive, desiring and self-regulating, managing and manageable.[34] Whatever the possible social functions of these discordant subjectivities may have been, it remains that they are, first, sustained by the hypothetical presence of a superior subjectivity,[35] a scientific observer, and, second, are given meaning through the evocation of common cultural images and forms. Two specific usages of cultural imagery and beliefs figure prominently in the early modern textbooks: the use of ordinary understandings and cultural stereotypes of self and other, and the deployment of characteristics of reality associated with more legitimate sciences. The first usage is illustrated by E. W. Scripture's introductory textbook and the second by a sample of textbook descriptions and illustrations of reality that rely on a reality depicted in other sciences.

A textbook published in the late 1890s furnishes examples of what might be called "coordinated" or "mercurial" subjectivities. Scripture's *The New Psychology* defends introspection while promulgating a "new" experimental psychology. Written by a psychologist at an elite institution, the work assumes an audience of socially advantaged students. In the introductory pages of the text, Scripture described the subjectivity of the new psychology in terms of the "vagaries of the human mind" and its untrustworthiness caused by the unavoidable operations of prejudices and unconscious alterations: "Our passions, our prejudices, and the dominant opinion of the day are abundant sources of dangerous illusion."[36] Scripture freely extended this conceptualization to himself, citing everyday examples of his untrustworthy self. However, this same precarious subjectivity makes possible its opposite, the masterful observer, initially through a faithful accounting of unfaithful mental processes and then through similar accountings of others' mental acts.

Scripture's trustworthy confession, and elaborate descriptions of psychological methods that follow, confirm both forms of subjectivity – the one and the other. Prefatory comments about "uncultivated observers" and their primitive mind-sets prepare the stage for an elaboration of characters.[37] It will suffice here to describe two strategies through which this elaboration is accomplished. First, Scripture used the existing social structure to define the "other" subjectivity, that configuration of complex mental processes with limited cognitive powers of self-control, which constituted the object of modern psychology. This is the subjectivity of "uncultivated observers" who remember favorable events but forget unfavorable ones, who associate changes in the weather with changes in the moon, and who are duped by a "whole race of prophets and quacks." These subjects, upon visiting Berlin, notice the shop windows in the Kaiser Gallerie but remain "unconscious of the watchful policeman around the corner," which is actually more characteristic of Berlin than the shops.[38] In defining psychology's object, then, Scripture relied on caricatures of the common "man"; this reliance occurs even in discussions of laboratory experiments. For example, his account of experimental work on "time of sensation," or reaction time in visual identification, demands a prior and cultural understanding of the ordinary reader. In these descriptions, the "observer" (subject in the experiment) acts like the "uncultivated": "He attempted to name the letter even when he had seen only part of it. Hereby he often named it correctly when he had seen only a little of it, and, on the other hand, he often thought he had recognized a letter clearly which was not present at all." Scripture then recounted other experimental studies in which securing the observer's correct recognition proved "a hopeless case." He suggested several ways to make reading more accurate but parenethetically quoted another experimentalist's conclusion that such innovations would undoubtedly shock public taste and create new confusions. In these samples, experimentation, or the reporting of it, captured and reenacted cultural forms of ignorance and cognitive shortcomings.[39]

Scripture also enlisted common understandings of cultural difference to demonstrate differences in subjectivities. By assuming a Western male reader, Scripture could readily differentiate a masterful subjectivity from the "other" one. Thus, the positive influence of mental effort on volition was exemplified by comparing "intelligent Europeans" with Africans, and "intelligent mechanics" with "common labourers." Using the same textual strategies, he illustrated the incremental effect of intellectual excitement on physical power with culturally specific cases: The "lecturer actually becomes a stronger man as he steps on the platform" and the mother bear protects her young "when in a state of fear."[40] In these examples "intellectual excitement" is gendered; productive and reproductive activities are gender-specific. Consequently a hierarchical arrangement of subjectivities is further asserted. When several female subjects attained the highest scores in a mental test of finger tapping, their performances were discounted on the basis of their extraexperimental pastimes (playing baseball in one case and playing the violin in another).[41] Again differentiation of subjectivities is declared by drawing on culturally established cognitive hierarchies. These hierarchies also are implicated in discussions of will, where a better mental condition, and more practice and training, are claimed to enhance volition. Thus effort, striving, and motivation are described, both explicitly and implicitly, as Western and male. Subjectivities are differentiated in these passages and the readers are persuaded not only because the differentiations are foregrounded with their cultural understandings but also because the readers' subjectivities can, at almost any time in the text, be identified as being *not* a member of the class of "uncultivated observers."

These textual practices enabled a smoothing of apparent contradictions between the motivated and knowing subjectivities attributed to readers, and the confused and inefficient subjectivities that constituted the object of psychological science. The two forms of subjectivities not only serve as a rhetorical device to engage and persuade readers – would-be consumers of modern psychology – but they functioned in relation to one another. The needy subjectivity of the ordinary actor enabled a believable construal of the masterful subjectivity of the expert observer. Further, the recurrent reliance on cultural markers, which repeatedly signaled difference and hierarchy among subjectivities, verified a world of dichotomous subjectivities while drawing an ambiguous and permeable line between them.[42] (This textual strategy of using cultural meaning to create an audience is similar to the textual tactics for construing "virtual witnesses" in early scientific writing.)[43] While the readers often could locate themselves outside the class of subjectivities investigated by psychological science, they were not entirely or always free to make this dissociation.

The second example of cultural forms used as persuasive devices in textbooks concerns the ways in which reality is depicted. The ambitious readers, motivated by personal and professional aspirations, needed to be directed toward an accurate perception of reality. Considerable textual work was devoted to directing perception and, consequently, relocating reality (some of this work is common to scientific writing and ultimately is what sets it apart from nonscientific writings). Introductory texts after 1890 no longer directed the readers simply to the authors' beliefs, or even to those opinions nested among other writers' ideas.

Nothing was posed as so exciting, so promising, in the new psychology textbooks as reality. The real can get us beyond epiphenomena and illusion, and more than that: Reality promises to eradicate the confusions of fleeting, multiple, and sometimes contradictory experiences. Entering this "temple of reality," as Ladd described it, is the ultimate objective of the new science and, hence, it is the subject of discursive work throughout the new psychology textbooks.[44] Despite some philosophical differences among the books, reality or the real was accorded several common attributes. First, the real *exists* and its existence is confirmed, on the one hand, by the possibility of scientists' objective gaze and, on the other hand, by examples of this gaze. Thus, in discussing "scientific imagination," James Mark Baldwin attributed to certain men a great "emotional soberness" and an ability to "see deeply," which enables them to have "direct reference to our knowledge of the world and things."[45] The examples of this access to reality are found throughout the books, but none are so convincing as illustrations. Here the unseen reality is made visible: The invisible organs are sketched, lines of energy are drawn, levels of consciousness are mapped, and magnitude and duration of memories are charted. In addition, these textbooks contain a healthy number of illustrations that initially obscure any obvious reality and then enable the author to explain the real nature of that veiled reality.

The second alleged attribute of psychological reality is that it was at once *natural* and *subjective* material and yet not biological. Mental experiences had to be rendered natural if they were to become objects of science. This was done by setting up a series of correspondences, between psychological states (sensation, perception, intention) and physical states. However, the correspondences usually are of similarity or parallelism and not identity. In other words, sensation was claimed to be more than, yet in some way aligned with, nervous impulses. In aligning mental experiences in this way, they could be presented as natural, thus real, and at the same time subjective, in the sense of being experienced internally *and* having that internal experience subject to observation (and eventually to control).

From these qualities of mental experience it followed that the person experiencing does not – and, in many instances, could not – have access to the "real nature" of subjective experience. Thus reality was given the third attribute of *uneasy or indirect accessibility*. Psychology goes beyond "the narrative, or the dramatic and artistic description of life" to observe "real nature," the causal relations underlying this psychic life.[46] Willing, sensing, feeling, thinking, seeing, dreaming, and hating are not what they appear to be to the subject. Insofar as the psychologist has access to reality whereas others do not, William James held that the psychologist becomes a critic. Critique, he continued, was necessary given the fallibility of subjective experience and the mere fact that "no subjective state, while present, is its own object; its object is always something else."[47] By the early twentieth century, this obscured reality was consistently sought in the data, not in the subject *who* experiences.

These textbooks shared a commitment to a constructed reality that was presented as natural, subjective, and difficult to know accurately. It was portrayed as a reality of amazingly complex mental transformations that nevertheless could be codified through mechanical laws and descriptions, on the one hand, and through data charts and sheets, on the other hand. The books presuppose, outline, and even detail these mental transformations, these subjective realities, as an objective reality or at least as a reality that could be known objectively. Except for an alliance with and dependence on physiology, the textbooks do not investigate any material reality. This abeyance persists even when a psychological event is dependent on material conditions, say hunger, pain, death. In these textbooks, either mental transformations are substituted for material transformations, or those mental transformations are mapped onto some taken-for-granted material condition. They encourage attention to and reflection on the mental, not any other reality.

More dramatic than the language of reality, then, was the visual representation of mental life. Things were no longer a matter of belief: In Bruno Latour's words, "This is *seeing*."[48] And seeing became increasingly important: Of six analyzed textbooks published between 1870 and 1887, several contain no illustrations and none exceeds 17. Of the analyzed texts published between 1888 and 1907, only two books (and these were brief "primers") had no visual representations; the remaining texts averaged 32 illustrations per book. Several qualities of these representations exemplify their strategical function in redirecting perception. The first quality has just been mentioned: Illustrations constituted a move from *believing* to *seeing*. That is, they offered another cognitive resource for persuading the reader to perceive in a particular fashion. Second, the graphics were overwhelmingly items "borrowed" from other sciences, notably biology; hence, additional cognitive authority was marshaled to persuade the reader. Third, the images are partial: They restrict observation to parts of bodies or systems. These decontextualized and defamiliarized images – detached from ordinary experiences and perception – increase the reader's reliance on the author's interpretation.

Visual representations certainly were not the only strategy for directing the reader's perceptions, for persuading them that psychology offered a superior access to reality and a means to experience the real rather than the epiphenomenal. However, along with textual depictions of reality, these visual aids are revealing of how perception was redirected and readers were persuaded.

Conclusion

Scientific textbooks, although generally considered "secondhand knowledge" by scientists and historians alike, actually represent genuine scientific activity. At the turn of the century most scientists spent considerable time teaching, and their instructional practices, like their laboratory activities, reflect the cultural nature of their larger project.[49] As science of the nineteenth century was moved from the public domain to the private territory of universities, boundaries were established to delineate *what* was taken as knowledge and *who* were the masters or generators of that knowledge. As Sally Kohlstedt has argued, education was instrumental in the emergence of a "cultural outlook in which the study of science gained a fundamental place."[50] If read from this vantage, and without the assumptions typically made about scientific education, psychology textbooks become historical resources for exploring that cultural outlook.

Given its subject matter, psychology was immediately implicated in cultural understandings and visions. Teaching and textbooks illustrate the dynamic interplay whereby psychology was at once produced through particular cultural projects and productive of those projects. The enterprise of forging a scientific definition of subjectivity contained a set of expectations that could not be realized through laboratory procedures alone: That definition had to correspond, at some level, with emerging subjectivities in the modern world. The scientific project of defining and scrutinizing subjectivity was constituted by certain conceptualizations of subjectivity, albeit conceptualizations that were ambiguous and far from agreed upon. Psychology textbooks reveal the complicated search for a universal subjectivity and, at least during the early years of modern psychology, they show how psychologists imagined a subjectivity that was sometimes local, mutable, and multiple.

Notes and references

1 Scientists' disdainful attitude toward textbooks and the act of writing textbooks is well known. Historians and other analysts of science have tended to reproduce this sentiment even when their objective entails debunking of scientific practice. Thus, for instance, Stephen Brush's frequently cited study of historical myths in science textbooks can be taken to provide testimony on the constitutive flaws of textbooks. Likewise, a number of studies of the biases, omissions, and misinterpretations in psychology texts, although intended to simply document some inadequate aspects of psychology, actually can be seen as confirming the overall derivative and flawed status of these works. See Stephen G. Brush, "Should the History of Science Be Rated X?" *Science*, 1974, *183*, 1164–1172. Examples of empirical studies of psychology textbooks include R. Michael Brown and Roma Brown, "Bias in Psychology and Introductory Psychology Textbooks," *Psychological Reports*, 1982, *51*, 1195–1204; C. J. Buys, "Freud in Introductory Psychology Texts," *Teaching of Psychology*, 1976, 160–157; Stuart J. McKelvie, "Left-wing Rhetoric in Introductory Psychology Textbooks: The Case of Mental Illness," *Psychological Reports*, 1984, *54*, 375–380; Douglas R. Miller, "An Analysis of the Treatment of 'Jensenism' in Introductory Psychology Textbooks," *Teaching of Psychology*, 1980, *7*, 137–139; Robert Sommer and Barbara Sommer, "Mystery in Milwaukee: Early Intervention, I.Q., and Psychology Textbooks," *American Psychologist*, 1983, *38*, 982–985. Some of these investigations do attend to historical and contextual conditions surrounding the production of texts and, therefore, do not imply that the textbook genre, in itself, is biased and second-rate knowledge. See, for instance, Ben Harris "Whatever Happened to Little Albert?," *American Psychologist*, 1979, *34*, 151–160; Ned Levine, Colin Worboys, and Martin Taylor, "Psychology and 'Psychology' Textbooks: A Social Demographic Study," *Human Relations*, 1973, *26*, 467–478.
2 For varied examples of such a revised conception of science, see Bruno Latour, "The Impact of Science Studies on Political Philosophy," *Science, Technology, and Human Values*, 1991, *16*, 3–19; A. Rabinbach, *The Human Motor: Energy, Fatigue, and the Origins of Modernity*, New York: Basic Books, 1990; and Steven Shapin and Simon Schaffer, *Leviathan and the Air Pump: Hobbes, Boyle and the Experimental Life*, Princeton: Princeton University Press, 1985.
3 Thomas B. Lawler, *Seventy Years of Textbook Publishing: A History of Ginn and Company, 1867–1937*, Boston: Ginn, 1938, p. 9. Many early twentieth-century psychologists identified William James's *Principles of Psychology*, New York: Henry Holt, 1890, to be the boundary marker of a new era for psychology and psychology textbooks. See Michael M. Sokal, "Introduction," in *Psychology: Briefer Course*, by William James, Cambridge, MA: Harvard University Press, 1984, pp. xi–xii.
4 Some of these texts are reviewed in Jay W. Fay, *American Psychology before William James*, New Brunswick, NJ: Rutgers University Press, 1939.
5 These numbers have been derived from my own bibliographic search of first edition, introductory psychology textbooks published in the United States. The numbers undoubtedly will be adjusted as additional texts are located and as texts are found not to meet one of the criteria for inclusion.

6 Michael W. Apple, *Teachers and Texts: A Political Economy of Class and Gender Relations in Education*, New York: Routledge & Kegan Paul, 1986, p. 82.

7 In addition, the publishing industry is not composed of standardized relations among the actors involved but, rather, is segmented by different industrial forms and by different types and structures of human relations. See Lewis Coser, Charles Kadushin, and Walter Powell, *Books: The Culture and Commerce of Publishing*, New York: Basic Books, 1982.

8 Although this claim implied a linear influence of human relations (both economic and social) on cultural products, the connection is far more complex and fluid. In the case of school textbooks, numerous researchers have documented the ways in which standardized written materials have transformed classroom activities, teachers, and educational objectives. See, for instance, David L. Elliott and Arthur Woodward, eds., *Textbooks and Schooling in the United States: Eighty-ninth Yearbook of the National Society for the Study of Education*, Chicago: University of Chicago Press, 1990; Henry J. Perkinson, *Early American Textbooks, 1775–1900*, Washington, DC: U.S. Department of Education, 1985; Apple, *Teachers and Texts*.

9 I use terms such as "mediate," "prestructure," or "produce" with awareness that the dynamics of the relations are yet unknown and certainly complex. Implicit in my position is a contrast between the textual analyses I attempt and the poststructuralist analysis of texts, which denies the existence of subjectivities with specific historically conditioned interests (that analysis assumes, paradoxically perhaps, a universal power dynamic underlying all cultural products, and which takes texts to be constructing the "real"). For critical commentaries on different versions of poststructuralist approaches, see Judith Newton, "Historicism New and Old: Charles Dickens Meets Marxism, Feminism, and West Coast Foucault," *Feminist Studies*, 1990, *16*, 449–470; Steven Shapin, "History of Science and Its Sociological Reconstructions, *History of Science*, 1982, *26*, 157–211; "Talking History: Reflection on Discourse Analysis," *Isis*, 1984, *75*, 125–130. The dichotomies presented in these commentaries warrant further exploration, especially in terms of the working definitions of discourse, interests, and practice. See Steve Woolgar, "On the Alleged Distinction between Discourse and *Praxis*," *Social Studies of Science*, 1986, *16*, 309–317.

10 Lawrence R. Veysey, *The Emergence of the American University*, Chicago: University of Chicago Press, 1965; Burton Bledstein, *The Culture of Professionalism: The Middle Class and the Development of Higher Education in America*, New York: Norton, 1976

11 Thomas Camfield, *Psychologists at War: The History of American Psychology, and the First World War*, unpublished Ph.D. dissertation, University of Texas at Austin, 1969, pp. 43–44.

12 See Bledstein, *Culture of Professionalism*; Camfield, *Psychologists at War*; Fay, *American Psychology before James*; Veysey, *Emergence of the University*.

13 Bledstein, *Culture of Professionalism*; Richard Ohmann, *Politics of Letters*, Middletown, CT: Wesleyan University Press, 1988; T. J. Lears, *No Place of Grace: Antimodernism and the Transformation of American Culture, 1880–1920*, New York: Pantheon, 1981.

14 G. Stanley Hall, "The New Psychology as Basis of Education," *Forum*, *17*, 713–719.

15 See Christopher Wilson, "The Rhetoric of Consumption: Mass-market Magazines and the Demise of the Gentle Reader, 1880–1920," in R. Fox and T. J. Lears, eds., *The Culture of Consumption: Critical Essay in American History, 1880–1980*, New York: Pantheon, 1983, 41–64. Also see Ohmann, *Politics of Letters*; Veysey, *Emergence of the University*.

16 Hall, "New Psychology"; Veysey, *Emergence of the University*, p. 61.

17 Hofstader quoted in Thomas L. Haskell, *The Emergence of Professional Social Science*, Urbana: University of Illinois Press, 1977.

18 Charles Rosenberg, "Toward an Ecology of Knowledge: On Disciplines, Context and History," in A. Oleson and J. Voss, eds., *The Organization of Knowledge in America*, Baltimore: Johns Hopkins University Press, 1979, p. 443.

19 E. J. Hamilton, *The Human Mind: A Treatise in Mental Philosophy*, New York: Robert Carter & Brothers, 1883, p. iii.

20 Later in this essay I note that in the new texts a certain passivity of the reader was presumed. This later account of passivity refers not simply to the social roles of teachers and students or to the gentleness of readers, but also to an assumed cognitive incompetence on the part of readers.

21 Edwin A. Kirkpatrick, *Inductive of Psychology,* Winona, MN: Jones & Kroeger, 1893, pp. 3–4.

22 Colin S. Buell, *Essentials of Psychology,* Boston: Ginn, 1898, p. iv.

23 William Krohn, *Practical Lessons in Psychology,* Chicago: Werner, 1894, p. 20.

24 George T. Ladd, *Primer of Psychology,* New York: Scribner, 1894, pp. 7, 8, 21.

25 James Drever, *The Psychology of Everyday Life,* London: Methuen, 1921, p. v.

26 William James, "Introduction," in Edward L. Thorndike, *The Elements of Psychology,* New York; A. G. Sieler, 1905, p. vii.

27 M. Millious quoted in Ch. Perelman and L. Olbrechts-Tyteca, *The New Rhetoric: A Treatise on Argumentation,* translated by J. Wilkinson and P. Weaver, Notre Dame: University of Notre Dame Press, 1969, p. 20.

28 Perelman and Olbrechts-Tyteca, *New Rhetoric,* p. 33.

29 Buell, *Essentials of Psychology,* p. 4; Robert M. Yerkes, *Introduction to Psychology,* New York: Henry Holt, 1911, p. 13.

30 Harvey Carr, *Psychology: A Study of Mental Activity,* New York: Longmans Green, 1925, p. 13; Fleming A. C. Perin and David B. Klein, *Psychology: Its Methods and Principles,* New York: Henry Holt, 1926, pp. 17–18.

31 Historians and sociologists of education have reported that textbooks influenced practice and participants: Textbooks promoted simplified and flattened accounts, contributing to students' disinterest and to the deskilling of teachers, among other things (see note 8). William James remarked on such effects of textbooks in his introduction to Thorndike's 1905 text. James wrote "Can it be, I thought, that the author's long connection with the Teachers College is making him a high-priest of the American 'textbook' Moloch, in whose belly living children's minds are turned to ashes, and whose ritual lies in text-books in which the science is pre-digested for the teacher by every expository artifice and for the pupil comminuted it to small print and large print, and paragraph headings, and cross-references and examination questions, and every other up-to-date device for frustrating the natural movement of the mind when reading, and preventing that irresponsible rumination of the material in one's own way which is the soul of culture." In Thorndike, *Elements of Psychology,* p. vi.

32 These studies include Roy F. Baumeister, "How the Self Became a Problem: A Psychological Review of Historical Research," *Journal of Personality and Social Psychology,* 1987, *52,* 163–176; John C. Burnham, "The New Psychology: From Narcissism to Social Control," in J. Braeman, R. H. Bremmer, D. Brody, eds., *Change and Continuity in Twentieth-Century America: The Nineteen-twenties,* Columbus: Ohio State University Press, 1968; Philip Cushman, "Why the Self Is Empty: Toward a Historically-Situated Psychology," *American Psychologist,* 1990, *45,* 599–611; Kurt Danziger, *Constructing the Subject: Historical Origins of Psychological Research,* Cambridge: Cambridge University Press, 1990; William Kessen, "The American Child and Other Cultural Inventions," *American Psychologist,* 1979, *34,* 815–820; Jill G. Morawski, "Contextual Discipline: The Unmaking and Remaking of Sociality," in R. Rosnow and M. Georgoudi, eds., *Contextualism and Understanding in Human Psychology.* New York: Praeger, 1986, pp. 47–66; Nikolas Rose, "Individualizing Psychology," in J. Shotter and K. J. Gergen eds., *Texts of Identity,* London: Sage, 1989, pp. 199–232; "Psychology as a 'Social' Science," in I. Parker and J. Shotter, eds., *Deconstructing Social Psychology,* London: Routledge, 1990, pp. 103–116; Edward E. Sampson, "Psychology and the American Ideal," *Journal of Personality and Social Psychology,* 1977, *35,* 767–782; "Cognitive Psychology As Ideology," *American Psychologist,* 1981, *36,* 730–743; Couze Venn, "The Subject of Psychology," in J. Henriques, W. Hollway, C. Urwin, C. Venn, and V. Walkerdine, eds., *Changing the Subject: Psychology, Social Regulation, and Subjectivity,* London: Methuen, 1984, 199–152.

33 Yerkes, *Introduction to Psychology*, p. 13.

34 Close analysis of that socially elevated observer subjectivity indicates that it, too, is composed of more than one subjectivity. Jill Morawski, "Maturation of the Psychologist's Two Selves," paper presented at the American Psychological Association Meetings, Boston, August 1990. That study, along with the present analysis, suggests that the scientific conceptualization of subjectivity, which constituted a major project for late nineteenth-century psychologists, was more complicated than choosing between humanism and science, between self as sensing subject and self as object. For a somewhat different account of that dilemma see David E. Leary, "The Psychologist's Dilemma: To Subject the Self to Science – Or Science to the Self?" *Theoretical and Philosophical Psychology*, 1990, *10*, 66–72.

35 The relations between cultural conditions and psychology's theories have been examined through various models of knowledge generation. For instance, Philip Cushman has explored some of the connections between increased production of goods and the development of psychological theory that posits needy or empty selves, selves in search of gratification. His thesis suggests that subjectivity was constructed not just as self-contained but also as an ongoing process of desire, a process that required both regulation and repair. Cushman, "Why the Self Is Empty." For a related interpretation of the labeling and management of anger, see Carol S. Stearns and Peter N. Stearns, *Anger: The Struggle for Emotional Control in America's History*, Chicago: University of Chicago Press, 1986.

36 E. W. Scripture, *New Psychology*, New York: Charles Scribner's Sons, 1897, pp. 3–4. For an analysis of recent construction of subjectivities in psychological writing, see Jill G. Morawski and Robert S. Steele, "The One and the Other: Textual Analysis of Masculine Power and Feminist Empowerment," *Theory and Psychology*, 1991, *1*, 107–131.

37 Scripture, *New Psychology*, p. 3.

38 Ibid., pp. 3–6.

39 Ibid., pp. 103–107.

40 Ibid., pp. 219–220.

41 Ibid., pp. 129–130.

42 The demarcation of subjectivities, however mercurial or ambiguous, is part of the "boundary work" of psychological science. For an excellent elucidation of boundary work, see Thomas F. Gieryn, "Boundary-work and the Demarcation of Science from Non-Science: Strains and Interests in Professional Ideologies of Scientists," *American Sociological Review*, 1983, *48*, 781–795.

43 Steven Shapin, "Pump and Circumstances: Robert Boyle's Literary Technology," *Social Studies of Science*, 1984, *14*, 481–520.

44 Ladd, *Primer of Psychology*.

45 J. M. Baldwin, *Handbook of Psychology*, New York: Henry Holt, 1891, pp. 45, 236.

46 Ladd, *Primer of Psychology*.

47 James, *Principles*, pp. 196–197.

48 Bruno Latour, *Science in Action: How to Follow Scientists and Engineers through Society*, Cambridge, MA: Harvard University Press, 1987, p. 48.

49 Stanley M. Guralnick, "The American Scientist in Higher Education, 1820–1910." In N. Reingold, ed., *The Science in American Context: New Perspectives*, Washington, DC: Smithsonian Institution Press, 1979, pp. 99–141. Also see Peter S. Buck and Barbara C. Rosenbrantz, "The Worm in the Core: Science and General Education," in E. Mendelsohn, ed., *Transformation and Tradition in the Sciences*, Cambridge: Cambridge University Press, 1984.

50 Sally G. Kohlstedt, "Parlors, Primers, and Public Schooling: Education for Science in Nineteenth-Century America," *Isis*, 1990, *81*, p. 445.

Part III

Early antecedents

9   The naturalized female intellect

Lorraine Daston

Introduction

It was predestined that the history of gender and the history of science and medicine would converge, for they share a central preoccupation with the understanding and uses of nature.[1] They also share a framework for analyzing conceptions of nature and their applications, that of naturalization. Reduced to its essentials, "naturalization" refers to ways of fortifying various social, cultural, political, or economic conventions by presenting them as part of the natural order. Naturalization is a leitmotif of gender studies, many of which show how forgers and enforcers of gender identities have appealed ceaselessly to the authority of nature, and how the interpreters of nature – natural philosophers, natural scientists, and physicians – have often aided and abetted that transfer of authority. In the context-dominated science studies of the last decade, naturalization has been the bridge carrying the heaviest traffic between science and its social context: Galileo, for example, "naturalizes" the shaky political legitimacy of the Medicis by christening the newly discovered moons of Jupiter in their honor; Darwin "naturalizes" the contested theories and practices of British political economy in the theory of natural selection. In both gender and science studies, naturalization is ideology at full strength, hardening the flimsy conventions of culture into the immutable, inevitable, and indifferent dictates of nature.

In this essay, I would like to use the history of early modern conceptions of the female intellect to challenge the notion of naturalization as it is currently deployed in both gender and science studies. Not only does this notion take the sharp boundary between "nature" and "culture" largely for granted – otherwise it would make no sense to talk about illegitimate "smuggling" across that border; it also routinely projects a relatively recent conception of nature back onto periods which understood that term quite differently. Where conceptions of nature diverge, so do the strategies (now emphatically in the plural) of naturalization. Naturalization is not the same

This chapter is reprinted from *Science in Context* 5, 2 (1992), pp. 209–235, where it is called "The Naturalized Female Intellect," by Lorraine Daston.

tactic when marshaled in, say, eighteenth-century France as in nineteenth-century Britain. Although the authority of nature is invoked in both cases, the meaning of that authority depends crucially on whether nature is understood normatively or descriptively, within the framework of the natural laws of jurisprudence or the natural laws of mechanics. My quarrel is not with the claim that naturalization is a subspecies of ideology, nor with the claim that it is often a peculiarly potent form of ideology. Rather, I question the propriety of using a single term to blanket a multitude of meanings, of very different political valences. In short, I aim to historicize and thereby differentiate naturalization and, with it, the broader rubric ideology.

The early modern period, here construed as embracing the sixteenth through the eighteenth centuries, offers unusually stark contrasts between various meanings of nature and of naturalization. Within the compass of three centuries, the denotative center of gravity of the word "nature" shifted from essences to matter, for what is desirable to what is inevitable, from the sovereignty of reason to that of physical necessity. Writings about the female intellect during this period are peculiarly well suited to reflect and focus these changes for three reasons: first, as with so many aspects of gender identity, what was distinctively female about women's way of thinking was usually alleged to be part and parcel of their "nature"; second, the political and social implications of the female intellect were debated heatedly and at unprecedented length; and third, the actual content of beliefs about what traits sex the intellect as female remained relatively constant during this period, despite sharp differences of opinion over their putative "natural" causes. It is thus possible to isolate and track these naturalist explanations as a pure exercise in changing forms and standards of explanation per se, without addressing the conflating issue as to how new *explananda* might have influenced the course of these changes.

My argument is divided into four parts. I first briefly examine the terminology of intelligence in order to point out fundamental distinctions between modern and early modern conceptions and thereby attempt to forestall anachronisms. Second, I review at some length early modern descriptions of the female intellect in order to establish its alleged causes and characteristics. The third section contrasts the notions of "nature" that undergirded the explanations of the female intellect, calling attention to points of contrast and historical development that splinter the apparent unity of the term. For these latter purposes, I make some brief excursions into the nineteenth century, in order to amplify contrasts between early modern and modern views of naturalization. In conclusion, I consider the implications of these different forms of naturalization for the treatment of female intellectuals, as well as for conceptions of the female intellect. Throughout, I draw most heavily though not exclusively on French texts for my evidence. This preference has two grounds: First, the French literature on the female intellect, from the *Querelle des Femmes* of the seventeenth century through the controversies over female suffrage during the French Revolution, is at once the most voluminous, politically pointed, and influential of the early modern writings on this topic (Ascoli 1906; Hoffmann 1977). German and British writers who took up these themes, such as Immanuel Kant and Mary Wollstonecraft, did so in reaction to French authors, especially Jean-Jacques Rousseau. Second, the dramatic changes in the concept of nature toward the end of the eighteenth century, which paved the way for ideology in the modern sense, appear to have emerged and taken root first in France, only gradually and with difficulty infiltrating German and British intellectual life, as the intoxication with *Naturphilosophie* in the one case and the persistence of natural theology in the other bear witness. By the turn of the nineteenth century, French intellectuals had largely become wary of both ways of infusing nature with sense and sensibility, and it is an avowedly neutral nature that is a precondition for the familiar version of naturalization.

Before intelligence

Before taking stock of early modern representations of the female intellect, a word about terminology and its load of anachronism is in order. Intelligence as currently and conventionally understood by psychologists is a brashly modern notion. In contrast to theories about the intellect from antiquity through the mid-nineteenth century, the intelligence measured by such tests as the Stanford-Binet is general, quantitative, and, at least in principle, distinct from personality and moral character. This modern conception of intelligence did not arrive full-blown but rather emerged by fits and starts; it was general before it was quantitative, and quantitative before it was morally neutral. Herbert Spencer's and Hippolyte Taine's discussions of a general "intelligence," which matched the internal order of mental representations with the external order of phenomena (Spencer [1855] 1966, 1:410), antedate Francis Galton's first attempts to quantify what he called "natural ability" (Galton [1869] 1972, 26). Similarly, moralized intelligence survived the definitive quantification of intelligence (see Binet 1898; Terman and Merrill [1916] 1937),[2] albeit not for very long; witness Catharine Cox's 1926 attempt to estimate retrospectively the IQs of three hundred past eminences such as Copernicus, Voltaire, Goethe, and John Stuart Mill, which included a character rating of, *inter alia,* their "degree of sense of humor," "trustworthiness," "family affection," "pure-mindedness," and "neatness" (Cox 1926, chaps. 11–13).

Cox's ratings were almost the last overt vestige of an ancient tradition of moralizing the intellect. Although mid-twentieth-century psychologists divorced, at least in principle and in public pronouncements, intelligence from personality and character,[3] such connections were still vigorously and unabashedly advanced throughout the nineteenth century. For example, Darwin identified genius with "unflinching, undaunted perseverance" (Darwin 1870, 1:328); Galton claimed that "natural ability" was compounded of capacity, zeal, and "an adequate power of doing a great deal of laborious work" (Galton [1869] 1972, 77). The congeries of concepts used by early modern writers to chart the kinds and relationships of mental faculties were still more permeable to the influences of morals and character. For example, the central notion of sensibility (*sensibilité, Sinnlichkeit*) in late seventeenth- and early eighteenth-century psychology referred to both perceptual and emotional sensitivity to impressions. Thus sensibility was at once the precondition for empirical knowledge and for the reasonable emotions of charity and compassion, which bound society together (Baasner 1986). Reason was still more closely identified with morality, for it was through the "natural light" of reason that, according to jurists, humans came to recognize all forms of truth, including "the eternal distinction between good and evil, the inviolable rule of justice [that] receives without difficulty the approbation of every man who reflects and who reasons" (d'Alembert and Diderot [1757] 1969, 2:684, s.v. "Loi naturelle").[4]

The exercise of reason not only revealed moral principles; it also sometimes required them. The patience and concentration needed to "combine in sequence a long chain of ideas; [the] attention that annihilates all objects in order to see only one and to see that one in its entirety" (Thomas 1772, 109) were at once integral parts of discursive reason and of an upright character. More than one early modern author disqualified women from philosophical contemplation on the grounds that they lacked the self-discipline and stamina to follow long demonstrations and intricate arguments: "It is true that women ordinarily have less application, less patience for reasoning in sequence, less courage and resolution than men" (Fleury 1686, quoted in Ascoli 1906, 56). As this example shows, the interdependence of moral and intellectual traits opened a channel through which social norms and cultural values could flow. It is not difficult to see how character is shaped by social role, and insofar as intellect is in turn shaped by character, it, too, is firmly anchored within the social order. Because of this interdependence, and the central role it played in the gendering of intellectual abilities, I use the term "intellect" rather than the putatively neutral "intelligence" in what follows, to underscore the differences between early modern and modern conceptions.

However, it is also somewhat misleading to use the singular term "intellect" when referring to early modern theories of mental abilities, for it suggests an approximation of our monolithic, general intelligence. In fact, seventeenth-century theories posited a collection of faculties and talents residing in the mind, and a correspondingly intricate division of intellectual labor. No single one or even simple sum of these faculties coincides with our concept of intelligence. For example, a census of possible eighteenth-century French candidates culled from the *Encyclopédie* would include: *intelligence* (the ability to "seize with ease the most difficult things" but meaning also concord between individuals, or information) (d'Alembert and Diderot [1757] 1969, 2:482, s.v. "Intelligence"); *raison* (the God-given faculty for "knowing the truth," especially innate truths) (ibid., 3:200, s.v. "Raison [Logique]"); *intellect* ("the soul insofar as it forms concepts" from the raw materials of sensation) (ibid., 2:482, s.v. "Intellect [Grammaire et Philosophie]"); *entendement* (the faculty for abstract thought, as distinct from the imagination) (ibid., 1:1180, s.v. "Entendement [Logique]"); and *esprit* (a mixture of "judgment, genius, taste, penetration, scope, grace, finesse," or "ingenious reason") (ibid., 1244, s.v. "Esprit [Philosophie et Belles-Lettres]"). In seventeenth- and eighteenth-century psychological treatises these comprehensive mental capacities might be supplemented by the more specific faculties of perception, imagination, memory, and judgment, plus abstraction, taste, or various "sentiments," according to the author's predilection. The early modern mind was a crowded place, crammed with separate but not always wholly distinct faculties that together orchestrated the life of mind and heart.

Sexing the mind

It is within the framework of this moralized, pluralist intellect – rather than within that of a neutral, general intelligence – that early modern discussions of a distinctively female intellect were firmly lodged. Given this profusion of faculties and functions, one might expect early modern psychologists to have been preoccupied with group and individual differences along each of these many dimensions. If twentieth-century theories of general intelligence sustain such investigations, then the myriad possibilities of a dozen or so faculties, with character differences to boot, must have highlighted human diversity still more dramatically, or so one might think. However, individual and group differences in intellectual endowment excited relatively little interest within early modern theories of mind. To be sure, degrees of superiority and inferiority in the "liveliness of our conceptions" or in the speed of mental combinations were duly noted, but uniformities rather than deviations, shared mechanisms rather than individual differences, commanded center stage. As Thomas Reid remarked of judgment: "The judgments grounded upon the evidence of sense, of memory, and of consciousness, put all men upon a level" (Reid [1785] 1969, 540).

There were religious as well as theoretical grounds for this apathy concerning individual differences among human beings, which were dwarfed, according to theologians, by the differences between humans and animals.

This latter distinction completely overshadowed the minor distinctions among human minds. Souls, and therefore minds, come only in one kind, according to orthodox Christian theology since Augustine, a position reinforced by Aquinas (Lloyd 1984, 31, 35). Although neither Augustine nor Aquinas nor their theological successors were particularly generous in their opinion of female capacities and rights, the tenet that rational minds have no sex surfaced again and again in early modern defenses of the feminine intellect: "The unique form and difference of that [human] animal consists only in the human soul" (Gournay 1622, 18; cf. Agrippa [1566] 1670, 3; Schurman 1641, 21; Le Moyne 1660, 284; Poullain de la Barre [1673] 1984, 60; Hippel [1792] 1979, 66–68).[5]

That the female intellect required such defenses points to the single most glaring exception to the claim that individual and group differences kindled little interest among early modern writers. Although the topic seldom featured prominently in treatises devoted exclusively to philosophical psychology, it did command the attention of a large number of medical and legal writers, as well as engaging numerous other authors in polemics over the moral, intellectual, and political status of women. This early modern polemical literature centered on the moral fitness of women. For example, the opening salvo in the seventeenth-century *Querelle des Femmes,* Alexis Rousset's *Alphabet de l'imperfection et malice des femmes* (1617), rehearsed female vices from "Avarice" to "Zelus Zelotypus" (i.e., jealousy) but barely spared a sentence for the intellectual debilities of women, aside from complaining that they talked too much (Olivier [Alexis Rousset] [1617] 1646, 93).[6] However, just because moral and intellectual virtues overlapped in early modern philosophy, debates over women's morals often widened willy nilly into debates over their intellect as well.

The Renaissance and early modern literature about the female intellect contained few novel substantive claims or justifications for these claims, although some writers did revalue allegedly female traits as equal or superior to allegedly male traits. The *locus classicus* for sex differences in all species during this period remained a passage from Aristotle's *Historia animalium* (608a19–608b12), so influential as to merit quotation at length:

> In all genera in which the distinction of male and female is found, nature makes a similar differentiation in the characteristics of the two sexes. This differentiation is the most obvious in the case of human kind and in that of the larger animals and the viviparous quadrupeds. For the female is softer in character, is the sooner tamed, admits more readily of caressing, is more apt in the way of learning; as, for instance, in the Laconian breed of dogs the female is cleverer than the male. . . . In all cases, excepting those of the bear and the leopard, the female is less spirited than the male; in regard to the two exceptional cases, the superiority in courage rests with the female. With all other animals the female is softer in disposition, is more mischievous, less simple, more impulsive, and more attentive to the nurture of the young;

the male, on the other hand, is more spirited, more savage, more simple and less cunning. . . . The fact is, the nature of man is the most rounded off and complete, and consequently in man the qualities above referred to are found most clearly. Hence woman is more compassionate than man, more easily moved to tears, at the same time is more jealous, more querulous, more apt to scold and to strike. She is, furthermore, more prone to despondency and less hopeful than the man, more void of shame, more false of speech, more deceptive, and of more retentive memory. (Barnes 1984, 1:948–949)[7]

Both in its form and in its content this passage reverberated through centuries, indeed millennia, of European debate about the differences between male and female. The polar opposition between complementary male and female intellects was not fully dissolved into a continuum until the late nineteenth century;[8] the intertwining of intellect and character persisted into the twentieth; the specific claims concerning docility, cunning, learning, memory, and so on are with us still. Complementary thinking about male/female differences structured early modern views about sex differences, even with respect to moral injunctions purportedly binding on all Christians. Thus to violate the passive virtues, chief among them chastity, was the cardinal sin for women but merely a peccadillo for men; conversely, timidity was the most easily excused fault in women and the least in men (Maclean 1977, 19; Kelso 1956, 24–27). Claims about the female intellect conformed to this structure of polarities strung together by loose analogy to the major rubrics of female passivity and male activity, although these primary poles could not capture all the nuances of alleged contrasts between men and women. As Ludmilla Jordanova points out, it would be misleading to isolate any single polarity from the web that sustained them all and defined each with reference to all the others (Jordanova 1989, 20–25).

What traits clustered around the feminine pole? Taking Aristotle's claims in the *Historia animalium* passage as their departure point, early modern philosophers, jurists, theologians, and physicians generally agreed that women excelled in memory, ability to learn (where "learning" was understood in the context of taming and therefore strongly associated with docility and pliability of character), cunning, and all aspects of mental mutability, including a quicksilver imagination and hair-trigger emotions. Just as women were alleged to have less aptitude for the active virtues, such as courage, so they were also branded inferior to men in active intellect, including the exercise of speculative reason (Maclean 1977, 11–19; 1980, 15, 51, 64).

Until well into the eighteenth century, these intellectual traits were corporeally grounded, largely determined by women's allegedly cold, moist bodily complexion. Sensory impressions, stamped upon the brain as a seal upon wax, therefore adhered more easily, distinctly, and durably in the soft, humid female matter than in that of the hot, dry male. Hence women excelled in memory and also in imagination, for the same complexion was linked to mutable mental impressions – as well as to levity, capriciousness, deception, and more intense passions (Maclean 1980, 34–42). Defenders of the female intellect in the sixteenth and seventeenth centuries sometimes thought these good grounds for admitting women into the company of the learned, deliberately transforming traditional infirmities into advantages: "One reproaches them [women] with the humidity of their complexion: but one will not reproach them if one recalls that humidity is the stuff of which the images employed by the sciences are formed: that it [humidity] is the proper temperament of memory, which is the depositary and nourishment of the sciences" (Le Moyne 1660, 285–86; cf. Agrippa [1566] 1670, 60). Neither the claim – women excel in memory and imagination – nor its causal justification – humoral physiology – had changed here, only the valuation.

Some of these early modern shifts in valuation of what were still thought to be distinctively feminine mental traits reflect upheavals in the global organization of scholarship, especially humanist-inspired attacks on the institutions and the acrimonious debating style of university scholasticism. Juxtaposed to the formal, dry consistency of scholastic argument and disputation, the vivacious, ornamental qualities associated with the female intellect were seen in a more favorable light. The Jesuit Pierre Le Moyne linked women with a philosophy more "agreeable and not less instructive" than that professed in the Schools, one that "embellished [axioms and decisions] in exquisite fashion, with curious and intricate figures," adding "luster to force; and endowing solidity with grace and dignity" (Le Moyne 1660, Preface). To someone as hostile to scholasticism as the Cartesian François Poullain de la Barre, women's lack of a proper university education was a positive advantage, for they were thus preserved from pedantry and dogmatism ([1673] 1984, 28–30).[9]

However, even for writers who did not welcome the polished, parry-and-thrust repartee of the salons (Lougee 1976, 27–30) as an improvement over the arid disputations of university scholastics, the perceived essence of the feminine intellect in the eighteenth century was its sociability. The mind of Rousseau's Sophy, educated to be the quintessential woman and ideal mate, was a work of social camouflage, amiable because perfectly accommodating: "Sophy's mind is pleasing but not brilliant, and thorough but not deep; it is the sort of mind which calls for no remark, as she never seems cleverer or stupider than oneself" (Rousseau [1762] 1974, 358). Tenacious memory, vivid imagery, swift and surprising associations, brief attention span, penetrating intuitions, excessive curiosity, the aim to please and be pleased – for admirers and detractors alike, these allegedly feminine mental traits converged on polite learning, as opposed to solitary, technical study. Defenders of the female intellect praised its grace and iridescence, so well suited to the social exercise of conversation: "Indeed if one considers in what manner men and women produce what they know, one will judge that the men are like those workers who work tediously on wholly unformed, rough-hewn stones; and the women are like Architects, or clever Lapidaries who polish and easily work at their own good speed what they have in hand" (Poullain de la Barre [1673] 1984, 33). Detractors turned the same traits and images against women: "Is it not true that their [women's] impatience and natural desire to change, resulting from fleeting and rapid impressions, does not permit them to follow the same studies for years on end, and thus to acquire profound and vast knowledge? One knows that there are qualities of mind which exclude one another. The same hand cannot cut the diamond, and dredge the mine" (Thomas 1772, 116). Despite diametrically opposed views on the value of the female intellect, polemicists on both sides were largely united in believing there was such a thing, and in their characterizations of it.

Friend and foe were not only in basic agreement about the description of the female intellect and its complementarity to that of the male; they also mostly concurred as to its underlying causes. Although the principal seventeenth- and eighteenth-century explanations mostly tethered differences in mind to differences in body, the precise character of these latter differences changed during this period. Medieval complexion-based explanations were still common currency in the late seventeenth century, but they were gradually superseded in discussions of gender differences by appeals to the relative "delicacy" of female organs. Thus the Sieur de Saint-Gabriel called on the authority of "the Philosophers and the Doctors" to support his claim that because of the "tenuousness of their skin and the delicacy of their flesh" women had "more vivacity of understanding, having a more subtle imagination" (Saint-Gabriel 1660, 42). These feminist appeals to bodily delicacy were a bizarre twist on an ancient Aristotelian theme, namely the inferiority of matter to form (intimately linked to the soul and its faculties, in its Christian version). However, whereas Aristotle had quite pointedly identified matter with the female principle of generation, and form with that of the male, in *De generatione animalium* (738b18–30), the late seventeenth-century version of the distinction opposed the female to gross matter: "As for delicacy, apparently those who make this a subject of accusation to them [women] have not followed Aristotle's opinion: they would then have known that the most delicate temperament is the least charged with matter; the most pure and best suited to be penetrated by lights of the mind [*lumières de l'Esprit*]; the best prepared for beautiful images and the impression of the sciences" (Le Moyne 1660, 286).

The male trait complementing female delicacy was strength, both of body and of mind. Eighteenth-century writers intent on restricting the influence and educational opportunities of women converted "delicacy" into "weakness" and made it the key to the feminine character, intellect, and social situation. Thus jurists pronounced men "by the prerogative of their sex and by the force of their temperament" to be "naturally capable of all kinds of employments and engagements," while simultaneously excluding women, "due to the fragility of their sex and their natural delicacy" (d'Alembert and Diderot [1757] 1969, 1:1377, s.v. "Femme [Jurisprudence]"). Most authors traced female weakness to childbearing and child-care responsibilities (Poullain de la Barre [1673] 1984, 21–23; Thomas 1772, 129); Voltaire anomalously reversed the explanation – because women are weak, they stay at home to look after the children: "Little able to labour at the heavy work of masonry, carpentry, medalling, or the plough, they are necessarily entrusted with the lighter labours of the interior of the house, and above all, with the care of children" (Voltaire [1764] 1824, 390).

Whichever way the causal arrow pointed, and whatever the political sympathies of the author as to the justice of current social arrangements, there was wide consensus in the second half of the eighteenth century that woman's weakness relative to man was the grounds for her confinement to the home and subordination to her husband. Rousseau praised the wisdom of nature, which made female cunning – still, as for Aristotle, a standard part of the female intellect – the counterweight to male strength, without which "woman would be man's slave, not his helpmeet," but recognized that cunning alone could not rescue woman from a life of submission to the stronger man (Rousseau [1762] 1974, 334–35). Condorcet branded both the domestic subordination and political disenfranchisement of women unjust, but he was as convinced as Rousseau that because woman was "weaker than man, it is natural that she lead a more retired, more domestic life" (Condorcet [1790] 1847–49, 10.128).

The most elaborated medical version of the weakness thesis can be found in the work of Pierre Roussel, who literally bodied out Rousseau's claim that "the male is only a male now and again, the female is always a female, or at least all her youth; everything reminds her of her sex; the performance of her functions requires a special constitution" (Rousseau [1762] 1974, 324). According to Roussel, not only the reproductive organs, but also the skeleton, ligaments, tissues, nerves, and vessels are "marked by the differences that display the functions to which woman is called, and the passive state to which nature destines her." Female organs are, Roussel claimed, soft, delicate, small, and elastic in comparison to those of the male, and from this fundamental distinction he read off all the clichés of feminine intellect and character. The mobility and sensitivity of her tender organs endow woman with the ability to seize at a glance "an infinity of nuances, of items of detail, and relationships that escape the most enlightened man"; her morality is dictated by sentiment and compassion; her good memory, mental agility, and animated conversation repair the omissions of the long studies her fragile frame cannot support without draining her "vital forces" (Roussel [1775] 1809, 9, 17–19, 59–64).[10]

Almost none of the traits, moral or intellectual, that Roussel derived from his global anatomy of female frailty was new, nor was the anchoring of these traits in bodily constitution. Memory, imagination, intuition, and sociability dominated the female intellect, and compassion and docility the female character, just as thoroughly when they had been chalked up to a cold, moist complexion as when they were adduced from "cellular tissues." However, the doctrine of physical weakness, in conjunction with the ever more insistent emphasis on women's confinement to home and hearth because of that weakness, did ultimately reorient the complementarity between male and female intellects along a new axis, that of the abstract versus the concrete.

A limited sphere implied limited experience and limited activity, and experience and activity came to be seen as increasingly important to intellectual development in the last quarter of the eighteenth century. Even the old female bastions of memory and imagination could not withstand the call to broad experience and vigorous activity: the "sedentary and soft life" of women could at best foster an imagination of pretty scenes and tender emotions, but this paled beside the imagination of the "always active man . . . nourished on mountain peaks, at the edge of volcanoes, at sea, in battlefields, or in the midst of ruins" (Thomas 1772, 112–13). This particular vision of adventure elevating the poetic imagination owed much to the aesthetic of the sublime and was steeply slanted in favor of male talents. However, similar views can also be found in Mary Wollstonecraft's severely rational, ardently feminist *Vindication of the Rights of Women* some twenty years later. Wollstonecraft firmly rejected Rousseau's contention that nature intended a double standard of virtue for the two sexes, arguing that "the prevailing notion respecting a sexual character was subversive to morality." The appearances that spoke in favor of such distinct characters were in fact artifacts of women's neglected education and men's tyranny. Yet, although Wollstonecraft maintained that men and women were equally endowed with reason and therefore with the capacity for the same kind of virtue, she also conceded that because men were physically stronger, "they seem to be designed by Providence to attain a greater degree of virtue" (Wollstonecraft [1792] 1982, 21, 54, 68).

Nor did Wollstonecraft shrink from the association between bodily and mental vigor, thus challenging over a century's worth of feminist claims that male scholars, like women, were of a weak disposition (Le Moyne 1660, 286–87; Roussel [1775] 1809, 60–61): "I find that strength of mind has, in most cases, been accompanied by superior strength of body, – natural soundness of constitution, – not that robust tone of nerves and vigor of muscles which arise from bodily labour, when the mind is quiescent, or only directs the hands" (Wollstonecraft [1792] 1982, 91). Wollstonecraft admitted nature may have made women in general weaker than men in general, but she exhorted women at least not to exacerbate their frailty by inactivity, deluded by the conventional opinion that delicacy added to their charms. Activity and breadth of experience, particularly in childhood, were indispensable to the development of bodily and mental force, for girls as well as boys: "Most of the women, in the circle of my observation, who have acted like rational creatures, or shewn any vigour of intellect, have accidentally been allowed to run wild – as some of the elegant formers of the fair sex would have it" (ibid., 101).

The experience of women, confined as they were by their domestic duties, was necessarily narrowed to social relations, which taught them "effects and modifications" but not the "simple principles" yielded by the scientific study of nature (ibid., 61). Wollstonecraft would have nothing to do with those who argued that feminine debilities in virtue and intellect were irremediable – her dedicatory epistle to Talleyrand called for a national education in revolutionary France and elsewhere that would include women and correct these infirmities, to make women "more masculine and respectable" in both reason and virtue. However, in her description of these infirmities and her association of them with physical weakness and the narrow experience apparently dictated by that weakness, her views closely resembled those of such writers as Roussel and Cabanis, for whom sexual character admitted only of slight modification (Roussel [1775] 1809, 10).

Moreover, Wollstonecraft concurred with many late eighteenth- and early nineteenth-century writers on sex differences in underscoring how women's limited sphere barred them from the abstract, general principles necessary for science and for justice.[11] In the late eighteenth and early nineteenth centuries the age-old oppositions between female memory and imagination versus male discursive and speculative reason were reformulated and condensed into an opposition between the female grasp of concrete details and the male mastery of abstract principles. Kant for example firmly discouraged women from deep study in metaphysics and mathematics on the grounds that their "beautiful understanding [*schöner Verstand*]" was incompatible with "abstract speculations or knowledge, which are useful but dry" (Kant [1764] 1968, 230). Rousseau's formulation was characteristically peremptory: "The search for abstract and speculative truths, for principles and axioms in science, for all that tends to wide generalisation, is beyond a woman's grasp; . . . works of genius are beyond her reach, and she has neither the accuracy nor the attention for success in the exact sciences; as for the physical sciences, to decide the relations between living creatures and the laws of nature is the task of that sex which is more active and enterprising, which sees more things, that sex which is possessed of greater strength and is more accustomed to the exercise of that strength" (Rousseau

[1762] 1974, 349–50). Regardless of whether these authors thought the distinction corrigible or inevitable, regrettable or fortunate, they concurred in recognizing its existence and in interpreting it as a consequence of women's limited sphere, itself in turn a consequence of women's physical weakness.

It is at this point that the history of general intelligence and that of the female intellect cross decisively. Had the late eighteenth-century opposition between concrete details and general principles remained one of several oppositions, attached to the several mental faculties that distinguished the male from the female, it would have been only a minor variation on an ancient theme. However, in the middle decades of the nineteenth century, psychologists increasingly preferred a single, overarching intelligence to a mind crammed with disparate faculties. The defining property of this new, general intelligence was the ability to synthesize general principles from the teeming detail of experience. Thus, with the ascent of general intelligence the intellect effectively became masculinized to an unprecedented degree. Distinctively female mental abilities, like distinctively female virtues, had almost always been classified as abilities and virtues of the second magnitude. However, they had been abilities and virtues nonetheless. With the homogenization of the intellectual faculties into a single, all-purpose intelligence, and the identification of that intelligence with the capacity for extracting general principles from experiential particulars, the link between "female" and "intellect" was all but severed.

The new concept of general intelligence excluded not only women but also savages and children. Hippolyte Taine contended that children show merely animal intelligence until they are capable of "extracting, remarking, and connecting two abstract terms" and of rising from particulars to "simple and fixed laws" (Taine [1870] 1888, 2:245); Herbert Spencer claimed that women and the "smaller brained races" were typically enmired in first impressions, "incapable of balancing evidence" ([1855] 1966, 1:581). For Spencer, as for late eighteenth-century writers on sex differences, this penchant for the particular and the concrete among women, the uncultivated, and the uncivilized stemmed in part from limited experience: "While throughout the lower grades of human intelligence, the concrete objects and acts within a narrow range of experience are reproduced in thought, and the imagination is thus almost exclusively reminiscent, that development of the conceptions which we have traced, implying a continually-wider excursiveness of thoughts more numerous, more heterogeneous, more involved, and bound together more variously and less coherently, makes possible new combinations of thoughts." Those minds denied this "excursiveness" were also thereby denied "abstract conceptions" and "truths of higher generality" (ibid., 2:603–4; Spencer 1873).

For Spencer, limited experience was no longer the exclusive cause of inferior, concrete intelligence. Rather, it was one of several factors, combining with "underdeveloped nervous systems" and small brain size, to cramp intelligence (Gould 1981; Tedesco 1987, chaps. 3–6). Despite its similarity to late eighteenth-century discussions of male and female intellects at the descriptive level, Spencer's theory of intelligence unfolded within a different explanatory space, recognizably ordered along the division between nature and nurture. In Spencer this division had not yet solidified; he could still countenance hybrid use/disuse explanations, in which experience, both individual and racial, somehow enlarged the brain and fortified the nervous system. Nature and nurture, though now distinct terms, were not yet necessarily mutually exclusive. However, later theorists of intelligence such as Galton separated the two cleanly into either/or components, ultimately to be quantified by correlational statistics (Galton [1869] 1972, 26, 56; Mackenzie 1981, 171–75). Although Galton himself plumped for the nature side in the debate over the causes of natural ability, opponents on the nurture side were just as tightly wedged into the same explanatory framework. Since debates about intelligence, female and other, are still waged within this framework, we must return once again to the eighteenth-century discussion of male and female intellects in order to appreciate its contingency and novelty.

The changing nature of nature

At first glance, the eighteenth-century framework for explaining gender differences, including those of intellect, looks reassuringly familiar. "Nature" and "education" are regularly invoked, usually in opposition to each other. Moreover, "nature's" dictates are generally expressed by bodily facts – be those facts cold, moist humors, a wandering uterus, physical weakness, or soft organs and tissues. The exact relation between these "facts" and what they purportedly explained admitted of several possibilities: causal, functional, and/or analogical. In the case of female mental traits, for example, cold, moist humors *caused* heightened imagination and memory by a straightforward, if crude, material mechanism of imprinting sensations on brain matter; physical weakness *functioned* to form women for their duties as wives and mothers with a suitable intellect and character; soft, elastic tissues *analogized* compassionate, mutable minds. All three forms of explanation survived well into the nineteenth century: small, underdeveloped brains *caused* low female intelligence (Broca 1861, 152–54); superior male strength relative to competitors *functioned* to win females (Darwin 1870, 2:316–17); the "quiescent" ovum *analogized* the "more passive, conservative, sluggish, and stable" female metabolism and character (Geddes and Thomson [1889] 1901, 18, 289).

Yet despite these parallels, the natures of the mid-eighteenth and mid-nineteenth centuries were different entities, and appeals to the authority of nature consequently rested on different grounds. To simplify the contrast for the sake of clarity: early modern nature was benevolent, purposeful, and sovereign through enlightened assent; modern nature was indifferent, aimless, and sovereign through physical necessity. Early modern nature could serve as an explicit source of social values because openly value-laden; modern nature, only as an implicit source because amoral. Early modern nature was incapable of "hard" facts, in the sense of unpleasant truths that vitiate ethical norms, for nature and enlightened morality joined together in prearranged harmony. Modern nature abounded in bitter revelations about the illusions of ethics and social reform, for nature was ruthlessly amoral. This does not mean that modern depictions and invocations of nature were any less ideological than their early modern counterparts, only that the ideology was hidden behind a façade of studied neutrality. More precisely, the concept of ideology in the sense of naturalization became possible in the middle decades of the nineteenth century, for only then did the embedding of social norms in nature come to be seen as necessarily fraudulent.

The concept of natural law still current throughout the eighteenth century throws these contrasts into relief. European jurists inherited the concept of natural law from Roman law, but seventeenth- and eighteenth-century treatises on the subject simultaneously widened the legal and social significance of natural laws and deepened their justification.[12] Natural laws transcended and superseded statute laws in their universality and validity: "The most general Rule for Human Actions, that is, that [rule] which one must follow qua Reasonable Animal, is what one ordinarily calls the *Right of Nature,* or *Natural Law,* and which one also could call *Universal Law,* because all of human kind is bound to observe it, or *perpetual law,* because it is not subject to change, as Positive Laws are" (Pufendorf [1682] 1734, 1:192). The necessity of natural laws was that of mathematical demonstrations, for we come to know and accept natural laws because "Human Understanding has the ability to discover clearly and distinctly, in reflecting on the nature and the constitution of man, the necessity of conforming its conduct to natural laws" (ibid., 217). Natural laws commanded assent in much the same way that mathematical demonstrations did – by the coercion of reason, not that of physical constraint.

Thus natural laws were at once necessary and violable, while laws of nature, such as the laws of motion, were neither. The laws of nature were physically irrefragable but rationally on a par with the positive laws of human legislatures, for God might well have ordained others (d'Alembert and Diderot [1757] 1969, 3:200, s.v. "Raison [Logique]"). In contrast, the natural laws that governed society could muster all the force of reason behind them but were nonetheless broken daily. Neither self-evidence nor self-interest could compel unenlightened governments and/or their unen-

lightened subjects to square conduct with, for example, the natural necessity to form a peaceable society. Custom, ignorance, bad education, vice –
all conspired to silence, though not wholly to efface the "impression of the
eternal reason that governs the universe" engraved upon the human soul
(ibid., 2:685, s.v. "Loi naturelle").

Nature and education were thus sometimes paired as antagonists in
eighteenth-century writings, but they were also sometimes yoked together.
The "natural" was opposed to both the supernatural and the artificial,
but the opposition was not symmetric. The natural and supernatural were
mutually exclusive, separated in theory if not in practice by a sharp boundary. The natural and the artificial, however, could overlap, and the boundary between them was often blurred. In one sense, the artificial encompassed everything that required human labor (including, for example,
training in eloquence or an education in affability as well as handicrafts and
manufactures). But in another sense all objects, even man-made ones,
belonged to nature; and in yet a third sense, all of nature was potentially
artificial, waiting to be put to human use (ibid., 2:1006, s.v. "Naturel [Méta-
physique]").

Hence the relationship between the natural and the artificial in general,
and between nature and education (or upbringing) in particular, was never
so starkly complementary as that between nature and nurture. Even the
most ardent proponents of a female nature, grounded in anatomy and natural law, could not have posed a crisp either/or question about the relative
contributions of nature and education. First, female nature, like natural law,
could be intensified or diluted by education. Rousseau's most influential
pronouncements about female nature occur in the middle of a long treatise
on education: the young Sophy must be painstakingly reared in order to
realize her true nature as a woman. Hers was, to be sure, a highly circumscribed education, lest it corrupt that nature, "for to make woman our
superior in all the qualities proper to her sex, and to make her our equal in
all the rest, what is this but to transfer to the woman the superiority which
nature has given to her husband?" (Rousseau [1762] 1974, 345). Similarly,
the physician Roussel worried that the entire scheme of female anatomy
and physiology might be undermined by education and custom (Roussel
[1775] 1809, 21–22). Only in the nineteenth century did anatomy – and all
other "natural" endowments – become destiny; the hold of eighteenth-
century nature was feeble by comparison and all too easily subverted.

Attempts to subvert the dictates of nineteenth-century nature were
deemed futile; attempts to subvert those of eighteenth-century nature, perverse. Natural law not only bore the imprimatur of reason, it also displayed
the benevolent wisdom of the creator or of a pantheistic nature. Nowhere
was this smug teleology more blatant than in discussions of female nature
and the rights and duties derived therefrom. Just because the hold of natural

law on actual conduct was so precarious, needing to be propped up by education and voluntary submission, it was essential to underscore that the natural order was also the most desirable one: "You must follow nature's guidance if you would walk aright. The native characters of sex should be respected as nature's handiwork. . . . Nature herself has decreed that woman, both for herself and her children, should be at the mercy of man's judgment. . . . What is, is good, and no general law can be bad" (Rousseau [1762] 1974, 326; cf. d'Holbach 1773, 123, 135; Charlton 1984, 161–63). Nor was teleology restricted to the sphere of manners and morals; anatomy and physiology provided equally explicit examples of how the female body was ideally constructed for its natural tasks (Schiebinger 1986; Hoffmann 1977, 165).

In the final decades of the eighteenth century, the wise, provident face of nature began to harden, at least in France. Drawing on the writings of Diderot, d'Holbach, Laclos, and de Sade, A. E. Pilkington has argued that "a new use of the idea of nature emerges: nature is now argued to be ethically neutral and blindly amoral" (1986, 55). Neither teleology nor values disappeared from the natural sciences; however, they did go underground. The overt harmony between what is and what is good had dissolved into a dissonance between hard facts and utopian hopes. Nature no longer revealed to reason what should be; rather, nature set stern limits as to what could be. Indifferent to human concerns, and therefore incorruptibly neutral in human disputes, the new nature was also inexorable. The reasonable necessity of natural laws had given way to the physical constraint of laws of nature. Whether or not enlightened reason dictated, for example, that girls should receive the same educational opportunities as boys, the "hard facts" of inferior female intelligence pronounced the expenditure of effort and resources futile. The hallmark of nature coupled with nurture was that nurture was powerless to change nature. What belonged to nature and what to nurture was (and is) furiously debated; but once a trait was consigned to the natural, no human will could alter it. Justice no longer counted as an argument in the natural realm. Once a weapon for progressives or even radicals in the eighteenth century, the standard against which the social status quo could be measured and found wanting, nature was more often than not enlisted on the side of conservatism in the nineteenth century.

It is important to bear in mind three points concerning this transformation in the meaning of nature as they relate to debates about the nature of women. First, the old, sometimes even ancient claims, and the cultural values that underpinned them, were easily assimilated within the new framework. Despite protests of neutrality, nineteenth-century biologists and psychologists who studied gender differences often decked out the age-old platitudes, and the social attitudes that went with them, in the new scientific language of evolutionary theory, cell physiology, and mental measurement.

Indeed, these claims redoubled their force, now vaunted as neutral descriptions of an indifferent nature by disinterested scientists. Second, nineteenth-century expositors of the "laws of nature" governing gender roles were no more successful than eighteenth-century proponents of "natural laws" in eliminating disobedience. Although nature was now allegedly immune to the corruptions and corrections of nurture, the nineteenth-century literature on gender differences is strewn with stern reminders to women reformers to submit themselves to the laws of their nature, although there presumably should have been little choice in the matter. Third, the new categories of nature versus nurture as applied to gender differences owed little or nothing to the attempts of Roussel, Cabanis, and others to base these differences in anatomy and physiology. Materialist medical explanations had been a staple of the literature on gender differences since time immemorial; "inscribing" sexual difference in the body did not begin at the turn of the nineteenth century.

What was new was the interpretation of these "natural" differences as incommensurable with values and as immiscible with education. For the first time medical materialism implied medical determinism in this realm. Naturalization as a strategy of legitimation underwent a parallel transformation. Nature never relinquished its authority as last court of appeal, but its authority was now of a palpably different kind. It ruled no longer through the principle of sufficient reason or even through that of enlightened self-interest; it now ruled through the iron necessity of matter. Its decrees were no longer reasonable and tending to safeguard human welfare; they were indifferent to human values and ends. The chasm between nature and culture yawned wider than ever before, and attempts to bridge that chasm were policed more severely than ever before. Those who read the cultural into the natural stood accused of anthropomorphism and ideology; those who read the natural into the cultural, of scientism and reductionism. The modern understanding of naturalization depends on this fault line, and is read back into earlier historical geographies only at the peril of distortion.

Conclusion

What difference did these different senses of naturalization make? Naturalizers drew the boundaries between the natural and the nonnatural, and regulated the traffic across the frontier: eighteenth-century naturalizers distinguished sharply between the natural and the conventional but permitted the moral to pass freely between both realms, mingled the psychological with the somatic in both causal directions, and invoked education to correct or corrupt nature; nineteenth-century naturalizers barred the moral from the natural, made the body the causal substratum of character and intellect, and opposed obdurate nature to pliable nurture.

It is important to realize that although each of these forms of naturalization had a global political affinity, reformist or conservative, it was possible – indeed, inescapable – for both sides of a political debate to couch arguments in the terms dictated by the then reigning framework of naturalization. Not only did Wollstonecraft and Condorcet enlist nature to support their case for the educational and political emancipation of women; they invoked much the same image of nature that Rousseau and d'Holbach had in summoning women back to hearth and husband. Similarly, when John Stuart Mill in 1869 protested against the subordination of women, he understood "natural" capabilities in the same immutable sense that Galton (who was persuaded of the inferiority of women's intelligence) did. Hence Mill and other reformers were forced to argue either that the extent of such capabilities could not yet be fairly judged or that they were irrelevant for suffrage or other rights (Mill [1869] 1970, 190–91). Naturalization is not just the weapon of one or another side of a political controversy, nor is it always monopolized by conservatives. Rather, it is the framework within which all combatants must erect their positions and arguments if they hope to tap or circumvent the formidable authority of nature.

Why nature, however understood, should wield such authority in Western societies has yet to be explained satisfactorily. Very little comparative work, either cross-historical or cross-cultural, has been brought to bear on the assumption that nature's authority is always the highest, perhaps because the assumption has so long had the status of a self-evident truth. However, if the meanings of nature, and therefore the *kinds* of authority it radiates, change historically, there exist at least *prima facie* grounds to think that the *degree* of authority has also changed. Although it would be difficult to find a period in European history since the twelfth century when nature was not a concept to conjure with, particularly with regard to the nature of sexuality and the relations between the sexes (Brundage 1987, 7, 16, and passim), nature's authority, and consequently attempts at naturalization, seem to have been steadily increasing since the late seventeenth century. However, it would be premature to argue (a) that these changes took place abruptly, once and for all, or (b) that they were simple, direct consequences of the Scientific Revolution. *Pace* Alexandre Koyré and E. A. Burtt, meaning and value were not banished from nature, or even from natural philosophy, with the triumph of Newtonianism (Koyré 1957; Burtt [1924, 1932] 1954). When theologians sought the advice of natural philosophers in apologetics, as Richard Bentley did from Isaac Newton in drafting his Boyle Lectures, the bedrock of justification in society had indeed shifted decisively. But the causes of this shift, and the twists and turns of the subsequent history of naturalization, have yet to be charted.

The female intellect – and a good many other putatively female traits – had long been naturalized, but the import of that naturalization changed dramatically during the eighteenth and early nineteenth centuries. Without ever leaving the realm of the "natural," the specific justifications for these assertions changed as well. Anabolic metabolisms replaced cold, moist humors; sexual selection replaced the natural law of the jurists; brain size replaced physical delicacy. What did not change markedly was the content of these assertions, however diversely naturalized. The passages on sexual character in Darwin's *Descent of Man* differ little from eighteenth-century descriptions, opposing male energy and "inventive genius" to female compassion, imitation, and "powers of intuition" (Darwin 1870, 2:316, 326–27). Darwin's identification of these female faculties with "the lower races" was a characteristically nineteenth-century addition, but otherwise the description could have been taken from Rousseau.

Given that the content of the descriptions of the female intellect remained largely constant, and that the explanations (however these may have differed in their specifics) remained largely "natural," we can study the difference made by a shift in the meaning of naturalization for beliefs about the female intellect detached from these potentially conflating factors. One particularly sensitive index for detecting this difference is the portrayal of female intellectuals. Although their numbers were never large, there were women in early modern Europe who pursued lives of learning and who sometimes even made a living out of learning (Grafton and Jardine 1981; Schiebinger 1989, chaps. 2–3). Whether they enjoyed an international reputation, as did the physicists Emilie de Châtelet and Laura Bassi, or remained local celebrities (or notorieties), as did the astronomer Maria Winkelmann and the naturalist Maria Sibella Merian, these women confronted reigning beliefs about the female intellect with flesh-and-blood counterexamples. Nineteenth century writers on the female intellect had to deal not only with a somewhat larger group of such counterexamples but also, at least in the final decades of the century, with campaigns to open the universities to women. How did those who described and explained the female intellect respond to these challenges, and did the entrenched framework of naturalization matter to their responses?

Before surveying these responses by period, it should be made clear that almost no one welcomed the prospect of women deserting their familial duties in droves for the life of the mind. This claim holds true even for authors who believed that women were intellectually equal or superior in some respects to men. For example, Le Moyne collected scores of instances in which women throughout history had distinguished themselves in philosophy, government, religion, and even on the battlefield, and argued on physiological and theological grounds that women's intellectual parts were at least the equal of men's: "In all this it is certain that there is nothing which the mind of women cannot achieve, nothing is above their abilities, and the paths which nature has opened for them. Why would they not be as

capable as we of contemplation and of the sciences of speculative philosophy?" Yet Le Moyne protested that he did not thereby intend for women to
abandon domesticity, for "it is not my intention to call women to the
colleges . . . to exchange their needles and wools for astrolabes and
spheres. I respect the boundaries that separate us too well" (Le Moyne
1660, 285, 288–89). Even the most fiery eighteenth-century defenders of
women's educational and political rights, writing in the heat of the French
Revolution, respected these boundaries. Condorcet imagined that the political emancipation of women would in no way disturb the household status
quo; Wollstonecraft thought that education for women would make them
better wives and mothers (Condorcet [1790] 1847–49, 10:128; Wollstonecraft [1792] 1982, 114–16). More conservative writers were even more em-
phatic that a woman's place was in the home and that this precluded
strenuous intellectual activities (Jordanova 1986; Charlton 1984, 162–163). I
have been able to locate only one early modern source that followed the
logic of female intellectual equality to its practical conclusion, imagining
women as professors at universities, ministers in churches, magistrates in
courts, and generals commanding armies (Poullain de la Barre [1673] 1984,
57, 76ff.). For the most part, however, the learned woman was an object of
ridicule, at best useless and at worst a renegade who had deserted her
rightful duties. Molière could find no better way of damning the bluestock-
ing Armande in *Les Femmes savantes* (1672) than by having her scorn
marriage and children in favor of intellectual pursuits (Molière 1688, I:i).

It is important to distinguish these early modern responses to women
intellectuals from the debate about whether and how women should be
educated, and also from the controversy waged over the salons. Although
critics such as Molière often linked the *femmes savantes* to the salons, the
salonneuses were as persuaded as their enemies that the essence of the
female intellect was its sociability, its penchant for vivid details, its tenacious memory, its lightning imagination. The battle waged over the salons
was "not whether women should become scholars, but whether women
should continue to play their [political] role in the salons" (Lougee 1976,
30). In what follows, I shall be concerned with responses only to those
learned women whose interests ran counter to beliefs about the strengths of
the female intellect. Many critics who puzzled or ranted over a woman's
taste for, say, metaphysics might well have strongly recommended that she
be educated in some other, more appropriate discipline, such as moral
philosophy. Women novelists who probed the psyche and anatomized morals and manners were seldom the target of such attacks.

At the heart of the early modern response to the learned woman was the
sense of the denatured, variously expressed as absurdity, revulsion, or
wonder. The French fabulist La Bruyère compared the learned woman to
an exquisitely carved firearm, useless except as a curious "pièce de cabinet"

(La Bruyère [1688] 1693, 148). Kant thought the accomplishments of "learned ladies" worse than useless – "they might awaken a certain cold admiration by dint of rarity, but will at the same time weaken the charms which give them sway over the opposite sex" – and freakish to boot, like the bearded woman at the fair (Kant [1764] 1968, 229). Neither Kant nor La Bruyère doubted the authenticity of the achievements of these female prodigies. But both found something ludicrous in the very notion of the woman intellectual, a certain comical inappropriateness in a woman's serious interest in Greek philology or the foundations of mechanics (Kant explicitly mocked the classicist Dacier and the physicist du Châtelet), when she might instead have dabbled in the more feminine fields of belles lettres and geography. The impression of absurdity was heightened by the apparent futility of such studies: If women were destined never to leave the home, queried these critics, what possible use could such learning be to them or to anyone else?

For those who could only too well imagine women forsaking the bosom of the family for the glittering conversation of the salon or, still worse, for solitary scholarship, the woman intellectual was not merely absurd but revolting. The French physician Cabanis thought intense intellectual work to be incompatible with femininity: "She [woman] is rightly frightened by mental work . . . ; she chooses that which demands more tact than science, more imagination than reasoning" (quoted in Hoffmann 1977, 165). The woman who defied these "natural" preferences thereby perverted her nature and became monstrous. The denatured female intellect here took on darker colors, those of the things and acts branded *contra naturam* and therefore morally loathsome. This response to the woman intellectual drew on the deep moral reserves still present in Enlightenment conceptions of nature, ultimately rooted in medieval Christian sexual taboos (Brundage 1987, 212–13, 286–87, 533, 571; Boswell 1981, 312–13).

In some contexts the woman intellectual could evoke more positive associations, if her sheer rarity was uppermost in the response. In the early modern period a learned woman capable of conversing with male scholars on their own terms was always an anomaly, and anomalies could be interpreted as wonders as well as abominations, as *praeter naturam* as well as *contra naturam*. The Bolognese physicist Laura Bassi seems to have fallen into this category of wonders, crowned with laurels (sometimes literally) at home by leading citizens bent on making her a symbol of Bologna's cultural aspirations, and admired abroad by such as Voltaire (Elena 1991). Yet the very magnitude of Bassi's reputation and the honors heaped on her underscored her status as prodigy rather than as woman intellectual. Bassi's career as professor of philosophy at the University of Bologna and member of the Istituto delle Scienze was almost sui generis for the period,[13] never intended as a model for more than a handful of other learned women – if for no other reason than that such imitators would have destroyed Bassi's title to uniqueness, to near miraculous status.

Moreover, the highly ceremonial existence that Bassi led was, as Paula Findlen has shown, redolent of ancient mythological associations, routinely apostrophizing her as "most learned virgin" or even as the virgin goddess Minerva, not to mention the obligatory comparisons to various muses (Findlen forthcoming). By transforming Bassi into a living allegory, her admirers at home and abroad intensified the aura of the wondrous. That her fame throughout the Enlightenment Republic of Letters was owed mostly to this aura rather than to her international influence can be concluded from her meager record of publications outside of Bologna (Elena 1991, 514–16). Learned women who also happened to be of royal blood, such as Princess Elizabeth of Bohemia and Queen Christina of Sweden, also partook of the wondrous, their rank and accomplishments admitting them into the realm of the preternatural and the admirable rather than that of the unnatural and the abhorrent.

Whether absurd, monstrous, or wondrous, the denatured woman intellectual of the late seventeenth and eighteenth centuries was never impossible. Until the final decades of the eighteenth century, it was the appropriateness not the authenticity of such pursuits that called down laughter, shock, or wonder. This is wholly in keeping with a framework of naturalization that was materialist without being determinist or amoral. Physician though he was, Cabanis was still willing to accept the existence, if not the desirability, of women intellectuals, without thereby calling into question the anatomy that should have inclined the entire sex in other directions. Enlightenment critics may have bemoaned the misguided education that had fitted a woman for natural philosophy or philology, but they were all too conscious that such unnatural upbringings were possible – and therefore to be reproached all the more severely. For the sternest of these writers, to stray from the course of nature was a matter of moral lassitude but not of miracles. In those few cases in which women intellectuals counted as wonders rather than as absurdities or abominations, they were treated as benign marvels, akin to the aurora borealis or a volcano, rare and unexplained but still credible.

Not so within the more rigid framework of mid-nineteenth-century naturalization, in which the prevailing tone was one of skepticism or paradox. Once "natural laws" had hardened into "laws of nature," violations could no longer be a matter for reprimand but only for incredulity. When the violation was too well attested to be simply dismissed out of hand, as in the case of the novelist George Sand or the chemist Marie Curie, critics insinuated that all genuine achievement could be traced back to male lovers and/or associates (Slama 1980, 213–43; Pycior 1987, 191–215). Cesare Lombroso, in his study of genius, doubted a priori whether women, who like children were "notoriously misoneistic," could ever muster the originality required to inaugurate new movements in art, science, or politics. The rare exceptions were, according to the inexorable logic of the new naturalization, disqualified as women: "Even the few [genial women] who emerge have, on near examination, something virile about them. As Goncourt said, there are no women of genius; the women of genius are men" (Lombroso [1888] 1891, 138). This retreat to paradox was a perfectly consistent response to exceptions within the nineteenth-century framework of naturalization, which demanded that exceptions be at all costs either discredited or reclassified. The denatured woman intellectual had become an impossibility.

Frameworks of naturalization may sometimes ascribe necessity to nature, but they themselves are contingent creatures of history. The conditions for their rise and fall, their longevity and modification have barely been granted existence, much less attracted investigation. The example I have sketched here – that quite similar beliefs about the female intellect could be differently naturalized – is more a kinematics than a dynamics of such a history, contrasting end states rather than unearthing causes. It is meant more as an existence proof by instantiation than as a full-dress account even of this brief episode in the history of naturalization. Naturalizations come in the plural, and their varieties matter to how and why the social and the natural come to be fused in specific instances. Without making frameworks of naturalization themselves objects of investigation, as well as engines of explanation, we cannot understand what "the authority of nature" meant and means, much less the sources of its power.

Acknowledgments

I would like to thank Mitchell Ash, Gerd Gigerenzer, and an anonymous reader for their comments on an earlier version of this essay. Much of the research for this paper was conducted at the Center for Advanced Study in the Behavioral Sciences, Stanford, with the help of NSF Grant DIR-8911169: I am grateful for both hospitality and support.

Notes

1 Among recent book-length studies at the intersection of history of science and history of gender, see Lloyd 1983; Keller 1985; Jordanova 1989; Schiebinger 1989; Russet 1989.
2 On the early history of intelligence measurements and mental testing, see Peterson 1925, chap. 5; Sokal 1987.
3 As far as the connection between intelligence and sex was concerned, male and female intelligences were virtually defined as equal in the revision of the Stanford-Binet test (Terman and Merrill [1916] 1937, 22, 34). For discussions and criticisms of recent psychological research on sex differences in intelligence, see Macoby and Jacklin [1966] 1974; Bleier 1988; Fausto-Sterling 1985, 13–60.

4 Unless otherwise noted, translations are my own.

5 Although a controversial passage in Aristotle's *De generatione animalium* (775a9–20) suggesting that women were monsters excited some comment, no one seems to have seriously doubted their humanity and therefore their possession of a rational soul; see Maclean 1977, 8–9; also Castiglione [1528] 1967, 219–20, for a firm refutation of the imperfection view.

6 On the *Querelle des Femmes* in general, see Maclean 1977, 35–48.

7 On the Renaissance and early modern influence of this passage, see Maclean 1977, 11; 1980, 41.

8 On the importance of the polarity structure in classical thought, see Lloyd 1966; on the relation of Aristotle's views on sex differences to ancient Greek society, see Lloyd 1983, 94–105; on how quantification ultimately dissolved the polarity between male and female intelligence, see Daston 1989.

9 See also Algarotti 1739, lvii–lviii, which aimed "to polish and ornament society, instead of drying out the mind." On seventeenth-century attempts by scientific academies to reform boorish scholastic manners, see Shapin 1988, 1991; Daston 1992.

10 See Hoffmann 1977, 130–56, for a full discussion of Enlightenment theories of female physiology.

11 Cf. Kant's distinction between *äoptierte* and *echte Tugend* as it parallels the distinction between *schöner* and *edeler Verstand,* in Kant [1764] 1968, 217–20, 228–43.

12 On the natural law tradition in early modern jurisprudence, see Gierke 1934.

13 Bologna had some tradition, perhaps in part legendary, of women taking degrees and instructing students: Maria Delfini Dosi took a law degree there in 1722; Christina Roccati Rodigina, a medical degree in 1751; Maria Gaetana Agnesi was offered an honorary chair in mathematics in 1750; Clotilde Tambroni became professor of Greek in 1790: See Findlen forthcoming.

References

Agrippa, Henry Cornelius. [1566] 1670. *Female Pre-Eminence: Or the Dignity and Excellence of That Sex, above the Male,* translated by H[enry] C[are]. London.

d'Alembert, Jean, and Denis Diderot, eds. [1757] 1969. *Encyclopédie, ou Dictionnaire raisonné des sciences, des arts et des métiers.* Vols. 1–35. Paris: Chez Briasson. Compact edition. 5 vols. New York: Readex Microprint.

Algarotti, F. 1739. *Le Newtonianisme pour les dames, ou entretiens sur la lumière, sur les couleurs, et sur l'attraction,* translated from Italian by Du Perron de Castera. Paris: Montalant.

Aristotle. See Barnes 1984.

Ascoli, Georges. 1906. "Essai sur l'histoire des idées féministes en France, du XVIᵉ siècle à la Révolution." *Revue de synthèse historique* 13:25–183.

Baasner, Frank. 1986. "The Changing Meaning of 'Sensibilité': 1654 till 1704." *Studies in Eighteenth-Century Culture* 15:77–96.

Barnes, Jonathan, ed. 1984. *The Complete Works of Aristotle.* Revised Oxford translation, 2 vols. Princeton: Princeton University Press.

Binet, A. 1898. "La Mesure en psychologie individuelle." *Revue philosophique* 46:113–23.

Bleier, Ruth. 1988. "Sex Differences Research: Science or Belief?" In *Feminist Approaches to Science,* edited by R. Bleier, 147–64. New York: Pergamon.

Boswell, John. 1981. *Christianity, Social Tolerance, and Homosexuality.* Chicago: University of Chicago Press.

Broca, P. 1861. "Sur le volume et la forme du cerveau suivant les individus et suivant les races." *Bulletin de la Société d'Anthropologie de Paris* 2:139–207.

Brundage, James A. 1987. *Law, Sex, and Christian Society in Medieval Europe.* Chicago: University of Chicago Press.

Burtt, E. A. [1924, 1932] 1954. *The Metaphysical Foundations of the Modern Sciences.* Garden City, N.Y.: Doubleday/Anchor.

Castiglione, Baldesar. [1528] 1967. *The Book of the Courtier,* translated by George Bull. Harmondsworth: Penguin.

Charlton, D. G. 1984. *New Images of the Natural in France: A Study in European Cultural History 1750–1800.* Cambridge: Cambridge University Press.

Condorcet, M. A. J. N. [1790] 1847–49. "Sur l'admission des femmes au droit de cité." In *Oeuvres,* 15 vols., edited by A. Condorcet-O'Connor and F. Arago. Paris: Firmin Didot Frères.

Cox, Catharine Morris. 1926. *The Early Mental Traits of Three Hundred Geniuses.* Stanford: Stanford University Press.

Darwin, Charles. 1870. *The Descent of Man, and Selection in Relation to Sex,* 2 vols. London: John Murray.

Daston, Lorraine. 1989. "Weibliche Intelligenz: Geschichte einer Idee." In *Jahrbuch des Wissenschaftskollegs zu Berlin 1987/88,* edited by Wolf Lepenies, 213–29. Berlin: Nicolaische Buchhandlung.

———. 1992. "Baconian Facts, Academic Civility, and the Prehistory of Objectivity." *Annals of Scholarship* 8.

Elena, Alberto. 1991. " 'In Lode della Filosofessa di Bologna': An Introduction to Laura Bassi." *Isis* 82:510–18.

Fausto-Sterling, Anne. 1985. *Myths of Gender: Biological Theories about Women and Men.* New York: Basic Books.

Findlen, Paula. Forthcoming. "Science as a Career in Enlightenment Italy: The Strategies of Laura Bassi (1711–1778)." In *Gender and Scientific Patronage,* edited by Pnina Abir-Am, Dorinda Outram, and Londa Schiebinger. New Brunswick, N.J.: Rutgers University Press.

Galton, Francis. [1869] 1972. *Hereditary Genius: An Inquiry into Its Laws and Consequences.* Gloucester, Mass.: Peter Smith. Reprint of 2nd ed. of 1892.

Geddes, Patrick, and J. Arthur Thomson. [1889] 1901. *The Evolution of Sex,* rev. ed. London: Walter Scott.

Gierke, Otto. 1934. *Natural Law and the Theory of Society 1500–1800,* translated by Ernest Barker. Cambridge: Cambridge University Press.

Gould, Stephen Jay. 1981. *The Mismeasure of Man.* New York: Norton.

Gournay, Marie de. 1622. *Egalité des hommes et des femmes.* N.p.

Grafton, Anthony, and Lisa Jardine. 1981. *From Humanism to the Humanities.* Cambridge, Mass.: Harvard University Press.

Hippel, Theodor Gottlieb von. [1792] 1979. *On Improving the Status of Women,* translated and edited by Timothy F. Sellner. Detroit: Wayne State University Press.

Hoffmann, Paul. 1977. *La Femme dans la pensée des lumières.* Paris: Editions Ophrys.

d'Holbach, Baron Thierry. 1773. *Système social, ou Principes naturels de la morale et de la politique avec un examen de l'influence du gouvernement sur les mœurs,* 3 vols. London.

Jordanova, Ludmilla. 1986. "Naturalizing the Family: Literature and Bio-Medical Sciences in the Late Eighteenth Century." In *Languages of Nature: Critical Essays on Science and Literature,* edited by Ludmilla Jordanova, 86–116. London: Free Association Books.

———. 1989. *Sexual Visions: Images of Gender in Science and Medicine between the Eighteenth and Twentieth Centuries.* Madison: University of Wisconsin Press.

Kant, Immanuel. [1764] 1968. *Beobachtungen über das Gefühl des Schönen und Erhabenen.* In *Kants Werke,* 9 vols., edited by the Königliche Preussische Akademie der Wissenschaften, 2:205–56. Berlin: Walter de Gruyter.

Keller, Evelyn Fox. 1985. *Reflections on Gender and Science.* New Haven: Yale University Press.

Kelso, Ruth. 1956. *Doctrine for the Lady of the Renaissance.* Urbana: University of Illinois Press.

Koyré, Alexandre. 1957. "The Significance of the Newtonian Synthesis." In his *Newtonian Studies*, 3–24. Cambridge, Mass.: Harvard University Press.

La Bruyère, Jean de. [1688] 1693. *Les Charactères de Théophraste traduits du Grec, avec les charactères ou les mœurs de ce siècle*, 7th ed. Brussels.

Le Moyne, Pierre. 1660. *La Gallerie des femmes fortes*. Leyden: Elsevier.

Lloyd, G. E. R. 1966. *Polarity and Analogy: Two Types of Argumentation in Early Greek Thought*. Cambridge: Cambridge University Press.

   1983. *Science, Folklore and Ideology*. Cambridge: Cambridge University Press.

Lloyd, Geneviève. 1984. *The Man of Reason. "Male" and "Female" in Western Philosophy*. London: Methuen.

Lombroso, Cesare. [1888] 1891. *The Man of Genius*. London.

Lougee, Carolyn C. 1976. *Le Paradis des Femmes. Women, Salons, and Social Stratification in Seventeenth-Century France*. Princeton, N.J.: Princeton University Press.

Mackenzie, Donald. 1981. *Statistics in Britain 1865–1930: The Social Construction of Scientific Knowledge*. Edinburgh: Edinburgh University Press.

Maclean, Ian. 1977. *Woman Triumphant: Feminism in French Literature 1610–1652*. Oxford: Oxford University Press.

   1980. *The Renaissance Notion of Woman*. Cambridge: Cambridge University Press.

Macoby, Eleanor, and Carol Nagy Jacklin. [1966] 1974. *The Psychology of Sex Differences*. Stanford: Stanford University Press.

Mill, John Stuart. [1869] 1970. *The Subjection of Women*. In *Essays on Sex Equality by John Stuart Mill and Harriet Taylor Mill*, edited by Alice S. Rossi. Chicago: University of Chicago Press.

Molière [Jean-Baptiste Poquelin]. 1688. *Les Femmes savantes*. Paris: E. Michellet.

Olivier, Jacques [Alexis Rousset]. [1617] 1646. *Alphabet de l'imperfection et malice des femmes*, rev. ed. Rouen: Iean Berthelin.

Peterson, Joseph. 1925. *Early Conceptions and Tests of Intelligence*. London: George G. Harrap.

Pilkington, A. E. 1986. "Nature as Ethical Norm in the Enlightenment." In *Languages of Nature: Critical Essays on Science and Literature*, edited by Ludmilla Jordanova, 51–85. London: Free Association Books.

Poullain de la Barre, François. [1673] 1984. *De l'Egalité des deux sexes*. Paris: Fayard.

Pufendorf, Samuel. [1682] 1734. *Le Droit de la nature et des gens, ou Système général des principes les plus importans de la morale, de la jurisprudence, et de la politique*, 2 vols., translated from Latin by Jean Barbeyrac. Amsterdam.

Pycior, Helena M. 1987. "Marie Curie's 'Anti-natural Path': Time Only for Science and Family." In *Uneasy Careers and Intimate Lives: Women in Science, 1789–1979*, edited by Pnina Abir-Am and Dorinda Outram, 191–215. New Brunswick, N.J.: Rutgers University Press.

Reid, Thomas. [1785] 1969. *Essays on the Intellectual Powers of Man*, edited by Baruch A. Brady. Cambridge, Mass.: MIT Press.

Rousseau, Jean-Jacques. [1762] 1974. *Emile*, translated by Barbara Foxley. London: Dent.

Roussel, Pierre. [1775] 1809. *Système physique et moral de la femme*, 5th ed. Paris.

Russet, Cynthia Eagle. 1989. *Sexual Science: The Victorian Construction of Womanhood*. Cambridge, Mass.: Harvard University Press.

Saint-Gabriel, Sieur de. 1660. *Le Mérite des dames*, 3rd ed. Paris.

Schiebinger, Londa. 1986. "Skeletons in the Closet: The First Illustration of the Female Skeleton in Eighteenth-Century Anatomy." *Representations* 14:42–82.

   1989. *The Mind Has No Sex? Women in the Origins of Modern Science*. Cambridge, Mass.: Harvard University Press.

Schurman, Anna Maria von. 1641. *Dissertatio, de ingenii mulieris ad doctrinam, & meliores litteras aptitudine*. Lugd. Batavor: Elsevier.

Shapin, Steven. 1988. "The House of Experiment in Seventeenth-Century England." *Isis* 79:373–404.

1991. " 'A Scholar and a Gentleman': The Problematic Identity of the Scientific Practitioner in Early Modern England." *History of Science* 29:279–327.

Slama, Béatrice. 1980. "Femmes écrivains." In *Misérable et glorieuse: La Femme du XIXe siècle,* edited by Jean-Paul Aron, 213–43. Paris: Fayard.

Sokal, Michael, ed. 1987. *Psychological Testing and American Society 1890–1930.* New Brunswick, N.J.: Rutgers University Press.

Spencer, Herbert. [1855] 1966. *The Principles of Psychology,* 2 vols. Osnabrück: Otto Zeller. Reprint of 3rd ed. of 1899.

1873. "The Psychology of the Sexes." *Popular Science Monthly* 4:30–38.

Taine, Hyppolyte. [1870] 1888. *De l'Intelligence,* 5th ed., 2 vols. Paris: Hachette.

Tedesco, Marie. 1987. *Science and Feminism: Conceptions of Female Intelligence and Their Effects on American Feminism, 1859–1920.* Ph.D. diss., Georgia State University.

Terman, Lewis A., and Maud A. Merrill. [1916] 1937. *Measuring Intelligence: A Guide to the Administration of the New Revised Stanford-Binet Tests of Intelligence.* Cambridge, Mass.: Riverside Press.

Thomas, Antoine Léonard. 1772. *Essai sur le caractère, les mœurs et l'esprit des femmes dans les différens siècles.* Paris: Moutard.

Voltaire, François Arouet de. [1764] 1824. "Women." In *A Philosophical Dictionary,* 2nd ed. London: John and Henry L. Hunt.

Wollstonecraft, Mary. [1792] 1982. *A Vindication of the Rights of Woman: Strictures on Political and Moral Subjects,* edited by Ulrich H. Hardt. Troy, N.Y.: Whiston.

Suzanne R. Kirschner

As Kenneth Gergen and his colleagues have reminded us, the correspondence of psychological theory with empirical fact is tenuous and problematic.[1] The psychological theories we construct are heavily laced with long-standing concerns, patterns, and images that are not derived from empirical observation. If this is the case, then surely one of the main purposes of a metapsychology is to study psychological theory as a means of illuminating the concerns and values that are most compelling to us as a culture. In exploring the theoretical frameworks currently in use, and the broad cultural lineages from which they are derived, we thus can learn a great deal about ourselves. As cultural documents, contemporary theories of human nature and development may be analyzed in terms of how they embody past and present ways in which we have constructed the dilemmas of existence and attempted to resolve them.

Few themes are more long-standing and pervasive in Judeo-Christian culture areas than that of an anticipated salvation or redemption from the woes and imperfections of human life. It is perhaps not surprising, therefore, that this concern continues to inform the assumptions and aspirations we bring to psychological theory to this day. In this chapter, I explore the persistence of the theme of redemption in psychoanalytic developmental psychology. By "psychoanalytic developmental psychology" I refer to three interrelated psychoanalytic schools or loosely affiliated groups of theorists under the broader umbrella of "psychoanalysis." These are ego psychology, object relations theory, and self psychology. All of these psychoanalytic theories trace the development of the ego and/or the self and its way of relating to "objects" (usually other persons), whether in actual interpersonal interaction or in intrapsychic fantasy. In contrast to classical psychoanalytic theory, in which the primary imperative of development is instinctual renunciation, the essential imperative of development in these post-Freudian theories is seen to be separation and individuation.[2] First I briefly review the work of several developmental psychologists who highlight the theological origins of the idea of development in nonanalytic psychology. Then I explore the question of whether the psychoanalytic narrative of development partakes of the same cultural lineage. I suggest that it, too, bears the imprint of a Judeo-Christian religious heritage. However, while cognitive-developmental psychology and other nonpsychoanalytic developmental theories draw mainly upon Enlightenment and evolutionist transmutations of religious doctrines, the psychoanalytic narrative owes more to the Romantic secularization of the Biblical historical design.

Theological sources of the idea of development

During the past two decades, several eminent developmental psychologists – including William Kessen,[3] Sheldon White,[4] and Bernard Kaplan[5] – have brought to our attention the fact that the idea of development in developmental psychology evinces a theological ancestry. They have pointed out that there are certain assumptions about the direction and ends of change from infancy to adulthood that are derived from the story of mankind's history and destiny as told in the Bible. They emphasize two assumptions in particular. First, Biblical history is prospectivist. It is infused with the salvationist assumption that the best is yet to be, that man is destined for a future of moral and material well-being. Second, the Biblical narrative evinces an eschatological orientation. In other words, there is a belief that the historical process necessarily moves toward this ameliorated end. This eschatological vision has been translated into the concept of teleology in psychology.

These scholars have highlighted the fact that Biblical history was translated into secular form in Enlightenment beliefs about reason and progress, and in subsequent nineteenth-century philosophies of history and social evolutionist schemes (which wedded the emergent scientific authority of biological evolution to the neoeschatology of teleology). It was via translation into these secular theories, then, that Biblical prospectivism and eschatology came to influence the child study and protodevelopmentalist movements that emerged in the final decades of the nineteenth century.

In their discussions of the theological sources of developmental theory, these psychologists refer mainly to cognitive-developmental and organismic paradigms (Kessen includes behaviorism as well), but Kessen and Kaplan also consider psychoanalytic theory to be an heir to Biblical eschatology and prospectivism. Thus, Kaplan argues:

Freud and Jung both assumed an immanent telos of development – a movement toward genitality or toward individuation – and both worked or claimed to work to remove certain factors inhibiting the relative attainment of such relatively advanced modes of being-in-the-world. Unfortunately, these two great minds were inclined to take their teloi as immanent in the biographical-historical process: ineluctable, if only the inhibiting forces could be overcome. Freud was, of course, far more pessimistic than Jung concerning the possibility of eliminating the inhibiting forces, and thus his teleological assumption is less obvious.[6]

It is true that psychoanalytic theories partake of the basic developmentalist assumption that the psychological maturity normally characteristic of adulthood is a higher, more advanced, more developed state than childish immaturity, which is more or less equated with primitivity. We also can ascertain a teleological element in psychoanalytic theory, both in the psychosexual movement toward genitality and (most notable in post-Freudian theories) in the movement toward individuation. Phylogenesis as well as ontogenesis moves in this direction toward greater rationality and civilization. This assumption is present in Freudian metapsychology, as well as in those post-Freudian schools known as ego psychology, object relations theory, and self psychology. In a sense, then, psychoanalysis is "prospectivist" in the tradition of Biblical history and its Enlightenment and evolutionist descendants.

Yet, although the developmental trajectory in psychoanalytic theory (whether psychosexual or ego-developmental) certainly evinces this inbuilt teleology, and hence can be read as Kaplan reads it, nevertheless there is a significant difference between psychoanalytic developmental psychology and other developmentalisms. In order to highlight this discrepancy, we must look more closely at the theories' respective depictions of the ends of the developmental process.

Kaplan has defined developmental psychology as

a practico-theoretical discipline . . . concerned with the perfection (including the liberation or freedom) of the individual. Its aim is to facilitate development . . . as an ideal movement toward freedom, autonomy, individuation, liberation from the various forms of bondage, external and internal.[7]

In this definition, I read the assertion that "perfection" in this developmental sense is strongly linked to the attainment of autonomy. "Autonomy," in turn, is used as a word that has several different senses: a movement toward greater rationality (i.e., the perfecting of one's capacity to apprehend ontological and moral truth), a movement toward greater individuation and independence, and – perhaps as a consequence of these two – a movement toward freedom from external constraint and internal conflict. Additionally, the end state of development (e.g., the perfected capacity to reason) seems to be conceptualized as unitary, untroubled by conflict or qualification (at least in principle).

Do contemporary psychoanalytic theories of development conform to this vision? Post-Freudian psychoanalytic theories which trace the development of the ego and/or the self and its modes of relating to objects also tell a story of psychological development. Yet in these theories we find descriptions of the highest developmental achievements that are framed in quite different terms from those described earlier. In order to understand how the psychoanalytic developmental trajectories diverge from those depicted in the other theories, let us take a close look at one such trajectory and then pay particular attention to its end.

Theories of ego psychology, object relations, and self psychology all chronicle an allegedly necessary and universal sequence. Over the course of development, the individual's sense of distinctiveness and individual identity develops out of an original state in which it experiences a sense of omnipotence that is concomitant to its actual situation of extreme dependence. Margaret Mahler (1897–1985), an ego psychologist whose "separation–individuation" theory is one of the most influential and lucid of these theories, called the infant's initially undifferentiated psychic state "symbiosis." She defined it as "hallucinatory or delusional omnipotent somatopsychic fusion with the representation of the mother and, in particular, the delusion of a common boundary between two physically separate individuals."[8] In Mahler's trajectory, which in this respect is representative of the entire family of post-Freudian theories, the infant is propelled in the direction of self-consciousness by two factors. One of these is an innate drive for and toward individuation (i.e., the autonomous exercise of its capacities and functions), and the other is simply his growing awareness of the problematic and often disappointing and frustrating nature of reality itself, as experienced in his own powerlessness to have all his wishes fulfilled. The overall task of development is to come to terms both with one's separateness and with the conflicting desires one feels for both individuation and a return to symbiotic fusion. These conflicts and contradictions are seen to be a permanent part of the human situation and character. Although a provisional balance between them is supposed to be struck by the age of 3, they are seen to flare up again particularly strongly during adolescence. And it is only as this later developmental period's crises and struggles begin to subside that a mature sense of individual identity, and the interpersonal capacities necessary for mature intimacy, are attained. Even then, these accomplishments are considered to be approximate and a matter of degree, rather than the enduring attainment of an absolute.

It is true that these psychoanalytic theories do not deny that autonomy – that is, individuation and rationality – is a necessary and central aspect of development. Yet their descriptions of the course and ends of development offer a rather more tempered vision, one in which there is an appreciation of the fact that autonomy and rationality always stand in tension with opposing tendencies and longings. According to this vision, the most developed forms of maturity entail an integration of both "progressive" and "regressive" tendencies: of individuation and fusion, rationality and impulse. In the most abstract sense, the highest development is considered, in these theories, to evince a reintegration of severed elements – most notably of subject and object – at a higher level than that of the original undifferentiated unity. Most often, this occurs in a "relationship" that preserves the

self's individuation and ego functions but also expresses and partially grati-
fies the psyche's opposing tendencies and longings.

What, then, can be said about the ends of development in Mahler's
narrative? At first glance, they seem to be similar to those voiced by
Kaplan. Certainly one crucial end is indicated by the name of Mahler's
theory: *separation and individuation*. Psychoanalytic developmental psychologists assert that the development of an enduring sense of separate
selfhood – of independence and self-direction – is an absolutely essential
aspect of maturity. *Rationality* also is valued as an end of development: All
of these psychoanalytic theories partake of the Freudian tenet that the
improved rationality and enhanced insight of the strengthened ego endow
the individual with a bit more control and freedom, and hence the capacity
for greater satisfaction of her needs, if not her fantasies. There is a teleological aspect to these theories as well – for example, in Mahler's notion that
individuation strivings are innately programmed into the individual. So far,
then, the ends of development in these psychoanalytic theories seem similar
or analogous to the ends of development as I described them for the nonpsychoanalytic developmental theories.

Yet the maturity that they conceptualize actually is more complex than
this. This is a vision of human development in which the self – even if
manifestly at a pinnacle of autonomy, self-reliance, and rationality – is
always beset by opposing tendencies and inclinations, tendencies that are
not eradicated but rather stand perennially in tension with these manifestly
"desirable" ends. According to psychoanalytic metapsychology (beginning
with Freud), the human condition is essentially a tragic one. This is so for
several reasons. First, by nature the human being has within him conflicting
tendencies, wishes, and needs. Second, the longings and fantasies that
originate *within* the individual psyche inevitably clash with certain imperatives of physical and social reality. Third, these conflicts and tensions
continue to impinge upon (indeed, they constitute) the human character
from birth to death, from psychological immaturity to psychological maturity.

What this means is that nothing – not maturity, not insight, neither
nature nor reason – can ever entirely eradicate this tragic dimension. Even
manifestly unconflicted and unproblematic rational functioning, even the
attainment of subjective states of satisfaction and joy, even the highest
moral judgments and acts, entail compromise and renunciation, a balancing
of so-called antisocial instincts and tendencies with opposing inclinations
and imperatives. Civilization would not *be* civilization without its discontents.

For Mahler and the other post-Freudians, the tragic story is less about
impulses and instincts than about the boundaries and limitations of the
other's powers and of one's own, of splits and ruptures both within and

outside the self. But for these theorists, as for Freud, the end point of development cannot be understood as a unitary or perfected state but rather as a complex integration of divergent or opposing needs and tendencies. The most fundamental tensions for Mahler are between symbiotic and narcissistic needs and longings on the one hand, innate individuation strivings on the other, and (on the third hand) certain imperatives and limitations inherent in interpersonal relationships.

Yet – and this is important – for all this pessimism, there is nonetheless also a triumphant or transcendent dimension in these theories, much more so in the post-Freudian theories than in Freudian texts. This transcendent dimension is not a denial or an effacement of life's tragedy. Rather, this vision of the last things takes account of the fact that since we cannot (and perhaps should not) hope to disabuse ourselves of the wish for reunion with our objects, and of other impossible longings, maturity must entail an integration of both individuating and symbiotic tendencies. This is less a picture of man (or woman) perfected by an ascent to individuation and rationality, than one in which the end of development entails an integration of both individuation and fusion, rationality and impulse, and – in a limited and partial, somewhat illusory, yet vital way – of self and object.

To be more specific: The story of development as told by Mahler and the others is not just a movement out of symbiosis toward autonomy and self-reliance. Rather, as I have explained, these theories also include the postulate that one always struggles (usually unconsciously) with the longing for reunion. They hold that even if one has developed to a higher, more securely individuated state, as one must, one still seeks out relationships in which this desire for oneness can be integrated with the imperative of separateness. Thus the end state of development is both autonomy and (perhaps an even higher end) the capacity to engage in certain types of limited and partial experiences of reunion with one's objects, but without losing the sense of separate and distinctive identity that one has struggled to achieve. Significantly, Fairbairn calls his end of development, not "independence" but "mature dependence."

There are several varieties and intensities of reunion-in-separateness that these analytic theorists have posited as indexes of mature integration. Of these, surely the one currently most emphasized is "mature intimacy." Both the "regression in the service of the ego" of falling in love and the more diffuse and ongoing "relationship" are seen to entail simultaneous and/or sequential integrations of dependency, "regression," and permeability of ego boundaries, on the one hand, and the intrapsychic sense of separateness and autonomy, on the other.[9]

In addition to mature intimacy, the creative process – for some individuals at least – is seen to entail a kind of experience of reunion of the individual self with the object world. In such a reunion, the self's awareness of its true boundaries is, paradoxically, preserved. In her book, *On Not Being Able to Paint*, psychoanalyst Joanna Field (Marion Milner) says of artistic creation:

It is surely through the arts that we deliberately restore the split and bring subject and object together into a particular kind of new unity. . . . [T]he experience of the inner and the outer coinciding . . . is consciously brought about in the arts, through the conscious acceptance of the as-if-ness of the experience and conscious manipulation of a malleable material.[10]

In short, this psychoanalytic vision of the ends of development differs significantly from the other developmentalisms discussed in this chapter. The question I wish to pose at this point is, What does this indicate about its cultural inheritance? Given psychoanalysis's more tempered and "ambivalent" view, its lack of a simple prospectivism vis-à-vis either individuals or society, does this mean that psychoanalytic developmental psychology is not a legatee of the Biblical historical design?

Kessen, Kaplan, and White have drawn our attention to the ways in which developmental psychology is continuous with a pervasive Judeo-Christian historical design. They have made a crucially important point about the cultural patterning of contemporary psychological theory. What I have argued here is that not all psychological developmentalisms are exactly alike, and that therefore there is more work to be done to discover the genealogy of the different branches of the Biblical-historical family tree. Specifically, I would suggest that psychoanalytic developmental psychology is heir to a different tradition of Biblical interpretation than the tradition that has been highlighted by Kessen et al. Moreover, we need to appreciate that this tradition of Biblical interpretation underwent its own process of secularization, culminating not in Enlightenment doctrines and social evolutionist theories but rather in the Romantic movement of the late eighteenth and early nineteenth centuries.[11]

The cultural genealogy of psychoanalytic developmental psychology

The post-Freudian narrative depicts maturity as the self's capacity for a reunion with its object at a higher level, but in such a way that the self's sense of its individuated distinctiveness is preserved. I have suggested that this is less an Enlightenment vision than a Romantic one. By Romantic thought I refer to that movement initiated among English and German artists and intellectuals during the last decade of the eighteenth century and the first two decades of the nineteenth. Those who participated in the Romantic movement – including the poets Blake, Wordsworth, Coleridge, and Hölderlin and the philosophers Fichte, Schelling, and Hegel – were individuals who were especially attuned to what they perceived to be the costs and losses of the Enlightenment, and to the mixed blessings of scientific and industrial progress. They felt that rationalism and empiricism provided an inadequate vision of reality and that the secularized prospectivist vision embedded in these philosophical positions offered an impoverished depiction of human potential. They became particularly disillusioned with the veneration of reason when the French Revolution (that brainchild of the Enlightenment) failed to fulfill what they had perceived to be its initial salvationist promise.

Thus disappointed, the Romantics sought to construct new, naturalistic modes of salvation, as the literary critic M. H. Abrams amply demonstrated in his study of Romanticism and its sources, *Natural Supernaturalism*.[12] They appreciated that earlier hopes for millenarian perfection (first anticipated in literal religious doctrines, and then in the initial optimism of the Enlightenment doctrines of progress) could not be sustained in the old way in the post-Enlightenment world.

They knew they could not return to the old religious cosmology – that this had to be a system of *worldly* salvation, which had both its beginning and its end, to quote Wordsworth, "in the very world which is the world of all of us, the place in which, in the end, We find our happiness, or not at all."[13] Therefore they attempted to translate the Biblical narrative, to divest it of explicitly theological terms such as the soul (or even, for the most part, God), inserting in its place the Mind or Self.

The Biblical narrative that they thus transformed, however, was not the straightforward Providential historical account cited by Kessen, White, et al., but rather a distinctive *version* of that account. The Romantics, in other words, drew upon a tradition of Biblical exegesis that combined the linear design of Biblical history with Neoplatonist mystical themes. From the age of Plotinus (third century A.D.) onward, such Christian mystical narratives had been elaborated by numerous and diverse religious thinkers. With the advent of the Reformation, mystical themes and patterns came to be integrated into certain Protestant sectarian doctrines as well. Thus Christian mysticism began to take a form that was more worldly and, eventually, more interiorized (seen as pertaining to the inner life of the individual spirit or soul, sometimes even negating the literal interpretation of the narrative as the external history of mankind). Romantics came into contact with Neoplatonized Biblical history mainly (though not exclusively) in its Protestant incarnations, and then they secularized and interiorized it still further and more definitively.

The Romantics are often represented as sentimental, celebrating regression and a return to the primitive and to original innocence. But this is by no means the whole story. Many Romantic thinkers articulated in their work a more or less generic narrative of the Mind's development in which it was necessary for the subject to undergo severance from nature and to further undergo a difficult process of growth and development. In this process, the fall into self-consciousness and the strife of conflicting tendencies within the mind are deemed not a hindrance but ultimately a spur to greater growth. The mind is enriched and deepened and thus may attain its highest state, a reconciliation with nature in which its differentiated distinctiveness is preserved. Blake postulated a spiritual developmental trajectory that moved from innocence to experience to a higher or organized innocence. Coleridge described the end state as one in which all individuation and diversity survive, as "distinctions without division." Like many Romantics he asserted that the higher unity of man with nature is achieved most fully in aesthetic experience, in what he and others called the act of imagination. This of course accords to artists an extremely high place on the developmental scale (a belief about which psychoanalysts are far more ambivalent than the Romantics were). Imaginative perception was seen to entail a reunification of mind and nature, a reconciliation of subject and object, that preserves the intervening differentiations. Romantic development thus is neither a simple regressive circle, nor linear like Biblical history. Rather, it is a spiral, since its end is, as Abrams called it, a reversion to a higher unity.

Of course, the Romantics harbored a lofty set of ambitions regarding how the human imaginative reunion with the world could renovate the human condition. In this their hopes far surpassed those of psychoanalysts, who even at their most lyrical are much more modest in their appraisal of the potential of the mature self and its relatedness literally to transfigure the world. In Romanticism, the sense of disjunction between the subjective experience of higher reunion and the reality of separation is perhaps less definitive and absolute than is the case in psychoanalysis, which is more explicitly materialist in its metaphysical assumptions. But the pattern of the developmental narrative, and especially the structure given to its end, appear to preserve Romantic concerns and sensibilities to a far greater extent than do nonpsychoanalytic developmentalisms.

Thus we can trace a series of cultural transformations in which a Judeo-Christian narrative was made more worldly (and in some cases interiorized) in the form of Protestant doctrines, and then became fully secularized in eighteenth- and nineteenth-century movements in philosophy, arts, and letters. In the case of nonpsychoanalytic developmentalisms there is a stronger inheritance from Enlightenment, positivist, and evolutionist doctrines, whereas in the case of contemporary psychoanalytic developmental psychology there is a stronger inheritance from Romantic doctrines.

This is not to say that it is quite this clear-cut, of course: Both Freudian psychoanalysis and the post-Freudian developmental narrative evince, in different ways and to different degrees, Enlightenment as well as Romantic patterns and values. And cognitive-developmental and organismic paradigms bear the imprint of both "inner light" Christian mysticism (via rationalism) and Romantic dialectics. Thus the sociologist Benjamin Nelson appears to have been correct when he wrote of the "various blendings of Protestant conscience, character, and culture,"[14] both literally religious and secularized, which have come to comprise so many different folk and high cultural discourses in Euro-American society. In any case, we need a more complex depiction of the religious and cultural genealogy of developmental-isms than is currently available.[15]

One might be tempted to suggest that, because developmental theory is a living embodiment of culturally constituted, theologically derived assump-tions, it is an inappropriate model for psychological science, which should be an empirical one. Yet from the point of view of the metapsychologist, it would be misleading to espouse the notion that if we begin the psychological-scientific enterprise anew we can come up with a more "em-pirically derived," truly "objective" (in the sense of veridical) system. The adequacy of this sort of objectivism as a theory of knowledge has come increasingly to be challenged for all forms of psychological and social the-ory, and arguably for knowledge in other domains as well.[16] However, if we consider that psychological theory may have important and valuable func-tions and meanings other than that of straightforward mimesis, then it becomes possible to appraise the value and import of psychoanalytic devel-opmental theory in other terms. From such a standpoint, it could be argued that the linkage of psychoanalytic developmental psychology to the counter-Enlightenment aspect of Romanticism renders this paradigm especially val-uable and worthy of preservation today, for it continues to convey meanings analogous to those intended by the Romantics in their work. The Roman-tics, after all, perceived that the disenchantment of the world deprived humanistic discourse of some crucial aspects of our spiritual and moral heritage. The contemporary psychoanalytic model of human nature and development – viewed in juxtaposition against both nondevelopmentalist models and nonpsychoanalytic developmentalisms – seems to best preserve at least some of what the Romantics sought to reconstruct. Although now couched in terms very different from those of the Neoplatonized Judeo-Christian history of the soul, in this model we can see a disenchanted, reconstructed version of one of our culture's most sophisticated and pro-found constructions of the dilemmas of human existence.

Notes and references

1 See, e.g., Kenneth J. Gergen, "Introduction: Toward Metapsychology," in Henderikus J. Stam, Timothy B. Rogers, and Kenneth J. Gergen (eds.), *The Analysis of Psychological Theory: Metapsychological Perspectives* (Washington, DC: Hemisphere Publishing, 1987), pp. 1–21.
2 For an exploration of the reasons for the ascendance of these post-Freudian theories in the United States and Great Britain, see Suzanne Kirschner, "The Assenting Echo: Anglo-

American Values in Contemporary Psychoanalytic Developmental Psychology," *Social Research* 57 (Winter 1990), pp. 821–857.

3 William Kessen, "The American Child and Other Cultural Inventions," *American Psychologist* 34 (1979), pp. 815–820; "The Child and Other Cultural Inventions," in Frank Kessel and Alexander W. Siegel (eds.), *The Child and Other Cultural Inventions* (New York: Praeger, 1983), pp. 26–39; Lectures at Wesleyan University, May 1985, and Harvard University, March 1986; *The Rise and Fall of Development* (Worcester, MA: Clark University Press, 1990).

4 Sheldon White, "The Idea of Development in Developmental Psychology," in R. M. Lerner (ed.), *Developmental Psychology: Historical and Philosophical Perspectives* (Hillsdale, NJ: Lawrence Erlbaum, 1983).

5 Bernard Kaplan, "A Trio of Trials," in Lerner, *Developmental Psychology*, pp. 185–228; "Value Presuppositions in Theories of Human Development," in Leonard Cirillo and Seymour Wapner (eds.), *Value Presuppositions in Theories of Human Development* (Hillsdale, NJ: Lawrence Erlbaum, 1986), pp. 89–103.

6 Kaplan, "A Trio of Trials," p. 189.

7 Kaplan, "Value Presuppositions," p. 96. It is true that not all developmentalist theories are self-consciously intended to promote the perfection of the human being or of some particular aspect of him or her: Some are merely intended as descriptions of how development does take place. Even such allegedly nonnormative theories, however, tend to be more normative, value-laden, and prescriptive than they allege.

8 Margaret S. Mahler, Fred Pine, and Anni Bergmann, *The Psychological Birth of the Human Infant: Symbiosis and Individuation* (New York: Basic Books, 1975).

9 See, e.g., Martin Bergmann, "Psychoanalytic Observations on the Capacity to Love," in John B. McDevitt and Calvin Settlage (eds.), *Separation-Individuation: Essays in Honor of Margaret Mahler* (New York: International Universities Press, 1971), pp. 15–40.

10 Joanna Field, *On Not Being Able to Paint* (Los Angeles: J. P. Tarcher, 1967), p. 131.

11 It is beyond the scope of this chapter to discuss the channels by which Romantic patterns were transmitted to these psychoanalysts. I will simply note that most Central Europeans or Englishmen with even a fairly rudimentary liberal education could not help but encounter the most basic Romantic patterns and themes. Not only were they present in the widely studied poets and philosophers I name in this chapter. They also persisted into nineteenth- and twentieth-century European and American arts and letters.

12 M. H. Abrams, *Natural Supernaturalism* (New York: Norton, 1971).

13 *The Prelude* (London: Penguin Classics, 1988), X, p. 442.

14 "Self-images and Systems of Spiritual Direction in the History of European Civilization," in S. Z. Klausner (ed.), *The Quest for Self-Control* (New York: Free Press, 1965).

15 See Suzanne R. Kirschner, *The Religious and Romantic Origins of Psychoanalysis: Individuation and Integration in Post-Freudian Theory* (Cambridge: Cambridge University Press, 1996).

16 See, e.g., Richard J. Bernstein, *Beyond Objectivism and Relativism: Science, Hermeneutics and Praxis* (Philadelphia: University of Pennsylvania Press, 1983); Kurt Danziger, "Generative Metaphor and the History of Psychological Discourse," in David E. Leary (ed.), *Metaphors in the History of Psychology* (Cambridge: Cambridge University Press, 1990), pp. 331–356.

11 The historical vicissitudes of mental diseases: Their character and treatment

Harry F. M. Peeters

Over the centuries the theories and practices concerning the mentally disturbed or the insane have been subject to continuous change. The determinants of these changes are predominantly to be found in social cultural developments, alterations in belief systems, or changes within the medical-psychiatric-psychological discourses. Changes in treatment, however, are not entirely the result of such influences. Alterations in behavior have also had effects on treatment and theory. The spread of melancholy, hypochondria, vapors, or spleen in the eighteenth century, for instance, contributed to a change in the treatment of the mentally disturbed and caused the therapist to turn professional (Foucault, 1961; Lepenies, 1972; Starobinski, 1960). The rise of hysteria at the end of the nineteenth century and the forms in which it found expression were also important determinants for transformations in psychiatry and psychology. Psychoanalysis as a theory, method of research, and technique of treatment largely owes its existence to such phenomena (Ellenberger, 1970). At the same time, in the genesis, spread, and disappearance of behavioral disturbances, socio-cultural conditions are also involved. After all, people are not *homines clausi,* individuals isolated from the outside world and, more particularly, from their social surroundings. They are social creatures from the cradle onward. Any form of human behavior, no matter whether it involves perception, motivation, learning, thinking, or emotionality, invariably is a form of social behavior at the same time. Therefore people will run into difficulties if they, for whatever reason, cannot or will not adapt to the values, norms, or expectations of their social environment.

In this chapter an attempt will be made to unravel this network of inter-, intra- and extradiscursive relations – in terms of Foucault (1968) – by means of giving an analysis of two distinct lines. First a brief overview will be given of the historical stages in the character and treatment of the mentally ill. In the next section the determinants that have played a part in conceptual formations and transformations will be analyzed in the case of the age-old problem of melancholy. Finally, I will discuss conclusions the present-day therapist should draw from this historical argument.

204

The Middle Ages: Rise and fall of the isolation and privatization of the insane

The medical-psychiatric theory and practice in the Middle Ages concentrated on four nosological entities: *insanity* (mania and melancholy), *frenesy* or madness combined with fever, *epilepsy* or falling sickness or lunacy, and *rabies* or canine madness. All of them were exogenous psychoses, disturbances in behavior brought about by external causes. Endogenous psychoses, psychosomatic disorders, and neuroses were not recognized or did not exist as such. As a consequence, the methods used for treatment were *evacuating:* bloodletting, scarification, and trephination (Beek, 1969; Peeters, 1982). The system of official medical science, however, was not so rigid or dominant that it decided on treatment under all circumstances. More often than not, the physician had to admit openly that he was at a loss, apart from the fact that he was too expensive to be consulted or inaccessible. In fact, the treatment was an amalgam of beliefs, magic, and science. The physician, realizing his powerlessness, often resorted to magic-religious remedies. Popular medical practice made use of herbs and techniques (e.g., bloodletting) symbolizing the therapeutical process and executing it simultaneously. The church developed a special collection of saints, each of whom offered an adequate remedy to a precisely defined group of patients; there was also a large variety of relics, all possessing the saint's undivided power to be worshiped by the pilgrims, who expected recovery as a result.

The mentally ill, belonging to a certain community, were neither isolated nor institutionalized by their fellow citizens. Fellow Christians sent them to religious centers where they received guidance and were given a short but intensive treatment, and sometimes they were left to be provided for in a village community established uniquely for their needs. The family, however, was held responsible for them and looked after them as long as they possibly could, and the law showed consideration for their diminished responsibility and legal capacity. This is not to say that the mentally ill were not made fun of or treated with harshness. Those from outside the community often fell victim to violence. They were expelled from town and, if a possibility presented itself, sent along with merchants and pilgrims. Like all other lame ducks in society, they either suffered merciless cruelty or were shown great compassion. Only those who became raving mad and had to be tied up because of their wild and aggressive behavior were temporarily locked up in mobile "nut-huts," small, jail-like cabins.

In the late Middle Ages the first asylums and institutions were introduced, in imitation of the Arabic countries where they had already been used for years. At first, these small institutions were no more than manifestations of charity, so many expressions of guilt and sincere regret, established by people who, at the end of their lives, were filled with remorse over their disregard for the weak and defenseless in society (Ackerknecht & Akert, 1964; Chatel & Jof, 1975; Chamberlain, 1966; Neugebauer, 1978).

The classical period: Differentiated confinement

The seventeenth century marked the beginning of the process of confinement, isolation in separate institutions and expulsion from "normal" society. Michel Foucault (1961), among others, has described this process, but he has highly exaggerated its impact. It was not until the latter half of the nineteenth century that isolation on a large scale was put into practice; institutionalization in the seventeenth century pales by comparison with later developments. Nevertheless, the isolation of the mentally ill did get under way and gradually a climate favorable to massive confinement was created. Initially, isolation went hand in hand with enormous economic, social, and religious crises, with uprooting people from their familiar surroundings, cutting them off from their homes and leaving them in frustration. The isolation of the mentally ill was also connected with the formation of states, with the changed appreciation of labor, the growing uneasiness about deviant behavior, and the tendency to restore order and keep oneself to oneself and stick to one's own group. Often the mentally ill were locked up in vacant leper houses together with the work-shy, beggars, idlers, the down-and-outs, and adventurers, because work was considered as an ethical value and as a means to maintain social order. Those who were not able to come up to the prevailing standards or did not conform were locked away.

Sufferers of melancholy, hypochondria, and vapors or spleen, common disturbances in those days, were mainly to be found in members of the upper classes. The causes of these illnesses, as understood at the time, were also class related: idleness, parental lovingness, a life of ease and sensuality, the torments of heart and mind, or the use of coffee, tea, and tobacco (Raulin, 1759; Pomme, 1760; Ellenberger, 1970; Blackmore, 1725; Cheney, 1733). Melancholy, particularly, was an honorable disease. It was considered to affect only highly talented people (Klibansky, Panofsky, & Saxl, 1964; Wittkower & Wittkower, 1969). At the same time, however, the meaning of melancholy underwent a metamorphosis. To the medieval monk melancholy was a sign of desolation. A studious person in the sixteenth century became a melancholic because he could not bridge the gap between his humanistic ideals and social reality (Burton, 1621). The Renaissance artist fell victim to melancholy as a result of the tearing apart of the order and pattern of the cosmos, and the disturbing fact that words no longer referred to things and vice versa (Babb, 1951). In the eighteenth century French aristocrats and German citizens became prey to melancholy because they no longer could play a major role in society and were forced to take refuge in etiquette or seek refinement in *Kultur* (Lepenies, 1972; Schings, 1977). In the nineteenth century people tended to be depressed because they had become alienated from themselves or had become too vulnerable in their intimate contacts with others.

All these historical forms of melancholy were accompanied by a loss of contact, but in every cultural period this contact was defined differently: It was a loss of contact with God, the classical ideals, the cosmos, the presumed role in society, or oneself or one's intimates. At the same time, people began to pursue a new order to escape the existing chaos. They sought refuge in asceticism, religious and social utopias, the cultivated order of formal contact and spiritual refinement, and a cult of self-reflection and self-fulfillment (Lepenies, 1972; Tellenbach, 1976). Until then the physical isolation of the "simple" fool and the spiritual isolation of the talented and high-class melancholic, hypochondriac, or sufferer of spleen or "affections vaporeuses" had run their separate courses. Physical isolation favored treating the lunatic as an animal (keeping him nude and enchained in a cold cell) and, as a consequence, he became an animal and behaved as such. Spiritual isolation resulted in increasing privatization. These two lines came together at the end of the eighteenth and at the beginning of the nineteenth century: The "simple" fool was released from prison, the house of correction or the place where he was detained together with other useless people, but only to be put away again, without delay, in an institution or asylum together with the "distinguished" mentally disturbed who had hitherto been free to go and do as they pleased.

The romantic period: Specific confinement and "moral treatment" (1800–1850)

Similar to the transition of the medieval to the classical model, the transition of indifferentiated isolation to specific isolation and "moral treatment" about 1800 was accompanied by broad sociocultural shifts. The economic need for manpower and the enlightened and romantic ideas about human nature and society brought about the isolation in asylums of the mentally ill on the one hand, and inspired optimistic confidence in the beneficial effects of change of environment and the therapeutic power of moralizing medical science on the other hand (Tuke, 1813; Foucault, 1961). But this transition was also affected by new behavioral disturbances, which demanded different treatment and up-to-date professionalization. In the institutions the new disturbances were given every possible chance to develop: Personal guilt of the sufferer was unquestionably at the root of the disturbance; insanity was regarded as the expression of personal inadequacy. The isolation was twofold: Not only was the patient isolated, the asylum was isolated as well.

It was preferable to build the asylums in the country, far from the built-up centers. Thus, patients were no longer exposed to dangerous stimuli. A different environment was supposed to be beneficial to the patients and, at the same time, there were better possibilities of subjecting the inmates to a strict, internal surveillance.

From now on the guilty, dependent, and isolated patient was confronted with the self-assured, powerful physician, invested with authority, such as Heinroth, Ideler, Willis, Esquirol, Pinel, Tuke, Rush, and Haslam – the names of the "great strong men" in the history of psychiatry (Carlson, 1960; Ey, 1978). According to Pinel, for instance, the patient had to submit to the physician's wish. The patient had to subject himself and had to be restrained "by making him entirely dependent on a man who, by virtue of his moral and physical properties, was eminently suited to exercise authority over him and to change his mad associations of ideas." Thus, the patient would quickly learn "that he had better give in and that the doctor's will is a hard and fast rule," and after some time he would realize that "putting up resistance against this will is as useless as opposing the laws of nature." The physician had to be in the possession of "a penetrating look" and a desire to impress others"; he was advised to catch the patient's eye immediately as he entered the cell (Kraepelin, 1918; Vandermeersch, 1982).

This period in the history of psychiatry was generally characterized by self-assurance and optimistic hopes of the progress of science. On account of his being institutionalized and having access to the physician's skill and authority, the patient could be cured. This period from 1800 till 1850, approximately, was a transitional phase in the history of psychiatry. It finally concurred with the period of the medical model and the large-scale isolation.[1]

Medical model and large-scale isolation (1850–1960)

Toward the mid 1800s inter- and intradiscursive factors played an important role in the treatment of the mentally ill. Sciences such as biology and physiology began to serve as a pattern for other sciences. In psychiatry, as Kraepelin put it, natural scientific observation came to replace philosophy and the moralizing approach (1918). From then on psychological disturbances were regarded as diseases of the brain and a new nosology developed, supported by biological-physiological laboratory research. The relationship between the mentally disturbed and the therapist turned into one of patient–physician, with all the consequent rites and obligatory examinations. Nursing was entirely restricted to the physical care of the mentally ill, and the organization of the asylum was modeled on a general hospital with a senior medical officer in charge. This period of the medical or organic-somatic model continued till the 1960s, uncontestedly and without interruption. It was the period of the great psychiatrists, such as Griesinger and Neisser; Kraepelin, the legendary classifier of mental diseases; and Arnold Meyer, his American counterpart. In this period the privatization of the mentally ill continued to develop. The medical model was exclusively directed at the individual (i.e., at his body): When making a diagnosis or in case of treatment – if any – the emphasis was put on the pathological-anatomical abnormalities of the brain, on defects in the functioning of the nervous system, and on the composition and activity of the bodily fluids. Even in psychologically oriented psychiatry, the patient was considered to be detached and isolated from his surroundings. The theoretical model in psychiatry was based on a disunion of inside and outside. The psychiatric vocabulary referred almost entirely to interior processes, taking place independently of their surroundings (Kraus, 1961; Elias, 1971).

Along with the increasing privatization and individualization of the patient, there was a rise in the physical isolation. Across Western Europe the population of mental institutions soared within a matter of decades (Blasius, 1979). In the Netherlands the number of patients in mental homes increased from 39 to 264 per 100,000 inhabitants over the period 1849–1928. The absolute number of patients admitted rose from 4,771 in 1884 to 26,217 in 1965. In this period the number of institutions increased from 14 to 38, 6 of which were mammoth institutions accommodating more than a 1,000 patients. Similar, quantitative shifts occurred in other West European countries and the United States. England took the lead in this development, by admitting 160 patients per 1,000 inhabitants as early as 1869, whereas France and the German states only admitted as many as 75 and 32, respectively (Köhler, 1977; Panse, 1964; Dörner, 1969; Peeters, 1982). Impulses toward order and shame had already caused the locking up of a number of the mentally ill in the seventeenth and eighteenth centuries. However, their number paled in significance by comparison with those institutionalized after the 1850s. It was not surprising that England set the trend and not without significance either; after all it was the country that saw the first industrial revolution. Huge numbers of destitute and handicapped were thrown out of employment and, consequently, excluded from society. And, just as in England, national and regional authorities in other countries were not eager to make provisions for this large body of unemployed persons and outcasts. But even so, the institutions were set up in larger numbers and they were more massive than at the end of the Middle Ages and the beginning of the classical period. And, where government failed to take action, private associations and organizations took the initiative. This increase in the population of mental homes was not so much caused by intradiscursive factors, such as the development of psychiatry as a science and the professionalization of the psychiatrist. A number of reasons can better explain this steady growth, to wit: the vicinity of asylums, outpatient clinics and health centers, and the financial position of municipalities (Kraus, 1933). The driving force behind this increase, however, was the incipient modern state, which, as a result of its highly specialized demands, rendered a rising group of people unfit for employment and unsuited to play a constructive role in community relations.

Contemporary breakdown of the medical model

In the 1960s it looked as if the social model would predominate in the theory and treatment of psychiatric patients. However, during this period the prevailing image of the mentally disturbed inside and outside psychiatry underwent a considerable change. Psychiatry left its ivory tower; there was a drastic change in the organization of mental homes; and the psychiatric patient began to talk about himself. These changes had already been initiated before World War II (think of Simon's "Aktivere Therapie"), but it was not until the 1960s that they manifested themselves on a large social scale. In particular, the movement called antipsychiatry provided fresh impetus for these changes and became the mouthpiece for new ideas. In the 1960s we thus witnessed a rejection of the medical model, of the mental homes as a system of locking up people and of psychiatry as a means of exerting social control. Furthermore, there were expressions – not univocally shared (Trimbos, 1975) – of positive appreciation for psychotic disturbances (notably of schizophrenia).

The antipsychiatry movement was hardly alone in its undermining of the medical model and its institutional realizations. Other movements and schools, such as interaction psychiatry (Sullivan), social etiology (Redlich and Hollingshead), social psychiatry, clinical psychology, and attribution theory, had an influence on the breaking down of the framework of traditional institutions and ideas. Therapies and therapeutical approaches, such as family therapy, group therapy, and the therapeutic community, also played an important role; and the use of psychopharmaceutical drugs was a crucial step in the speeding up of the transformation process. Each of these developments formed a necessary condition for social changes in psychiatry. However, these determinants should also be situated in the entire matrix of the social shifts in the 1960s and 1970s. Socializing and democratizing processes dramatically changed the image of the psychiatric patient, mental diseases, and treatment. The individualistic-medical and, at the same time, authoritative models were brought under severe question, and together with this shift in understanding the number of patients in the mental homes gradually decreased. In the Netherlands there was a drop of 11.5% between 1955 and 1974. For the first time in ages one could witness a major decline in the physical isolation of the disturbed, even when the number of people seeking psychiatric or psychological help strongly increased. The causes of disturbances of behavior in the present are mainly to be found in social dysfunctioning and the influence of society. Therefore social therapies have become symbols of hope. Once again, this tendency runs parallel to change in life patterns, and links up with the breakthrough of family privatization, and the breaking down of the taboo on death and development in criminal law (Peeters, 1982).

Formation and transformation of the concepts of melancholy, acedia, and depression

The preceding account attempts to make clear the importance of political factors in combination with sociocultural and economic factors in the institutional history of people suffering from behavioral disturbances. A contrasting case will now be considered, one in which these extradiscursive factors are surely active, but which demonstrates more fully the force of intra- and interdiscursive factors. Our concern, then, is to examine the transformation of the concepts of melancholy, acedia, and depression. Their lengthy and well-documented history would appear to indicate most clearly what kind of driving forces come into play in the genesis and development of the psychiatric-psychological discourse. Their history also shows to what degree behavioral disturbances have become internalized and psychologized over time. From their history it will also appear that in the course of time we have increasingly come to rely on "psychological language in making sense of ourselves and others" (Gergen, 1991, 227).

Throughout their lengthy history, melancholy and depression have witnessed "a parade of theories," all of them giving an explanation of their origin and development and making suggestions about how treatment should be given. After a domination of the humoral theory which lasted about 2,000 years, the past four centuries have witnessed a rapid succession of atrochemical notions, hydrodynamic conceptions, mechanical explanations, theories of nervous transmissions and electrical charges and discharges, disease theories of the brain and nervous constitution, and neuroendocrinometabolic concepts, more often than not related to shifting understandings in the natural sciences (Jackson, 1986, 386–389). In addition, the present century has offered us a series of psychologically oriented explanations, derived from psychoanalysis, *Daseins*analysis, phenomenology, and cognitive psychology (Tellenbach, 1976; Beck, 1972, 1979). Throughout these centuries melancholia and depression have denoted a disease, a troublesome condition of a certain severity and duration, a temperament, or type of character. In spite of all the differences of theory and denotions there has always been a common denominator of complaints and symptoms: sadness, loss of contact, sleeplessness, loss of appetite, loss of weight, anxiety, self-derogatory concerns, suicidal inclination, delusions.

And so, Jackson had some reason to call his thorough and elaborate historical study on melancholy and depression "tracing the variations in a remarkable consistency" (Jackson, 1986, 27–246). And yet, this apparent "consistency" does not alter the fact that the various symptoms and complaints
tend to show marked differences in meaning for both patient and environment and that different theories have been formulated to account for this.
Therefore we would rather not talk about "remarkable consistency" so
much as a "family resemblance" of complaints and symptoms.

In the following I intend to give a description of the historical vicissitudes
of the concepts of melancholia, depression, and their relative, acedia. I
would like to point out that linguistic structures, traditional language conventions, metaphors, theoretical foreconstructions, presumptions of daily
life, and scientific concepts are embodied in a complex system of interdependence and interaction. In the history of the three concepts – dating from
500 B.C. to the present day – a number of processes can be distinguished,
which, in connection with the processes of treatment described earlier, and
with varying success and importance, have been essential in the setting of
standards for deciding who was ill and who was not, what could be regarded
as etiology and symptomatology, what therapy was appropriate, and who
was qualified to give treatment.

Imagination substantielle

As far as we know the term "melancholy" was used for the first time in a
writing *About Air, Water, and Place* dating from the fifth century B.C.,
which is to be found in the *Corpus Hippocraticum*. It deals with the influence of the climate on the well-being and ill health of people and in chapter
10 it says: "If a black summer with fierce northerly winds is followed by a
dry autumn, also characterized by prevailing northerly winds, this will be
beneficial to the phlegmatic and the moist type but most harmful to the
choleric types because the latter run the risk of being dehydrated too much,
for there is a possibility that they will contract dry inflammations in the eyes
and run high and persistent fevers, some will even sink into melancholy."
According to Flashar (1966, 22–23), a specialist in the critical-philosophical
study of medical theories in antiquity, this text allows three conclusions:

1. Melancholy is regarded as a disease that certain types of people will develop under certain circumstances, but not inevitably.
2. The vulnerable type is called choleric and not the "black bilious" type as
   one would expect. This can be explained from the fact that in the writing in
   question the concepts of melancholic and black bile are not yet mentioned.
3. The text does not give a picture of the melancholy syndrome and does not
   make clear whether there is a psychological disorder that is connected with
   the disease; the cause of the illness, however, is indicated: It is the thickening of the bile and the dehydrating of the moist elements.

The origin of the term "melancholy" can be explained as follows: The thickening of the bile was established by checking the consistency of the bilious substance and melancholy was diagnosed by the degree of the discoloration of vomit, feces, and urine. A dark discoloration meant an excess of dark fluids. On these grounds it can be concluded that at the beginning melancholy was not regarded as a state or condition, dominated by black bile, but as a disease, characterized by a dark discoloration of the bile (Flashar, 35). In a tract of later date from *Corpus Hippocraticum,* in the third book on *Epidemics* (17.2), mental complaints and symptoms such as drowsiness, lack of appetite, insomnia, excitement, and depression were mentioned for the first time. At the end of the tract it is remarked that "the frame of mind is melancholic." This pronouncement corresponds to one of Hippocrates' aphorisms: "If fear and sadness continue for any length of time, this is an indication of a melancholic state of mind." However, it took a considerable time for the black bile to be introduced as a bodily fluid in its own right. This eventually happened about 400 B.C. in a tract *About the Nature of Man,* presumably written by Hippocrates' son-in-law Polybus. The fundamental idea in this tract was that man is formed from the fluids blood, phlegm, light or yellow bile, and black bile. An unbalanced mixture of these fluids causes illness.

It is remarkable that the recognition and naming of the bodily components and the qualities related to them are physiognomic in character, or in Tellenbach's words: "alles Geistige tritt leibhaft in Erscheinung, alles Leibhafte bringt sich geistig zum Austrag" (Tellenbach, 1976, 13). This mode of thinking in analogies has been termed by Bachelard *l'imagination substantielle*.

In order to explain the causes of the symptoms and to gain insight into the treatment of the diseases, one had to form a picture of the bodily processes. To obtain this, all bodily processes were reduced to four roots: waters, juices, or fluids of corporality and their mutual interchange of mixing and demixing. This was further analogous to Empedocles' ideas about the four roots or elements of the world (air, fire, water, and earth). By thinking in these analogies, the microcosmos was connected with the macrocosmos and the four fluids were associated with the four phases of life, the four seasons, and the four directions of the wind. Thus, melancholy could be linked with the dry and cold earth and with the autumn in its quality of a phase of life and a season. A person was called healthy if the qualities, the fluids, and the elements were on balance with each other and bore the right proportion or *temperamentum*. The balance could be disturbed, however; it could shift into eight different directions: One of the primal qualities could be too dominant or two primal qualities could outweigh the other ones to such a degree that one of the humors would get the upperhand.[2] Someone was called melancholic or began to suffer from

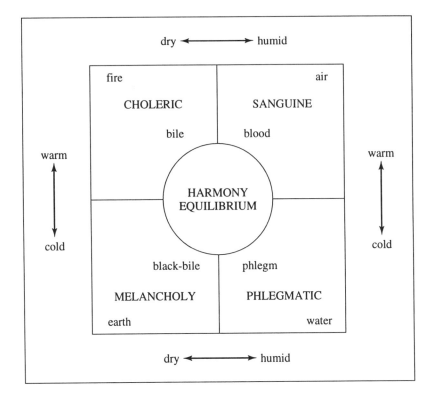

Figure 1. System of analogies.

melancholy if there was too much black bile in the body, or as a result of the predominance of black bile owing to coldness and dryness. The dominance of black bile in its turn could be caused by light, climate, food, physical exercise, phase of life, season, sorrow, loss of normal contact, and rhythm (see Fig. 1)

This system of analogies was also reflected in the modes of therapy. All therapeutic rules and interventions were directed at restoring the lost balance. Thus, melancholy had to be treated with evacuating remedies, such as the swallowing of an extract of the roots of hellebore (in order to stimulate diarrhea, vomiting, and a black, bloody bowel movement) and bloodletting to weaken the black bile and restore the humoral balance. In addition, the health regime was aimed at keeping the balance even; moderation in everything, in movement, food, drink, light, and air, was the source of well-being. In this respect Werner Jaeger is right in pointing out that Greek medicine was first and foremost *paideia,* the education of body and soul (Starobinski, 1960, 10).

This way of observing and thinking was also evident in the language used when talking about human behavior and psychological experiences. A straightforward picture of motivation and feelings in mental concepts was not possible (Sarbin, 1964, 523–523). Psychological situations could only be expressed in terms of concrete and external objects. Melancholy was "black bilousness" because it was seen as the product of black bile, and this black bile was a concrete object and manifestly present in the body. Similar "substantiated" descriptions were equally evident in other disorders. They, too, were distinguished and described in the same practical, visual way of thinking and in concrete language. Thus, in the case of hysteria, the coming loose of the husteron (the lower part of the uterus) was seen as the direct cause of the symptoms. Blaming the humors of the husteron for the illness was "modern" in comparison to what had been regarded as the cause of mental disturbances until the fifth century B.C. In the earlier time the stirrings of strong emotions, such as *ate* (a temporary blotting out of the normal conciousness or a partial or temporary insanity) and *menos* (a sudden flux of energy, trust, and courage), a disease like epilepsy (a blow dealt from outside) and admonitions (an idea suddenly hit upon, or an unexpected recognition or recollection), were attributed to gods, the fates, and demons. In the fifth century B.C. the "psychological interventions" of supernatural beings began to give way to more proximal and substantial causes, at least as far as the social and cultural elite was concerned (Dodds, 1957, 3, 5, 8, 9, 11–18, 66, 68, 185). The bodily humors were an example of this development.

An interdiscursive fusion

From the early Christian days onward till the end of the Middle Ages, acedia was regarded as a persistent trial of the soul. In the heat of midday, hermits and monks could be tempted by it and were made to doubt whether, after all, there was anything worth living for. Especially those who, more than others, had sought to be in touch with God were struck with spiritual inertia and suicidal aggression. Acedia changed their relationship with God, whom they no longer cared for, no more than He cared for them.

The original meaning of the word akedia (Greek for noncaring or careless; also uncared for, such as a corpse left without burial) was narrowed down to *negligentia* (negligence) of God by early Christian writers such as Chrysostom (fourth century), Evragius (fourth century), Cassian (fifth century), and Gregory the Great (sixth century). Negligence of God, in combination with *pigritia* (indolence) and *otiositas* (idleness), was the most fundamental characteristic of acedia. *Taedium* (dejection), *desperatio* (despair), and *tristitia* (sadness) completed the picture. It is quite likely that, at first, each of these triads used to be two different types of acedia (Wenzel, 1960, 160; Jackson 1986, 72). The concept of acedia, classified as a cardinal sin, retained its basic idea of boredom, spiritual torpor, dejection, or even disgust with fulfilling one's religious duty over a period of many centuries. About A.D. 1500 the term disappeared and fell practically into disuse. Did the emotion disappear along with the term? According to Rom Harré this is exactly what happened. After all, the very existence of the emotional state acedia was connected with the duty to God fulfilled in spiritual exercise. Along with the loss of this moral order, acedia disappeared as well, and with it the concept and the term (Harré, 1986, 220–227). Finlay-Jones takes the view that the original notion of acedia became corrupted and that, gradually, acedia meant no more than personal laziness. In A.D. 1215 the fourth Lateran Council ruled that the faithful had to confess their sins regularly. In order to search their conscience the faithful could avail themselves of a list of sins, which they had to learn by heart. Acedia did not show on this list because as a concept it was too complicated and too sophisticated. In addition to this, the diligent citizen began to look upon acedia as the "sloth of idle nobility" (Finlay-Jones, 1986, 227–233).

The disappearance of acedia, however, can also be regarded as a fusion of two traditions that, in different discourses, drew similar conclusions. On the one hand, there was a discourse about acedia in the church with ecclesiastical authors as authorities and, on the other, there was a medical discourse about melancholy with Aristotle, Hippocrates, and Galen as the most important sources of reference (Hersant, 1984, 45–46). Indeed, the symptoms described in both discourses overlapped considerably: One finds the same aversion to life, the preoccupation with death, the same sense of collapse and desolation, the same withdrawal in silence and isolation (Hersant, 1984, 47). However, another, more decisive factor that contributed to the fusion was the fact that over the years melancholy had acquired a moral connotation and as such it had begun increasingly to resemble acedia. Melancholy was increasingly regarded as a fertile breeding ground for Satan's work: *Melancholia balneum diaboli*. Melancholy might even be Satan's own creation, a means to exercise his evil influence. This interchange between Satan and melancholy had already been described in a most penetrating way by Saint Hildegard von Bingen. The moment that Adam sinned in taking the apple "melancholy curdled in his blood as when a lamp is quenched, the smouldering and smoking which remains reeking behind and his gall was changed to bitterness, and his melancholy to blackness" (Klibansky, Panofsky, & Saxl, 1964, 79–80). The merging of the Christian-moral tradition and the medical-humoral tradition was possible because the latter had turned into a Christian moral tradition itself. Melancholy had absorbed acedia, or the other way round, because when "le semblable mange le semblable, on ne sait trop lequel, du mangeur ou du mangé, en verité absorbe l'autre" (Hersant, 1984, 48). The fusion between melancholy and the triad, dejection-despair-sadness, was the most significant.

I hold the view that, owing to the fusion of two traditions (to which the pastoral simplification, already mentioned, had also contributed), Rom Harré's thesis need not be wrong as such, but needs modifying. Acedia did not disappear at the end of the Middle Ages, but faded out one or two centuries later as a result of a process of secularization. This decline was obscured by the fact that, for a considerable time, the emotional state of acedia continued to be regarded as an integral part of the concept and term melancholy.

From melancholy to depression: A struggle of professionals

It is not always easy to determine for what reason a certain term in psychiatry becomes obsolete and disappears from the official nosography. It may be due to an internal reorganization of the taxonomical order with the aim of obtaining a more precise and better differentiated indication of a syndrome or illness. Another explanation is that the psychiatric terminology adjusts itself to new discoveries and new forms of therapy. Finally, it may occur that new and other forms of mental disturbances and deviant behavior necessitate a change of terminology. Whatever the reason, ever since the beginning of the nineteenth century the psychiatric profession has had the last word. From the moment that medical specialists began to take an interest in the theory of insanity and wanted a say in the treatment of the mentally ill, they have shown a total disregard for the laymen and, with them, for their language. The "psychiatrizing" of the terminology became an instrument for the "professionalizing" of the psychiatrist and, as such, gave the psychiatrist the right to distinguish the pathological from the normal (Fedida & Postel, 1977, 18). This is, in short, what happened to the old, time-honored melancholy in the nineteenth century.

"Le mot mélancholie, consacré dans le language vulgaire, pour exprimer l'état habituel de tristesse de quelques individus, doit être laissé aux moralistes et aux poètes qui, dans leurs expressions ne sont pas obligés à autant de sévérité que les médecins," according to the early nineteenth-century psychiatrist Etienne Esquirol in his work *De la lypémanie ou mélancholie* (Esquirol, 1976, 398). With his suggestion to reserve the term melancholy for moralists and poets, Esquirol gave expression to the general idea of equipping the psychiatric medical science with a tight methodology, clinical observation, and a rational causal explanation. The term melancholy with its century-old aura of imaginative and intuitive force had to give way to terms based on "faits observables." Metaphysical, religious, or mythical obscurantism was no longer acceptable. An obscure notion like melancholy, originating from bodily fluids, could not be tolerated in the era of psychiatric positivism.

The theme of feeling "weighed down," the sensation of heaviness, can lay claim to a history as old as that of melancholy. From the seventeenth century onward, the term "depression" began "to absorb the traditions of the weighed down and heaviness metaphor" (Jackson, 1986, 398). Hence, a form of physiognomical observation and physical perception could function as the initial stage of what later became a technical term. Depression as a distinct mental disease was formulated as such for the first time by Kraepelin, the famous classifier of diseases, in the 5th edition (1896) of his *Psychiatrie. Ein Lehrbuch für Studirende und Aertze*. According to him, depression, which he called "das manisch-depressive Irresein," had to be regarded as a disease unit because, in spite of its manifold forms, it was clear that it could be recognized by a certain uniformity of symptoms and complaints and it knew a specific pathogenesis and a particular progress and a particular outcome. Kraepelin regarded depression as an endogenous disease. Kraepelin's assertions formed the beginning of serious disagreement among professionals about classification.

Adolf Meyer, a dominant figure in American psychiatry between 1895 and 1940, was not long in taking up the gauntlet. He focused attention on the patient's life story. He also challenged Kraepelin's idea of discrete disease entities and regarded psychiatric disorders as maladaptive reaction patterns that depended on constitution and life experiences (Meyer, 1951; Lidz, 1966). The battle continued on all kinds of fronts. Was depression an endogenous disease and, if so, what exactly did endogeny mean (was it a degenerative constitution, something hereditary, a "biologisches Gesamtgeschehen")? Was depression an exogenous or reactive disease and, if so, what environmental factors or events were pathogenic, or was depression an endogenous–exogenous disease and, if so, what was the interaction between predisposition and environment, susceptibility and circumstances? Other borderline fights within the controversy over the classification of depression concerned the distinction between neurotic and psychotic depressions, vital and personal, unipolar and bipolar depressions, and primary and secondary depressions.

It is perhaps not surprising that discussions about depression as a disease unit have grown idle. Psychiatrists and clinical psychologists no longer talk about depression as a disease unit but see it as a complaint, a symptom, a syndrome. Basic disagreements simply remain suspended (Kuilman, 1971). In the authoritative *Diagnostic and Statistical Manual of Mental Disorders* (DSM-III-R, 1987) issued by the American Psychiatric Association, depression is depicted solely in terms of its symptoms – for example, loss of interest or satisfaction in all or nearly all normal activities and pleasures, eat and sleep disorders, a sense of worthlessness and guilt, problems of concentration, preoccupation with death, and suicidal tendencies. Interestingly, the ancient term melancholy remains now at the fringes, now reserved for a severe form of a depressive episode.

The historical constructionist-contextualistic model

Must we conclude from the preceding that systems of pathology, categories of mental illness, and treatment forms simply change unsystematically and chaotically over time? Surely we cannot predict the course of history in these matters. However, it is possible to generate analytic tools that may enable a more systematic assessment of stability and change across time. It is useful in the present request to outline a constructionist-contextual approach to understanding historical change, an approach that derives heavily from Hutschemaekers's (1990) history of neurosis in the Netherlands.

Briefly put, any array of behavior deemed problematic by a given culture (or subculture) generates three interrelated forms of reaction. There is, first of all, a labeled behavior and its etiology. People come to label the behavior in a certain way, to believe that it is one kind of thing and not another. However, it is also difficult to translate aberrant behavior into meaningful motives and aims with the help of commonsense theories. As a result, experts relate the complaints and symptoms "responsible" for this stagnation to other phenomena. Psychiatrists and psychologists in our days link them with character problems, somatic aspects, psychosocial stressors, and the global level of functioning by means of the DSM-categorization. The form and content of these attributions and constructs largely depend on the theoretical points of departure. Similar to the humoral theory used to construct a dominance of the black bile as a result of distal and proximal causes and the Kraepelian pathology that could point out an organic defect, so psychoanalysis constructs an unconcious conflict, phenomenology constructs an outlook on life, and cognitive psychology constructs a "cognitive triad" of negative conditions, interpretations, and expectations of the self (Hutschemaekers, 1990, 122–126; Beck, 1972, 1979). The constructs employed, in turn, determine the social consequences of melancholy or depression. It is maintained that the old-time melancholic should try and find another climate or study less and that the modern melancholic should adopt a more adequate cognitive template. Stagnation of meaning, construction of meaning, and social consequences are context-bound. They are shaped and determined in specific situations. They are also historical and social insofar as they change, assume, and influence each other in a process of mutual feedback. In Figure 2 this model has been represented schematically.

Mutual feedback domains

The mutual feedback relation between stagnation of meaning, construction of meaning, and social consequences is realized primarily through what Moscovici regards as social representations (Moscovici, 1976, 1981, 1984, 1988). These social representations, which in their quality of cognitive

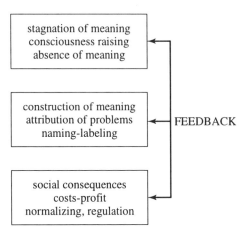

Figure 2. The historical-contextualist model (Hutschemaekers, 1990).

matrices interrelate ideas, words, images, and perceptions, enable patients, therapists, and the culture more generally to understand each other. Through social representations, meanings become acceptable to all parties and enable them to accept the consequences. Thus, social representation – as a framework of meaning – forms the background and foundation of specific constructs, attitudes, and attributions. Representation determines the limits of social significance and dialogue. However, representations have their own history; they are in a constant process of being created by people in the community. They also move away from their original context and form by means of transformation processes of objectivation and person-ification, figuration and ontologisation (Moscovici, 1988). In these processes newly created constructs are constantly being embedded in familiar and safe situations. This process, called anchoring or grafting, leads to the creation of new, specific constructs, which are constantly being assimilated into old social representations. Old social representations are also accom-modated to new specific constructions and events. A striking description of this proces of assimilation and accommodation of social representations has been given by Zeegers (1988), who used the metaphor of walking islands. By force of a continuous wind from the west, an island will slowly but certainly crumble away unnoticed, while at the east coast, simultaneously, alluvial land will be formed, absorbing the old coast. In this process of assimilation and accommodation "social construction" takes place at two levels: at the level of the massive cognitive matrices and at the level of specific constructs, attributes, and attitudes. In Figure 3 this model has been represented schematically.

Global representations often exist for centuries (as we have seen in the

Processes of decoding and transference

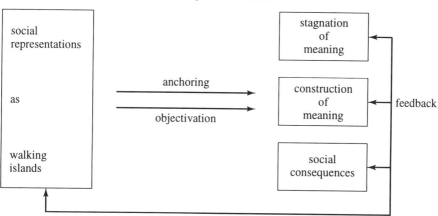

Figure 3. Transformation of representations.

case of the history of the classical melancholy), while the more specific constructions such as attitudes can transform suddenly (as a result of the demands of professionalization or a new legislation) and continue to exist for some time. However, sometimes it happens that social representations suddenly reappear after having been out of sight, "below sea level," for centuries, to give expression to a recognizable reality in a renewed form. Social representations, represented here as "walking islands," suggest that the representations with their various processes of assimilation and accommodation, crumbling away and depositing alluvial land, remain always recognizable. Thus, in the history of melancholy and depression the differing theories regarding origin were accepted as useful constructions and productive bases of treatment, since they originated from and were linked to the more general representations of body and mind (Speak, 1990), and thus promoted meaningful contact within the various cultural settings (Lepenies, 1972).

The historicity of therapy: The healing properties of time

Let us finally give the contextual-construction model a practical application. About a century ago the well-known French psychiatrist Pierre Janet saw on the horizon a "pédagogie sérieuse" that would enable him and his contemporaries to recognize crimes in advance, redress perverse instincts, cure the unhappy and those suffering in body and in mind, and bring relief to those who, so far, had been considered incurable (Janet, 1894–1895). Janet's optimism proved to be unfounded. Large-scale research into the results of "psychotherapy" shows that in spite of vast efforts to perfect the therapeutic processes, its effectiveness appears to be very meager indeed (Lazarus, 1968; Bergin & Strupp, 1972). But perhaps, at bottom, today's therapy with all its specialist requirements is not so much of a problem after all. As can be concluded from the social constructionalist-contextualist approach presented here, it is imperative that therapist and patient belong to the same system of social representations. On the base of this the two of them form constructs, understand each other, and help one another. Three historical examples, among which is a recent one from East Germany, may serve to illustrate this point of view.

Well into the eighteenth century, Johann Joseph Gassner, a simple "village priest," was a successful exorcist. On a large scale he exorcized the devil from the possessed in all layers of society. Before he started exorcizing he made sure whether the patient believed in Jesus Christ. If so, he set to work. In a solemn Latin and with ritual gestures he began challenging the demon (had he power over the right arm? – the right arm convulsed straightaway; power over the left leg?), and if the demon had sufficiently been provoked, Gassner thought fit to drive him out of the body. But then, Gassner lived in a time that belief in demons was on the wane. People wanted a rational explanation of their disturbances and wanted a therapy based on the latest scientific findings. It was only a matter of years that exorcism had to give way to Mesmer's animal magnetism – a spiritistic aura that connected people and made use of a *baquet* for physical device, which had much appeal to the enlightened minds at the end of the eighteenth century owing to its assumptions, practice, and rational and natural historical approach (Ellenberger, 1970, 53–68). At that moment falsification of history set in. There was no way for Mesmer to explain his predecessor's success but to declare that Gassner, unknowingly, had made use of animal magnetism. Fortunately, Mesmer was never asked to attend to Gassner's former patients.

A century later Pierre Janet, already mentioned, faced the same problems of a cognitive short-circuit as Mesmer. In his essay "Un cas de possession et l'exorcisme moderne" (1894), he mentioned a patient – called Achilles in order to avoid possible identification – who, in 1890, showed all classical signs of being possessed. After having tried without avail to get in touch with Achilles and many fruitless efforts to calm him down, Janet finally sought the assistance of a chaplain, attached to the Salpêtrière. But the chaplain had lost all confidence in his powers. He restricted his efforts to offering some comfort, trying to make a distinction between true faith and diabolical superstition. According to the chaplain the patient was a madman and in urgent need of medical care rather than religious help. According to the chaplain's doubts as to diabolical superstition, Achilles could not be cured by him (Janet, 1894–1895).

After the German unification psychotherapists in what used to be East Germany seem to be under a greater emotional stress than their patients. "Many patients break off treatment, even after two or three hours," complains a psychotherapist from Dresden. "Their overpowering concern is with their making a living and they cannot be bothered with working on their inner conflicts; the therapist on the other hand has not yet familiarized himself with a sort of person that takes initiatives and shows perseverance." The therapist regards himself as insincere when he takes an optimistic view, or as a gullible fool or even as a traitor who suddenly has to advocate the formerly hated market economy. The sudden changes in the social representations of the individual and society cause the therapist to feel "powerless," paralyzed in the exercise of his profession (Moser, 1991).

To reiterate my point, it will not be possible for a therapist and patient to reach an understanding and start treatment unless they are part of the same system of cultural meanings.

The therapies change with the time, change with the social representations and specific constructs. A therapy has to be tailored to those representations and constructs. If this is not the case, either as a result of the theory being fixed in the past or too much anticipating the future, it will fail to be effective. In addition to the manifold requirements a (psycho)therapist has to meet in any case, there is one that should be most needed: immersion in the contemporary meaning system. Only on this condition is time prepared to heal all wounds.

Notes

1 For the Netherlands the period of the moral treatment came too early. This is probably due to the small-scale asylums and their particularistic form of government. Contrary to the practice in other West European countries there was no central government interference. Regional and local particularism caused the isolation and treatment of the mentally ill and their supervision to belong to the competence of the regents and local authorities. Central government had yet to learn how to deal with these affairs and local government was too slow and too backward to follow the international development.
2 The characterization of the four types of humors (temperaments) continued to develop during the postclassical period until it found its definite form around the twelfth century (Flashar, 1966, 117).

References

Ackerknecht, E. H., & Akert, K. (1964). Wechselnde Formen der Unterbringung von Geisteskranken. *Schweizerische Medizinische Wochenschrift, 44*, 1541–1546.
Aristotle. (1927). *The works of Aristotle translated into English*, ed. W. D. Ross. Vol. 7: *Problemata*, trans. E. S. Forster. Oxford: Oxford University Press.
Babb, L. (1951). *The Elizabethan malady: A study of melancholia in English literature*. East Lansing: Michigan State University Press.
Beck, A. T. (1972). *Depression: Causes and treatment*. Philadelphia: University of Pennsylvania Press.

Beck, A. T. (1979). *Cognitive therapy and the emotional disorder*. New York: New American Library.

Beek, H. H. (1969). *Waanzin in de middeleeuwen. Beeld van de gestoorde en bemoeienis met de zieke*. Nijkerk: G. F. Callenbach.

Bergin, A. E., & Strupp, H. H. (1972). *Changing frontiers in the science of psychotherapy*. Chicago: Aldine Atherton.

Blackmore, R. (1725). *A treatise of the spleen and vapours: Or hypocondriacal and hysterical affections*. London: J. Pemberton.

Blasius, D. (1979). *Der verwaltete Wahnsinn: Eine Sozialgeschichte des Irrenhauses*. Frankfurt am Main: Suhrkamp.

Burton, Robert. (1621/1977). *The anatomy of melancholy*. New York: Vintage Books.

Carlson, E. T. (1960). The psychotherapy that was moral treatment. *American Journal of Psychiatry, 117*, 519–524.

Chamberlain, A. S. (1966). Early mental hospitals in Spain. *American Journal of Psychiatry, 123*, 143–149.

Chatel, J., & Jof, B. (1975). Psychiatry in Spain, past and present. *American Journal of Psychiatry, 132*, 1182–1186.

Cheney, G. (1733). *The English malady; Or, a treatise of nervous diseases of all kinds*. London: G. Strahan & J. Leake.

Diagnostic and statistical manual of mental disorders. (1987). 3rd ed. Rev. DSM-III-R. Washington, D.C.: American Psychiatric Association.

Dodds, E. (1957). *The Greeks and the irrational*. Boston: Beacon Press.

Dörner, K. (1969). *Bürger und Irre: Zur Sozialgeschichte und Wissenschaftssoziologie der Psychiatrie*. Frankfurt am Main: Europäische Verlagsanstalt.

Elias, N. (1971). Sociologie en psychiatrie. *Sociologie en Geschiedenis*. Amsterdam: Van Gennep (123–156).

Ellenberger, H. F. (1970). *The discovery of the unconscious: The history and evolution of dynamic psychotherapy*. New York: Basic Books.

Esquirol, Etienne. (1976). *De la lypémanie ou mélancholie*. In *Classics in psychiatry. Etienne Esquirol. Des malades mentales*. New York: Arno Press (vol. 2, 398–481).

Ey, H. (1978). La notion de "maladie morale" et de "traitement" moral dans la psychiatrie française et allemande au début du XIX siècle. *Perspectives Psychiatriques, 1*.

Fedida, P., & Postel, J. (1977). *Etienne Esquirol. De la lypémanie ou mélancholie*. Toulouse: Privat.

Finlay-Jones, Robert. (1986). Accidie and melancholy in a clinical context. In Harré, R. (ed.), *The social construction of emotions*. Oxford: Basil Blackwell (227–233).

Flashar, Hellmut. (1966). *Melancholie und Melancholiker in den medizinischen Theorien der Antike*. Berlin: Walter de Gruyter.

Foucault, M. (1961). *Folie et déraison: Histoire de la folie à l'âge classique*. Paris: Union Générale d'Editions.

Foucault, M. (1968). Réponse à une question. *Esprit, 36* (371), 850–874.

Foucault, M. (1969). *L'archéologie du savoir*. Paris: Gallimard.

Gergen, K. J. (1990). Die Konstruktion des Selbst im Zeitalter der Postmoderne. *Psychologische Rundschau, 41*, 191–199.

Gergen, K. J. (1991). *The saturated self: Dilemmas of identity in contemporary life*. New York: Basic Books.

Griesinger, W. (1867). *Die Pathologie und Therapie der psychischen Krankheiten*. Stuttgart: Krabbe.

Harré, R. (1986). *The social construction of emotions*. Oxford: Blackwell.

Hersant, Y. (1984). Acedia. *Le Débat, 29*, 44–48.

Hutschemaekers, G. (1990). *Neurosen in Nederland, Vijfentachtig jaar psychisch en maatschappelijk onbehagen*. Nijmegen: Sun.

Jackson, S. W. (1986). *Melancholia and depression: From hippocratic times to modern times*. New Haven: Yale University Press.

Janet, P. (1894–1895). Un cas de possession et l'exorcisme moderne. *Bulletin de l'Université de Lyon, 8* (2), 42–43.

Klibansky, R., Panofsky, E., & Saxl, F. (1964). *Saturn and melancholy: Studies in the history of natural philosophy, religion and art.* London: Nelson.

Köhler, E. (1977). *Arme und Irre: Die liberale Fürsorgepolitik des Bürgerstums.* Berlin: Wagenbach.

Kraepelin, E. (1896). *Psychiatrie. Ein Lehrbuch für Studirende und Aertze.* Leipzig: J. A. Barth.

Kraepelin, E. (1918). Hundert Jahre Psychiatrie. *Zeitschrift für die gesamte Neurologie und Psychiatrie, 38,* 210–211.

Kraus, G. (1961). *Krankzinnigheid in Nederland. Een sociaal-psychiatrische studie.* Leiden: Stenfert Kroese.

Kuilman, M. (1971). *Klinische en psychologische beschouwingen over de endogenie.* Lochem: De Tijdstroom.

Laurentius, Andreas. (1500/1939). *A discourse of the preservation of sight; of melancholike diseases; of rheumes and old age.* Trans. R. Surphlet. London. Reprint Shakespeare Association Facsimiles, 102.

Lazarus, R. S. (1968). *Patterns of adjustment and human effectiveness.* New York: McGraw-Hill.

Lepenies, W. (1972). *Melancholie und Gesellschaft.* Frankfurt am Main: Suhrkamp.

Levinus, Lemnius. (1561). *De habitu et constitutione corporis.* Antwerpen.

Lidz, T. (1966). Adolf Meyer and the development of American psychiatry. *American Journal of Psychiatry, 123,* 320–332.

Meyer, A. (1951). A review of *Recent problems of psychiatry.* In Winters, E. E. (ed.), *The collected papers of Adolf Meyer.* Baltimore: Johns Hopkins Press (vol. 2, 331–385).

Moscovici, S. (1976). *La psychanalyse, son image et son public.* Paris: Presses Universitaires de France.

Moscovici, S. (1981). On social representations. In Forgas, J. P. (ed.), *Social cognition: Perspectives on everyday understanding.* London: Academic Press (181–209).

Moscovici, S. (1984). The phenomenon of social representations. In Farr, R. M. & Moscovici, S. (eds.), *Cognitive analysis of social behavior.* The Hague: Martinus Nijhoff (3–69).

Moscovici, S. (1988). *Le Dieu à faire des machines.* Paris: Arthème Fayard.

Moser, T. (1991). Interview in *Die Zeit,* June 6, 1991.

Neugebauer, R. (1978). Treatment of the mentally ill in medieval and early modern England: A reappraisal. *Journal of the History of Behavioral Sciences, 14,* 158–169.

Panse, F. (1964). *Das Psychiatrische Krankenhauswesen.* Stuttgart: Thieme.

Peeters, H. F. M. (1982). Historische fasen in aard en behandeling van geesteziekten. In Binneveld, J. M. W., Brinkgreve, C., Lameijn, A. J., Peeters, H. F. M., Vandermeersch, P., Vos, C. P. & Vijsclaar, J. (eds.), *Een psychiatrisch verleden. Uit de geschiedenis van de psychiatrie.* Baarn: Ambo (11–25).

Peeters, H. F. M. (1984). Theoretical orientations in a historical psychology. In Gergen, K., & Gergen, M. (eds.), *Historical social psychology.* Hillsdale, N.J.: Lawrence Erlbaum (61–81).

Peeters, H. F. M. (1990). Limits of social constructionism: Beyond objectivism and relativism. In Van de Vijver, F., & Hutschemaekers, G. (eds.), *The investigation of culture.* Tilburg: Tilburg University Press (77–90).

Pomme, P. (1760). *Traité des affections vaporeuses des deux sexes.* Paris: Desaint et Saillant.

Raulin, J. (1759). *Traité des affections vaporeuses du sexe.* Paris: Hérissant.

Sarbin, T. R. (1964). Anxiety: Reification of a metaphor. *Archives of General Psychiatry, 10,* 632–633.

Schings, H. J. (1977). *Melancholie und Aufklärung.* Stuttgart: J. B. Metzler und C. E. Poeschel.

Starobinski, Jean. (1960). *Geschichte der Melancholiebehandlung von den Anfängen bis 1900.* Acta psychosomatica, no. 4. Basel: Documenta Geigy.

Tellenbach, H. (1976). *Melancholie. Problemgeschichte-Endogenität-Typologie-Pathogenese-Klinik.* Berlin: Springer-Verlag.

Trimbos, K. (1975). *Antipsychiatrie. Een overzicht.* Deventer: Van Loghum Slaterus.

Tuke, S. (1813). *Description of the retreat, an institution near York for insane persons of the society of friends.* York: W. Alexander.

Vandermeersch, P. (1982). *De religie en het ontstaan van de psychiatrie.* In Binneveld, J. M. W., Brinkgreve, C., Lameijn, A. J., Peeters, H. F. M., Vandermeersch, P., Vos, C. P., & Vijselaar, J. (eds.), *Een psychiatrisch verleden. Uit de geschiedenis van de psychiatrie.* Baarn: Ambo, (11–25).

Wenzel, S. (1960). *The sin of sloth: Acedia in Medieval thought and literature.* Chapel Hill: University of North Carolina Press.

Wittkower, R., & Wittkower, M. (1969). *Born under Saturn: The character and conduct of artists: A documented history from antiquity to the French revolution.* New York: Norton.

Zeegers, W. (1988). *Andere tijden, andere mensen. De sociale representatie van identiteit.* Amsterdam: Bert Bakker.

12   Women as mothers and the making of the European mind

Brigitte Niestroj-Kutzner

Bildung is a human right.
  – Graffiti, Psychologisches Institut, Freie Universität Berlin

To Hanus and Mechthild Papousek

Over the past quarter century the topic of the "woman as mother" has achieved a recognizable if somewhat isolated place in sociohistorical research (Welter, 1966; Bloch, 1978; Badinter, 1980; Treckel, 1989; Todd, 1980; Nash, 1981; Wilson, 1984; Dixon, 1988; Lewis, 1989; Atkinson, 1991). Separate from this history, another topic of research has been able to establish itself: the "history of childhood" (van den Berg, 1956; Ariès, 1960; DeMause, 1974; Peeters, 1975; Arnold, 1980; Borstelmann, 1983; Schlumbohm, 1983; Boswell, 1988; Shahar, 1990). Parallel to these concerns there has developed a further branch of research that aims to pursue historically the relationships between parents and children (Hunt, 1970; Demos, 1970; DeMause, 1974; Greven, 1977; Kagan, 1977; Ozment, 1983; Pollock, 1983; Houlbrooke, 1984; Ottmüller, 1991).

In reviewing literature in these areas it is noticeable that there is a lack of reciprocal permeation. The history of the woman as mother has left virtually no mark on the history of the parent–child relationship, in which a distinction is seldom made between father and mother (Crawford, 1986), and which fails to give even the slightest of hints that a history of the woman as mother might prove a sensible object of research. On the other hand, in studies of the woman as mother, points of contact with the history of childhood are scarcely detectable. Our experience is no different when we look at the history of developmental psychology (Anderson, 1956; Anandalakshmy & Grinder, 1970; Reinert, 1976; Cairns & Bornstein, 1979; Bornstein, 1979; Borstelmann, 1983; Cairns, 1983; Smuts & Hagen, 1985) as well as the history of infant care (Stendler, 1950; Vincent, 1951; Wolfenstein, 1953; Schlossman, 1981). We more readily find a connection

I wish to thank Kenneth Gergen for his support.

227

to the history of the family, history of childhood, history of the woman as mother, and developmental psychology in the literature on the history of family education (Lawrence, 1962; Schlossman, 1976; Weiss, 1978; Gadlin, 1978; Marre, 1986; Wrigley, 1989).

For developmental psychology, an analysis of its inherent concepts, especially regarding the woman as mother, has yet to be made. It comes as something of a surprise that developmental and child psychology, in which the mother–child relationship is researched the most intensively, has scarcely been affected by the present discussion of the woman as mother. To the best of my knowledge the demand made by Klapper (1971), that the relationship of feminism and developmental psychology be reflected anew, has had no further influence on research work. Chodorow and Contratto (1982) repeated this demand with the added insight that a history or theory of motherhood comes to a dead end if it does not reflect on and question theories of child development.

Feminists have been trying to build a theory of mothering without examining or noticing that a theory of mothering requires a theory of childhood and child development as well. . . . Feminist theories of motherhood have not been able to move further because, as we have suggested, they are trapped in the dominant cultural assumption and fantasies about mothering, which in turn rest on fantasied and unexpected notions of child development. (pp. 69–70)

But does this mean that we would rid ourselves and our research from "cultural assumptions"? Can there be an "objective truth" about the nature of child development and mothering? Is, for example, our concern for "intersubjectivity" the result of more thorough and intensive research into mother and child, as Benjamin (1990) seems to suggest, and thus a form of scientific progress? Or does this "revolutionary discovery" of the newborn as capable of reciprocal interaction with hidden social and cultural demands coincide with the feminist age and the emphasis on intersubjectivity?

A major purpose of this essay is to show that our assumptions regarding human development in general and the mother and child in particular have their roots in a Christian-humanistic tradition. I also wish to locate the origins of the discourse on the mother and child within a critical historical review of notions of a changing anthropology of the human subject. The working hypothesis is as follows:

A changing view of the human being is associated with a changing approach to child care and child development. This changing approach to the child is accompanied by a "new woman." Women are newly constructed when children, and thus a future society, are defined.

Thus the understanding of motherhood and its cultural ideology may be enhanced by linking the history of motherhood with the history of child development and the making of the European mind. The latter, including as it does the emerging beliefs in "the man of reason," has enormous impact on the definition of motherhood as well as on that of childhood.

The Christian-humanistic legacy in theories of mother and child

The mother–child relationship and its influence on the developing child is so well established as a focus of psychological research that the underlying assumptions about the nature of women as mothers and of children has scarcely been examined. The constructs used in psychological research are seldom recognized as constructs, that is, as conscious products of the research community and not necessarily as "nature"-given or reflecting "pure" reality. Typically the assumptions remain hidden or as untouchable taboos. I wish to discuss and highlight one particular assumption, the seemingly nature-given relationship between intimacy and reason, that still awaits critical-theoretical, and in this case sociohistorical, discussion. The belief frames research on the early mother–child relationship and its correlation with cognitive and social development. I wish to emphasize that the making of the European mind and the discourse of the mother–child relationship are highly related. This seems to me the most marked difference, at least in the sources available, between ancient-medieval and modern times in relation to the changing attitudes to mother and child. This changing attitude coincides with various other changes, which, I believe, are no mere accidents.

In earlier publications (1985, 1987) I have stated that with Christian humanism, as represented in Vives (1492–1540) and Erasmus (1466–1536) and their writings on motherhood and the developing child, we have a completely new interpretation of the mother–child relationship; the shaping of the child's mind and thus of the future new man is highly dependent on this interaction. (Let us recall that humanism is regarded as the cradle of modern man.) In her book on childhood in the Middle Ages, Shulamith Shahar confirms this finding. She agrees that in former times (before Erasmus and Vives) "medieval churchmen, and to a large extent fathers as well, regarded her (the mother), as being exclusively responsible for the child's welfare and physical safety. Medieval authors . . . stressed the need to treat small children under 7 gently and lovingly. They did not, however, stress the importance of the mother's role as the inculcator of speech or the influence of early education on emotional development" (1990: 115). The Middle Ages knows no special justification for love between people and for human care. Salimbene von Parma mentions in his chronicle the experiment conducted by Kaiser Friedrich II (1215–1250), who had some children grow up in isolation in order to determine which language they would develop. This "delusion," as Salimbene writes in 1285, ended in failure, for "without the care and touching, without the smiling and tenderness of their nurses or those caring for them they could not in fact live" (quoted from Niestroj, 1987: 31). Consider Erasmus's statement at the beginning of the sixteenth century: "We cannot stress enough that the first few years of life are of utmost importance for the future life of the child." Analysing sources written prior to Erasmus, Shahar confirms that this Erasmian sentence "could not have been written by a medieval writer" (Shahar, 1990: 115). The present chapter furnishes a tentative account of why this is so and its implications for later developmental theory.

Vives and Erasmus are not only standing at the beginning of a new historical development, they also reflect a previous development, especially regarding attitudes toward "language." The general insight of the humanists, to put it simply, could be summarized as follows: Every aspect of life, including language and meaning, can be related to a dynamic rather than a fixed truth. Between the fourteenth and sixteenth centuries a shift took place, "the shift from referential to relational semantics, from regarding the meaning of language as a given object of reference to regarding it as a dynamic function of use" (Waswo, 1987: 13). During this period the relationship between language and meaning is reconsidered and defined anew because of "observations such as: historical changes in the forms and meanings of words; their context dependency; their systematic functions; their possession of multiple referents; their ability to constitute knowledge, shape feeling, and mold behaviour; their domination by social usage." It is only in the Renaissance and during the time of humanist influence that all those different aspects were seen 'to be mutually relevant or to cohere sufficiently to provide a sustained challenge to the dominant model of meaning" (Waswo, 1987: 17). The humanists' discourse on language and the mother–child relationship will only be taken up again during the eighteenth century.

In Germany with the reception of Locke, Rousseau, and Kant, a vast amount of literature appears again with exactly those concerns just mentioned. In the eighteenth century, the authors are much more precise; child development and woman as mother have become, then, well established as theoretical objects (Niestroj, 1985; Kittler, 1985–1991). This is also a reason why I think it worthwhile for psychologists to concern themselves with those early writings; the Christian-humanistic tradition – its anthropology, its vision of the autonomy of man and the importance of the "mind – is exactly the tradition that we find in research on the mother–child relationship in the twentieth century. What some might regard as an anthropological "given" we can reconstruct as being man-made. I am not claiming that there is a direct line of descent (Christian-humanism to the Enlightenment to twentieth-century science), but we are entitled to draw this line as a hypothesis because of the underlying mutual assumption concerning the importance of the early mother–child relationship and the developing mind extant in the various theories. We do not find this development, in the French tradition with Montaigne (1533–1592) already opposing Erasmus's emphasis on "culture," in Rousseau (1712–1778), nor in theories of child development written in the nineteenth century, or in Jean Piaget. It is mainly in the second half of the twentieth century that psychologists rediscovered "interaction and the socialization of cognition" (see, e.g., Isbell & McKee, 1980; Shweder, 1984).

Man is "fashioned not born" (Erasmus)

Usually we refer to Immanuel Kant when the impact of culture, of education over "nature," is historically emphasized. But it was Erasmus, in fact, who first claimed that man is not born but fashioned. This assumption of man being fashioned has, to my mind, enormous consequences for the definition of women as mothers. Erasmus in his *On an Early Scientific Education of Children* (1529) writes the sentence in a context in which he emphasizes the function of the mother in "fashioning" the child. When the plasticity of man becomes a conscious cultural value, women as the first educators, as the first to "select" reality for the child, seem to be indispensable for language development, for social, moral, and cognitive development, indeed, for shaping the whole personality of the child. Whereas the tendency in centuries prior to Erasmus was to stress caring and ensuring the child's survival, the trend in the Christian-humanistic literature was toward the child's cognitive development and toward personality in relation to "the other." The concept of imitation and thus of interpersonal influence has a long history, but the stress placed on the mother's capacity for influencing the child's social as well as cognitive functioning seems to be an "invention" of the modern period. Erasmus applies ancient Greek philosophical wisdom to the mother–child relationship: Love, authority, and learning are highly related, as is illustrated in the following quotation taken from the *Colloquia familiaria* (about 1518/1965):

Even if it made no difference what milk a delicate child drinks, or what saliva it swallows with the pre-chewed food, or even if you came across a nurse of the sort I doubt exists, do you imagine anyone can put up with all the irksomeness of nursing as a mother can – the filth, the sitting up late, the bawling, the illnesses, the never sufficiently attentive watching? If there's any woman who lives like a mother, it will be one who cares like a mother. Yes, and what's more, your son may love you less, his natural affection being divided, as it were, between two mothers; and your devotion to him will cool in turn. The result will be that when he's older, he'll be the less willing to obey your commands and you'll care less for him – you'll see the nurse in the way he behaves. Now one of the main steps in the learning process is mutual affection between teacher and pupil. (Erasmus, 1965: 283)

To this philosophical wisdom Erasmus adds his own novel insight in stressing the importance of the early years for the development of the child and the significance of an exclusive interaction within the mother–child relationship. Historically speaking, this is no small achievement.

Rousseau in his *Emile* (1762) follows a similar principle for the teacher–pupil relationship, but he is far from attaching great importance to the early years and especially to women educators of their children. Rousseau is quite content to see women breast-feed their own children but he has no other claims to make and does not link early love to desired results in the child's development. How different are Erasmus and the many German writers on child development in the post-Enlightenment period in the late eighteenth century; from the beginning of life man is seen as in need of dialogue and of friendship, of human social interaction. This is the new anthropology, developed over the centuries, which Erasmus has transferred for the first time to the early period of human life: Man's reason is the product of intersubjective relations. When Erasmus wrote that the prime condition of all learning is reciprocal love we can take this as the result of a long historical process in which man experienced himself as powerful. This "intersubjectivity," however, is not meant as an end in itself. Medieval writers, and later Rousseau, might have anticipated, in respect to maternal love, the writings of Freud and Bowlby. However, Erasmus anticipated the mood and demand of the eighteenth and twentieth centuries: the conviction that *man* is social, *knowledge* is social, and *meaning* is social. Dialogue, language development in the child, friendship, those intersubjective aspects are part of the condition for the developing mind. The ideal of the "man of reason" is associated with an anthropology in which man is seen as a being of dialogue. The thinking and reflective mind needs and requires the freedom of discussion.

Man as a being in need of *dialogue*, and thus in need of *intimacy*, furnishes a complete change of outlook on man's position in the world. When knowledge and meaning are social, when "truth" and "reason" are negotiable, then man is the maker and interpreter of his world. Human dialogue and intersubjectivity become a new "value" for creating the European mind.

Mother: The silent force of modernity

With this historical background we now find "intimacy" is not an end in itself; "intimacy" is seen and interpreted in our context as a precondition of "mind." This construct, which has its beginnings in the Christian humanists, is part of the underlying assumption in child and developmental psychology. This is the link between "intimacy and reason," or, in modern terms "intimacy and cognition." Whatever we wish to call it – intersubjectivity, interpersonal sensitivity, intimacy, or the socialization of cogniation – the provider for all this, in the modern view, is the mother. The silent force of modernity, of human progress, of the making of the "man of reason," is woman as mother in her combined functions of nurturing and teaching. Thus, the ideal early mother–child relationship as formulated by the humanists is linked to the growing importance of language and writing, to the perfectibility of the child and thus mankind, to greater awareness of individualism, and, most of all, to "reason" as the new savior of mankind implying that human nature is destined for change and progress. The notion of "change" and "progress" seems to be highly characteristic of the Christian-humanistic tradition and not to be found in other cultures. This idea of progress is also highly related to the notion of controlling, shaping, and molding future events and "products" – like the social, moral, verbal, and cognitive development of the child: "fashioned not born" as Erasmus asserted to mothers. Future man can be created by the human community itself. The humanists experience themselves as being part of the creation of a new, just, and better world.

Continuing the tradition: The developmental psychology of Joachim Heinrich Campe

The humanist themes were reflected in a wide variety of Enlightenment writings. Foremost among them were the works of Joachim Heinrich Campe (1746–1818), who in my opinion was the author of the first great book in developmental psychology, and who related the development of the child to the function of the woman as mother. His 1785 book (1985), *On the Earliest Development of the Minds of Young Children in the First and Second Year of Childhood,* is also one of the most important precursors of contemporary developmental theory. Campe emphasized scarcely anything more strongly than that man, as a child, is of society and a social being. He makes an "instinct for human love" the foundation of the mental development of the child, furnishing as well the significance of woman as mother. The basis for cognitive development for Campe is the organically determined capacity for sensual perception already present, as it were, in man. But Campe relates the realization of this capacity to the presence of the mother as the source for intimacy *and* stimulation. The infant's perception and experience of its environment is effected largely via its senses: This makes possible sensual knowledge of the world on the basis of experience and active dealing with the world. Campe's book accords a central place to the child's sensual knowledge. Bahrt (a colleague of Campe), in an introduction to the revised edition of Campe's works, points out that the main aim of education is to accustom the child to sensual perception so as to enable it to learn truth from these early insights into elementary order and "as a result to make them through self-thought the property of his own mind, to provide early training in the necessary powers of concentration, of abstraction, etc., and guide him to reasoned thought" (Bahrt, 1785: 30).

For Campe the child's assimilation of the world depends, then, on its cognitive *and* social, naturally given abilities: "Only man alone depends for his education wholly on that which surrounds him, on what of importance he observes in others of his species and especially in those who stand in closest relationship to him. He is an imitative animal and that he had to be, *because he was to be a social one*" (1785: 131; emphasis added). Through Campe's postulated "instinct for human love," his presentation of the development of the child is marked by a unity that has not yet again been achieved despite the various approaches in today's child and developmental psychology.

As we have seen, the humanistic tradition contributes substantially to the assumption that man can change and reform himself. Contemporary beliefs about the relationship between mother and child continue to be informed by this assumption. The emphasis placed on "emotional attachment" today, with the empirically determined importance it places on the linguistic, social, and cognitive development of the child, reflects this influence. The importance of present experience as the moment deciding future behavior, the belief in a "sensitive phase" in the development of a person that molds the future, is then a reflection of a far earlier discourse. To extend this view, it may be said that the emphasis placed today on progress, plasticity, and the predictability of man (along with the relationship of these to each other) owes much to the humanists and Enlightenment thinkers. The humanist Erasmus of Rotterdam, the philosopher, doctor, and pedagogue John Locke (1632–1704), and the cofounder of behaviorism John B. Watson (1878–1950) all made the impressionability and the susceptibility to manipulation of human behavior the center of their "educational theories." They share the basic assumptions of man as "unimal educandum," "animal symbolicum," "white paper," and "tabula rasa." To educate a child means, according to these approaches, feeling a duty toward the future, but also having hope for a more just and self-determined human society. In spite of its many problems, behaviorism surely stood at first for the liberation of man, and opposed to the last remnants of the conservative ideology of "social Darwinism."

More broadly, it might be conjectured that what for the modern age and the Enlightenment was "education" is for the twentieth century "socialization." Both are related to the hope that social change might be brought about through local, interpersonal means. The power – or, rather, powerlessness – that provides the bourgeois subject with the illusion of participation in social processes by means of change within the area of intimate relationships has declared this to be its own strength. This partially euphoric belief in the education of the mind as a force for social change must also be regarded as compensation for the experience of powerlessness regarding the ability to participate actively and regulatively in social processes. The cultivation of the human mind, and the related role of the mother–child relationship, may also be regarded as an attempt to reconcile the individual with human society, to transcend the experience of distance and distancing between individuals and groups.

In behaviorism, no inner, psychical relationship-structures are seen as being essential to this development. Man is to be "freed" from the psyche, at least in research. This concept of freed intelligence culminates not in man but in artificial intelligence, which simultaneously redeems a promise to the bourgeois subject. It is the consequence of a history of the human control of the passions: Artificial intelligence needs no such control. Thus it is understandable that academic developmental and child psychologies, which were biologically and physiologically orientated as was psychology itself, do not at first show interest in the mother–child relationship; this was left to psychoanalysis. Only in the 1970s was there a boom in mother–child research, in biologically and humanistically orientated psychology. But cognitive developmental psychology, hitherto context-free, again discovered an area that had for decades completely disappeared from scientific view: social intelligence.

As early as 1978 Kuhn criticized in developmental psychology a tendency to consider social and cognitive development as separate. In doing so, the cognitive development of the child is frequently taken to be anchored in the organism, whereas the process of social development is regarded essentially as external, resulting from conditioning and imitation. Also in the 1970s the social ability, intersubjectivity, and cognitive curiosity of the newly born infant, is *re*discovered and proclaimed to be the beginning of a new scientific revolution (Klaus, 1979). To my mind, it is not sheer coincidence that those two areas of academic research with their emphasis on cooperation and intersubjectivity in infants (e.g., Papousek & Papousek, 1977, 1979; Trevarthen, 1980) and on prosocial behavior, social cognition, and social intelligence (Mussen & Eisenberg-Berg, 1977) were taken up simultaneously in the 1970s. These movements coincide with the awareness that our Western world is in urgent need for improved moral quality – consideration and sympathy for others, generosity, and cooperation – and in less need for egotism and self-seeking behaviors (Mussen & Eisenberg-Berg, 1977).

The theories on the mother and her child suggest that a reliable perspective is possible for observing the world, for knowledge, and for structuring life. Thus origin and identity – interpersonal activity and home – are deemed comparable in a world in which there seems to be no longer any home. In theories of mother and child the first years of life are quite often seen as the home of man (e.g., Winnicott, 1986). In a world in which home encompassed more than just these first years of life, such a statement could perhaps be accepted. But in a deeply "homeless" world, such a statement seems to contain a declaration of bankruptcy to mankind; this sort of home is the last hope to which man, for better or worse, may cling.

Conclusions

My initial purpose was to show that the link between motherhood and notions of child development has a long history. This history intermixed with deep-rooted cultural values and expectations. Notions of child development were (and still are) a product of a changing anthropology, a hope in human progress, in which women were (and are) ascribed a special function. It is equally important to realize that the notions of human progress and of child development have almost always been related to a redefinition of woman, as well as to a desire to change social institutions and human relations via changing the mother–child relationship. (This has also been true for theories of socialization; see Danziger, 1971: 15ff.) This is part of our Christian-humanistic legacy. Vives and, particularly, Erasmus have theoretically and programmatically given the Western world a new image of women as mothers, a view that has been strengthened over the centuries and which has turned into an anthropological "given." It has found its established place in child and developmental psychology. Psychological research has been concerned with the entire question of early experience and its effect on social and cognitive growth. We thus regard as common knowledge "the fact" that the mother is the principal figure in the child's development. By tracing such assumptions back to the humanists and putting them in a much broader historical context, we better understand why cultural views are so firmly implanted that they appear as "given" and are so resistant to change.

I shall conclude this essay with a sentence from Steven Schlossman: "The very real possibility that the focus upon the mother–child relationship will (has) become a substitute for, rather than a prelude to, more concerted efforts at social change is perhaps the best reason for continuing to probe its history to understand its varied meanings and uses in the past . . . and our link with that past" (1976: 467).

References

Anandalakshmy, S., & Grinder, Robert E. (1970) Conceptual emphasis in the history of developmental psychology: Evolutionary theory, teleology, and the nature–nurture issue. *Child Development,* Vol. 41, pp. 1113–1123.

Anderson, John E. (1956) Child Development: An historical perspective. *Child Development,* Vol. 27, pp. 181–196.

Ariès, Philippe (1960) *L'enfant et la vie familiale sous l'ancien régime.* Paris: Plon.

Arnold, Klaus (1980) *Kind und Gesellschaft in Mittelalter und Renaissance.* Paderborn: Ferdinand Schöningh.

Atkinson, Clarissa W. (1991) *The oldest vocation: Christian motherhood in the Middle Ages.* Ithaca, N.Y.: Cornell University Press.

Badinter, Elisabeth (1980) *L'amour en plus.* Paris: Flammarion.

Bahrt (1785) Abhandlung. Über den Zweck der Erziehung überhaupt. In *Allgemeine Revision des gesammten Schul – und Erziehungswesens. Von einer Gesellschaft praktischer Erzieher.* Herausgegeben von Joachim Heinrich Campe. Hamburg: Carl Ernst Bohn.

Bloch, Ruth H. (1978) American feminine ideals in transition: The rise of the moral mother, 1785–1815. *Feminist Studies,* Vol. 2, pp. 100–126.

Borstelmann, Lloyd J. (1983) Children before psychology: Ideas about children, from antiquity to the late 1800s. In William Kessen (Ed.), *Handbook of child psychology,* Vol. 1. New York: Wiley, pp. 1–40.

Boswell, John (1988) *The kindness of strangers: The abandonment of children in Western Europe from late antiquity to the Renaissance.* London: Allen Lane.

Cairns, Robert B. (1983) The Emergence of developmental psychology. In William Kessen (Ed.), *Handbook of Child Psychology,* Vol. 1, *History, theory and methods.* New York: Wiley, pp. 42–102.

Cairns, Robert B., & Bornstein, Peter A. (1979) Developmental psychology. In Eliot Sandford Hearst (Ed.), *The first century of experimental psychology.* Hillsdale, N.J.: Lawrence Erlbaum.

Campe, Joachim Heinrich (1785) *Allgemeine Revision des gesammten Schul – und Erziehungswesens. Erster und Zweiter Theil.* Hamburg: Carl Ernst Bohn.

Campe, Joachim Heinrich (1985) *Über die früheste Bildung junger Kinderseelen.* Ed. B. H. E. Niestroj. Berlin: Ullstein (originally published 1785).

Chodorow, Nancy, & Contratto, Susan (1982) The fantasy of the perfect mother. In Barrie Thorne & Marily Yalom (Eds.), *Rethinking the family.* New York: Longman.

Crawford, Patricia (1986) "The sucking child": Adult attitudes to child care in the first year of life in seventeenth-century England. *Continuity and Change,* Vol. 1 (1), pp. 23–52.

Danziger, Kurt (1971) *Socialization.* Harmondsworth: Penguin.

DeMause, Lloyd (Ed.) (1974) *The history of childhood.* New York: Psychohistory Press.

Demos, John (1970) *A little commonwealth: Family life in Plymouth Colony.* Oxford: Oxford University Press.

Dixon, Suzanne (1988) *The Roman mother.* London: Croom Helm.

Erasmus, Desiderius (1965) *The colloquies of Erasmus.* Trans. Craig R. Thompson. Chicago: University of Chicago Press.

Erasmus, Desiderius (1985) *Collected Works of Erasmus.* Vols. 25 and 26. Toronto: University of Toronto Press.

Gadlin, Howard (1978) Child discipline and the pursuit of self: An historical interpretation. In H. W. Reese & L. P. Lipsett (Eds.), *Advances in child development and behavior.* Vol. 12, New York: Academic Press.

Greven, Philip (1977) *The Protestant temperament: Patterns of child-rearing, religious experience, and the self in early America.* New York: Alfred A. Knopf.

Houlbrooke, Ralph A. (1984) *The English Family 1450–1700.* London: Longman.

Hunt, David (1970) *Parents and children in history: The psychology of family life in early modern France.* New York: Harper & Row.

Isbell, Billie Jean, & McKee, Lauris (1980) Society's cradle: An anthropological perspective on the socialisation of cognition. In J. Sants (Ed.), *Developmental psychology and society.* London: Macmillan.

Kagan, Jerome (1977) The child in the family. *Daedalus,* Vol. 106, pp. 33–56.

Kittler, Friedrich A. (1985) *Aufschreibesysteme 1800–1900.* Munich: Wilhelm Fink.

Kittler, Friedrich A. (1991) *Dichter – Mutter – Kind.* Munich: Wilhelm Fink.

Klapper, Zelda, S. (1971) The impact of the women's liberation movement on child development books. *American Journal of Orthopsychiatry,* Vol. 41, pp. 725–732.

Klaus, Marshall (1978) Foreword. In E. B. Thoman (Ed.), *Origins of the infant's social responsiveness.* Hillsdale, N.J.: Lawrence Erlbaum.

Kuhn, Deanna (1978) Mechanisms of cognitive and social development: One psychology or two? *Human Development*, Vol. 21, pp. 92–118.

Lawrence, K. Frank (1962) The beginnings of child development and family life education in the twentieth century. *Merrill-Palmer Quarterly*, Vol. 8, pp. 207–227.

Lewis, Jan (1989) Mother's Love: The construction of an emotion in nineteenth-century America. In Andrew E. Barnes & Peter N. Stearns (Eds.), *Social history and issues in human consciousness: Some interdisciplinary connections*. New York: New York University Press.

Marré, Beatrice (1986) *Bücher für Mütter als pädagogische Literaturgattung und ihre Aussagen über Erziehung (1762–1851). Ein Beitrag zur Geschichte der Familienerziehung*. Weinheim: Beltz.

Mussen, Paul, & Eisenberg-Berg, Nancy (1977) *Roots of caring, sharing, and helping: The development of prosocial behavior in children*. San Francisco: W. H. Freeman.

Nash, Carol S. (1981) Educating new mothers: Women and the Enlightenment in Russia. *History of Education Quarterly*, Vol. 21, pp. 301–316.

Niestroj, Brigitte H. E. (1985) Die Mutter–Kind-Beziehung im Kontinuum von Neuzeit und Moderne. In Joachim Heinrich Campe: *Über die früheste Bildung junger Kinderseelen*, B. H. E. Niestroj, Frankfurt am Main: Ullstein, pp. 7–73.

Niestroj, Brigitte H. E. (1987) Modern individuality and the social isolation of mother and child. *Comparative Civilizations Review*, Vol. 15, pp. 23–40.

Ottmüller, Uta (1991) *Speikinder – Gedeihkinder. Körpersprachliche Voraussetzungen der Moderne*. Tübingen: Edition discord.

Ozment, Steven (1983) *When fathers ruled: Family life in reformation Europe*. Cambridge, Mass.: Harvard University Press

Papousek, Hanus, & Papousek, Mechthild (1977) Mothering and the cognitive head-start: Psychobiological considerations. In H. R. Schaffer (Ed.), *Studies in mother infant interaction*. London: Academic Press, pp. 63–85.

Papousek, Hanus, & Papousek, Mechthild (1979) The infant's fundamental adaptive response in social interaction. In Evelyn B. Thoman (Ed.), *Origins of the infant's social responsiveness*. Hillsdale, N.J.: Lawrence Erlbaum.

Peters, Harry F. M. (1975) *Kind en jeugdige in het begin van de moderne tijd (ca. 1500–ca. 1650)*. Amsterdam: Boom Meppel.

Pollock, Linda A. (1983) *Forgotten Children: Parent–child relations from 1500 to 1900*. Cambridge: Cambridge University Press.

Reinert, Günther (1976) Grundzüge einer Geschichte der Human-Entwicklungspsychology. In H. Balmer (Ed.), *Die Psychologie des 20. Jahrhunderts*. Vol. 1. Zürich: Kindler.

Rousseau, Jean-Jacques (1977) *Emile*. Trans. B. Foxley with introduction by P. D. Jimack. London: Dent.

Schlossman, Steven L. (1976) Before home start: Notes toward a history of parent education in America, 1897–1929. *Harvard Educational Review*, Vol. 46, pp. 436–467.

Schlossman, Steven L. (1981) Philanthropy and the gospel of child development. *History of Education Quarterly*, Vol. 21, pp. 275–299.

Schlumbohm, Jürgen (Ed.) (1983) *Kinderstuben. Wie Kinder zu Bauern, Bürgern, Aristokraten wurden*. Munich: Deutscher Taschenbuch Verlag.

Shahar, Shulamith (1990) *Childhood in the Middle Ages*. London: Routledge.

Shweder, Richard A. (1984) Anthropology's romantic rebellion against the enlightenment, or ther's more to thinking than reason and evidence. In R. A. Shweder & R. A. LeVine (Eds.), *Culture theory: Essays on mind, self, and emotion*. Cambridge: Cambridge University Press.

Smuts, Alice Boardman, & Hagen, John W. (Eds.) (1985) History and research in child development. In *Monographs of the society for research in child development*, Vol. 50 (4–5).

Stendler, Celia B. (1950) Psychologic aspects of pediatrics. Sixty years of child training practices. Revolution in the nursery. *Journal of Pediatrics*, Vol. 36, pp. 122–134.

Todd, Margo (1980) Humanists, Puritans and the spiritualized household. *Church History,* Vol. 49, pp. 18–34.

Treckel, Paula A. (1989) Breastfeeding and maternal sexuality in colonial America. *Journal of Interdisciplinary History,* Vol. 20, pp. 25–51.

Trevarthen, Colin (1980) Communication and cooperation in early infancy: A description of primary intersubjectivity. In M. Bullowa (Ed.), *Before Speech: The beginning of interpersonal communication.* Cambridge: Cambridge University Press.

van den Berg, Jan Hendrik (1960) *Metabletica. Über die Wandlung des Menschen. Grundlinien einer historischen Psychologie.* Göttingen: Vandenhoeck & Ruprecht. (Dutch edition, 1956.)

Vincent, Clark E. (1951) Trends in infant care ideas. *Child Development,* Vol. 22, pp. 199–209.

Vives, Juan Luis (1913) *Vives: On Education.* Trans. Foster Watson. Cambridge: Cambridge University Press.

Waswo, Richard (1987) *Language and meaning in the Renaissance.* Princeton: Princeton University Press.

Watson, John B. (1982) *Psychological care of infant and child.* London: Allen & Unwin.

Weiss, Nancy Pottisham (1978) The mother – child dyad revisited: Perceptions of mothers and children in twentieth century child-rearing manuals. *Journal of Social Issues,* Vol. 34, pp. 29–45.

Welter, Barbara (1966) The cult of true womanhood: 1820–1860. *American Quarterly,* Vol. 18, pp. 151–174.

Wilson, Stephen (1984) The myth of motherhood a myth: The historical view of European child-rearing. *Social History,* Vol. 9, pp. 181–198.

Winnicott, Donald W. (1986) *Home is where we start from.* London: Norton.

Wolfenstein, Martha (1953) Trends in infant care. *American Journal of Orthopsychiatry,* Vol. 23, pp. 120–130.

Wrigley, Julia (1989) Do young children need intellectual stimulation? Experts' advice to parents, 1900–1985. *History of Education Quarterly,* Vol. 29, pp. 41–75.

Part IV

Lived history

13 Emancipation – a failed project? Remarks on the discourse of radical critique

Irmingard Staeuble

A quarter century ago, students of my generation turned to a radical theoretical and practical critique of social science, the university, and society at large. Keenly ambitious to grasp social totality, we rediscovered the radical classics, which had remained in oblivion even after the end of fascism. Sit-ins, teach-ins, and demonstrations changed our views of history and of society. Critical theory seemed to provide the key to a conscious practical transformation of the world. The nature of social reality as well as the means of changing it became fiercely contested. Before long, students became teachers faced with students who rejected the tyranny of totalization. The dream of social revolution faded in favor of subversion and a concern with the microphysics of power and the state of the subject in the metropoles. In the meantime, the social world around us kept changing rapidly, inconsiderate of the critics' confusion and in utterly unforeseen directions. Will the triumph of market economy and mass migrations from the poorhouses of the world mark the end of critical social theory and its projects for a better society? Or can there be another attempt consciously to make history?

Bewildered by the vicissitudes of the radical discourse on social science, I would like to attempt a self-critical review of the motives and goals, discouragements and regained visions, that inspired, altered, and fragmented the radical project under the impact of changing social conditions. As the socially constituted knowledge interests involved in the critical discourse have hardly been reflected on during the dynamic ups and downs of the radical movement, my account can at best be a preliminary to what might some day become a historiography of oppositional movements in social science. I will start from the subjective, inevitably partial perspective of a participant in those projects of the student movement which aimed at an interdisciplinary critique of social science, for the sake of social transformation. When it comes to the fragmentation of the radical project

I would like to thank Kenneth Gergen and the editors of this volume for many valuable suggestions and criticisms on an earlier draft, and for their generous assistance in making my paper readable English.

243

and the changing paradigms of critical theory, the perspective will become more distanced, indicating tensions between the original aims and the appeal of new approaches. In order not to mislead readers, I should mention that the radical discourse on psychology will not play the key role in my review. As our critique of social science aimed at regaining a comprehensive view of history, society, and subjectivity, it opposed disciplinary specialization. From our interdisciplinary perspective, psychological discourse played a marginal role, especially as it had little to offer to our concern with subjectivity. In particular, I will ask (1) what social motives and goal orientations inspired the student movement, and how changing social conditions subsequently affected the participants' views of the social world; (2) what impact the changing paradigms of critical theory had on the critique of social science; and (3) how these changes affected the critique of traditional psychological discourse.

Fascination with solidarity: The discovery of Marxism

Like other centers of the student movement, the Free University of Berlin was the site of some focal events that, in the mid-1960s, contributed to a rapid political radicalization of masses of students who so far had been apathetic. The postwar restoration of West Germany became a major theme when in 1965 a discussion of "restoration or new beginning," scheduled by the Student Board, was not allowed to take place in the main lecture hall. When we went there, we wanted to listen to the opinions of a well-known leftist journalist, Erich Kuby. But we were to participate in the first sit-in, protesting in front of the closed lecture hall. A year later, the Vietnam War became the focus of our worries about imperialist offensives, and the city saw the first anti–Vietnam War demonstration. A few colored eggs thrown at the Amerika Haus (House of U.S. Culture) during the demonstration caused a big stir, so that the Academic Senate banned further political discussions from university rooms. The conflict between oppositional students and the university plus city authorities escalated to the point when, in 1967, during the violent dispersion of a demonstration against the Shah of Iran by the police, a student was killed by a policeman. We were stunned, the democratic facade had crumbled. "Pull the liberal mask and you'll see a fascist face" became one of the slogans of those days.

Global political problems, antiauthoritarian revolt, and academic life seemed to be equally close, demanding theoretical efforts and direct action. Schools and universities were to be democratized, and curricula were to be made "socially relevant." What had the role of social science been during fascism? How was emancipatory educational practice to be developed? As we got no answers within the system of "Fachidiotentum" ("expert idiocy," a widely used student slogan), we decided to find them by ourselves: In winter 1967, we started the "Critical University," offering our own courses on subjects not covered by the Free University curriculum – from antiauthoritarian education to postcolonial liberation movements. The model was meant to develop into a full-blown counteruniversity, but it lasted only for two semesters.

For most of us, the silence which surrounded the fascist past had long been a major stimulus to the quest for knowledge. Having studied the émigré left's explanations of the link between capitalism and fascism, we short-circuited this insight with our discontent. We provoked our teachers, asking many questions and staging "relevancy" discussions during lectures. In conspirational groups we discovered Marx, and the exciting and revealing experience of "reading *Capital*" was to become the core rationale for a critical social science.

Emancipation from authoritarian constraints, poor working conditions, provincialism, and power politics was our enthusiastic goal. From Berkeley to Prague, revolution seemed in the air, stimulating utopian visions. In this "project of collective and individual autonomy" (Castoriadis 1987–1988), socialism was the promise of solidarity, cosmopolitan openness, and a world to be shaped according to needs.

In the beginning, our critique of social science was marked by the notions of "manipulation" and "establishment." Discontent with the industrial and military applications of social science led to a concern with the question of how we could challenge the "servants of power" (Baritz 1960), and their partial views of society and the individual. The positivism dispute (Adorno et al. 1976) generated into a wave of polemical ideology critique, demasking the manipulative knowledge interests that were served by social research. Our simplistic version of class struggle allowed for an easy answer to the question of "Which side are you on?" Theoretically or practically, one either served the interest of capitalist economy or that of the proletarian masses.

When the industrial strike movements in France and Italy reached a peak in 1969, the issues of class struggle and trade-union strategies gained practical relevance. The problem was that in Germany the workers did not seem to know their proper interests. What, then, prevented their "objective interests" from coming to the fore? How was class consciousness to be raised? The obvious importance of these questions for a revolutionary strategy caused a split between "theoreticists" and "practicists." While the latter resumed factory jobs to agitate the workers (an experience from which some returned with subtly changed views), the former attempted to reorientate social science around social class analysis and problems of class struggle. Discovering the absence of notions of social class and class conflicts in sociology, and the lack of any psychological contributions to questions of class consciousness, we set out to subject both disciplines to a systematic critique of their implicit norms of social harmony and conformism.

Soon it became clear that a substantiation of such critiques would take major efforts. Why not spend these efforts directly on the development of a new social science? A split among the "theoreticists" themselves was foreshadowed, which was soon to grow into a fierce controversy between the adherents of a radical critique and the "reformists." For the protagonists of a new psychology, in the interests of "the workers" or "the people," the question was whether to start from Reich or the Frankfurt School, venture into sexual politics, or renew Freudian Marxism? Was Marx at all reconcilable with Freud? Was not the Cultural Historical School of Vygotsky and Leontev a sounder source of inspiration? On the other hand, those who stuck to the idea of a radical critique of social science struggled with the problem of how to reconcile ideology critique with our vague notion of a dependence of scientific theories on processes of economic change (Bernal 1965) and the concept of knowledge interests suggested by Habermas (1968/1977). What could it mean to criticize social science from an emancipatory interest, in order to transform it?

Critical social science

The theoretical aim as envisaged in the late 1960s was a critical social science that would provide an orientation for the radical transformation of society. Revolution would take long-term efforts and the question of proper strategies had become highly controversial. As intellectuals, we had to prepare the theoretical ground. "Without theory no revolution," underneath a portrait of Marx, became one of the favorite plastic bag imprints. Drawing from Marx's critique of political economy, we viewed the social sciences as a comprehensive body of systematically distorted social knowledge. A radical critique was to uncover this distortion, as well as the interests that had led to the fragmentation of the social sciences. We were to restore the "true" body of societal knowledge. Our task was nothing less than developing a comprehensive theoretical analysis of modern society in its complexity, including those tendencies and active forces out of which a better reality might be formed.

The main difficulty we faced was the transfer of Marx's elaborate concept of ideology into the specialized social sciences. As a model, Marx's critique of Hegel or of classical political economy aimed at the disclosure of the false assumptions in culturally influential theories. As we saw it, the piecemeal theories we were faced with in the specialized disciplines were distorted descendants from classical political economy and social theory. In order to develop a comprehensive account of history, society, and the individual, we had to raise the specialized disciplines to a level of coherence from which transdisciplinary critical analysis could be undertaken.

Reconstructing psychology's "true" subject

As to the psychological part of the project of a critical social science, the aim was a critique of psychology that would reveal its core deficiencies, located in the definition of its subject matter, and at the same time develop a more adequate approach to its "proper" subject matter – that is, the subjective dimension of socioeconomic developments (Pressedienst Wissenschaft 8, 1972). This critique seemed to require a preparatory sociohistorical account of social science in terms of the origins of its specializations. The question was why social totality had been cut like a cake into "economic," "sociological," and "psychological" slices (Staeuble 1976). A comprehensive sociohistorical critique of psychology was to account for both, the historicity of psychology and the historicity of subjectivity. On the one hand, it was to explain why psychology took the shape it actually did. For instance, why does psychological discourse favor ahistorical concepts of mind at the expense of sociohistorical concepts of subjectivity? On the other hand, and more important, it was to unearth the various knowledges of subjectivity that remained precluded from academic psychology. For instance, how was the mentality of industrial workers conceptualized in the labor movement?

In order to account for psychology's distortions, we tried to reconstruct the social contexts of its origins in bourgeois society (Staeuble 1972; Jaeger & Staeuble 1978) and its modern applications (Maikowski, Mattes, & Rott 1976). In search of the social origins of modern psychology, we turned to the conceptualizations of "empirical subjectivity" in eighteenth-century Germany, for instance in the first programs for an empirical psychology. We hoped that by tracing the route from these beginnings to the academic institutionalization of psychology, we might be able to demonstrate how psychological discourse became narrow and socially biased. As a theoretical framework we used a social class perspective. From the respective views of the bourgeoisie and the working people, which were the main problems the social classes had with their own subjectivity, how did each class view the problems of the other? Not surprisingly, eighteenth-century sources offered rich evidence of the emerging bourgeoisie's concern with individualization, as well as abundant programs of a psychosocial formation of the working class. The project of modernity clearly'had a psychological dimension. So had the nineteenth-century oppositional project of a radical social transformation as designed since the days of Fourier and Owen. Insofar as modern psychology claimed a monopoly on knowledge of subjectivity, it could, indeed, be challenged with having abandoned many knowledge resources accumulated over two centuries, and favoring human engineering rather than an understanding of the sociocultural constitution of subjectivity.

Still, the results did not encourage a continuation of this type of sociohistorical reconstruction. The closer we got to the institutionalization of modern academic psychology, the less evidence there was of social knowledge interests that could be attributed to social class views. The differentiation of explicitly stated psychological research interests provided a messily incoherent picture, and it was matched by the increasingly diverse views of social problems held by working-class organizations, thus shattering the totalizing social perspectivist approach. What proved viable in the long run was no more than the attempt at explaining particular formations and changes of psychological research areas in terms of practical problems social agencies had with empirical subjects. On this line, however, historical critique was hardly distinguishable from sound social contextual historiography.

In retrospect, the expectations as to what a historical critique might achieve have been at the same time surmounted and disappointed by recent historiography of psychology. On the one hand, studies by Rose (1985), Hildebrandt (1990), and Danziger (1990), to mention but a few, have provided a far more coherent view of the formation of modern psychology than I would have ever thought possible. This view portrays – and I think adequately portrays – the limited reality on which psychological knowledge has been based. Faced with this small world, it does seem odd to have loaded the discipline with claims to emancipation. Surely, a critical theory of subjectivity was not to be won by reconstructing the deficits of psychology. It took a while to notice that the fallacy of this assumption was not least due to having taken the universalized knowledge claims of psychology at face value.

The great transformation of social science was to remain a chimera. The vision of a comprehensive theory of history, society, and subjectivity became increasingly questionable, as Marxist contributions accumulated. Political economies of science and the educational system, ideology critiques of sociology and psychiatry, historical critiques of specialized disciplines and materialist studies of everyday consciousness – all of these attempts brought about new specializations.

This is not to say that the predominantly Marxist period of critique had made no impact on traditional psychological discourse. For instance, as most of the conceptions of the mind favored by traditional empirical psychology were being called into question for their ideological bias, the naturalist assumption of "psychological reality" as a given has widely yielded to the notion of its social construction. The debate on social relevance also gave rise to a psychological discourse that is more historically and socially situated. To some extent, the emancipatory claims may also have contributed to turning the object domain of psychology into a lively contested area. Though the current pluralism in psychological discourse seems largely due to the professional reorientation toward clinical psychology, an increasing awareness of the social origins of the clients' complaints is obvious even in the by now inflationary talk of "psychosocial" problems. Perhaps, the current pluralism provides a chance for renewed attempts at making social psychology more social (Graumann & Moscovici 1986a, 1986b, 1987) and more historical (Gergen & Gergen 1984), or at historicizing the approach to subjectivity (Jüttemann 1986; Reuter 1990; Sonntag 1990; Staeuble 1991).

Rejecting the tyranny of totalization

In the early seventies, the student movement's revolutionary enthusiasm had withered away. After the failure of the strategy of mass mobilization, especially with regard to the West German emergency bill of 1968 and the 1969 strikes in the Italian and French car industry, sectarianism spread among Stalinist, Trotskyist, and Maoist student groups, and increasingly stale "marxologist" interpretations of the classics slowed down the quest for comprehensive social theory. Disillusionment spread when it became clear that the university reform of 1970 had brought about a technocratic modernization, which radical student demands had helped to realize. The model of student participation in faculty decisions, a reformist concession to our radical demands for democratization, was undermined by a 1972 Supreme Court decision in favor of professors' majority and subsequently reduced to symbolic student presence. Job bans against leftist radicals disrupted the "long march through the institutions" and slowed down the younger students' spirit of revolt. On the other hand, the integrative potential of the welfare state was no longer to be underestimated. But welfare state analysis proved a tiresome exercise for academics, with little appeal to students. Hardly noticeable at first, student mood shifted from the utopia of a societal alternative toward the "currently intolerable," and the common denominator of the intolerable seemed to be excessive social control.

Foucault's writings provided a response to various discontents. His anti-scientistic rhetoric entailed the promise of a radical undermining of the scientific status of the human sciences, and his provocative writings on the microphysics of power allowed for both an analysis of the functioning of particular institutional practices of human degradation and issue-centered direct intervention. Lending a voice to the insane and the imprisoned seemed a liberating turn against silencing institutions. Also, the strategic notion of power being divided among various parties and social agencies, permanently changing hands between social actors, was closer to the experience of provocative direct action than the notion of class struggle. Playing subversive games, one could win or lose, and the result would be temporary.

Archaeology and genealogy of the human sciences

For Marxist attempts at a social history of the human and social sciences, Foucault's linkage of discourses and practices seemed valuable. At least, I thought so when I halfheartedly agreed to put Foucault on the agenda for a University of California course on approaches to the history of social science. However, when the generalized notion of "disciplinary society" (Foucault 1977) tended to get the better of "capitalist society," the relationship looked less close. As an institutional model of the subjection of individual bodies, the prison might equal schools, factories, and barracks, but viewing society as a totalized institution was certainly far from a dialectic model.

An archaeological critique of knowledge and a complementary genealogical historiography of the human sciences as presented in Foucault's inaugural lecture at the Collège de France aimed at both, an unmasking of discursive rules of exclusion, and an analysis of the power practices that gave rise to the particular discourses. The emphasis on the productive aspect of power practices suggested a possible extension of the Marxist paradigm of production, just as the postulated convergence of the will to truth – "that enormous machinery of exclusion" (Foucault 1974, 15) – with the will to power radicalized the critique of instrumental reason.

Had Foucault not so strongly encouraged an unsystematic use of his ideas, we might have given more thought to the inconsistencies in his proposals. For instance, insofar as genealogical historiography is used to demonstrate the convergence of the will to knowledge with the will to power, it must unearth the knowledges that have been excluded from the human science discourse. Our reading of Foucault was that the knowledges of psychiatric patients, the imprisoned, gays, and blacks provide perspectives that transcend the power-knowledge regime. However, genealogical historiography itself also claimed a privileged knowledge position beyond the power-knowledge regime. With this claim, problems of the Marxist ideology critique reappeared. But unlike Marxist ideology critique, which turns the privileged perspective of proletarian class consciousness into a practical perspective of liberation, genealogy rests content with mere historiography.

Deconstructing the subject

When Foucault turned from the techniques of subjection to the techniques of the self, to the practices by which individuals act upon themselves (e.g., confession), producing a self-referential subjectivity, he modified his approach. His genealogy of desiring subjects is to trace the forms and modalities of self-referentiality by which being is historically constituted as experience (Foucault 1984a, 1984b). Analyzing the modern experience of oneself as the subject of a "sexuality," he opens a range of questions that refer to the conditions of self-concern: By means of which truth games do humans think of their own being when regarding themselves as insane, sick, or criminals, or reflecting upon themselves as living, talking, and working beings (Foucault 1984a)?

Foucault-inspired approaches to the historiography of psychology have been strongly based on the disciplinary model of society. Sonntag (1988) who combined the demasking of psychology with the production of the individual stressed the political and administrative regulations of a psychologized population. His plea for a historiography of the individual justly warns of the illusion that one could discover the "real" mental makeup of humans, the kind of "thing in itself" missed by psychology. Instead, an "historical psychology" would have to look for the sociohistorical and intellectual relations and means of production that allowed for the construction of "subjectivity," "consciousness," and "self." Still, accounts of the techniques of the self (e.g., Hahn & Kapp 1987) have yet to flourish in the discourse on psychology.

The nuclear threat: Limits of the emancipatory project

Around 1980, visions of a great transformation of society had faded in favor of issue-centered protest movements. Antinuclear, feminist, ecological, and alternative life-style initiatives flourished, and antinuclear campaigns found support in large parts of the population. The university had ceased to be the center of political protest. Attempts at resuming the project of a critical social science came with the imminent stationing of the Pershing II and the conservative political "turn" of 1983, the symbol-laden and much debated fiftieth year after the beginning of fascism. Joining peace movement demonstrations, blockades of nuclear plant and Pershing II sites, and symbolic declarations of "nuclear free zones" revived a sense of solidarity, but we soon felt it was not a sufficient response to the expansion of the civil and military nuclear threat. Small groups of students and teachers set up peace initiatives in various departments, to discuss the nuclear condition, and to search for more adequate theoretical and practical responses. Some seminars and invited lectures also focused on special aspects of the nuclear problem. Learning more technical and economic facts about nuclear rearmament, collecting the materials provided by the antinuclear organizations of physicians and physicists, and rereading Günther Anders's (1956/1980) reflection on the human condition in the nuclear age was an important process. However, the expectation that this focus would generate a renewed discourse of critical social science was soon to be disappointed.

Anders's challenge of traditional as well as critical social theory made it clear that our previous attempts at theorizing modernity in terms of class struggle and the chances for social revolution had been far too simplistic. Since Hiroshima, the problem of *how* societies are to be organized has been overshadowed by the problem of *whether* life on earth can continue. Technology has reached a point where humankind is endowed with the negative omnipotence of its self-destruction, an omnipotence we cannot get rid of as it is inscribed as "know-how" in the very system of science and technology. The nuclear condition casts doubts upon the lasting critical function of the category of human labor on which the emancipatory project has been based. As this notion of labor is associated with objectivation and self-realization, it still implies a problematic anthropocentrism, which, in Occidental ethics, has always had a counterpart in the association of objectivation and domination, from the biblical "subject the earth to thyself" to Kant's license for using everything, except humans, as mere means. In his essay on the Hiroshima bomb, Anders argues convincingly that it is impossible to think of nuclear weapons in terms of means and ends. Not only would the logic of instrumental reason itself collapse in the actual use of such "means." From the beginning of nuclear "testing," these "experiments" have been events of historical reality, accumulating irreversible contamination. The products of nuclear technology are but extreme examples of the long chain of effects of which we are no longer in command. With technology becoming the "subject" of history, limits of the emancipatory project make themselves felt. The question is no longer who is to promote whose emancipation, but rather what kind of emancipation is at stake.

The fatal cleavage between technomind and moral imagination

In his diagnosis of the human condition in the nuclear age, Anders emphasizes the phenomenon of a "Promethean" disproportion between our technological capabilities and our inability to imagine, let alone handle responsibly, the world-transformative effects of technology. Moral evil is thus no longer a matter of ill-doing or ill-willing, it is inherent in the structure of our deficient imagination and sense of responsibility vis-à-vis the system of our products. The modern industrial revolution with its spiraling dynamic has increasingly outbalanced the relationship between the technical and socio-moral capacities of humans. Millions of people can be killed by simply pressing a button, but we cannot imagine or mourn over more than a few victims. Compassion and institutionalized inhibition from violating or killing other people work hardly beyond the realm of concrete interpersonal relations.

For Anders, the merging of the classical dichotomy of *making* (poiesis) and *doing* (praxis) into a *serving* of industrial and political machines is the core problem of fragmented subjectivity of which Eichmann or Hoess are the prototypes. This fragmentation has reached an extent that makes the chance of resynchronizing the organizer of death factories with the after-hours loving family father, or the manager of poison gas production with the nice sport on the tennis court, extremely fragile.

One might have expected closer investigations into the technological transformation of both social relations and human capacities to flourish. Still, the concern with "human obsolescence" has hardly gone beyond reinterpretations of Anders's challenge of philosophy and social science (Althaus 1989; Brentano 1987; Staeuble 1987, 1988). Proposals for cross-disciplinary approaches to the technonuclear condition remained marginal, due not least to an increasingly tight organization of teaching and learning along the lines of disciplinary specialization. The problem of the nuclear condition may also in itself be a too big problem to encourage a reshaping of critical social science. The envisaged goal of individual and collective autonomy would require that societies all over the world develop the ability of consciously and responsibly deciding over the kind of technology they use and the way in which they use it. Yet how would one conceptualize the global pattern of sociotechnological conditions in a way that would allow to estimate the opportunities and limits of establishing technological alternatives? The cross-disciplinary study groups and colloquia established in response to the Chernobyl catastrophe dissolved within a short period, as participants felt they could not reconcile radical theoretical ambitions with the emotional perplexity caused by the nuclear pervasion of everyday life.

The ambiguous appeal of difference

The conservative turn with its nonetheless modernist program of nuclear energy extension, more freeways, and high-tech communication marked the end of social democratic reform and leftist visions of a great transformation. The economic recession brought the postwar model to an end. This model had been based on Keynesian economic regulation, welfare state compensation for social risks, and the nation-state as the political unity of action (Altvater 1983). As a consequence of stagnant world production, structural mass unemployment was now about to marginalize potentially one-third of society. The end of "working society" seemed imminent, and it proved difficult to even imagine viable alternative modes of a societal regulation of the economy.

The combination of nuclear threat and economic crisis entailed a growing sense of "no future," which widely nourished the appeal of posthistoire and postmodernism. If the declared end of the social, the political, and the agony of the real suggested that we may not at all be dealing with real phenomena, but only with nominalist scriptures, its impact on the radical discourse grew, nevertheless. Baudrillard's (1975, 1978) parodies on production, the revolt of the signs, and the implosion of power drew attention to symptoms of derealization and dissuasion and at the same time dissuaded attempts at an explanation of these symptoms. Lyotard's (1984) dismissal of the modern metanarratives, the idea of social emancipation, solidarity, and self-determined activity even suggests that there is nothing lost and nothing to deplore. Social conflicts and the resulting misery in the world are no longer ascribed to objective causes, but to the fact that humans still hold on to the values of autonomy and self-determination.

The appeal of postmodernism in social theory is largely due to its epistemological concern with fragments, fractures, and difference, which corresponds to a political concern with minorities. The notion of difference suggests a concern with sensitivity to "otherness" and tolerance of plurality instead of the antagonisms of social classes and the bellicose dichotomies of progress and reaction, rationality and irrationality, and the like (Huyssen 1986). However, different forms of social life are not self-sustaining entities. They depend on one another, interact, or clash. In case of conflict, Lyotard's (1983) model provides for local and temporary negotiations and agreements. Provisional social contracts can be entered in all sexual, cultural, familial, and international affairs. But what if the differences turn out to be irreconcilable? The sweeping dismissal of the universal principles of modernity tends to leave us with Hobbesian conditions of civil war.

Postmodern challenges to social science

Recent attempts at interpreting postmodernity in terms of economic, social, and cultural changes indicate that the critical tradition is still a helpful guide to the analysis of puzzling cultural experience. Jameson (1984) used hallucinatory city images mirrored from glass facades as an entry to the question of the situatedness of the individual in the postmodern space, interpreting the aesthetic experience of "intensity" in terms of the classic topos of stateliness. For him, the fascination with the surface of mirrored mirror images points to the difficulty of grasping the global system of multinational capitalism; situated in this hyperspace, our mode of perception proves obsolete, unable to gain distance. Harvey's (1989) account of the transition to "flexible accumulation" by new organizational forms and technologies in production, and of their bearing on the postmodern experience of space and time has provided a convincing argument for the structural relationship between intensified acceleration of accumulation and the role of volatility and ephemerality of fashions and labor processes, media images, and social practices.

Critiques of social science based on the postmodernist trend have focused on the objectivistic and universalistic knowledge claims established by modern social analysis. In anthropology, the emphasis on culturally constituted meaning systems, indigenous notions of personhood and emotion, and the communicative aspects of ethnographic research practices have considerably undermined the ethnocentric predicament of modernization. Decolonization and the emergence of indigenous voices in social science have undoubtedly spurred the ethnographers' inclination toward critical self-reflection and their search for variegated new approaches. Tracing the social origins of postmodernist shifts in sociology would require a more complex task of sorting disciplinary transfers of the "ethnological view," revivals of phenomenological approaches directed either at an improvement or a rebuttal of Marxist analysis, trendy adaptations, and attempted transformations. As observed by Bauman (1989), sociology has responded to the postmodern cultural setting through mimesis, unable to conceive of itself as a particular historical response to a changed social reality. Though I cannot follow his reduction to mimetic adaptation, I agree with the corollary insofar as a reconceptualization of the subject matter and subjects of sociology is still lacking. To use Bauman's example of the social space beyond the nation-state, this social space can no longer be viewed as a mere "territory for action"; considering the people who live there and speak and act for themselves, it needs to be acknowledged as a "source of action."

From distant cultures to different cultural groups at home, an increased sensitivity to otherness has pervaded social and historical studies. Even in psychology where knowledge claims used to be most strongly shaped by the science model, there is substantial evidence that participant observation, narrative analysis, and social constructionism have begun to make an impact (Kvale 1992). Still, in my view, the postmodern challenge to social science consists in heterogeneous tendencies that undermine the traditional knowledge claims of single disciplines within the confines of these disciplines, but do not amount to a generative alternative able to radically reconceptualize the domain of history and society.

Shattered illusions

When I wrote this paper in 1991, it was with a gloomy sense of the inadequacy of the new left discourse in general and my own contribution in particular. Before the collapse of communism, the decentering of the Marxist paradigm had seemed to offer the opportunity of gradually reworking critical social theory. Rethinking modernity in terms of humankind's potential nuclear and ecological self-destruction was, no doubt, vitally important. Shifting the focus of analysis from the relations of production and dominance to the microphysics of power and the cultural practices of meaning production could be taken as a learning process favoring subtler views of our life world. For many, this was not meant to be a departure from the project of emancipation; it meant expanding the theoretical tools of promoting it, especially since Gorbachev's "perestroyka" nourished widely shared expectations of democratic transformations in the Eastern societies and the beginning of nuclear disarmament achieved some success.

The extent of economic bankruptcy, political surveillance, and mass political compliance exposed in the collapse of the state socialist regimes was a shocking revelation. The Gulf War had hardly ceased to shock pacifists with the prospects of a Pax Americana, when civil war began to rage in former Yugoslavia. Fascinated by new theoretical approaches, had we not too much indulged in marginal aspects of Western culture, at the expense of serious analysis of the global condition? Entangled in the thicket of everyday business, had we not too easily allowed former commitments to slacken, and thus lost touch with reality? At the turn to 1994, in rewriting the last part of my essay, I still wonder if stronger commitment to the discourse of critical social science might have made a difference, in terms of theoretical and practical responses to the unexpected sociopolitical transformations in Eastern Europe and beyond.

In this still breathtaking process it has become increasingly difficult to put in efforts toward "regaining ground in the daily process of losing ground" (Haug 1990). Pondering today's news it is difficult to recall the events of yesterday, not to mention placing events in historical perspective in order to develop some sense of political judgment. New vistas are badly wanting, but their development will inevitably take time. Thus the left, scrupulous about political intervention unless clear perspectives can be offered, has remained noticeably silent.

In the discourse of German unification, the former promoters of critical social theory have hardly made an impact. Dominated by those who had always "known" that everything is wrong with Stalinist regimes, socialist perspectives, and Marxist theory, the discourse derides the economic, ecological, and cultural state of affairs in East Germany. Intellectuals from the GDR who in 1989 had rallied with citizens chanting "we are the people" resentfully withdrew when it became clear that a democratic socialist renewal of the GDR within some form of German confederation was not what most people wanted. Most dissenters found it too difficult to articulate generative political perspectives.

Violent racism has been one of the most disturbing signatures of unification, along with the expansion of ultrarightist parties and groupings, and a veritable renaissance of nationalist and fascist discourse in public culture. Considering the top priority of the issue of fascism in the early days of radical commitment, one might have expected a discourse of critical social science to gain momentum in the face of these related phenomena. But 20 years of obvious liberalization of West German society had nearly put into oblivion the concern with the social and psychological origins of fascism. Was the model of the authoritarian personality still valid? And what updated alternative could be substituted for the plea for a "socialist decision" (Tillich 1933/1980)? Perplexed with too many questions, we uneasily joined candle rallies, hardly challenging the ongoing dissociation of the related phenomena of a new rightism. In comments and media debates, the racist attacks, mostly committed by young activists, were described in vague terms of frustration and aggression, with moralistic overtones of loss of sound family ties; the rise of rightist parties was normalized by comparison with neighboring countries, and respectable publishers and feuilletons started rehabilitating rightist thinkers of the past. At the same time the debate on political asylum and the subsequent change of the constitution could be declared as a due response to popular unrest, notwithstanding the fact that politicians and social scientists raving about an imminent "deluge of refugees," "pseudoapplicants for asylum," and the "boat being full" had all along fueled the unrest. Leftist interventions, it must be admitted, rarely went beyond moralistic appeals to preserve the once constitutional response to the Holocaust.

Unless silence and moralism are to draw us ever deeper into compliance with political developments detrimental to democracy, their origins need to be seriously scrutinized. There have been few autocritical attempts at reviewing the roots and lasting effects of the 1968 protest, but they suggest a yet unresolved emotional tension in the mentality which took shape in the early protest against the central West German ideology of anticommunism. In a debate carried out in 1992 by the editors of the social science journal *Leviathan,* this problem was aptly termed our "anti-anticommunism." As children of the fascist generation, our informed but no less emotional rejection of fascism made us identify with the communist heroes of the antifascist opposition. The extent to which GDR antifascism was derided in West Germany sufficed to turn the GDR into the imaginary representative of a "better" Germany, preventing us from closer scrutiny of the mix of denazification politics and mere state ideology. Although the first discoveries of positive aspects of existing socialism did not last, some belief in its transformative potential remained. The lasting effect was a defensive attitude toward existing socialism, even against better knowledge, just in order to avoid any misunderstanding of our criticism as an agreement with anticommunism. Unable to resolve the dilemma of pleading for socialism and at the same time criticizing the scandals of existing socialism, the new left largely abstained from public criticism. It may have been symptomatic that it never produced any systematic analysis of the Soviet system comparable to the lucid insights presented by radical Eastern dissidents (Fehér, Heller, & Markus 1983).

Coming to terms with the problematic responses to the fascist past in West and East Germany would require joint inquiry into the distorting mutual projections involved in the political experience of three generations. When the GDR State Security archives were opened, some former dissidents tried to provide some kind of forum for such learning processes, proposing the establishment of round-table dialogues among GDR citizens concerning their reasons for collaboration with the secret service and other forms of compliance with the system. Unfortunately, a political culture that would support such experiments was entirely wanting. In the media, individualized revelations of collaboration remained the rule, and representatives of the "Hitler Youth" generation who in West Germany had once been reluctant to engage in a debate on fascist collaboration were the first to heap blame and scorn upon accused GDR citizens. In support, the once liberal press organs turned to near univocal disdain for the student movement generation and its political concerns.

Thanks to the initiative of one woman, at least a single event was to highlight the potential of dialogical working through the past. Brigitte Rauschenbach, a philosopher and political psychologist, brought together social scientists and writers from East and West Germany to analyze and compare the lasting impact of the national socialist past on the modes of coping with the two German societies and their reunion (Rauschenbach 1992). Though the national research funding agency turned the project down for "unclear scientific purpose," support was scratched together so that in February 1992 an unusually exciting conference could take place at the Free University of Berlin. The speakers outlined central aspects of the political experience of three generations, and subsequent discussion encouraged members of the audience to engage in a dialogue on their own experiences. Amazingly, participants from the East began to talk openly about guilt and shame, and after some hesitation Western leftists also joined, recalling their projective views of antifascism. In these talks, an intense awareness emerged of the intricate links of politics and subjectivity, of disappointed expectations still to be worked through and conditions of compliance to be analyzed further. Although participants expressed their desire for follow-up meetings, so far no one has carried on.

Should the project of emancipation be dispensed with?

The collapse of expectations for socialism makes us question the desirability of new global alternatives. On the other hand, the social problems involved in the ongoing global transformation require renewed efforts to figure out viable routes toward social justice. As the shaping of future social conditions, both conflict and prospects for peace, begins with the imaginative investments of the present, I can see no substantial reason for dispensing with the project of emancipation. Required, however, is a substantial revision of both the moral objectives to be achieved and the role of critical theory in designing viable routes.

Parting with the Marxist illusion that a planned collective economy will automatically bring about social justice does not imply that one also has to part with Marx's insight that the moral goal of social justice depends on the establishment of suitable economic relations (Tugendhat 1991). The question being reopened is, What kind of distribution of material resources could increase the chances of moderating the cleavage between the rich and the poor, within Western countries and the marketizing socialist countries, and between the industrialized regions and poorhouses of the world? Imaginative economic thought is still on the agenda.

For the conceptual outline of a just world order, the just distribution of resources is an essential moral objective, but not the only one to be considered. In her daring approach to a theory of international justice, Janna Thompson (1992) suggested no less than four goals: "promotion of individual liberty, respect for the communities which individuals do or could value, a distribution of resources which would ensure that all individuals are able to exercise their liberty and maintain their community life, and peaceful relations among communities based upon principles or procedures which all can agree are fair" (Thompson 1992, 188). Having discussed the difficulty of making these objectives compatible, she also draws attention to the possibility that they might not be shared universally. As they have been formulated from a Western perspective, people from other cultures might value objectives that are incompatible with those valued by us, a problem that can only be resolved in a negotiating dialogue across cultures.

Reviewing the role of critical theory in the process of emancipation, Markus (1986) has come to similar conclusions concerning the inevitability of cross-cultural dialogue. In his reformulation of the historical materialist model of critical theory, he suggested that the dichotomous notions of the paradigm of production – material content and social form, social relations of production and subjective productive forces – be taken as practical-historical distinctions that can only be made with reference to existing radical needs. Departing from empirically observable discontents, critical theory attempts to explain them in terms of their origins in existing forms of social life, and to interpret them in terms of subjective forces that potentially transcend the existing social system. Thus new vistas of an imaginable better future can be opened up. With regard to the relationship between critical theory and its addressees, the collective subject of revolutionary action cannot, as in the Marxist model, be itself constructed. Critical theory can only incite a learning process in which the participants articulate their claims and try to work out ways of realizing them. Further and beyond Marx, critical theory can no longer be conceived in the singular; it must reckon with a plurality of "radical subjects," within a particular society or from various societies. The way in which the Marxist model itself eventually dissolved into a plurality of Marxisms was but one instance of different vistas resulting from different social experience.

Acknowledging that critical subjects come from and value different cultures amounts to a serious calling into question the Western self-image as civilizing avant-garde of world history. So far, even critical theory has largely been articulated from the perspective of Western democracies. Its objectives cannot be claimed to be of universal validity, much as Western philosophical discourse tends to their normative foundation. It needs to be made quite clear that the degree of civil liberty, individuality, and reflectivity valued by us is a result of human efforts in particular historical conditions. In principle, of course, we know this. But in order to engage in a dialogue with people from different cultures, we still have to learn reflective self-distance. Considering the difficulties encountered, for instance, by feminists or gays within Western culture to make people listen to a different voice and acknowledge different life-styles, the challenge can hardly be overestimated.

Currently, there is an abundance of critical voices that convey differentiated views of the past reality of state socialism and the concerns and goals involved in the transformative process. There is also an increasing number of indigenous writers and social scientists from the remotest parts of the world who speak for themselves and their own societies and concerns. After centuries of cultural monologue, we would be well advised to begin listening to what they have to say.

If the task of negotiating across cultures the objectives and mode of critical theory appears deterringly Sisyphean, I hasten to add that there is much to be gained from listening. Ethnographers have been among the first to appreciate the decentering of Western notions of personhood and self. They have since turned to self-reflective deconstructions of the subject matter of anthropology and the romanticist construals of subjectivity in foreign cultures (Staeuble 1992, 1993). Listening to voices from other cultures may also increase our perceptive sensitivity toward the threat which the West represents for people in non-Western societies. Indigenous novelists offer abundant observations on the aftereffects of colonial inferiorization as well as evidence of lasting vulnerabilities. Migrant novelists also convey some sense of the subtle and intriguing encounters between cultures. Learning to listen is a first step toward an intelligible global discourse.

References

Adorno, T. W., Albert, H., Dahrendorf, R., Habermas, J., Pilot, H., & Popper, K. R. (1976) *The Positivist Dispute in German Sociology*. New York: Harper Torchbooks.

Althaus, G. (1989) *Leben zwischen Sein und Nichts. Drei Studien zu Günther Anders*. Berlin: Metropol.

Altvater, E. (1983) Politische Überlegungen ein Jahr nach der Wende. *Leviathan, 11*, 580–599.

Anders, G. (1956/1980) *Die Antiquiertheit des Menschen* [The obsolescence of man]. 2 vols. Munich: Beck.

Baritz, L. (1960) *The Servants of Power: A History of the Use of Social Science in American Industry*. Middletown, Conn.: Wesleyan University Press.

Baudrillard, J. (1975) *The Mirror of Production*. St. Louis: Telos Press.

Baudrillard, J. (1978) *Kool Killer oder Der Aufstand der Zeichen*. Berlin: Merve.

Bauman, Z. (1989) Sociological Responses to Postmodernity. *Thesis Eleven, 23*, 35–63.

Bernal, J. D. (1965) *Science in History*. London: C. A. Watts.

Brentano, M. von (1987) Günther Anders' Philosophie des Atomzeitalters. In C. Schulte (Ed.), *Friedensinitiative Philosophie: Um Kopf und Krieg*. Darmstadt: Luchterhand, 13–30.

Castoriadis, C. (1987–1988) The Movement of the Sixties. *Thesis Eleven, 18–19*, 20–31.

Danziger, K. (1990) *Constructing the Subject: Historical Origins of Psychological Research*. Cambridge: Cambridge University Press.

Fehér, F., Heller, A., & Markus, G. (1983) *Dictatorship over Needs*. Oxford: Blackwell.

Foucault, M. (1974) *Die Ordnung des Diskurses*. Inaugural Address to Collège de France, 2 December 1970. Munich: Hanser.

Foucault, M. (1977) *Discipline and Punish: The Birth of the Prison*. New York: Pantheon Books.

Foucault, M. (1984a) *Histoire de la sexualité*. Vol. 2. *L'usage des plaisirs*. Paris: Éditions Gallimard.

Foucault, M. (1984b) *Histoire de la sexualité*. Vol. 3. *Le souci de soi*. Paris: Éditions Gallimard.

Gergen, K. J., & Gergen, M. M. (Eds.) (1984) *Historical Social Psychology*. Hillsdale, N.J.: Lawrence Erlbaum.

Graumann, C. F., & Moscovici, S. (Eds.) (1986a) *Changing Conceptions of Crowd and Behavior*. New York: Springer-Verlag.

Graumann, C. F., & Moscovici, S. (Eds.) (1986b) *Changing Conceptions of Leadership*. New York: Springer-Verlag.

Graumann, C. F., & Moscovici, S. (Eds.) (1987) *Changing Conceptions of Conspiracy*. New York: Springer-Verlag.

Habermas, J. (1968/1977) *Knowledge and Interests*. Boston: Beacon.

Hahn, A., & Kapp, V. (Eds.) (1987) *Selbstthematisierung und Selbstzeugnis: Bekenntnis und Geständnis*. Frankfurt: Suhrkamp.

Harvey, D. (1989) *The Condition of Postmodernity: An Enquiry into the Origins of Cultural Change*. Oxford: Blackwell.

Haug, W. F. (1990) *Versuch beim täglichen Verlieren des Bodens unter den Füßen neuen Grund zu gewinnen: Das Perestrojka-Journal*. Hamburg: Argument.

Hildebrandt, H. (1990) *Zur Bedeutung des Begriffs der Alltagspsychologie in Theorie und Geschichte der Psychologie. Eine psychologiegeschichtliche Studie anhand der Krise der Psychologie in der Weimarer Republik*. Frankfurt: Peter Lang.

Huyssen, A. (1986) Postmoderne – eine amerikanische Internationale? In A. Huyssen & K. R. Scherpe (Eds.) *Postmoderne. Zeichen eines kulturellen Wandels*. Hamburg: Rowohlt, 13–44.

Jaeger, S., & Staeuble, I. (1978) *Die gesellschaftliche Genese der Psychologie*. Frankfurt: Campus.

Jameson, F. (1984) Postmodernism, or the Cultural Logic of Late Capitalism. *New Left Review, 146*, 53–92.

Jüttemann, G. (Ed.) (1986) *Die Geschichtlichkeit des Seelischen. Der historische Zugang zum Gegenstand der Psychologie*. Weinheim: Psychologie Verlags Union/Beltz.

Kvale, S. (Ed.) (1992) *Psychology and Postmodernism*. London: Sage.

Lyotard, J.-F. (1983) *Le Différend*. Paris: Les Éditions de Minuit.

Lyotard, J.-F. (1984) *The Postmodern Condition: A Report on Knowledge*. Minneapolis: University of Minnesota Press.

Maikowski, R., Mattes, P., & Rott, G. (1976) *Psychologie und ihre Praxis. Materialien zur Geschichte und Funktion einer Einzelwissenschaft in der Bundesrepublik*. Frankfurt: Fischer.

Markus, G. (1986) *Language and Production: A Critique of the Paradigms*. Dordrecht: Reidel.

Pressedienst Wissenschaft 8 (1972) *Psychologie als historische Wissenschaft. Geschichte der psychologischen Theorien und der Berufspraxis von Psychologen mit dem Ziel der Entwicklung einer kritischen Psychologie*. Berlin: Freie Universität.

Rauschenbach, B. (Ed.) (1992) *Erinnern, Wiederholen, Durcharbeiten. Zur Psycho-Analyse deutscher Wenden*. Berlin: Aufbau-Verlag.

Reuter, M. (Ed.) (1990) *Black Box Psyche? Texte zur historischen Psychologie 1*. Pfaffenweiler: Centaurus.

Rose, N. (1985) *The Psychological Complex. Psychology, Politics and Society in England, 1869–1939*. London: Routledge & Kegan Paul.

Sonntag, M. (1988) *Die Seele als Politikum. Psychologie und die Produktion des Individuums*. Berlin: Dietrich Reimer.

Sonntag, M. (Ed.) (1990) *Von der Machbarkeit des Psychischen. Texte zur historischen Psychologie 2*. Pfaffenweiler: Centaurus.

Staeuble, I. (1972) Politischer Ursprung und politische Funktionen der pragmatistischen Sozialpsychologie. In H. Nolte & I. Staeuble, *Zur Kritik der Sozialpsychologie*. Munich: Hanser, 7–65.

Staeuble, I. (1976) *Die bürgerliche Gesellschaft als Problem und Probleme in der bürgerlichen Gesellschaft. Zur Kritik der Sozialwissenschaften*. Berlin: Diss. Druck.

Staeuble, I. (1987) Von der Schwierigkeit, über Günther Anders zu schreiben. *Leviathan, 15*, 305–317.

Staeuble, I. (1988) Das tödliche Mißverhältnis von Kopf und Herz. In G. Althaus & I. Staeuble (Eds.), *Streitbare Philosophie. Margherita von Brentano zum 65. Geburtstag*. Berlin: Metropol, 319–338.

Staeuble, I. (1991) "Psychological Man" and Human Subjectivity in Historical Perspective. *History of the Human Sciences, 4:* 417–432.

Staeuble, I. (1992) Wir und die Anderen. Ethno-psychologische Konstruktionen im Wandel. *Psychologie und Geschichte, 4* 1–2: 139–157.

Staeuble, I. (1993) Kolonialismus, Ethno-Psychologie, und die schwierige Vorstellung eines Miteinander auf der Welt. In H. Givsan & W. Schmied-Kowarzik (Eds.), *Reflexionen zur geschichtlichen Praxis. Helmut Fleischer zum 65. Geburtstag*. Würzburg: Königshausen & Neumann, 65–92.

Thompson, J. (1992) *Justice and World Order. A Philosophical Inquiry*. London: Routledge.

Tillich, P. (1933/1980) *Die sozialistische Entscheidung*. Berlin: Medusa.

Tugendhat, E. (1991) Das Friedensproblem heute. *Kursbuch 105*, 1–12.

14   The transcendental alarm

William Kessen

About 1,500 years ago, Augustine of Hippo thanked God for his mother's milk:

For neither my mother nor my nurses stored their own breasts for me; but Thou didst bestow the food of my infancy through them, according to Thine ordinance, whereby Thou distributest Thy riches through the hidden springs of all things. (Augustine, 400/1949, I, p. 7)

God was the active agent in the ordinary events of life; nothing moved or intended or played except under His prescription and with His knowledge. Of course, as the Western desire to know broadened, the Augustinian "hidden springs" subtly became a significant source of error and of evil. The task of the talented believer became not merely to accept what was but to change the present – and to change it for the better. Over centuries, the core notion of salvation escaped its eschatalogical boundaries and became – almost drunkenly, in the rational explosion of the seventeenth century – the guiding spirit of human action. The shift from salvation as a gift of God, delivered in eternity, over to an immediate and secular consequence of social service was a process that took centuries, that was confined largely to European cultures, and that has never been complete in any culture. The shift had several discernible components – the deification of Nature, the belief in human progress, and the opportunities of scientific analysis, chief among them. As we shall see, by the nineteenth century in the United States, you worked in life, not (only) to assure an eternity of grace hereafter but to find solutions to the problems that people faced now.

How matters had been transformed by the beginning of the twentieth century! William James came to New Haven in 1896 to tell the Philosophical Club about Harvard College "freethinking and indifference"; he hoped to share a "good old orthodox College conversation" with his more receptive audience in Yale as he asked his auditors to hear his "sermon on . . . justification *of* faith" (1897, all quotations from p. 1). James's case was made with his usual soft eloquence and is winning (James, 1897); what commands our attention, however, is the defensive and protective temper of his commentary. James recognized that he was swimming against a

263

strong current and that reflections about the logical legitimacy of religious belief – especially by a one-time social scientist like himself – were simply not done. Augustine's God was no longer in the intellectual domain and James stood near the opening of a new era, an era in which positive social science would solve all the problems that, in our ignorant days, we had left to the mercy of the Deity.

My uneasy goal, in these pages, is to outline the changes that occurred in the West between Augustine's proud declaration and James's pleading request. Further, I want to maintain that not long after God lost his transcendental epaulettes, the replacement God – Science – began to shiver on its pedestal. My attention will be on American social science and, specifically, often on psychology; there is a more general argument implied here about positivistic scientific enquiry in general (from physics to sociology) but I will present the more limited brief in illustration of several phenomena. Finally, I will turn for a moment to the question lying under the entire discussion: What shall we do now?

Changes in transcendental power

The movement of God between Augustine and James from the ever present, ever powerful mover of humanity to the Spectator Lord – the traffic cop of Nature – was an uneven, incomplete, and jagged set of events. The change, for most Westerners, was slight or marked an unnotable shift of practice; for the keepers of the culture – the priests, the intelligentsia, the writers of encyclopedias, the academicians – the change was profound and encompassed everything in the structure of their lives. The definition of knowledge, the methods of finding out, the sources of moral judgment, the place of power, the nature of civilization – all became *human* endeavors, at best guided and at worst only observed by the Almighty. The brilliant social commentator and ally of John Dewey, George Herbert Mead, caught the mathematical character of the shift in his observation that perfection was no longer merely a mark of God but also a mark of God's creation. "If God created the world for the fall and the salvation of man, . . . he would create it in a mathematical fashion so that a mathematical statement of it could be given" (Mead, 1936, p. 8).

Of course, the creation of the Bleacher Lord carried with it changes of the modern mind that persisted well into the twentieth century. The never eroding idea of man's salvation, apparently available in secular time by 1700, and the perfectibility of mankind, a demonstrated scientific principle by 1875, had become a governing Western idea of the past 200 years – the inevitable movement of human definition toward the better.[1] But, more and more after 1650, it was progress to be worked by the infallibility of Science now, not the infallibility of an omnipotent God on Judgment Day. There were hesitations in the change, and many scholars stayed true to God as well as to Science but, by the end of the nineteenth century doubts about the effective power of God had given place to an equally evangelical certainty about the effective power of science. When perfectibility became the grain of theories of human nature, and when scientific method was seen as at least as effective as prayer, the West was ready for the invention of the social sciences.

Emerson and Darwin

Parallel currents were running in mainstream American life during the nineteenth century. The national ritual of progress was shaped by a curious combination of political activity and commitment to social service. From Emerson to Franklin Roosevelt, an almost unchallenged principle reigned. Drawn again from its religious ancestry, the rule of service to others became a guide for Americans of a certain disposition, a guide that showed little diminution of monastic fervor between Saint Francis and Jane Addams. Emerson set the temper.

What we commonly call man, the eating, drinking, planting, counting man, does not, as we know him, represent himself, but misrepresents himself. Him we do not respect, but the soul. . . . When it breathes through his intellect, it is genius; when it breathes through his will, it is virtue; when it flows through his affection, it is love. (Emerson, 1841/1847, p. 387)

Let me hurry to say that my placing Emerson in the genealogy of American social sciences is not contrived; one of his editors wrote that "he was the teacher of America. What he said and wrote is still the gospel we most easily understand" (Atkinson, 1940, p. xxv). The problem for commentators at the end of the twentieth century is trying to figure out how the American academy has maintained Emerson's optimism as, first, God and, then, Science lost their transcendental luster.

Just a word about Emerson's time, to assure you that he did not sing the joys of Nature and the promise of the locomotive in an environment without pain. He wrote as the Irish immigration began, he was about to take an antipathetic position on slavery, he lived through the cicatrix in our history, the Civil War, and he faced Reconstruction and the abandonment of blacks, all without losing a jot of his conviction that Nature and the Oversoul would keep us secure and advancing. God sustained Emerson, but not the God of Augustine. Emerson's God was in his all-encompassing vision of perfect Nature.

Nature, for Emerson, was good, powerful, and fulfilling. He brought to the midcentury of the nation a spiritual promise that has dominated the rhetoric and the public oratory of the United States from his time unto our own. And it was a promise that permitted a secular interpretation; his

Essays were part of the preparatory apparatus of the people of the nineteenth century who gave themselves to the creation of juvenile courts and
settlement houses. Mostly dedicated women, they, just a hundred years
ago, made the care of children, immigrants, and the poor their consuming
lifework and, for all the recent debate, a basic principle of American
culture.[2]

But, of course, the tides of change helped Emerson's enthusiasm. While
he wrote the essay on the oversoul, Charles Darwin was elaborating his
vision of natural selection and, in the last half of the nineteenth century,
even as Emerson looked unseeing, Darwinian scientific biology gave muscle
to Emerson's hopeful message. The ideology of the oversoul needed an age
obsessed with the infinite possibilities of science. Darwin's message was
relatively simple. We now have a method, scientific study, and a theory,
natural selection, that gives the old salvationist story of heaven a worldly
form. Just by the processes of Nature, revealed by our impervious method,
we can be confident that the best, the brightest, the most benign folks will
survive and triumph. The conjunction of Emerson's quiet certainty about
humanity's future with the fervor of Darwin's apostles did the trick –
American progressivism was the central conviction of the culture and it
supported (it may even have helped to produce) the invention of the social
sciences in American colleges at the end of the nineteenth century. The
center of our established academic belief was about to shift again – from
Nature to Science.

Darwin had prepared the way. His gathering of the evidence demonstrated what earlier thinkers had supposed – that animal species were
related to one another in a great continuous uncoiling of progressive development. It was an exhilarating display for Western intellectuals, and the
hardly controlled enthusiasms of the evangelical churches were matched by
the enthusiasms of the Darwinians.

Not so widely noted in the transformations of the nineteenth century was
the shift – among intellectuals – of transcendental *passion* from religion to
nature to science. The conviction of certainty that had made the Crusades
and the Cathedral at Chartres, the intensity that animated Augustine and
Aquinas and Calvin, the sheer righteousness of truth, were transferred
without loss of fire from the old God to the new Science.[3] The human will
to believe, the almost desperate turn toward the transcendental, has never
been so vividly displayed as in the transfer of intensity that marked the
transformation of God as the source of all knowledge to Science as the
perfect method of finding out. The rhapsodic commitment of the new social
scientist measured up to the older extravagances of the pulpit. G. Stanley
Hall's words were to be different from Savanarola's but they were to shine
with a comparable fire. It was the power of a transcendental conviction.

The emergence of scientific psychology

In the intellectual turbulence of the nineteenth century, psychology as a discipline made its slow way. And, in an almost caricatural copy of the larger surround, psychology moved from the theological to the scientific mode. Two American headmasters and minor scholars of the nineteenth century stood near the beginning of psychology as an academic discipline and neither of them had doubts about the theological grounding of the field. Cyril Pearl's *Youth's Book on the Mind* stated the everyday obvious. "The study of the Human Mind is one of the most extensive and important that can be pursued. . . . It is the mind that raised man above the brute, that allies him to angels, and brings him near to God" (Pearl, 1842/1847, p. 1). And Henry Day was as clearheaded about understanding human nature; near the end of his *Elements of Psychology,* he wrote, "Love to God thus in its highest form is will to please him or will to glorify him" (Day, 1876, p. 246).

And close to the birth moment of academic psychology and near his own accession to the presidency of Yale College, Porter was unequivocal.

We do not demonstrate that God exists, but that *every man must assume that He is.* . . . We are not alone justified, we are compelled to conclude our analysis of the human intellect with the assertion, that its various powers and processes suppose and assume that there is an uncreated thinker, whose thoughts can be interpreted by the human intellect which is made in His image. (Porter, 1868, p. 662)

I am not maintaining that at some magic moment, in the late nineteenth century, the classical Western deity stepped aside and let Science slip onto His throne. You have only to look at the marvelously rich ambiguity of Rousseau's work and the variety of his discipleship to understand the complexities of the mental revolution that was transforming European civilization in the eighteenth and nineteenth centuries. If I were sketching a general story about the culture of the West, instead of hinting at changes in the hermetic academy, my emphasis would be more on the fragility and superficiality of the acceptance of science. Nor am I suggesting that the academy, uniformly and on schedule, changed its mind one day. There is no reference to God in Charles Eliot's presidential address at Harvard in 1869, but compulsory chapel attendance lasted in American colleges until yesterday; there are no prayers for the religious to be found in Mill or in Baldwin, but American presidents take their oaths to God. What interests me is the transformation of the social sciences in the academy from a grounding in theology to a grounding in secular science. The move was dramatic.

The clerical cast of early psychology is clear. Of the seven legendary founders of the discipline, three were themselves ordained (Fullerton, Hall, and Ladd) and three were the sons or the sons-in-law of clerics (Baldwin, James, and Jastrow). Only Cattell escaped the marks. And Hall, enthusiast for evolution and for Jesus, stung throughout his life by the *odium theologicum*, rejoiced in the affiliation of the old religion with the new science.

The new psychology . . . is I believe Christian to its root and center. . . . [Its mission is] . . . to flood and transfuse the new and vaster conceptions of the universe . . . with the old Scriptural sense of unity, rationality, and love. . . . The Bible is slowly being re-revealed as man's great textbook in psychology. (Hall, 1885, pp. 247–248)[4]

There were, however, many new psychologists at the turn of the century who seem to have doubted that the Bible had finished the job of textbook writing. In something like a feeding frenzy, the New Psychology produced piles of books and journals to invent the field – and a nonchurchly scientific field it quickly was. Within 10 years of the founding in Worcester in 1892, references to the religious origins and development of early psychology were gone; Munsterberg succeeded James, Sanford succeeded Hall, Scripture succeeded Ladd, Stratton succeeded Baldwin, Science succeeded God. If van Winkle had slept between 1880 and 1900, he would have missed the continental shift that took psychology the long stretch from essays on moral philosophy typically taught by the president of the college onto the Leipzig-dominated ideology of brass-instrument controlled experiments.[5]

And thus it was that, in the decades between Emerson's *First Essays* and the entrance of the United States into the First World War, the unthinkable happened – *God died*. The certainty that grew from a transcendental commitment, a certainty that had, with mixed success to be sure, sustained the West for a millennium or several, that certainty left the academy. The claims of sure science and sure evolution erased our need for theological comfort; we could *do*, we would prosper, with progress and the scientific method.

The fading of science

The commitment to God as the source of power has lasted for 2,000 years and (if truth be told) shows no sign of leaving the field. American social science as the source of transcendental trust and the origin of wise human action has made it for about 100 and is now in confused disarray.[6] We are too much in the midst of breakdown to look closely at all the possible causes of the flattening tire, but some major surrounding events can be seen dimly.

Forecaster of the end was history written as constantly improving, the story of the world for which Hegel had provided theoretical form in the days when Darwin was triumphing. No threat to technical science, the loss of history as a model of eternal human betterment marked the onset of disaster. The ovens of Auschwitz and the ovens of Hiroshima, the slaughters of Stalin and the mindless cruelty in China – all brought pause to the easy belief in the inevitable reach upward of history. But academic history lost more than the old-fashioned belief in improvement; it also lost the confidence of the sages in the possibility of provable historical events. Schama's (1991) recent experiment with plausible narrative testifies to the fragility of empirical truth in history making.

And, then, in another corner of the forest, still apparently at a safe distance from the biochemists and the sociologists, literary criticism took a turn away from the facts of form and the facts of biography to put forward a new (or, at least, a not recently popular) way of seeing text. Gadamer and Derrida became the names aquiver on tongues and, among literary commentators anyway, the word "hermeneutics" became as common as "soccer." More than that, the distance between criticism and science did not prove to be safe; in forms hardly disguised, the interpretative strategy appeared in the work of anthropologists and social psychologists and historians of science.[7] The wind, broken discreetly enough in English departments, had become a tornado.

Unfortunately for the confidence of social scientists, it was not just in the humanities – never positivistic enough – that the changes of epistemology were at work. For 20 years and more, Clifford Geertz has been sounding a tune that has nothing of the old, and still comforting, song of the simple and the universal. Almost any passage in his work will indict the positivistic dream but let us read, from 1983.

> The golden age (or perhaps it was only the brass) of the social sciences when, whatever the differences in theoretical positions and empirical claims, the basic goal of the enterprise was universally agreed upon – to find out the dynamics of collective life and alter them in desired directions – has clearly passed. (Geertz, 1983, p. 34)

More recently, Geertz has been joined by persuasive colleagues in several social scientists – at an angle, by James Clifford (1988), who inverts the classical paradigm by having culture drive anthropological method, and by Wolf Lepenies (1988), who tells us of the near miss by which sociology became scientific rather than literary.

The wind of change still blows; it blows in psychology as well as in history, criticism, and anthropology. The 1970s and 1980s have seen an expansion in the territory of critical or interpretative psychologists – the list is no longer as much a dean's list as it is a roll call – and their varied arguments have settled into a definable pattern. Bruner, Cole Gergen, Rogoff, and Shweder[8] have, from different generations and different preparations, been among the leaders calling for a reconstruction of psychology. The traditional view of normal mental science is under attack and the attack begins to have a hard epistemological core.[9]

The sum of the assessment is scaldingly simple. For all its spectacular achievements of the past centuries, *positive social science is only **one other** way of solving human problems.* It will not support the transcendental weight that the culture has laid on it; Science will not serve as God.

And so, as we enter the twenty-first century, the intellectual leadership of the West is without a transcendental center. In a world mad with variety and wealthy with possibility, neither established center has held and the transcendental alarm has been sounded in ways quiet and in ways bizarre. Where shall we turn now?

With neither God nor Science to prop us, a glance at our lives in this open moment may clarify the disorder; I cannot offer comfort.[10]

The prospects before us

In the remarks that follow, I have made two assumptions that may not be comfortable for all readers. First, I have assumed that there will continue to be a human need for a transcendental allegiance, a feeling of human insufficiency that calls for some sort of higher power or force that can sustain us. How typical is our call for language to meet the new dilemmas we face! Since James's attempt to stem the scientistic monsoon, no established psychologist has touched the problem of transcendental power and its place in mental life. We have tried to remove the pain by stopping the possibility of serious conversation. Our current equivocations probably measure well the inadequacies of our forms of discourse.

The second assumption I have made was more difficult; I must treat the contemporary bouillabaisse of partial solutions to the loss of God and the loss of Science as a stew warranting serious treatment. The temptation to slide off into comic exaggeration was appealing; the edges of the transcendental crisis – the assurances of astrology, the vision of sex as a therapy, the comfort of language unrelated to thought – invite attempts at humor. But I leave the black laughs to the journalists and the novelists.[11]

Money

Raw acquisition, always a sensuous affection of Americans, has become a commonplace of the New Transcendentalism. One more promotion, one more BMW, one more spouse, will solve the human tangle; the everyday injunction that you can be neither too rich nor too thin carries the message of the mass.

With changes in the meaning of paid work and the changes in the rewards of women in the society, there has been a dramatic falloff in the amount of free volunteer service in the American community. Necessary social tasks that were often performed as a duty or shared among friends have become income-producing work or have been taken over by new affiliations of volunteers. The most visible recent examples of modified volunteerism have been federally encouraged engagement (e.g., the Peace Corps) and small gatherings of women, usually young mothers and almost always working, who set up transient units to handle babysitting or to open discussions of modern life.

Money and service make an interesting contrast. The new acquirers have the intensity of transcendental commitment but almost no defensible ideology; the new servers are often reticent in what they do but they have an ancient and noble lineage of justification.

Health

Hard muscles, slow heart rate, low cholesterol, salvation. On the theme of healthy living and healthy eating, a vast and scarcely controlled *literature* exists; the properly dutiful reader may spend all his money and most of his time finding out about the nuances of the pancreas or the dangers of lead.

An adjunct to our obsession about health, and a rather peculiar one, is our obsession about animal rights. Saving the deer and the birds and the dolphins from injury is of importance far beyond the animals; fighting for animal rights has exactly the fervor and the certainty that sent the young people of Europe toward Jerusalem on the Children's Crusade. Here, the savagery of the transcendental believer joins in neat fit with the sense of righteous service.

Only one other current debate, also linked to the health movement, has the mixture of fervor and moral certainty that guided Dante, Fra Angelico, and the destroyers of the Albigenses. The fight over abortion draws on both theological and scientific arguments but it depends on neither. In a number of ways, the argument about the rights and prohibitions of pregnancy represents in full form the potentials of a new transcendental spirit in America.

Environment

Just a word about the new transcendental aura surrounding our care for the environment. The range of concern has become enormous, the bureaucracies grow as fast as does Bethesda, and the texts of commitment get more shrill and less forgiving by the day, sure marks of the call on a higher power. The next few years will tell us whether or not parts of the environmental movement will be colored with strident ideology and with blood.

If my assumptions are correct – if the community is bereft of God and of Science and if the void must be filled – then we face two staggering sets of problems. How shall we deal with the colossal political puzzles posed by a transcendental void? I have no wisdom to share on the political issues, save to remind us that the maneuvers chosen will be radically local and to share my fear that some of the maneuvers will be rending.

And, how shall we manage the problems that arise in redefining how social science knowledge – especially, knowledge in psychology – will be acquired and systematized? To be sure, the question is a literal reflection of the questions that lie about us in social and political and economic terms, but these epistemological questions are our own, the queries we were charged to answer as the knowers of the culture.

Here, the news is far better. The scholars who have led the assessment of the failings of positive social science have shifted their focus to the task of reconstruction. The emphasis on cultural variation, the promise of narrative as the source of systematic method, and the return of interest in theorists of communication – all contain strategies that will help us to continue, with joy and (if we are smart) with humility, the critical examination of the fields that John Stuart Mill aptly called "the moral sciences."

Notes

1 The literature on Western ideas about the directions of human change is multifarious. For examples, Bury (1920) treats largely of the philosophical aspects of progress's development; Lovejoy (1936) talks of the transition to biological science; Lasch (1991) lashes at some of the recent political implications of the idea. Our current understanding of the historical links between salvation and secular progress is insufficient.

2 The story of the Salvationist Women of turn-of-the-century America – Edith Abbott, Grace Abbott, Jane Addams, Julia Lathrop, Lillian Wald, and many others – remains to be told. Part of their biography will certainly link Emersonian optimism and progressivism with the settlement houses and the flood of human donation that illuminated the United States in the 1880s and the 1890s. See, however, Muncey (1991), Smuts (1995), and Sklar (1995).

3 The differences between a theological and a scientific vision of phenomena are many and important but my point here is a basic one. In the years between 1650 and 1950, the zeal of the missionary became the zeal of the academic researcher and the power of both seems of more than casual or accidental similarity.

4 Some scholar must explore the place of James McCosh of Princeton in the exile of God from psychology. His little monograph on Darwinian ideas not only influenced Baldwin directly and profoundly. When McCosh, the symbol and measure of Protestant orthodoxy, wrote, "I see nothing irreligious in holding that the bird may have been evolved by numerous transitions from the reptile, and the living horse from the old horse of the Eocene formation" (McCosh, 1876, pp. 36–37), he provided a *façon de parler* that permitted the believing scientist to pursue both of his commitments without apology.

5 The job of understanding the origins of professional psychology are eased by the small number of players and by the public heat of their controversies. For an example, Titchener's attempts to remake the American Psychological Association and the early years of his exclusive Society of Experimental Psychologists are neatly outlined by Furomoto (1988).

6 Doubts about the security of positivistic social science have existed throughout the golden years of psychology's growth. James quickly lost his tentative confidence in the American reading of Wundt's promise; Dewey offered a tough-minded alternative to the excitement of logical regularity and the experiment (see esp. Dewey, 1910, 1916). Neither thinker held on to strong followings in academic normal social science but, recently, the insistent criticism of Geertz and Bronfenbrenner and Gergen and Bruner and a host of younger

reappraising psychologists has tilted the study of humankind remarkably back toward what James and Dewey saw 90 years ago.

7 One of the hurtful strokes came from the evolutionary biologists who took apart the old conviction we thought we had from Darwin about the necessity of natural selection making better species. The central myth under attack was adaptationalism (see Gould and Lewontin, 1979) but the philosophical spread was much broader; gone were the grounds of (developmental) psychology in evolutionary inevitability. See my Werner Lectures, 1990.

8 Bruner's recent title (1990) does not equivocate about the essential shift from experiment to narrative; Cole (in press) has summarized his view, Gergen continues his long dissection of psychology (see Gergen, 1994); Rogoff (1990) explores novel ways of presenting data about children in culture; Shweder, the current champion of reform, states his case well in opening a treatment of cultural psychology (1990).

9 I will not ape my betters to write the declaration of new analysis but, at least, the following notions are in the center, however much we scold my idiosyncratic statement of them. (1) The social sciences are not nomological disciplines. What is the case is the case for a particular setting and for a particular time. (2) Certainty is not an attainable goal for social science. We must be pleased with plausible accounts. (3) The individualistic premises of Western tradition introduce deflecting biases into our social science at its base. (4) Most social science knowledge will turn out to be matters of clarified and tested folk knowledge.

10 For many reasons, I will not address the political changes that have taken place in Europe since 1989. There is something of an ironic surprise in the temporal parallel between the fall of science and the fall of European state communism but I dare not explore the conjunction here. However, the pictorial representation that I would choose to illustrate the transcendental alarm is the Patriarch of All the Russias in attendance at the ceremony initiating Mikhail Gorbachev's presidency.

11 Important issues of public action and political power have been raised during the twentieth century, the most important being the question of human rights – rights for minority citizens and for women. I will not discuss such ambivalences deeply rooted in our culture but I will save my brief remarks for those concerns, recently raised, that smell of a new search for transcendental loyalties.

References

Atkinson, B. 1940. *Ralph Waldo Emerson: Complete Essays and Other Writings*. New York: Modern Library.

Augustine of Hippo. ca. 400/1949. *Confessions*. New York: Modern Library.

Bruner, J. 1990. *Acts of Meaning*. Cambridge, MA: Harvard University Press.

Bury, J. B. 1920. *The Idea of Progress: An Inquiry into Its Origins and Growth*. London: Macmillan.

Clifford, J. 1988. *The Predicament of Culture: Twentieth-Century Ethnography, Literature, and Art*. Cambridge, MA: Harvard University Press.

Cole, M. In press. *Mind in Culture*. Cambridge, MA: Harvard University Press.

Day, H. N. 1876. *Elements of Psychology*. New York: G. P. Putnam's Sons.

Derrida, J. 1976. *Of Grammatology*. Baltimore: Johns Hopkins University Press.

Dewey, J. 1910. *How We Think*. Boston: D. C. Heath.

Dewey, J. 1916. *Essays in Experimental Logic*. Chicago: University of Chicago Press.

Eliot, C. W. 1869/1969. *A Turning Point in Higher Education*. Cambridge, MA: Harvard University Press.

Emerson, R. W. 1841/1847/1983. The Over-Soul. *Essays: First Series*. In *Emerson: Essays and Lectures*. New York: Literary Classics of the United States. Pp. 183–400.

Furomoto, L. 1988. Shared Knowledge: The Experimentalists, 1904–1929. In Jill G. Morawski (Ed.), *The Rise of Experimentation in American Psychology*. New Haven, CT: Yale University Press. Pp. 94–113.

Gadamer, H.-G. 1976. *Hegel's Dialectic: Five Hermeneutical Studies*. New Haven, CT: Yale University Press.

Geertz, C. 1983. *Local Knowledge: Further Essays in Interpretive Anthropology*. New York: Basic Books.

Gergen, K. J. 1994. *Toward Transformation in Social Knowledge*. 2nd ed. London: Sage.

Gould, S. J., & Lewontin, R. C. 1979. The Spandrels of San Marco. *Proceedings of the Royal Society of London (B), 205,* 581–598.

Hall, G. S. 1885. *The New Psychology*. Boston: Houghton Mifflin.

James, W. 1897. *The Will to Believe*. New York: Longman Green.

Kessen, W. 1990. *The Rise and Fall of Development*. Worcester, MA: Clark University Press.

Lasch, C. 1991. *The True and Only Heaven: Progress and Its Critics*. New York: Norton.

Lepenies, W. 1988. *Between Literature and Science*. Cambridge: Cambridge University Press.

Lovejoy, A. O. 1936. *The Great Chain of Being: A Study of the History of an Idea*. New York: Harper & Row.

McCosh, J. 1876. *The Development Hypothesis: Is It Sufficient?* New York: Robert Carter and Brothers.

Mead, G. H. 1936. *Movements of Thought in the Nineteenth Century*. Chicago: University of Chicago Press.

Muncey, R. 1991. *Creating a Female Dominion in American Reform, 1890–1935*. New York: Oxford University Press.

Pearl, C. 1842/1847. *Youth's Book of the Mind, Embracing the Outlines of the Intellect, the Sensibilities, and the Will*. Portland, ME: Hyde, Lord and Duven.

Porter, N. 1868. *The Human Intellect, with an Introduction upon Psychology and the Soul*. New York: C. Scribner.

Rogoff, B. 1990. *Apprenticeship in Thinking: Cognitive Development in Social Context*. New York: Oxford University Press.

Rousseau, J.-J. 1761/1950. *Émile*. New York: E. P. Dutton.

Schama, S. 1991. *Dead Certainties*. New York: Knopf.

Sklar, K. K. 1995. *Florence Kelly and the Nation's Work*. New Haven, CT: Yale University Press.

Smuts, A. B. 1995. *Science Discovers the Child 1893–1935* Unpublished manuscript.

Stigler, J. W., Shweder, R., & Herdt, G. H. 1990. *Essays in Comparative Human Development*. Cambridge: Cambridge University Press.

Author index

275

Subject index